# CHILDREN OF COLOR

REFERENCE BOOKS ON FAMILY ISSUES
VOLUME 25
GARLAND REFERENCE LIBRARY OF SOCIAL SCIENCE
VOLUME 1093

# REFERENCE BOOKS ON FAMILY ISSUES

# Children of Color
## Research, Health, and policy Issues

Edited by
Hiram E. Fitzgerald
Barry M. Lester
Barry S. Zuckerman

Garland Publishing, Inc.
a member of the Taylor & Francis Group
New York and London
1999

Library of Congress Cataloging-in-Publication Data

Children of color : research, health, and policy issues / edited by Hiram E.
   Fitzgerald, Barry M. Lester, and Barry S. Zuckerman.
         p.     cm.  — (Reference books on family issues ; vol. 25)
   (Garland reference library of social science ; vol. 1093)
      Includes bibliographical references and index.
      ISBN 0-8153-2288-7 (case: alk. paper)
      1. Children of minorities—Government policy—United States.
   2. Children of minorities—Services for—United States.   3. Children of
   minorities—Health and hygiene—United States.   4. Children of minorities—
   Research—United States.   I. Fitzgerald, Hiram E.   II. Lester, Barry M.
   III. Zuckerman, Barry S.   IV. Series: Reference books on family issues ;
   v. 25.   V. Series: Garland reference library of social science ; v. 1093.
   HV741.C536155   1999
   362.7'089'00973—dc21                                              98–42198
                                                                         CIP

Printed on acid-free, 250-year-life paper
Manufactured in the United States of America

# CONTENTS

# PREFACE

Proceedings of the Second Society for Research
on Child Development Round Table:
Children of Color

The second of three Round Tables brought together scholars from the disciplines of anthropology, education, family and child ecology, pediatrics, nursing, social work, sociology, and developmental psychology, to discuss past, current, and future research, health, and policy issues apropos of children from currently defined minority groups within American society.

Regardless of the time or the conditions under which various peoples came to North America, their presence has contributed to the rich diversity of cultures that now define American society and that link its citizenry to nearly every geographical region of the world. The only guarantee about the next century is that this diversity will continue to increase. The Immigration Act of 1990 paved the way for substantially more immigration to the United States than in the preceding decade, and, by the time the 1990s draw to a close, immigration will have accounted for more than half of the population growth of the United States during the decade. This immigration in combination with growth rates among minorities within the United States, forecasts an American population in the mid 21st century that will be slightly more than 50 percent non-white. However, knowledge about the diversity of cultures is not matched by an equal knowledge about the diversity of child development within those cultures. Neither is there a critical mass of researchers with sufficient cultural competence to address the methodological, theoretical, and pragmatic challenges that within-culture studies present. The Round Table was designed to frame these challenges and to focus attention on the need to develop innovative approaches to the study of child development that can strengthen our understanding of within-species diversity.

In Chapter 1, Vonnie McLoyd challenges researchers to focus attention on the factors that promote positive developmental outcomes for minority children, especially those who live in high risk environments. Part of this challenge is to shift from deficit and compensatory models and to broadly examine the way that researchers conduct their business. In Chapter 2, Jeanne Brooks-Gunn and her colleagues question the validity of instruments used in data collection and the constructs assessed across the breadth of minority groups. Specifically, they question the use of family race, ethnicity, and social class as explanatory variables in child development research. Dena Swanson and Margaret Beale Spencer (Chapter 3) respond to the challenge for innovations in theory and propose a phenomenological ecological systems theory for the study of risk, vulnerability, and resilience of urban youth who reside in high risk environments. In addition, they call for the construction of a normative developmental psychology of minority youth.

Such a normative psychology will require a broader understanding of culture, and John Ogbu's anthropological approach serves as a solid starting point (Chapter 4). Ogbu suggests that understanding culture is not sufficient, one also needs to develop a research corps that focuses less on "problem" children, attends more to the meaning of cultural competence, and emphasizes human development within its cultural context. For example, according to Mary Lou de Leon Siantz (Chapter 5), migration must be understood within the context of the Hispanic family, with its emphasis on family and cultural values (familism, respect, gender roles) in relation to child socialization. She proposes a mediational model for the study of mental health, academic performance, and social adjustment of Hispanic children. Al Bienstar del Niño is a program that focuses on the health needs of Mexican-American children and the strategies that their parents use to assist development of healthy lifestyles. In Chapter 6, Norma Olvera Ezzell and her colleagues report some of the findings from their study of this community based program. They found that mothers who had fatalistic views about health were less likely to use socialization techniques that would promote the internalization of good health practices among their children.

Our deficient knowledge of the health status of immigrant minority children is particularly distressing. In Chapter 7, Fernando Mendoza and Noel Rosales point out that building a national data base on the health status of immigrant children would facilitate development of effective policy and treatment decisions apropos of their health care. For example, Rubén Rumbaut and John Weeks (Chapter 8) present evidence indicating the low income immigrants from Mexico and Southeast Asia have unexpectedly positive perinatal outcomes. Paradoxically, however, their health risks increase as acculturation increases. Rumbaut and Weeks suggest that the high socioeconomic status of U.S. born individuals, may be offset by an increase in risky behaviors that contribute to medical, nutritional, and psychosocial disadvantage and, therefore, poorer perinatal outcomes. Here is a case where a strong national data base on minority health status could help to determine whether risky behaviors actually do increase with acculturation, for whom such behaviors increase, and what policy decisions would most likely counter the presumed negative effects of acculturation.

In Chapter 9, Rowena Fong and Colette Browne examine the impact of immigration policy on Chinese-American families. Chinese families place strong emphasis on filial piety, that is the individual is subsumed by the family. When immigration policy leads to intergenerational separation of family members, it attacks a set of family values that may never be replaced, especially by very young couples. Fong and Browne echo a recurrent theme in these chapters, namely, that grouping individuals into government defined categories masks the rich within-category diversity. This is as true for the peoples of Southeast Asia as it is for people from Latin America, Africa, and Europe.

How all of this diversity plays out in public policy decisions is a question that Harriette Pipes McAdoo believes requires stronger input from the research community. Obviously, all of this has implications for public policy. In Chapter 10, McAdoo proposes an action agenda for research with children and families. To generate an active agenda, the research community must increase its capacity to translate research into practice. McAdoo argues that researchers need to study the outcomes of public policy decisions, so that decisions about policy can be informed by science based outcomes. Cynthia García Coll and Katherine Magnuson point out that social policy affects children of color disproportionately because they are disproportionately represented among groups receiving the benefits of social policy (e.g., poor families). Finally, Melvin Wilson and his associates (Chapter 12) draw attention to the fact that minority families are embedded in a majority educational system. Thus, minority culture is learned at home, it is not part of the dominant culture, and the dominant culture knows little about how minority children are socialized into family.

These chapters, therefore, represent the proceedings of the Round Table. Each chapter represents an expansion of the 10–minute oral presentations made by the Round Table participants. Missing from this volume is the rich and active 20 minute discussion that followed each presentation, although authors had rough transcriptions of the discussions available as they prepared their final chapters.

As with the first Round Table, we would like to thank the members of the Society for Research in Child Development Executive Committee and the SRCD Liaison to Pediatrics program for their continued sponsorship of these discussions. Proceedings of the third Round Table, are in preparation and will appear in print in 1999. The Round Tables would not have taken place without the financial support of the Irving B. Harris Foundation, an organization that has provided broad infrastructure support for the clinical and scientific study of infants, children, and families. Finally, we thank all of the Round Table participants for their high spirits, patience, and good will during the twelve continuous hours of Round Table presentations and discussion.

Hiram E. Fitzgerald
Barry M. Lester
Barry S. Zuckerman
December 1998

# CONTRIBUTORS

JEANNE BROOKS-GUNN, PH.D.
Center for Children and Families
Teachers College
Columbia University
New York, NY

COLETTE BROWNE, D.P.H.
University of Hawai'i at Manoa
School of Social Work
Honolulu, HI

RAYMOND CHAN, M.A.
Department of Psychology
University of Virginia
Charlottesville, VA

JENNIFER H. COUSINS, PH.D.
Department of Medicine
Baylor College of Medicine
Houston, TX

HIRAM E. FITZGERALD, PH.D.
Department of Psychology and
    Applied Developmental Science
    Programs
Michigan State University
East Lansing, MI

ROWENA FONG, ED.D.
University of Hawai'i at Manoa
School of Social Work
Honolulu, HI

CYNTHIA GARCÍA COLL, PH.D.
Education Department
Brown University
Providence, RI

BARRY M. LESTER, PH.D.
Brown University Program
    in Medicine
Departments of Psychiatry
    and Psychology
E. Providence, RI

TAMA LEVENTHAL
Center for Children and Families
Teachers College
Columbia University
New York, NY

KATHERINE MAGNUSON, B.A.
Education Department
Brown University
Providence, RI

HARRIETTE PIPES MCADOO, PH.D.
Department of Family and Child
  Ecology
Michigan State University
East Lansing, MI

VONNIE C. MCLOYD, PH.D.
Department of Psychology and
  Center for Human Growth
  and Development
University of Michigan
Ann Arbor, MI

FERNANDO MENDOZA, M.D., M.P.H.
School of Medicine
Department of Pediatrics
Stanford University
Palo Alto, CA

JOHN U. OGBU, PH.D.
Department of Anthropology
University of California
Berkeley, CA

NORMA OLVERA-EZZELL, PH.D.
Office of Health Promotion
Baylor College of Medicine
Houston, TX

L. MICHELLE PIÑA, M.A.
Department of Psychology
University of Virginia
Charlottesville, VA

THOMAS G. POWER, PH.D.
Department of Psychology
University of Houston
Houston, Texas

VIRGINIA RAUH, D.SC.
Center for Population and Family
  Health
Columbia University School
  of Public Health
New York, NY

NOEL ROSALES
School of Medicine
Department of Pediatrics
Stanford University
Palo Alto, CA

RUBÉN G. RUMBAUT, PH.D.
Department of Sociology
Michigan State University
East Lansing, MI

MARY LOU DE LEON SIANTZ,
PH.D., R.N.
Psychiatric-Mental Health Nursing
Indiana University School of Nursing
Indianapolis, IN

DESIREE D. SOBERANIS, B.A.
Department of Psychology
University of Virginia
Charlottesville, VA

MARGARET BEALE SPENCER, PH.D.
Center for Health, Achievement,
  Neighborhood Growth and
  Ethnic Studies (CHANGES)
University of Pennsylvania
Philadelphia, PA

DENA PHILLIPS SWANSON, PH.D.
Center for Health, Achievement,
  Neighborhood Growth and
  Ethnic Studies (CHANGES)
University of Pennsylvania
Philadelphia, PA

JOHN R. WEEKS, PH.D.
San Diego State University
San Diego, CA

MELVIN N. WILSON, PH.D.
Department of Psychology
University of Virginia
Charlottesville, VA

CLAUDIA YAÑEZ, B.S.
Department of Public Affairs
Office of Health Promotion
Baylor College of Medicine
Houston, TX

BARRY S. ZUCKERMAN, M.D.
Department of Pediatrics
Boston University School
  of Medicine
Boston, MA

# SECTION 1
## RESEARCH ISSUES

# 1 CONCEPTUAL AND METHODOLOGICAL ISSUES IN THE STUDY OF ETHNIC MINORITY CHILDREN AND ADOLESCENTS

*Vonnie C. McLoyd*

More dramatic than at any time in the twentieth century, the past decade saw increases in the proportion of racial and ethnic minorities in the American population. Each of the four major ethnic minority groups increased as a proportion of the total American population, with even sharper increases occurring in the child and adolescent population. In 1980, of all American children between the ages of 10 and 19, 75.8% were non-Hispanic whites, 14.2% were African Americans, 7.8% were Hispanic, 1.5% were Asian/Pacific Islanders, and 0.8% were Native Americans. By 1992, the comparable figures were 68.8%, 14.8%, 12.1%, 3.4%, and 1%, respectively (U.S. Bureau of the Census, 1994). Growth among racial and ethnic minorities is projected to exceed that of non-Hispanic whites for several decades. Demographers predict that by 2010, non-Hispanic whites will constitute only 60.4% of Americans between the ages of 14 and 24, with African Americans, Latinos, Asian/Pacific Islanders, and Native Americans comprising 17.2%, 15.9%, 5.6% and 0.9% (39.6% total) (U.S. Bureau of the Census, 1994).

The recent and projected increases in the proportion of racial and ethnic minorities in the American population are driven primarily by two factors: (1) higher immigration rates of minorities, compared to immigration rates for non-Hispanic whites of European or Middle Eastern descent and (2) slightly higher fertility rates of immigrants, compared to native-born Americans. Prior to the late 1950s, most immigrants to America were from northern and western European countries, with Germany being the leading source as recently as the early 1950s (Martin & Midgley, 1994). However, by the 1980s, 85% of all immigrants arriving in the United States were from Asian and Latin American countries, whereas only 10% were from Europe. Mexico, the Philippines, Vietnam, China, and Korea, respectively, were the top five countries of origin. Caribbean countries, taken together, were the second-largest source of immigrants during the 1980s (following Mexico), most of whom were from the Dominican Republic (28%), followed by Jamaica (24%), Cuba (18%), Haiti (16%), and Trinidad and Tobago (4% combined) (U.S. Bureau of the Census, 1994).

Growth in the proportion of racial and ethnic minorities in the American population is occurring in the context of another significant demographic trend, specifically, a decline in the proportion of adolescents and young adults in the total American population. Between 1980 and 1992, the proportion of adolescents and young adults between the ages of 10 and 19 years old in the American population dropped from 17.4% to 13.8% (U.S. Bureau of the Census, 1994). This decline, first discernible in the early 1980s, is largely a function of lower birthrates and the huge generation that preceded the current cohort of American youth, commonly known as the baby boomers (Wetzel, 1987). It will translate into a reduction in the number of entrants into the labor force and, hence, a decline in the ratio of workers to retirees. The effect of this trend, combined with increases in the proportion of racial and ethnic minorities in the American population, is that as Americans age, they will be increasingly dependent on the productivity of African American, Hispanic, and Asian workers. In the coming decades, then, American's economic and social well-being will depend even more than at present on its ability to enhance intellectual and social competence and minimize problematic development in all its youth (Edelman, 1987; Wetzel, 1987).

Significant advancement toward the latter goals is likely to require a confluence of facilitating conditions. Arguably, the most important of these is a shift in governmental priorities toward policies and support programs that reduce childhood poverty and its adverse effects. As of 1993, 22.7% of children under age 18 were officially classified as poor (U.S. Bureau of the Census, 1994), a rate of childhood poverty markedly higher than those in most Western industrialized countries (i.e., Canada, Sweden, Germany, Netherlands, France, United Kingdom) (Smeeding & Torrey, 1988). This challenge will require considerably more information than is currently available about the precursors, moderators, and mediators of successful and problematic development in minority children and adolescents. In this chapter, the current state of knowledge about development in minority children is assessed and priorities for research on this topic are offered in light of these recent and projected demographic trends. Special attention is given to African Americans, the largest ethnic minority group in America (U.S. Bureau of the Census, 1994) and the one that most often has been at the center of controversy about psychological research on minorities (Guthrie, 1976; Jones, 1991; Myers, Rana & Harris, 1979).

During the past decade or so, a number of researchers conducted systematic analyses of data-based articles in child development journals in an attempt to characterize the current state of psychological knowledge about minority children. Focused primarily on the nature of empirical investigations of African American children, these analyses, along with critiques of specific lines of research, point to several limitations in the current knowledge base about development in these children. These limitations center on three issues, namely, the quantity of research available, conceptual biases, and research methodology.

## Paucity of Research on Minority Children

First and foremost, the field is at risk of being unable to help meet the challenges and informational needs created by changing demographics because it generates so little knowledge about minority children. The overwhelming majority of empirical studies published in major, nonspecialized child development journals (i.e., *Child Development, Developmental Psychology*) focus exclusively or primarily on non-Hispanic whites (Graham, 1992; Hagen & Conley, 1994; McLoyd & Randolph, 1985). Notably few are concerned with minority children. The rate of research on African American children is very low in absolute terms, but tends to be higher than rates for children from other minority groups (Hagen & Conley, 1994). Even so, recent years have witnessed a surprising decrease in the number and percentage of articles about African American children. The possibility that this trend holds for articles about all minority children is troubling.

In her analyses of empirical articles published between 1970 and 1989 in six journals of the American Psychological Association, Graham (1992) found a steady decrease in the number and percentage of articles about African Americans, defined as those articles in which the authors specifically stated that African Americans were the population of interest or analyzed their data by race. A linear increase in the number and percentage of relevant articles was observed between 1970 and 1974 (203 articles or 5.2%), followed by a steady drop in each of three subsequent publication periods—1975–1979 (165 articles or 4.1%), 1980–1984 (93 articles or 2.7%), 1985–1989 (65 articles or 2%). This pattern was evident in five journals, two of which publish a high percentage of articles concerning child and adolescent development (i.e., *Journal of Educational Psychology* and *Developmental Psychology*). A pattern similar to the one documented by Graham was found in *Child Development*. McLoyd and Randolph's (1985) analysis of this journal for the period 1936–1980 indicated that the number of articles on African American children increased through the early 1970s and declined thereafter. There are several plausible explanations for the decline in mainstream journal publication of research on African Americans, among them, a reduction in research funding (McLoyd & Randolph, 1985), increased desire to avoid the controversy and ethical and moral risks associated with empirical study of African Americans, and disciplinary shifts to topics less relevant to the study of African Americans (Graham, 1992).

A recent study of articles published in *Child Development* between 1980 and 1993 found that the rate of research on African Americans remained extremely low through the 1980s, but showed a slight recovery between 1990 and 1993. This increase was not an artifact of a special issue of *Child Development* devoted to research on ethnic minority children, published in 1990, as this issue was excluded from the analyses (Spencer & McLoyd, 1990). Whether this signals a real growth trend or is simply random variation remains to be seen. It also is noteworthy that this study found abysmally low rates of research on Hispanics and Asian Americans (Hagen & Conley, 1994).

*Conceptual Biases in Research on Minority Children*

Conceptual biases also contribute to the limited capacity of existing research to help address the challenges created by an increasingly heterogeneous population. Deviance and negative developmental outcomes have been the dominant foci of research on minority children. Relatedly, studies of minority children, like those of minority adults, rarely have samples that qualify as representative of within-race or within-ethnicity diversity (Jones, 1991). Commonly studied are children developing in high-risk contexts marked by, among other things, poverty, low parental education, parental unemployment, and dangerous neighborhoods (Allen & Majidi-Ahi, 1989; Gibbs, 1989; Inclan & Herron, 1989; LaFromboise & Low, 1989; McLoyd & Randolph, 1984; Ramirez, 1989). The problem is not the existence of such research per se, but rather the lack of a counterweight corpus of research that focuses on normative development, contributors to positive developmental outcomes, and minority children living in more benign environments.

Research on ethnic minority children is dominated by a race- and ethnic-comparative framework (i.e., African American children compared to non-Hispanic white children). In their analyses of articles about African American children published in *Child Development* between 1936 and 1980, McLoyd and Randolph (1985) found that the number of race-comparative studies was almost twice that of race-homogeneous studies (i.e., studies with only African American children as research participants). Almost three times as many race-comparative studies as race-homogeneous studies were identified in another study of articles about African American children published in over 20 journals between 1973 and 1975 (McLoyd & Randolph, 1984). Similarly, Graham's (1992) analyses revealed that of all studies of African Americans published in *Developmental Psychology* and the *Journal of Educational Psychology* between 1970 and 1989, 65% and 78%, respectively, were race-comparative.

This comparative framework is problematic on several counts. First, race- and ethnic- comparative studies are rarely guided by an explicit theoretical or conceptual rationale for the comparison. More often they are exploratory or designed to document the existence of mean differences based on the vaguest of notions about why race or ethnicity "matters." In his appraisal of psychological research on ethnic minority adults, Jones (1991) found a similar preoccupation with, and an atheoretical approach to, the study of race/ethnic differences. Although focused primarily on psychological research on minority adults, Jones' characterizations of this work are no less accurate than research on minority children and adolescents:

> The most common approach is to take an idea, a measurement instrument, or a finding in the literature, and see if Blacks differ from whites, if American Indians differ from Anglo-Americans, and if Asians differ from Hispanics and Blacks and Anglo-Americans, and so forth. . . . But a review of all the published studies in APA journals and some selected other journals such as *Child Development* . . . reveals very little systematic knowledge accumulation. . . . These studies are typically atheoretical. . . . The study of race differences has become an attempt to catalogue the array of ways people differ as a result of their location in society, their history, and their cumulative interactions within their group and between themselves and members of other groups. No unified theory of these kinds of sociocultural or historical effects exists, although we do often develop generalized notions that are used to "explain" findings. (pp. 32–33)

In other instances, discovery of race/ethnicity effects are simply by-products of statistical controls for race or ethnicity. That is, partitioning the amount of variance due to race or ethnicity often reflects nothing more than the researcher's strategy to reduce extraneous variance as much as possible to give the focal independent variables a chance to show their significance. Given the atheoretical nature of most race/ethnic-comparative research, the rarity of systematic efforts to determine what factors account for or mediate a documented race/ethnic difference is hardly surprising. This treatment of race and ethnicity has resulted in a desultory literature replete with studies of one-shot questions and reports of race/ethnic differences that are pedestrian, unexplained, and insubstantial in their scientific contribution. As Jones (1991) noted, one of the legacies of this tradition is minimal systematic accumulation of knowledge about ethnic minorities. Lack of attention to factors that mediate or account for race/ethnic differences is especially striking when compared to research on other equally complex demographic variables such as social class and poverty. Psychological research on social class and poverty has clearly shifted from description of effects to explanation of these effects, that is, analyses of processes by which social class and poverty affect psychological outcomes (Bronfenbrenner, 1986; House, 1981; Huston, McLoyd & García Coll, 1994). Inexplicably, research on the "effects" of race and ethnicity has shown no such advancement. This issue is discussed in more detail later in the chapter.

A related criticism of the race/ethnic-comparative framework is that it not only fosters atheoretical research, but also impedes development of psychological theory relevant to minority groups and programmatic examination of individual differences within different minority groups (Azibo, 1988; Howard & Scott, 1981; McLoyd & Randolph, 1984). Comparatively little is known about individual differences within minority groups or the sources of deviation from the norms of development within these populations. The importance of attending to intragroup variation is underscored by research demonstrating that variables which best explain differences within certain minority groups in, for example, achievement are sometimes different from those that best explain intergroup differences (Howard & Scott, 1981). Scholars also have criticized the race/ethnic-comparative framework for indirectly fostering a view of minority children as deviant. When race or ethnic differences are found, critics argue, they often are interpreted as deficiencies or pathologies in minority children, rather than in cultural relativistic, ecological, or systemic terms (Howard & Scott, 1981; Myers, Rana & Harris, 1979). Deficiency interpretations are not necessarily inherent to race/ethnic-comparative studies. However, they hold sway largely because of their compatibility with the pejorative and stigmatized view of African Americans in particular (Crocker & Major, 1989). This hegemony eclipses alternative explanations, obviates direct tests of mediating processes, and in general, stymies the formulation and empirical testing of psychological theory concerned within minority children, adults, and families.

## Methodological Problems in Research on Minority Children

The view of minority children as deviant is further advanced by the practice of comparing low-SES (socioeconomic status) minority children with middle-SES white children. This problem was present in almost one-fourth of race-comparative studies published in *Child Development* between 1936 and 1980 (McLoyd & Randolph, 1985). Graham's (1992) analyses of *Developmental Psychology* and the *Journal of Educational Psychology* revealed lower, but not insignificant, rates of confounding (14% and 19%, respectively, of all race-comparative studies). In addition, of the studies on African Americans in these two journals that used acceptable criteria to specify the social class of research participants (e.g., standard social class indices, indirect measures such as census data, information from school records, participation in compensatory education program), 25% of those in *Developmental Psychology* and 36% of those in the *Journal of Educational Psychology* compared low-SES African Americans with either middle-SES whites alone or to samples consisting of both low- and middle-SES whites.

Nonspecification of the race of the experimenter (examiner, interviewer, therapist) and use of instruments developed for use with white middle-class individuals is a common threat to the internal validity of research on minority children and adolescents (Myers, Rana & Harris, 1979). McLoyd and Randolph (1985) found that the experimenter's race was unspecified in 71% of all studies of African American children published in *Child Development* between 1936 and 1980. High rates of nonspecification were also found in their content analysis of articles published about African American children in several human development journals (McLoyd & Randolph, 1984). Likewise, Graham (1992) reported that between 1970 and 1989, 65% of articles about African Americans in *Developmental Psychology* and 88% of studies in the *Journal of Educational Psychology* failed to mention experimenter race. As she explained, concern about nonspecification of experimenter race is not necessarily predicated on the assumption that white experimenters have negative effects on African American children's behavior. Rather, the issue is the unknown and its sheer pervasiveness. In effect, experimenter race effects, where they exist, constitute error variance in the majority of studies of African American children published in premier journals in child development. Nonspecification of experimenter race makes impossible even crude estimates of how findings may be affected by experimenter race. It also hinders independent verification of findings, a task crucial to the advancement of fields of knowledge.

In addition to the internal validity problems created by the confounding of race, ethnicity, and social class, nonspecification of experimenter race, and use of instruments whose psychometric properties within minority populations have not been established, many studies of minority children have unknown external validity because of inadequate specification of the social class background of the children or that of the white comparison group. McLoyd and Randolph (1985) found that one-fourth of race-comparative studies published in *Child Development* up to 1980 did not even mention the social class of one or both of the groups. Moreover, Graham's (1992) analysis indicated that 45% of race-comparative studies in *Developmental Psychology* and 48% of such studies in the *Journal of Educational Psychology* used unacceptable criteria (e.g., subjective impressions) to specify the social class of research participants. Appropriate generalization of findings is dependent on adequate definition and description of the sample and the target and accessible population (Kerlinger, 1973). The problem of inadequate subject descriptions is not limited to studies of minority children. Indeed, Hagen and Conley (1994) found that between 50% and 70% of studies published in *Child Development* each year between 1980 and 1991 gave no information whatsoever concerning the ethnic or racial backgrounds of the research participants!

The prevalence of comparisons between lower-SES African Americans and middle-SES whites and nonspecification of children's social class led Graham (1992) to conclude that "empirical studies involving African Americans have remained remarkably insensitive to the complexities of race and class in this society" (p. 634). This insensitivity borders on social irresponsibility and scientific imprudence because it results in invidious comparisons, promotes racial group stereotypes, minimizes the existence and benefits of white privilege, and of course, leaves entangled the proportion of variance accounted for by race versus socioeconomic status (SES). Furthermore, race-comparative studies that fail to specify experimenter race racially neutralize the research context and researcher-participant relations, even while testing race as a significant source of variation in the dependent variable. None of these research practices is trivial, for ours is a nation transfixed and transformed by race and racial oppression since its inception, marked by de facto racial segregation in virtually all ecological and social contexts, and convulsed with regularity by heated debates on the interpretation of data on the relation of race to human behavior and social stratification (e.g., performance on IQ tests, school achievement, residential segregation, economic well-being) (Fairchild et al., 1995; Hacker, 1992; Herrnstein & Murray, 1994; Jacoby & Glauberman, 1995; Yee et al., 1993; Zuckerman, 1990).

Although the truth or validity of a particular study is impossible to prove, circumstances and factors that pose significant threats to validity are relatively common in research on minority children and adolescents. Approaches to the conceptualization of external validity typically emphasize population, and ecological and construct validity. However, in their analysis of the external validity of race-comparative research, Washington and McLoyd (1982) argued that such approaches do not provide an adequate framework for comparative research involving ethnic minorities. They call for systematic efforts to insure cultural as well as interpretative validity, seen as an empirical mechanism for the inclusion of intentionality and meaning in the research process.

Cultural validity is concerned with the procedures necessary to identify the rules that regulate conduct (i.e., norms) as well as those that define various practices and institutions. Rules of the first kind tell us that certain things ought to or may be done in a certain manner. Those of the second kind tell us how acts are to be performed, providing a system of rules that gives structure to such things as marriage, contracts, language, and religion. Ethnic segregation, but especially racial segregation, is a longstanding and omnipresent pattern within American society that is even more salient when social class is taken into account (Hacker, 1992; Massey, 1994). An important consequence of this segregation for the research process is that white scholars typically possess only a modicum of knowledge of the rules, norms, and nuances of minority cultures, especially as manifested in lower-SES strata of these cultures. Moreover, in many instances, their ethnocentrism and arrogance on the one hand, and minority individuals' suspicions of the motives of researchers on the other, are hindrances to white researchers' acquisition of this cultural knowledge. Commitment of energy and resources to bridge the longstanding, structurally rooted chasms that often separate white researchers from minority individuals is predicated on recognition and acknowledgment of deficits in cultural knowledge. These deficits, if not remediated, pose serious threats to the cultural validity of investigations of minorities.

Recent work by Brody and his colleagues (Brody, et al., 1994) provides a rare example within the field of child development of systematic efforts to reduce threats to cultural validity. Prior to undertaking their study of the effects of family financial resources on the academic competence and socioemotional adjustment of African American youth living in the rural South, Brody et al. formed focus groups comprised of rural African Americans who were representative of the population they planned to study. These groups assisted in the development of valid self-report instruments, suggesting changes in wording of scale items and deletion of items that they perceived as unclear or irrelevant to rural African Americans. They also recommended data collection procedures and contexts that they believed would yield the most sound data and that families would consider most acceptable.

Interpretative validity hinges on the premise that human actions are teleological or intentional. The basis for teleology is the individual making choices about goals and how to achieve them. The intentional nature of human action places the individual at the center of the explanation of action. It is the individual who is best able to describe the motivational background, goals, and perceived means to achieve goals that set the stage for action (Washington & McLoyd, 1982). The question of whether to utilize the words, motives, and purposes of the informants or to give priority to the interpretations of social scientists is one of the critical methodological questions in race/ethnic-comparative research. This dispute dates back to the debates between the anthropologists Leslie White and Franz Boas (Fisher & Werner, 1978). The Boas group contended that each culture has to be understood on its own terms and that it is the actor's interpretation of a phenomenon that is the basic datum of the discipline. White and his supporters, on the other hand, were advocates of a scientific approach in which causal explanation of phenomena is used in the search for "universal" dimensions of culture. In their search for a way out of this dilemma, Fisher and Werner (1978) argued that anthropology should begin with "the culturally constituted units, always listening to what people tell us, while looking for the theoretical structure that enables us to understand and interpret what we are hearing, and observing" (p. 215).

In view of the omnipresent racial and ethnic cleavages in American society and the myriad factors that act as barriers to communication among ethnic/racial groups within the general populace, Fisher and Werner's proposal is as relevant to psychologists studying America's ethnic minorities as it is to anthropologists conducting crosscultural research. One of the consequences of racial and ethnic oppression in American society is the creation of a series of myths and distorted images of the lives of minorities. For this reason alone, it seems important that researchers conducting race/ethnic-comparative research provide opportunities for participants to give their interpretations of the issues at hand. Empirical research in child development and child socialization has made virtually no progress in this area, largely because interpretative validity is not a criterion by which the quality of research is judged.

This is not to suggest that progressive trends are not evident on some fronts. In a special issue of *Child Development* devoted to research on minority children (Spencer & McLoyd, 1990), the number of race-comparative and race-homogeneous studies was about equal (as was the case for the total pool of manuscripts submitted for publication in the special issue). This may signal a growing acceptance of studying minority children in their own right and a weakening of the view that a comparison group comprised of white children is a prerequisite for adequate interpretation of research findings about minority children. In addition, many of the studies published in the special issue tested hypothesized processes (i.e., they were not strictly outcome-oriented) and focused attention on sources of variation within racial/ethnic groups (McLoyd, 1990).

## PRIORITIES FOR RESEARCH ON RACIAL AND ETHNIC MINORITY CHILDREN AND ADOLESCENTS

In view of minorities' growing representation in the American population, the urgency of increasing the rate and quality of research on minority youth and families has never been greater. Avoiding the methodological problems identified above, as well as undertaking procedures that reduce threats to validity, are important steps toward improving the quality of research. Priorities for research on minority children and adolescents are described in the next section. The goal is not to present an exhaustive list of specific topics, but rather to outline basic issues and questions that cut across content areas or domains of development. We especially need to (1) develop more culturally relevant conceptual frameworks for thinking about minority children and families; (2) proceed beyond cataloguing race and ethnic differences to systematic study of the factors that mediate these differences; (3) expand our knowledge about normative development and precursors of resilience in minority children; (4) better understand the etiology of problematic development, including whether and how race and ethnicity moderate etiology; (5) produce knowledge useful for the formulation of policy and for the development, delivery, and maintenance of intervention and prevention programs that address the needs of minority children and families; and (6) expand our understanding of processes that reduce racial and ethnic prejudice and facilitate transracial/transethnic understanding. We shall now examine each of these priorities.

### Culturally Relevant Concepts and Theoretical Frameworks

Existing developmental research, in the main, is undergirded by conceptual frameworks developed for thinking about white middle-class children and families. The concepts and values at the center of these frameworks often are incompatible with the experiences, beliefs, and values of major segments of minority populations. For example, for Native Americans, tribe or tribal grouping, rather than the nuclear family, is the important unit of analysis for understanding patterns of organization, family systems, and socialization. Likewise, whereas individual autonomy and competitiveness are strongly held values in white middle-class culture, in many minority groups, these values are tempered by or rejected in favor of values for interdependence and cooperation (Boykin, 1983; Harrison, Serafica & McAdoo, 1984; Harrison, et al., 1990).

Progress in understanding minority children and families will require formulating more culturally appropriate concepts and broadening and/or reframing theoretical conceptions of behavior and competence to reflect the cultural diversity that exists in American society—processes too often short-circuited in the research process (Dilworth-Anderson, Burton & Johnson, 1993; Laosa, 1989). Developing and reconfiguring analytic points of departure are part of the intricate and dynamic processes by which research is made culturally sensitive (Rogler, 1989) and are critically important determinants of the quality, content, and applicability of information yielded by investigations. The challenge, then, is not to create data bases on minority children that necessarily parallel those that exist on white middle-class children. More valuable is formulating culturally relevant constructs, developing sound measures of indicators of these constructs, and systematically studying their precursors and consequences. However, this kind of work is more arduous and slower-paced, partly because it demands a lot of "spade-work" and creative thought, is more dynamic than linear in nature, and often is not given high priority by funding agencies because its feasibility and payoffs are seen as more uncertain than is the case for traditional research.

## Mediators of Race and Ethnicity "Effects"

As we noted previously, most studies of minority children are race- or ethnic-comparative in design. They typify what Bronfenbrenner (1986) termed the "social address" model of analysis, contrasting children who differ in terms of race/ethnicity with no explicit consideration of intervening structures or processes through which race or ethnicity affect the course of development. Most scholars agree that race, like ethnicity, is a social, not a biological, category (Cooper & David, 1986; Gould, 1983; Montagu, 1964; Yee et al., 1993; Zuckerman, 1990). The concept of race as a marker of an immutable physical (i.e., biological, genetic) entity owes its emergence in American society partly to the economic-based need to singularize and stigmatize African Americans in order to justify slavery, foment white racism, and in turn, minimize class consciousness and obfuscate class oppression within white society (Bennett, 1966). As we note below, race persists as a powerful determinant of economic well-being and the availability of economic opportunities.

Given that race and ethnicity are categories defined by social characteristics, systematic inquiry into those social variables that account for the ever-expanding catalogue of race and ethnic differences in the psychological litera-ture is long overdue. Essentially, this involves the difficult work of dissecting out of the complex matrix of race and ethnicity certain process variables and relating them to developmental outcomes, much as has been done with pov-erty and social class (Huston, McLoyd & García Coll, 1994). House (1981) has argued persuasively that tracing the processes through which social struc-tures, positions, or systems affect the individual involves three theoretical tasks. Although directed toward understanding how and why socioeconomic status influences behavior, his analysis is instructive for understanding the mediators of race and ethnicity effects as well. First, according to House, we must un-derstand the multiple aspects, dimensions, and components of the social struc-ture, position, or system in question, and ultimately, develop conceptual frame-works that specify which of these are most relevant to understanding, in our case, observed race or ethnic differences in developmental outcomes.

Second, on the grounds that social structures, positions, or systems influence individuals through their effects on social interactional patterns, stimuli, and events that individuals experience in their daily lives, House (1981) maintains that we must understand the proximate social stimuli and interpersonal interactions that result from one's social location (i.e., race or ethnicity). In the case of race and ethnicity, these might include, among count-less possibilities, culturally distinctive family and peer socialization experi-ences, cultural belief systems that guide behavior and accord meaning to experiences, contacts with indigenous cultural institutions (e.g., churches representing various religious denominations), interactions and exposure to events that derive from race- and ethnicity-related ecological contexts (e.g., poor minority children are more likely to live in high-poverty neighborhoods than are poor white children; O'Hare, 1994), racial and ethnic socialization, and experiences of discrimination or inferiorization (Bowman & Howard, 1985; Boykin, 1983; Feagin, 1991; Jones, 1991). Finally, according to House, we need to understand when, how, and to what extent these proximate ex-periences affect behavior or dispositions, a task that requires documenting the psychological processes through which interactions and stimuli are per-ceived, processed, and accommodated. Systematic research of this nature is essential to forging a better understanding of the meaning and significance of race and ethnicity as they bear on development (Spencer, 1990).

## Normative Development and Precursors of Resilience

Adequate data bases about normative patterns of development in minority children from *diverse* economic backgrounds are the bedrock of genuine ethnic, racial, and class diversification of research on child and adolescent development. They are preconditions for the search for universals and the formulation of culturally valid definitions of both *deviance* and *resilience*. Relatedly, data on normative development could be enormously helpful in interpreting and according significance to findings from studies of environmental influences (e.g., after-school care) on minority children's development. A shift in priority from race- and ethnic-comparative research to race- and ethnic-homogeneous research may be a prerequisite of significant progress in assembling such data bases. Decisions about aggregating or distinguishing particular groups of ethnic and racial minority youths (e.g., Mexican Americans vs. Cuban Americans vs. Puerto Ricans; Chinese Americans vs. Japanese Americans) will need to be reached with a clear appreciation of the historical, linguistic, cultural, and ecological factors that separate these groups and the relevance of these factors for understanding the issues under investigation (Harrison, Serafica & McAdoo, 1984; Harrison et al., 1990; Portes & Rumbaut, 1990). Programs of research on normative development also will require development of new standardized measures or modification of existing ones to insure that they are valid and reliable and, in general, that they have good psychometric properties in minority populations.

Study of the developmental course and adaptation of children of immigrants from different cultures and geographic locations is critical. We need to understand the forces that determine how they resolve conflicting ideas and values of their parents versus native-born peers and adults; the multiple pathways to ethnic identity formation, resolution, and assimilation; and how these processes influence psychological functioning, school achievement, social behavior, and life chances. Within this broad agenda, study is needed of the dynamic interplay between the characteristics that immigrants and their children bring with them and the various features of the social contexts that receive them (e.g., school, church, neighborhood) and how this interplay influences the adaptation process and developmental outcomes. What factors, for example, determine whether a particular immigrant group assimilates into the mainstream middle-class sector of American society, as opposed to the underclass, or whether it preserves or relinquishes immigrant values, mores, and solidarity (Portes & Zhou, 1993; Rumbaut, 1995)?

Minority children in general are more likely than their white counterparts to be confronted with a range of chronic and acute stressors associated with problematic development (e.g., poverty, marital disruption, violence, and parental incarceration and death) (Gibbs et al., 1989). Nevertheless, many are intellectually dexterous, academically successful. and socially well-adjusted, despite such stressors. We need to learn what kinds of environmental supports and conditions enable them to defy the odds. Research on naturally occurring processes that lead to these positive outcomes is an important counterweight to inquiries into adverse effects of acute and chronic stressors, both for its contribution to basic knowledge and its potential implications for policy and practice. Because successful adaptation is more than the absence of negative development, research on resilience holds promise as a source of valuable information over and above what we learn from studying the precursors of problematic adaptation. This nascent area of research, coalescing around the concept of resiliency, is exciting, vital, and grappling with a host of conceptual and methodological issues (Cowen et al., 1990; Luthar & Zigler, 1991; Masten et al., 1990; Rutter, 1990; Werner & Smith, 1982). Unfortunately, little of this work focuses on African American children or other minority children (e.g., Clark, 1983; Jarrett, 1995; Williams & Kornblum, 1985).

### Etiology of Problematic Development

Many of the most pressing problems now facing the United States (e.g., school dropout, poor academic performance, violence, teenage pregnancy and childbearing, HIV infection) disproportionately affect children from ethnic and racial minority backgrounds (Gibbs et al., 1989). To a major extent, this circumstance is rooted in the greater socioeconomic disadvantage experienced by minority children of both native-born and immigrant parents. This disadvantage is reflected in higher rates of poverty and residence in concentrated poverty areas, among other factors. In 1991, Puerto Rican, African American, and Mexican American children under 18 years of age had poverty rates of 57%, 44%, and 36%, respectively, compared to a rate of 15% for non-Hispanic white children (Reddy, 1993; U.S. Bureau of the Census, 1992). Moreover, whereas poverty is primarily a transitory phenomenon among non-Hispanic whites, it is a chronic condition among certain groups of minorities (e.g., African Americans, Puerto Ricans) (Duncan & Rodgers, 1988).

Minority children also are more likely to live in high-poverty neighborhoods where institutional and social supports for children and families are relatively scarce and threats to positive growth and development are abundant. In 1980, for example, 39% of poor African Americans and 32% of poor Hispanics in the five largest American cities lived in high-poverty areas (i.e., areas with poverty rates no lower than 20%), compared to 7% of poor non-Hispanic whites (Wilson, 1987). A recent study of census tracts in the United States found that 80% of all children living in distressed census tracts were minorities (i.e., African Americans, Hispanics, and Asians), distressed census tracts being those with percentages at least one standard deviation above the national mean for all census tracts in at least four of five characteristics (unemployment, high school dropout, single-parent families, welfare receipt, and poverty) (O'Hare, 1994).

These negative economic conditions associated with minority status are strong predictors of problematic development. A plethora of studies link poverty to socioemotional and behavioral problems, developmental delays in intellectual functioning, and school failure (McLoyd, 1990; McLanahan, Astone & Marks, 1991). Moreover, chronic poverty, compared to transitory poverty, has been found to have much stronger negative effects on children's psychological and intellectual functioning (Duncan, Brooks-Gunn & Klebanov, 1994). Evidence also exists that neighborhood economic conditions, although less powerful than family-income differences, are significant predictors of negative developmental outcomes. For example, in comparison to having moderate-income neighbors, having low-income neighbors predicts more externalizing problems in young children, whereas greater concentrations of affluent neighbors predict higher IQs (Duncan, Brooks-Gunn & Klebanov, 1994).

Because we need better understanding of the etiology of problems disproportionately affecting minority children, ecologically sensitive research that identifies risk factors for problem behaviors and traces the pathways leading to these outcomes should go forward. Especially needed is information about sources of within-group variation and clarification of whether the correlates, antecedents, and pathways of problematic development differ as a function of race/ethnicity. This understanding is a prerequisite to well-designed, effective, and culturally sensitive prevention and intervention strategies (McKinney et al., 1994). Research on violence provides an excellent example of how information about ethnic differences in correlates and antecedents can inform the development of ethnically sensitive intervention and prevention programs (Hammond & Yung, 1993).

### Prevention, Intervention, and Policy-relevant Research

Empirical evaluation of prevention and intervention programs that target minority children are needed to clarify what programs are most effective, for whom, and why. Included here are studies of the effects of locally based and initiated prevention and intervention strategies (e.g., violence prevention, programs to prevent school failure), as well as the effects of national social policies especially relevant to minority children and their families (e.g., Family Support Act of 1988; Welfare Reform Law of 1996) (McKinney et al., 1994; McLoyd, 1994). Such research is of special significance to minority children because their social ecologies often include environmental risks that are amenable to intervention, prevention, and public policy influence (e.g., poverty, unemployment, poor medical care). Direct evaluation of existing programs and policies is not the only way researchers can influence policy. Basic child development research can also inform policy, but to do so, it must explicitly investigate factors that are "regulatable" and it must be framed in terms that can be translated into policies and programs. Because economic considerations are at the center of most policy goals and decisions, prospects of influencing policy are enhanced if researchers go beyond simply demonstrating that a particular program or policy has positive effects on children's development and attend to issues of cost-effectiveness (i.e., cost-benefit analyses) (Huston, 1994). Research of this nature can help resolve the conflict many scholars feel between generating knowledge for the sake of science and contributing to the solution of critical social problems (Huston, McLoyd & Garcia Coll, 1994).

## Racial and Ethnic Attitudes and Relations

A final research priority is perhaps more relevant to white children and adolescents than their minority counterparts. For several reasons, the "browning of America" arguably portends heightened racial/ethnic prejudice and conflict or at least sharper racial and ethnic cleavages. First, it is occurring against a venerable cultural backdrop of presumed white (European) superiority and longstanding white privilege. Second, the children of today's immigrants are notably less likely than their counterparts in the early twentieth century to believe that rejection of the values and folkways of their parents' homeland is a prerequisite to success in American society. Many espouse economic, but not cultural, assimilation into mainstream society. Third, today's immigrants are most likely to settle in inner-city neighborhoods, where assimilation often means joining a world that is antagonistic to the American mainstream because of its collective experience of racism and economic exploitation (Portes & Zhou, 1994; Sontag, 1993). Cultural ignorance, or lack of understanding of the other—the foundation for racial/ethnic prejudice—is difficult to overcome in American society partly because of the widespread racial and ethnic segregation in housing, schooling, and social relations (Hacker, 1992). For example, two-thirds of non-Hispanic whites currently live in neighborhoods that are at least 90% white (Edmondson, 1994). If heightened racial/ethnic prejudice and conflict are consequences of the changing ethnic and racial composition of the American population, parents, teachers, counselors, and other socialization agents will need insights into the antecedents and developmental course of ethnic/racial prejudice and ethnocentrism. Even more important, perhaps, they will require knowledge about the conditions that inhibit prejudice and facilitate acceptance and concern about those who are culturally different.

## CONCLUSION

The field of child development must grow and adapt to changing circumstances or suffer a fate of impertinence and languor. By their very nature, growth and adaptation are never free of challenge and discomposure. The rapid and significant changes occurring in the ethnic and racial composition of the American population obligate the discipline to give increasing priority to understanding the conditions that facilitate and disrupt positive development in minority children. To do otherwise is ethically indefensible and inimical to the long-term self-interests of the nation. A critical stance toward existing data bases is necessary, but not sufficient, for advancing the psychological study of minority children and adolescents. Students of minority child development should avoid replication of the problems in research design, sampling, and validity discussed in this chapter and, in general, hold to higher standards of conceptual and methodological rigor. We must move ahead with the development of theoretical perspectives that have robust explanatory power, are steeped in basic knowledge about minority cultures, and reflect the integrity of minority cultures. Meeting these challenges will necessitate proactive responses from all quarters of the discipline, including graduate training programs, professional societies, journal editors, funding agencies, and individual scholars in their roles as researchers, teachers, and reviewers of manuscripts and grant applications.

## ACKNOWLEDGMENTS

Portions of this paper were presented at the Children of Color Roundtable, convened by Hiram Fitzgerald, Barry Lester, and Barry Zuckerman and sponsored by the Society for Research in Child Development, the SRCD Liaison to Pediatrics Program, and the Irving B. Harris Foundation, March 28–29, 1995, Indianapolis, IN. The author expresses appreciation to Sheba Shakir and Sherri Slotman for their bibliographic and editorial assistance.

## REFERENCES

Allen, L. & Majidi-Ahi, S. (1989). Black American children. In J. Gibbs, L. Huang & Associates (Eds.), *Children of color: Psychological interventions with minority youth* (pp. 148–178). San Francisco: Jossey-Bass.

Azibo, D. (1988). Understanding the proper and improper usage of the comparative research framework. *Journal of Black Psychology, 15,* 81–91.

Bennett, L. (1966). *Before the Mayflower: A history of the Negro in America, 1619–1964.* Baltimore: Penguin Books.

Bowman, P. & Howard, C. (1985). Race-related socialization, motivation and academic achievement: A study of black youths in three-generational families. *Journal of the American Academy of Child Psychiatry, 24,* 134–141.

Boykin, A. W. (1983). The academic performance of Afro-American children. In J. T. Spence (Ed.), *Achievement and achievement motives.* San Francisco: Freeman.

Brody, G., Stoneman, Z., Flor, D., McCrary, C., Hastings, L. & Conyers, O. (1994). Financial resources, parent psychological functioning, parent co-caregiving, and early adolescent competence in rural two-parent African-American families. *Child Development, 65,* 590–605.

Bronfenbrenner, U. (1986). Ecology of the family as a context for human development: Research perspectives. *Developmental Psychology, 22,* 723–742.

Clark, R. (1983). *Family life and school achievement: Why poor black children succeed or fail.* Chicago: University of Chicago Press.

Cooper, R. & David, R. (1986). The biological concept of race and its application to public health and epidemiology. *Journal of Health Politics, Policy and Law, 11,* 97–116.

Cowen, E. L., Wyman, P. A., Work, W. C. & Parker, G. R. (1990). The Rochester child resilience project: Overview and summary of first year findings. *Development and Psychopathology, 2,* 193–212.

Crocker, J. & Major, B. (1989). Social stigma and self-esteem: The self-protective properties of stigma. *Psychological Review, 96,* 608–630.

Dilworth-Anderson, P., Burton, L. & Johnson, L. B. (1993). Reframing theories for understanding race, ethnicity, and families. In P. B. Boss, W. Doherty, R. LaRossa, W. R. Schumm & S. K. Steinmetz (Eds.), *Sourcebook of family theories and methods: A contextual approach.* New York: Plenum.

Duncan, G., Brooks-Gunn, J. & Klebanov, P. (1994). Economic deprivation and early-childhood development. *Child Development, 65,* 296–318.

Duncan, G. & Rodgers, W. (1988). Longitudinal aspects of childhood poverty. *Journal of Marriage and the Family, 50,* 1007–1021.

Edelman, M. W. (1987). *Families in peril: An agenda for social change.* Cambridge, MA: Harvard University Press.

Edmondson, B. (1994). The trend you can't ignore. *American Demographics, 16,* 2.

Fairchild, H., Yee, A., Wyatt, G. & Weizmann, F. (1995). Readdressing psychology's problems with race. *American Psychologist, 50,* 46–47.

Feagin, J. (1991). The continuing significance of race: Antiblack discrimination in public places. *American Sociological Review, 56,* 101–116.

Fisher, L. E. & Werner, O. (1978). Explaining explanation: Tension in American anthropology. *Journal of Anthropological Research, 34,* 194–215.

Gibbs, J. T. (1989). Black American adolescents. In J. Gibbs, L. Huang & Associates (Eds.), *Children of color: Psychological interventions with minority youth* (pp. 148–178). San Francisco: Jossey-Bass.

Gibbs, J. T., Huang, L. & Associates (Eds.) (1989). *Children of color: Psychological interventions with minority youth.* San Francisco: Jossey-Bass.

Gould, S. J. (1983). *The mismeasure of man.* New York: Norton.

Graham, S. (1992). "Most of the subjects were white and middle class": Trends in published research on African Americans in selected APA journals, 1970–1989. *American Psychologist, 47,* 629–639.

Guthrie, R. V. (1976). *Even the rat was white: A historical view of psychology.* New York: Harper & Row.

Hacker, A. (1992). *Two nations: Black and white, separate, hostile, unequal.* New York: Scribner.

Hagen, J. W. & Conley, A. C. (1994, Spring). Ethnicity and race of children studied in *Child Development,* 1980–1993. *Society for Research on Child Development Newsletter,* 6–7.

Hammond, W. R. & Yung, B. (1993). Psychology's role in the public health response to assaultive violence among young African-American men. *American Psychologist, 48,* 142–154.

Harrison, A., Serafica, F. & McAdoo, H. (1984). Ethnic families of color. In. R. Parke, R. Emde, H. McAdoo & G. Sackett (Eds.), *Review of child development research: The family* (vol. 7, pp. 329–371). Chicago: University of Chicago Press.

Harrison, A., Wilson, M., Pine, C., Chan, S. & Buriel, R. (1990). Family ecologies of ethnic minority children. *Child Development, 61,* 357–362.

Herrnstein, R. & Murray, C. (1994). *The bell curve: Intelligence and class structure in American life.* New York: Free Press.

House, J. (1981). Social structure and personality. In M. Rosenberg & R. Turner (Eds.), *Social psychology: Sociological perspectives.* New York: Basic Books.

Howard, A. & Scott, R. A. (1981). The study of minority groups in complex societies. In R. H. Munroe, R. L. Munroe & B. Whiting (Eds.), *Handbook of cross-cultural human development* (pp. 113–152). New York: Garland.

Huston, A. (1994). Children in poverty: Designing research to affect policy. *Society for Research on Child Development Social Policy Report, 8* (2), 1–12.

Huston, A., García Coll, C. & McLoyd, V. C. (Eds.) (1994). Special issue on children and poverty. *Child Development, 65.*

Huston, A., McLoyd, V. C. & García Coll, C. (1994). Children and poverty: Issues in contemporary research. *Child Development, 65,* 275–282.

Inclan, J. & Herron, D. G. (1989). Puerto Rican adolescents. In J. Gibbs, L. Huang & Associates (Eds.), *Children of color: Psychological interventions with minority youth* (pp. 251–277). San Francisco: Jossey-Bass.

Jacoby, R. & Glauberman, N. (Eds.) (1995). *The bell curve debate.* New York: Random House.

Jarrett, R. (1995). Growing up poor: The family experiences of socially mobile youth in low-income African American neighborhoods. *Journal of Adolescent Research, 10,* 111–135.

Jones, J. M. (1991). Psychological models of race: What have they been and what should they be? In J. D. Goodchilds (Ed.), *Psychological perspectives on human diversity in America* (pp. 7–46). Washington, DC: American Psychological Association.

Kerlinger, F. N. (1973). *Foundations of behavioral research.* New York: Holt, Rinehart & Winston.

LaFromboise, T. D. & Low, K. G. (1989). American Indian children and adolescents. In J. Gibbs, L. Huang & Associates (Eds.), *Children of color: Psychological interventions with minority youth* (pp. 114–147). San Francisco: Jossey-Bass.

Laosa, L. (1989). Social competence in childhood: Toward a developmental, socioculturally relativistic paradigm. *Journal of Applied Developmental Psychology, 10,* 447–468.

Luthar, S. S. & Zigler, E. (1991). Vulnerability and competence: A review of research on resilience in childhood. *American Journal of Orthopsychiatry, 61,* 6–22.

Martin, P. & Midgley, E. (1994). Immigration to the United States: Journey to an uncertain destination. *Population Bulletin, 49* (2), 2–45.

Massey, D. (1994). America's apartheid and the urban underclass. *Social Service Review, 68,* 471–487.

Masten, A., Morison, P., Pellegrini, D. & Tellegen, A. (1990). Competence under stress: Risk and protective factors. In J. Rolf, A. Masten, D. Cicchetti, K. Nuechterlein & S. Weintraub (Eds.), *Risk and protective factors in the development of psychopathology.* Cambridge, Eng.: Cambridge University Press.

McKinney, M. H., Abrams, L., Terry, P. & Lerner, R. (1994). Child development research and the poor children of America: A call for a developmental contextual approach to research and outreach. *Family and Consumer Sciences Research Journal, 23,* 25–41.

McLanahan, S. S., Astone, N. M. & Marks, N. (1991). The role of mother-only families in reproducing poverty. In A. C. Huston (Ed.), *Children in poverty: Child development and public policy* (pp. 51–78). New York: Cambridge University Press.

McLoyd, V. C. (1990). Minority children: Introduction to the special issue. *Child Development, 61,* 263–266.

McLoyd, V. C. (1990). The impact of economic hardship on black families and children: Psychological distress, parenting, and socioemotional development. *Child Development, 61,* 311–346.

McLoyd, V. C. (1994). Research in the service of poor and ethnic/racial minority children: Fomenting change in models of scholarship. *Family and Consumer Sciences Research Journal, 23,* 56–66.

McLoyd, V. C. & Randolph, S. (1984). The conduct and publication of research on Afro-American children: A content analysis. *Human Development, 27,* 65–75.

McLoyd, V. C. & Randolph, S. (1985). Secular trends in the study of Afro-American children: A review of *Child Development,* 1936–1980. In A. Smuts & J. Hagen (Eds.), History and research in child development. *Monographs of the Society for Research in Child Development* (pp. 78–92), *50* (4–5, Serial No. 211).

Montagu, A. (1964). *The concept of race.* Toronto: Collier-Macmillan.

Myers, H. F., Rana, P. G. & Harris, M. (1979). *Black child development in America, 1927–1977.* Westport, CT: Greenwood Press.

O'Hare, W. (1994). 3.9 million U.S. children in distressed neighborhoods. *Population Today, 22,* 4–5.

Portes, A. & Rumbaut, R. (1990). *Immigrant America: A portrait.* Berkeley: University of California Press.

Portes, A. & Zhou, M. (1993). The new second generation: Segmented assimilation and its variants. *Annals of the American Academy of Political and Social Sciences, 530,* 74–96.

Portes, A. & Zhou, M. (1994). Should immigrants assimilate? *Public Interest, 116,* 18–33.

Ramirez, O. (1989). Mexican American children and adolescents. In J. Gibbs, L. Huang & Associates (Eds.), *Children of color: Psychological interventions with minority youth* (pp. 224–250). San Francisco: Jossey-Bass.

Reddy, M. A. (Ed.) (1993). *Statistical record of Hispanic Americans.* Detroit: Gale Research.

Rogler, L. (1989). The meaning of culturally sensitive research in mental health. *American Journal of Psychiatry, 146,* 296–303.

Rumbaut, R. (1995). *The crucible within: Ethnic identity, self-esteem, and segmented assimilation among children of immigrants.* Unpublished paper, Michigan State University.

Rutter, M. (1990). Psychosocial resilience and protective mechanisms. In J. Rolf, A. S. Masten, D. Cicchetti, K. Nuechterlein & S. Weintraub (Eds.), *Risk and protective factors in the development of psychopathology* (pp. 181–215). Cambridge, Eng.: Cambridge University Press.

Smeeding, T. & Torrey, B. (1988). Poor children in rich countries. *Science, 242,* 873–877.

Sontag, D. (1993, June 29). A fervent "no" to assimilation in new America: Children of immigrants rewriting an axiom. *New York Times,* p. A6.

Spencer, M. B. (1990). Development of minority children: An introduction. *Child Development, 61,* 267–269.

Spencer, M. B. & McLoyd, V. C. (1990). Special issue on minority children. *Child Development, 61.*

U.S. Bureau of the Census (1992). *The Black Population in the United States: March 1991* (Current Population Reports, P20–464). Washington, DC: U.S. Government Printing Office.

U. S. Bureau of the Census (1994). *Statistical abstract of the United States: 1994.* Washington, DC.

Washington, E. D. & McLoyd, V. C. (1982). The external validity of research involving American minorities. *Human Development, 25,* 324–339.

Werner, E. & Smith, R. (1982). *Vulnerable but invincible: A study of resilient children.* New York: McGraw-Hill.

Wetzel, J. (1987). *American youth: A statistical snapshot.* New York: William T. Grant Foundation.

Williams, T. & Kornblum, W. (1985). *Growing up poor.* Lexington, MA: Lexington Books.

Wilson, W. J. (1987). *The truly disadvantaged: The inner city, the underclass, and public policy.* Chicago: University of Chicago Press.

Yee, A., Fairchild, H., Weizmann, F. & Wyatt, G. (1993). Addressing psychology's problems with race. *American Psychologist, 48,* 1132–1140.

Zuckerman, M. (1990). Some dubious premises in research and theory on racial differences: Scientific, social, and ethical issues. *American Psychologist, 45,* 1297–1303.

# Equivalence and Conceptually Anchored Research with Children of Color

*Jeanne Brooks-Gunn*
*Virginia Rauh*
*Tama Leventhal*

The struggle for equivalence in developmental research with children and families from different backgrounds has several origins. The first has to do with the transposition of methods from one group to others, specifically procedures based on primarily middle-class white children and families. The second has to do with the intersection of race, ethnicity, and social class, in the lives of children and their families as well as in our research paradigms. The third has to do with the meaning of community in the lives of children and families from different social class, ethnic, and racial groups. In this chapter, we present some examples of approaches that we have been using in order to portray in more nuanced and hopefully more realistic ways the lives of children in families.

Many of the other chapters in the volume outline approaches to studying children of color. One goal of this volume is to highlight multiple and, perhaps even more importantly, appropriate ways of studying America's children and families in order to reflect the manner in which ethnicity, race, and class inform the lenses through which childhood and parenthood are experienced. This chapter reflects work-in-progress, as we continue to experiment with new approaches and to incorporate the insights of our colleagues, and the families who work with us, into our development efforts and into our process-oriented analyses. We have been humbled by the difficulty of designing contextually sensitive measures and of deciding when it is appropriate to use similar constructs for groups differing with respect to race, ethnicity, or class, and when different constructs need to be applied.

The chapter is divided into three sections: The first is concerned with developmental outcomes, or child-level variables; the second deals with process variables, or family-level variables; and the third deals with neighborhood resource variables, or community-level variables. In the first section, a definition of equivalence is offered (primarily based on the work of Helms,

1992), followed by a discussion of when it is appropriate to use outcome measures developed with white middle-class samples for other groups defined by race, ethnicity, or class. We also raise the question of when it is appropriate to make comparisons across different groups of children and families and when single-group studies are most beneficial, vis-à-vis the study of child-level variables. The second section focuses on the use of family race, ethnicity, or class as explanatory variables in analyses. It is our premise that these so-called address variables are often used indiscriminately or as proxies for family-level mechanisms, even when process variables have not been explored or even included in research designs. Examples of the use of family process variables are included in this section. The third section has as its focus the examination of community-level variables. We argue that neighborhoods influence familial processes and child outcomes via the lenses of race, ethnicity, and class as well. We are particularly interested in how the social resources (or "social capital") of neighborhoods are transmitted, and how, if at all, these social resources might operate differently depending on the makeup of neighborhoods and friendship networks.

## Defining Equivalence for Developmental Outcomes

Many of us worry about the ways in which we conduct research, vis-à-vis our ability to describe the outcomes of development in a sensitive and realistic manner. That is, do the measures that have been crafted capture the dimensions for which they were originally intended? And furthermore, are the dimensions that developmentalists have outlined actually tapping the relevant aspects of children's lives? Typically, these issues have been addressed vis-à-vis a particular group of children—those that are white and from primarily working-class or middle-class families. Some developmental scholars (e.g., Clark & Clarke, 1988; García Coll, 1990; Hess & Shipman, 1965; Slaughter-Defoe, et al., 1990; Spencer, Brookins & Allen, 1985; Spencer & Markstrom-Adams, 1990) have studied other groups of children—children of color and poor children (of all colors). Anthropology has a long tradition of documenting the lives of families from many backgrounds (Burton, 1990; Jarrett, 1995; Stack, 1974). These pioneers in the study of children of color provided the impetus and the underpinnings for the current work on equivalence—whether or not the measures currently being used are appropriate for most groups of children in America and whether or not new, contextually specific measures are needed.

Using the frame of cultural equivalence is one approach to these two issues. Cultural equivalence may be defined in many different ways. We follow Helms (1992) in understanding equivalence as including functional, conceptual, and measurement domains (although a possible addition is suggested later in this chapter). Our interest is in equivalence for groups of families defined by race, ethnicity, or class (in this chapter we do not address definitions of culture, which in some cases, subsume ethnic or racial groups and in other cases may not).

Equivalence needs to be addressed in studies including families from different groups as well as in studies focusing on one relatively circumscribed group (Duncan & Brooks-Gunn, 1997). That is, even if attention is placed on a group—low-income rural white families or middle-income suburban black families—questions of equivalence arise. In general, this is because most studies, regardless of the race, ethnicity, or social class of its families, employ measures that have been developed on other groups of children and families—mostly white middle-class suburban or urban families. So, not surprisingly, the studies of white farm families in Iowa have employed so-called traditional measures of parent-child interaction, youth outcomes, and parent mental health (Conger, et al. 1997; Conger, et al., 1992, 1993). The same is true of ongoing work on suburban black families (Hughes, personal communication).

## Discrimination as an Aspect of Equivalence

Issues are most likely to be raised about the borrowing of measures that originated in studies of primarily white middle- to high-income families when the subject of inquiry is low-income nonwhite families. For example, the Baltimore Study of Teenage Parenthood, conducted by Furstenberg and Brooks-Gunn (Baydar, Brooks-Gunn & Furstenberg, 1993; Brooks-Gunn, Guo & Furstenberg, 1993; Furstenberg, Brooks-Gunn & Morgan, 1987; Furstenberg, Levine & Brooks-Gunn, 1990; Guo, Brooks-Gunn & Harris, 1996), a 30-year longitudinal study that is composed primarily of black families, has been criticized for using so-called traditional measures of success (i.e., completing high school, curtaining fertility in the teenage years, job attainment) (Leadbeater & Christman, 1989). It is unlikely that the Iowa Rural Family Study, as it follows low-income white youth into the young adulthood years, will be subjected to the same criticism. Why is this so?

One answer has to do with discrimination, especially in terms of lack of opportunities (i.e., job and housing or spatial discrimination). That is, the Baltimore youth may be less likely to be able to procure well-paying jobs than the Iowa youth, even if educational attainment in the two groups is the same. (To make the comparisons more accurate, we would need to study low-income youth in Baltimore and low-income black youth in Iowa; *see* Freeman (1991) for such an example of low-income urban white and black youth in Boston.) Consequently, discrimination has to be included in any discussion of equivalence. We favor including opportunity structure as a dimension of equivalence, adding it to the function, concept, and measurement domains identified in past work (Helms, 1992; García-Coll, et al., 1997).

## Functional Equivalence

The other way to address the issue of why one study might be faulted for defining developmental outcomes based on previous research with other groups is based on functional equivalence. That is, educational attainment may have different functions in different settings, in part due to differential job opportunities and in part due to the meaning of education. For example, education may not be seen as an avenue (or as a very sure avenue) to better-paying jobs when few jobs exist. Or education may be construed as a way into the middle class, and a move from a low-income neighborhood or community for some individuals or groups. For other groups, education may be seen as a means to provide for one's extended family while staying in one's (poor) community of origin. The measure itself would be equivalent, in the sense that high school graduation or the granting of a GED is standard across settings; however, the meaning of the degree may differ, as well as the opportunity to profit from it (Lewin-Epstein, 1986). In brief, functional equivalence of measures must be considered in any study, and differences in equivalence are critical when studying families who differ with respect to race, ethnicity, or class.

## Conceptual Equivalence

One important point of the preceding discussion is that the problem of equivalence is not avoided by conducting work on only one ethnic or class group. Indeed, it may be a bigger issue, in that the possibilities for detecting equivalence problems are severely restricted. That is, how might results of a study on family processes be interpreted if a particular outcome is not linked to any of the developmental processes measured? Were family-linked developmental processes not important, were the processes not measured adequately, or were the key processes left out of the equation altogether?

An interesting example is the work on the role of fathers in families in which the mother and father were never married. Some researchers have maintained that contact with absent fathers in single-parent, never-married households does not have much of an impact on child outcomes, over and above factors such as income, maternal education, and other contextual features (Furstenberg & Harris, 1993). Others do not even distinguish between never-married mother households and ever-married households (i.e., married, divorced, separated, or widowed), even though research demonstrates how critical this distinction is (Brooks-Gunn, 1994; McLanahan & Sandefur, 1994; Thompson & Walker, 1989). Ethnographic studies suggest that fathers are available to their children and play an important role in families headed by a never-married mother (Burton, 1990; Lancaster & Hamburg, 1986). McLoyd (1990; McLoyd, et al., 1994) has suggested that the lives of single black mothers and their children needs to be a focus of study, especially with regard to employment and family life. Trying to draw lessons from these various research lines, we have conducted several analyses using large data sets where we have looked at links between paternal contact and child support in two different groups of father-absent households—never-married households and ever-married households—and in two racial groups—black and white (Argys, et al., in press). Associations between income provided by and contact with the noncustodial father differed by type of household and by racial group. Such findings lead to a revision of the statement that father contact is not important, as it may have different effects in different settings. A related example comes from recent research on the degree of contact that unwed couples have when their children are very young. Using data from the children of the National Longitudinal Study of Youth (NLSY; Chase-Lansdale, 1991), McLanahan and colleagues (1998) are finding that a relatively large proportion of unwed couples are living together at the time of birth and when the child is two years of age. Clearly, father contact probably has a different meaning when the father is residing with the child than when he is not. These unwed co-habitation relationships are usually not differentiated from unwed, separate household relationships. Additionally, co-habitation rates vary by ethnicity.

This approach might be criticized in that the measures of interest are not very contextually specific. Indeed, the analyses with our colleagues just cited are based on the Children of the National Longitudinal Study of Youth. This data set employs quite traditional measures of family process and child outcome (Brooks-Gunn, et al., 1995). At the same time, large data sets are useful in distinguishing patterns of association among such process and outcome measures in different groups of children and families. Often, such data sets are used without dividing the sample into possibly contextually meaningful groups—such as the never-married and ever-married household analysis and the unwed, residential and unwed, nonresidential fathers analysis discussed. The examination of associations within specific groups of families (defined conceptually) often paints a very different picture than the examination of associations when controlling for group differences. In the analyses on effects of paternal contact and support just mentioned, associations with child outcomes were obscured in regression analyses including all families.[1] We would argue that the combination or separation of groups, for analytic purposes, should be decided conceptually. For example, in New York City, distinctions are made between American-born and Caribbean-born blacks (Waters, 1991). A distinction is also often made between Puerto Rican and Dominican Latino families in New York, even though both groups are from the Caribbean (McCarton, Brooks-Gunn & Tonascia, 1994; Rauh, Wasserman & Brunelli, 1990; Wasserman, et al., 1990).

## EQUIVALENCE AND FAMILY PROCESSES

Equivalence issues arise when studying the families of children of color. Even when considering relatively static family address variables (such as education and income), problems of equivalence arise. We present several examples of such problems in this section as well as examples from more process-oriented work.

### Comparability of Family Address Variables

Another issue in designing more contextually sensitive work is how to interpret differences in findings among different groups. Clearly, the fields of developmental psychology and sociology have been too quick to attribute a group difference to race or ethnicity. Betancourt and Lopez (1993) have documented the unfortunate tendency to conflate ethnicity, race, and class. They make the important point that most studies do not attempt to disentangle, or even define, these constructs—or, that assumptions are made about comparability across race or ethnic groups when social class is controlled.

We provide an example of this assumption from work using the Infant Health and Development Program, an eight-site trial of the efficacy of early intervention services for the health and development of low-birth-weight premature infants (Infant Health and Development Program, 1990; Brooks-Gunn, et al., 1993; Brooks-Gunn, et al., 1994). This study, by design, includes a relatively large number of black and white families across the social class spectrum. Of particular interest is that this longitudinal study of infancy and childhood includes low-income white families and middle-income black families (the two frequently omitted groups, as middle-income whites and low-income blacks have been studied most intensively of all race/class groups in developmental psychology).

Even in this study, however, the black and white low-income families were not comparable. For families who were at or below the poverty line, the black families still had lower maternal educational levels, experienced longer periods of poverty, and were more likely to reside in neighborhoods with high concentrations of poverty (Brooks-Gunn, et al., 1994; Duncan, Brooks-Gunn & Klebanov, 1994; Liaw & Brooks-Gunn, 1994; Smith, Brooks-Gunn & Klebanov, 1997). As another example, like many before us, we often divide this sample into three groups based on maternal education—less than high school, high school graduate, and more than high school. These distinctions obscure variations between black and white mothers; twice as many white mothers in the more than high school group graduated from college than black mothers in the same educational group (Brooks-Gunn, et al., 1992), whereas more black mothers in the high school graduate group have GEDs than do white mothers. Therefore, while the inclusion of families from a wide range of social class was a welcome addition to the Infant Health and Development Program, it is not possible to assume that the poor black and white families in this study (or in any other study) are living in similar conditions. Consequently, we may not assume that any differences in family process, for example, between the poor black and white mothers are due to race or cultural differences, since the two groups live in different situations.

## Comparability of Maternal Well-Being Variables

Of particular interest when studying child outcomes are family variables that go beyond the so-called address or social status variables mentioned thus far (i.e., income, educational level, family structure). A number of family processes are believed to influence parenting behavior, which in turn affects child outcomes (Sigel, 1986; Sigel, McGillicuddy-DeLisi & Goodnow, 1992). Social support, mental health (depressed or anxious affect), and coping skills are three that are mentioned, and examined, quite often (Barnard & Martell, 1995; Belsky 1984; Crnic, et al., 1984; Crockenberg, 1981). Are the measures that are traditionally employed equivalent across groups? Take, for example, maternal coping skills. Distinctions among forms of coping behavior have been made, especially among denial, passive coping, and active coping (Billings & Moos, 1982; Moos & Billings, 1982). It is assumed that effective coping involves an active orientation. However, what is seen as appropriate coping is likely to be influenced by the type of problem encountered and the acceptable ways one's referent group deals with such problems. For example, religious beliefs are probably critical. Many Christian faiths emphasize relying on prayer to overcome problems. God's will in many religions is considered a determinant of both outcomes and the occurrence of calamities. Passive coping, then, might be an appropriate response to some situations for many families. Another determinant of coping behavior is previous experience. If a woman of color has been turned down for many jobs in which she meets the qualifications as specified for the job, and if she sees white women with similar skills being hired for such jobs, after a time active coping (i.e., trying to enter a certain segment of the job market) may not seem possible or worth the effort (given the low probability for success). Do such experiences alter the ways in which coping behaviors are perceived and used? Does the meaning of terms such as "coping" change as a function of such experiences? Very little research addresses such questions.

Similar issues might be raised with respect to measures of depressive symptoms. It is unclear as to whether the meaning of the items typically included in such scales are equivalent. However, in contrast to the scant literature on coping, a great deal is known about depressed affect. The internal consistency of depressed affect scales seems to be similar across race and social class groups (Goodyer, 1990; Petersen, et al., 1993). At the same time, few studies have been conducted to see if depressed affect influences family processes differently in various ethnic, racial, or class groups.

## Comparability of Parenting Behaviors

Typically, dimensions of parenting behavior are presumed to be more or less universal, in that responsivity, provision of learning experiences, warmth, firm control and guidance, and lack of harshness, inconsistent parenting, and punitiveness are beneficial for children (Bornstein, 1995; Bradley, 1995; Maccoby & Martin, 1983). However, it is not clear as to whether the most frequently used measures are tapping these dimensions in an equivalent fashion (Benasich & Brooks-Gunn, 1996). The following is an example from the Home Observation for Measurement of the Environment (HOME scale; Caldwell & Bradley, 1984). In the Infant Health and Development Program, the home environment was assessed using the HOME when the children were 12 months and 36 months of age (Bradley, et al., 1994; Klebanov, Brooks-Gunn & Duncan, 1994). The HOME provides a rating of a series of behavioral items in the home, collected during a one-hour home visit (Caldwell & Bradley, 1984). During this time, a trained observer completes rating scales which are supplemented by maternal-report items gathered during a semistructured interview. Thus, the HOME is predominantly, although not exclusively, a naturalistic observation technique. The subscales of the HOME inventory include: Home Learning (e.g., Learning Materials, Language Stimulation, Variety of Stimulation), Warmth, Physical Environment, Acceptance/Punitiveness, and Modeling. Additionally, when the children were 30 months of age, they were observed and videotaped during interaction with their mothers during a clinic visit. One task involved problem solving, using the plexiglass devices designed by Sroufe and colleagues (using a stick to get something out of a box and a lever task) (Spiker, Ferguson & Brooks-Gunn, 1993). Measures of Quality of Assistance and Supportive Presence were rated from the videotapes. In an analysis conducted by Berlin and her colleagues (1995), the relative strength of the HOME ratings at age 12 months and the problem-solving ratings at 30 months were examined using receptive verbal ability scores from the 36-month assessment point. Of most relevance here is the fact that the videotape observational codes added to the prediction of child outcomes, over and above family structure and HOME scores (*see also* Sugland, et al., 1995, and Bradley, et al., 1994, for a discussion of possible differences in factor structures of the HOME for different racial and ethnic groups). As illustrated in Figure 2–1, an effect was found for adding in the ratings of maternal interactive behavior from the videotaped situations for the black mothers but was not found for the white mothers in these analyses (when regressions were run separately for the two racial groups). For example, the HOME scales were significantly associated with child outcomes in all of the regression models for the white sample, while the videotaped problem-solving task scores were not. In contrast, the HOME was a significant predictor of child outcomes in one of three regressions for the black sample and the problem-solving task scores in two of the three regressions.

Berlin and her colleagues (1995) speculate that the HOME and problem-solving tasks are tapping somewhat different constructs of parenting (even though the HOME and the problem-solving task each have a cognitive stimulation and an emotional support dimension). Additionally, it may be that the HOME scale does not adequately represent maternal cognitive stimulation for black mothers (or represents it less adequately than it does for white mothers). We provide three possible explanations: (1) Rater bias is more pronounced in coding that is done in the home (or live) than coding done in the laboratory, where other characteristics of the home or neighborhood are not evident. (2) Racial rater bias is more pronounced when all raters are white (in the Infant Health and Development Program, all of the HOME raters were white; the raters for the problem-solving videotaped task were from other groups as well). (3) Black mothers are on the whole less comfortable than white mothers when a stranger enters the home (especially a stranger from a different racial background). Discomfort could influence how mothers respond to questions and how they interact with their children during the visit (Doucette-Gates, et al., in press). All three of these factors may be operating; it is impossible, given the design of the IHDP, to infer

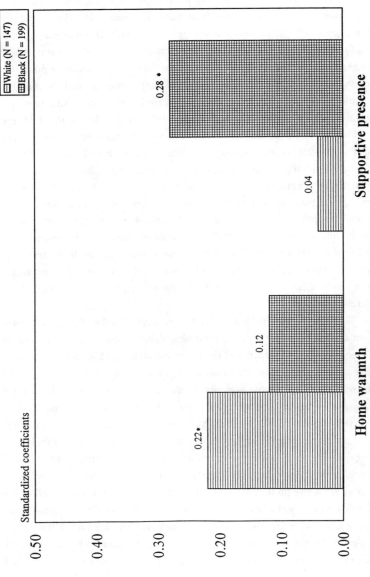

Figure 2–1. The association of HOME Warmth (36 months) and maternal supportive presence (30 months) on receptive language abilities at 36 months of age. (From Berlin, L. J., et al., 1995). Model controls for site, birth weight, gender, neonatal health, income, number of children, and maternal age; * p < 0.05.

which might be operating. The fact remains, however, that particular measures or settings may influence maternal behavior differentially as a function of class, race, or ethnicity (Chase-Lansdale & Brooks-Gunn, 1995; García Coll, et al., 1997).

In another set of analyses, our group has used the coding scheme originally developed by Baumrind (1973) and adapted by Hetherington and Clingempeel (1987), which is based on the constructs of warmth/responsivity and control. Four types of parenting behavior are coded—authoritative, authoritarian, disengaged, and permissive. In the free play observation at 30 months of age in the IHDP data set, three of these dimensions exhibited variability across a sample of 385 children and their mothers, where each dimension was scored on a five-point scale (Kohen & Brooks-Gunn, in press). When looking at associations with Stanford Binet scores at three years of age, we found differences for the black and white children (*see* Figure 2–2). Figure 2–2 presents the unstandardized coefficients for the three-year IQ (these coefficients are number of IQ points). We also examined the associations of authoritative, authoritarian, and disengaged parenting and IQ, controlling for site, treatment group, child birth weight, neonatal health, gender, maternal age, and maternal education. Results suggest that high authoritative parenting is associated with IQ scores for whites but not blacks. These findings are in line with Baumrind's (1972) earlier assertions about possible differences in the importance of authoritative parenting for different groups. However, authoritarian parenting was negatively associated with IQ in both groups (*see* Figure 2–2). Thus, contrary to earlier arguments, authoritarian parenting is not linked in a positive way to black children's IQ scores (Kohen & Brooks-Gunn, in press).

Similar types of analyses have been reported by García Coll and colleagues (García Coll, 1989; García Coll, et al., García Coll & Magnuson, in press; Levine, García Coll & Oh, 1985). In order to examine individual and contextual variables associated with mother-infant interactions in different cultural contexts, parallel analyses were conducted on a sample of low-SES adolescent mothers in San Juan, Puerto Rico, and a sample of lower middle-class white adolescent mothers in Providence, Rhode Island. In the Puerto Rican sample, individual (age) and contextual (child-care support, previous experience in child care) factors were associated with qualitative aspects of the mother-infant interaction rather than discrete maternal behaviors (García Coll, 1989; García Coll, et al., 1989; García Coll & Magnuson, in press). Among the white adolescent mothers, however, individual (ego development) and contextual (child-care support) variables predicted positive maternal behavior in a face-to-face interaction (García Coll &

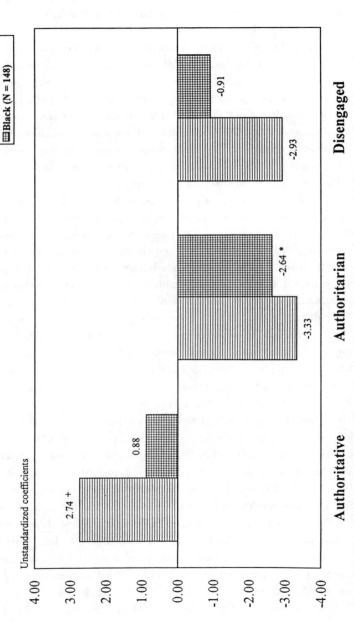

Figure 2–2. The association of parenting styles and Stanford Binet scores at 36 months by race. Model controls for site, intervention, birth weight, gender, neonatal health, maternal age, and maternal education; + p < 0.10; * p < 0.05.

Magnuson, in press; Levine, García Coll & Oh, 1985). As illustrated in these findings, context (i.e., child-care support) appears to operate differently on maternal-child interactions in these two culturally distinct groups.

In response to such findings, we have been developing new items to include in home inventories for studies of children of color. The purpose is to include items that may tap important aspects of parenting not being adequately measured by current inventories. This work, being funded by the Foundation for Child Development, has as its primary focus Latina mothers, specifically those from Puerto Rican, Mexican, and Dominican backgrounds. At the present time, we are not making any a priori hypotheses about the suitability of these new items for all three ethnic groups, but are piloting them in all three ethnic groups. Our approach has been to conduct focus groups of mothers and researchers from various Latino backgrounds, to discuss the current items in the HOME Inventory, and to suggest additions. The additions are then piloted with several families; the focus groups meet again to discuss these experiences and further refine the items. Presently, our group has gone through three iterations. Examples of new items identified through this process that tap aspects of acceptance are as follows, as well as examples of original HOME items.

Original Items on Acceptance Subscale of HOME:

- Parent does not scold or derogate child more than once during the home visit.
- No more than one instance of physical punishment during the past week.

New Items on Acceptance Subscale of HOME:

- If your child has a temper tantrum in a public place how do you respond? After the mother provides the answer, she is asked, "If that [technique] does not work, then what do you do?" After the mother provides the answer, she is asked, "If that [technique] does not work, then what do you do?" If the mother states that the child never has a temper tantrum, that response is coded, and then the mother is asked what she would do if the child did have a tantrum. We wish to allow mothers to describe real-life situations, in which the first parental response does not always result in a change in child behavior. We also wish to see whether a mother has experienced a particular problem. For example, if temper tantrums in public are completely unacceptable in a particular group, then children have had some socialization around the particular issue (in this case, acting out in public).

- The technique just described is used for the following situations identified in focus groups, that of refusing to eat what is served for dinner and refusing to clean one's room.
- Mothers could be asked to talk about their child for five minutes, and their response recorded on audiotape. General measures of warmth and acceptance may be rated from the tape after the interview. This procedure, adapted from Barnes-McGuire and Earls (1995), allows for coding of maternal speech vis-à-vis acceptance without the possible bias inherent in visiting a home. It is less costly than videotaping, and the rating takes less time than observational systems for videotaping.

While by no means perfect, this measurement development strategy is presented as a way to enhance the usefulness of widely used home inventories for specific groups. In fact, it may turn out that such additional items may be useful for white middle-class samples of mothers as well.

Other researchers have also recently attempted to develop culturally appropriate assessment tools. For example, Vazquez Garcia, et al. (in press) have created a culturally appropriate scale to assess family values and functioning of Puerto Rican adolescents. In a review of the literature and existing instruments, they identified Familism and Respecto as fundamental constructs to Latino families. Familism is "the strong identification, loyalty, attachment and solidarity of individuals within their families," and Respecto involves maintaining generational and gender-role boundaries in families (Vazquez Garcia, et al., in press, p. 2). Accordingly, items were developed to tap three dimensions of the family values of Familism and Respecto—personal beliefs, family practices, and perceived cultural expectations. They employed several focus groups and performed translation/back translation, as is standard procedure for measures that are translated or administered in multiple languages. Their findings suggest that changes in adolescents' family values are associated with migration and acculturation (Vazquez Garcia, et al., in press).

Clearly, we must reconsider many of our constructs regarding family-level processes to determine whether they are relevant across cultural context. As evident in the research on familial processes discussed in this section, current inventories of parenting beliefs and behaviors have proved insufficient in assessing families from different ethnic, racial, and social class groups. In particular, these measures lack the sensitivity to tap beliefs and behaviors that are meaningful to children and families of color. The development of culturally appropriate measures, such as those described above, indicates progress toward our goal of equivalence in assessing family processes. Employing new and innovative methods may prove a necessary means to this end (García Coll, et al., 1997).

## EQUIVALENCE AT THE COMMUNITY LEVEL

In our work, we are interested in how individual families derive benefits from communities rich in social resources, or, alternatively, how families manage to provide high-quality parenting for their children despite impoverished surroundings (Brooks-Gunn, et al., 1997a,b). Thus, we start with an interest in the intersection between class and race (here, defined in very rough terms as poverty and associated factors) (Chase-Lansdale & Brooks-Gunn, 1995; Huston, 1991; McCormick & Brooks-Gunn, 1989; Parker, Greer & Zuckerman, 1988) at the family and at the community levels. We have been especially interested in families' connections to, or isolation from, the communities in which they reside, and how this construct can be better measured. Specifically, we are interested in understanding how a family's connections to the social fabric of the community (1) directly affect the quality of the proximal caregiving environment, and (2) potentially moderate the impact of both family- and community-level conditions on child and family outcomes. Our focus was on Latino families and communities. Of particular relevance for this volume was the focus on community and the types of measures that might provide a better understanding of community connections in Latino families.

Following Coleman (1988), we used social capital as our organizing frame. We include the following dimensions as indicative of social capital—opportunity, norms and sanctions, interpersonal ties and reciprocity, information, stability, and quality of life (*see also* Furstenberg & Hughes, 1997; Korbin & Coulton, 1997; Sampson & Morenoff, 1997).

Our previous work has shown that both neighborhood and family poverty indices have adverse effects on the home environment (Chase-Lansdale, et al., 1997; Klebanov, et al., 1997; Klebanov, Brooks-Gunn, & Duncan, 1994). Specifically, neighborhood poverty has been shown to be associated with less maternal warmth/responsiveness, after taking into consideration the effects of individual-level factors (including maternal depressive symptoms and social supports). We tested the main effects of African American and Hispanic group membership, but did not explore the possible moderating effects of such group membership on the association of neighborhood-level conditions with patterns of child care or the proximal home environment.

Other work suggests that the effects of community variables on the caregiving environment are not uniform across ethnic groups. We reanalyzed data from a study of inner-city minority families (Shiono, et al., 1995). As part of a larger study of ethnic/racial differences in lifestyle during pregnancy, this subsample was followed prospectively for two years after delivery to obtain information about antenatal influences on child developmental outcomes. We selected this data set because it is multiethnic and also includes neighborhood-level information for each family. It was also comparable to work by Brooks-Gunn and colleagues with respect to aggregate and individual-level variables (Klebanov, et al., 1994).

We were interested in whether residence in a poor neighborhood was associated with adverse mother-child interactional patterns, regardless of individual demographic attributes, as hypothesized by Wilson (1991a, 1991b). Table 2–1 shows the results of Ordinary Least Squares (OLS) regression of Warmth as measured by the HOME scale, on (1) proportion of community residents earning less than $10,000, and (2) proportion of professionals in the community (a proxy for proportion of families earning more than $30,000), controlling for the effects of eight individual-level factors. In the IHDP data set, the proportion of families earning less than $10,000 had a significant negative effect on the Warmth subscale, even after taking individual factors into consideration. The same effect was present in the Lifestyles in Pregnancy data set. Neighborhood effects on HOME Learning subscales were substantially weaker, and this finding is also consistent with IHDP findings (Klebanov, et al., 1997; Klebanov, Brooks Gunn & Duncan, 1994). There were also significant individual- and family-level effects such that higher maternal education and greater maternal social support were significantly associated with higher HOME Learning scores, while female headship and large household size were associated with lower HOME Learning scores. These effects were consistent across both data sets.

Table 2–2 shows the results of the regression analysis within the Hispanic community only (N = 69). Although the sample size is small, the expected individual-level predictors of the home environment (such as education, social support, and household size) were significantly associated with the HOME Learning subscales, but not the Warmth subscale. The absence of neighborhood-level effects may be a function of the very small sample, especially since the standard errors are quite large. Alternatively, it may be that the choice of neighborhood-level measures was limited (Brooks-Gunn, Duncan & Aber, 1997b).

Following the lines suggested in the previous section on family-

TABLE 2–1. OLS Regression Coefficients and Standard Errors for Various Models of Effects of Neighborhoods on HOME Environment Scores

| Independent Variable | IHDP[a] (N = 719) | | | NYICM (N = 191) | |
|---|---|---|---|---|---|
| | Physical Environs | Home Learning | Warmth | Home Learning | Warmth |
| *Neighborhood Level* | | | | | |
| Fraction of families | −2.19* | −1.51 | −1.21* | 6.25 | −4.86 |
| with income < 10K | (0.57) | (1.61) | (0.56) | (4.65) | (2.35) |
| Fraction of families | −0.46 | 2.39 | −0.40 | 7.93+ | 0.57 |
| with income > 30K | (0.76) | (2.16) | (0.76) | (4.12) | (2.08) |
| *Family Level* | | | | | |
| Total family income | 0.02* | 0.04* | 0.00 | 0.10 | 0.10 |
| in thousands | (0.01) | (0.01) | (0.01) | (0.43) | (0.22) |
| Number in households | −0.10* | −0.29* | −0.03 | −0.37* | −0.14 |
| | (0.02) | (0.07) | (0.02) | (0.18) | (0.08) |
| Welfare status | −0.27 | 0.08 | −0.06 | 0.96 | 0.65 |
| | (0.15) | (0.42) | (0.15) | (0.92) | (0.47) |
| Teenage births | −0.14 | 0.43 | −0.27 | −0.48 | 0.03 |
| | (0.18) | (0.50) | (0.18) | (1.67) | (0.84) |
| Mother's education | 0.11* | 0.52* | 0.07* | 3.45*** | 0.48 |
| | (0.03) | (0.09) | (0.03) | (0.64) | (0.32) |
| Female headship | 0.06 | −0.43 | −0.21 | −2.44*** | 0.76+ |
| | (0.16) | (0.45) | (0.16) | (0.87) | (0.44) |
| Change in female | −0.08 | −1.81* | −0.13 | — | — |
| headship | (0.19) | (0.53) | (0.19) | | |
| Black | −0.33 | −3.02* | −0.61* | — | — |
| | (0.18) | (0.50) | (0.18) | | |
| Hispanic | 0.01 | −2.37* | −0.10 | — | — |
| | (0.25) | (0.70) | (0.25) | | |
| *Individual Level* | | | | | |
| Moos active behavioral | 0.03* | 0.09* | 0.01 | — | — |
| coping | (0.01) | (0.03) | (0.01) | | |
| Depression | −0.02* | −0.03 | −0.01 | −0.02 | 0.76+ |
| | (0.01) | (0.04) | (0.01) | (0.03) | (0.44) |
| Social Support | 0.01 | 0.38* | 0.05 | 0.26* | −0.02 |
| | (0.03) | (0.07) | (0.03) | (0.12) | (0.01) |
| $R^2$ (adjusted) | −0.29 | 0.46 | 0.14 | .07 | 0.14** |
| Constant | 4.84 | 8.80 | 4.26 | — | — |

[a] Source. Klevanov et al. (1994).
+ $p < 0.10$; * $p < 0.05$; ** $p < 0.01$; *** $p < 0.001$.

TABLE 2–2. OLS Regression Coefficients and Standard Errors for Various Models of Effects of Neighborhoods on HOME Environment Scores for Hispanic Families in the New York Inner-City Mothers Sample

| Independent Variable | NYICM | | | |
| --- | --- | --- | --- | --- |
| | Home | Learning | Warmth | |
| | M | SD | M | SD |
| Neighborhood Level | | | | |
| Fraction of families with income < 10K | 2.40 | 7.44 | 2.66 | 5.33 |
| Fraction of families with income > 30K | 10.05 | 7.45 | 3.46 | 5.41 |
| Family Level | | | | |
| Total family income | 0.37 | 0.75 | 0.67 | 0.54 |
| Number in households | −0.64 | 0.37 | −0.08 | 0.26 |
| Welfare status | 0.37 | 1.04 | 0.75 | 0.75 |
| Teenage births | 3.31 | 0.18 | −1.94 | 1.74 |
| Mother's education | 3.35* | 1.05 | 0.40 | 0.75 |
| Female headship | −0.88 | 1.06 | 0.17 | 0.75 |
| Individual Level | | | | |
| Depression | 0.01 | 0.05 | 0.03 | 0.03 |
| Social Support | 0.41 | 0.18 | 0.14 | 0.12 |
| $R^2$ adjusted | 0.39*** | | 0.14 | |

$+ p < 0.10$; $*p < 0.001$; $**p < 0.05$; $***p < 0.01$.

level variables, we have developed a series of items tapping acculturation and social isolation. We have hypothesized that the processes of acculturation and the degree of social connection in a community would affect the child-rearing environment directly. As an example of social isolation and connection, our focus groups lead to the addition of more detailed information about how the family celebrates special occasions, such as birthdays, holidays, and anniversaries. Special attention is paid to holidays from the country of origin (independence day, patron saint day). Questions have also been developed on the importance of specific customs, religious practices, and food to the Latina mother. Acculturation items from Marin, et al. (1987) are being augmented (e.g., questions related to differential language use in the home depending on the topic and the affect associated with the topic, contexts in which understanding or speaking Spanish is expected of children, maternal use of Spanglish).

In the context of our study, one question of primary importance is whether social connection/isolation and acculturation operate differently in communities as a function of social class and ethnic integration. Following Korbin (1994), as well as ethnographers (Jarrett, 1995), we suspect that while acculturation might be accelerated in neighborhoods with multiple ethnic groups, social connections might be more fragmented in more ethnically integrated neighborhoods. Our sampling frame is based on neighborhood composition, such that higher and lower social class and higher or low ethnic homogeneity of neighborhoods were the two factors that were used to sample neighborhoods (and families within neighborhoods). And, we are working with two Latino groups in Chicago—Puerto Ricans and Mexicans—to see if class and ethnicity of neighborhood have similar or different effects on maternal parenting beliefs and behavior.

As in previous sections of this chapter, we are advocating conceptually anchored research, to identify the constructs of interest and to use as a basis for designing new measures, if needed (*see* Hughes, Seidman & Williams, and Hughes & DuMont, 1993), for the discussion of a similar frame, culturally anchored research). We believe that the equivalence of community-level variables, like family-level variables, must be conceptually driven.

To further explore this issue, we examined a broader range of neighborhood-level conditions in the Lifestyles in Pregnancy sample of inner-city minority mothers. Previous studies have shown that characteristics such as median income, percentage of female-headed households, percentage of unemployed males, and proportion of high school graduates are highly intercorrelated (Brooks-Gunn, Duncan, Klebanov & Sealand, 1993). A summary measure of "Concentrated Poverty Area" may provide a more parsimonious measure of economic conditions. Following Wilson (1987) and Sampson, et al. (1997a,b), we defined "Concentrated Poverty Area" as those neighborhoods in which more than 40% of the residents fell below the poverty line. We then classified the sample into concentrated and nonconcentrated poverty areas (although the nonconcentrated poverty areas were not affluent, in the present sample). Subscales of the HOME were again used to measure aspects of the proximal home environment. Analysis of covariance and multiple regression techniques were used to assess the contribution of community-level variables to parenting practices, while adjusting for the effects of individual family characteristics. Hierarchical linear modeling approaches were not suitable for use with this data set because of the small number of cases in each census tract and the lack of a truly nested data structure.

Results are presented in Table 2–3, again using data from a minority sample of African American and Hispanic families. Families who reside in high-concentration poverty areas had significantly lower scores than families who reside in nonconcentrated poverty areas on the parent-child interactive subscales and physical stimulation subscales of the HOME, after controlling for the individual effects of maternal education and income. Analyses with the Hispanic subsample did not yield significantly different findings, although statistical power is marginal. However, we were encouraged by the results of this pilot work, which suggests that broad aspects of the quality of economic conditions in the community are quite powerful determinants of home conditions and parenting practices in particular (net of family characteristics), and these effects hold up among minority inner-city families (*see also* Chase-Lansdale, et al., 1997; Korbin & Coulton, 1997).

Table 2–3. Unadjusted Mean Scores on Parent-Child Interactive and Physical Stimulation Domains by Concentration of Poverty in the Lifestyles in Pregnancy Sample

| | Community Poverty Dimension | | |
|---|---|---|---|
| *Interactive Domain* | *High Concentration of Poverty (N = 49)* | *Low Concentration of Poverty (N = 66)* | |
| *Parent-Child Interactive Domain* | | | |
| Emotion/verbal responsivity | 6.84 | 7.74 | $p = 0.02$ |
| Encouragement of maturity | 4.92 | 5.83 | $p = 0.003$ |
| Emotional climate | 4.96 | 5.65 | $p = 0.02$ |
| *Physical Stimulation Domain* | | | |
| Growth fostering materials | 4.61 | 5.21 | $p = 0.07$ |
| Provision for active stimulation | 2.96 | 4.08 | $p = 0.001$ |
| Family participation in developmentally stimulating experiences | 3.00 | 3.74 | $p = 0.008$ |
| Aspects of the child's physical environment | 4.76 | 5.82 | $p = 0.002$ |

## CONCLUSION

In this chapter, we have addressed the issue of equivalence in research in terms of function, concept, and measurement as identified by Helms (1992), and we have suggested opportunity structure as another area in which to examine equivalence. Using examples from our own research as well as that of others, we discussed these dimensions of equivalence at three levels—

child-level variables, family-level variables, and community-level variables. We have argued for conceptually anchored research, which entails a more process-oriented framework. This approach leads to an inclusion of social stratification, position, or class variables (*see* framework developed by García Coll, et al., 1997). In addition, we have suggested that conceptually anchored research also must consider discrimination and segregation, both of which influence children of color more than white children, even when equating groups on social class. Most importantly, employing a conceptually anchored approach necessitates a reconsideration of our current analytic strategies, application of measures (particularly many commonly used inventories), and development of new measures. By using a more processoriented framework at different levels of our research, we may all strive to enhance our under-standing of America's children and families.

## ACKNOWLEDGMENTS

Versions of this chapter were presented in the Roundtable on Children of Color at the Society for Research in Child Development meetings, Indianapo-lis, March 1993 and in the Symposium on Assessing Families and Neigh-borhood Conditions in Hispanic Communities at the National Head Start Conference, Washington, D.C., June 1996. The research presented here was made possible by grants from the Foundation for Child Development, the March of Dimes Foundation, and the National Institutes of Child Health and Human Development (NICHD) and the NICHD Research Network on Child and Family Well-Being. We appreciate the support of the Foundation for Child Development and the NICHD Research Network on Child and Family Well-Being in the writing of this chapter. We also wish to thank our collaborators, who have helped us struggle with and for equivalence in re-search—Diane Hughes, Lindsay Chase-Lansdale, Linda Burton, Margaret Beale, Ana Mari Cauce, Monica Rodriquez, Robin Jarrett, Chris Moore, and Martha Zaslow. We also owe a debt of gratitude to Diane Hughes; we have obviously borrowed from her construct of culturally anchored research.

## NOTES

1. Steinberg and colleagues have made a similar point in the longitudinal study of high school students in California (Steinberg, Dornbusch & Brown, 1992; Steinberg, et al., 1991). They have argued that studies should never combine different ethnic groups. They should at least limit the combination to groups that are relatively large, such as white, black, Latino, Asian. In the case of the California study, the Latino group was primarily Mexican American; many suggest looking at Latino groups separately, given cultural differences among those from different countries of origin (the same is true of Asian groups).

REFERENCES

Argys, L. M., Peters, H. E., Brooks-Gunn, J. & Smith, J. R. (in press). The impact of child support dollars on child well-being. *Demography.*

Barnard, K. E. & Martell, L. K. (1995). Status and social conditions of parenting. In M. Bornstein (Ed.), *Handbook of parenting* (pp. 3–26). Hillsdale, NJ: Erlbaum.

Barnes-McGuire, J. & Earls, F. (1995). Coercive family process and delinquency: Some methodological considerations. In J. McCord (Ed.), *Coercion and punishment in long-term perspectives* (pp. 348–361). New York: Cambridge University Press.

Baumrind, D. (1972). An exploratory study of socialization effects on black children: Some black-white comparisons. *Child Development, 43,* 261–270.

Baumrind, D. (1973). The development of instrumental competence through socialization. In A. Pick (Ed.), Minnesota symposium on child psychology: Vol. 7. Minneapolis: University of Minnesota Press.

Baydar, N., Brooks-Gunn, J. & Furstenberg, F. F., Jr. (1993). Early warning signs of functional illiteracy: Predictors in childhood and adolescence. *Child Development, 64* (3), 815, 829.

Belsky, J. (1984). The determinants of parenting: A process model. *Child Development, 55* (1), 83–96.

Benasich, A. A. & Brooks-Gunn, J. (1996). Enhancing maternal knowledge and child-rearing concepts: Results from an early intervention program. *Child Development, 67,* 1186–1205.

Berlin, L. J., Brooks-Gunn, J., Spiker, D. & Zaslow, M. J. (1995). Examining observational measures of emotional support and cognitive stimulation in black and white mothers of preschoolers. *Journal of Family Issues, 16* (5), 664–686.

Betancourt, H. & Lopez, S. R. (1993). The study of culture, ethnicity, and race in American psychology. *American Psychologist, 48* (6), 629–637.

Billings, A. G. & Moos, R. H. (1982). Family environments and adaptation: A clinically applicable typology. *American Journal of Family Therapy, 10* (2), 26–38.

Bornstein, M. (Ed.) (1995). *Handbook of parenting.* Hillsdale, NJ: Erlbaum.

Bradley, R. H. (1995). Environment and parenting. In M. Bornstein (Ed.), *Handbook of parenting* (pp. 235–261). Hillsdale, NJ: Erlbaum.

Bradley, R. H., Whiteside, L., Mundfrom, D. J., Casey, P. H., Kelleher, K. J. & Pope, S. K. (1994). Early indications of resilience and their relation to experiences in the home environments of low birth weight, premature children living in poverty. *Child Development, 65,* 346–360.

Brooks-Gunn, J. (1994). Research on stepparenting families: Integrating disciplinary approaches and informing policy. In A. Booth & J. Dunn (Eds.), *Stepfamilies: Who benefits? Who does not?* (pp. 167–189). Hillsdale, NJ: Erlbaum.

Brooks-Gunn, J., Brown, B., Duncan, G. & Moore, K. A. (1995). Child development in the context of family and community resources: An agenda for national data collection. In National Research Council Institute of Medicine, *Integrating federal statistics on children: Report of a workshop* (pp. 27–97). Washington, DC: National Academy Press.

Brooks-Gunn, J., Duncan, G. & Aber, J. L. (Eds.) (1997a). *Neighborhood poverty: Context and consequences for children,* Vol. 1. New York: Russell Sage Foundation Press.

Brooks-Gunn, J., Duncan, G. & Aber, J. L. (Eds.) (1997b). *Neighborhood poverty: Policy implications in studying neighborhoods,* Vol. 2. New York: Russell Sage Foundation.

Brooks-Gunn, J., Duncan, G. J., Klebanov, P. K. & Sealand, N. (1993). Do neighborhoods influence child and adolescent development? *American Journal of Sociology, 99* (2), 353–395.

Brooks-Gunn, J. & Furstenberg, F. F., Jr. (1987). Continuity and change in the context of poverty: Adolescent mothers and their children. In J. J. Gallagher & C. T. Ramey (Eds.), *The malleability of children* (pp. 171–188). Baltimore: Brookes Publishing Co.

Brooks-Gunn, J., Gross, R. T., Kraemer, H. C., Spiker, D. & Shapiro, S. (1992). Enhancing the cognitive outcomes of low-birth-weight, premature infants: For whom is the intervention most effective? *Pediatrics, 89* (8), 1209–1215.

Brooks-Gunn, J., Guo, G. & Furstenberg, F. F., Jr. (1993). Who drops out of and who continues beyond high school?: A 20-year follow-up of black urban youth. *Journal of Research on Adolescence, 3* (3), 271–294.

Brooks-Gunn, J., Klebanov, P. K., Liaw, F. R. & Spiker, D. (1993). Enhancing the development of low-birth-weight, premature infants: Change in cognition and behavior over the first three years. *Child Development, 64* (3), 736–753.

Brooks-Gunn, J., McCarton, C. et al. (1994). Early intervention in low birth-weight, premature infants: Results through age 5 years from the Infant Health and Development Program. *Journal of the American Medical Association, 272* (16), 1257–1262.

Burton, L. M. (1990). Teenage childbearing as an alternative life-course strategy in multigenerational black families. *Human Nature, 1* (2), 123–143.

Caldwell, B. M. & Bradley, R. H. (1984). *Home observation for the measurement of the environment.* Little Rock: University of Arkansas.

Chase-Lansdale, P. L. & Brooks-Gunn, J. (Eds.) (1995). *Escape from poverty: What makes a difference for children?* New York: Cambridge University Press.

Chase-Lansdale, P. L., Gordon, R., Brooks-Gunn, J. & Klebanov, P. K. (1997) Neighborhood and family influences on the intellectual and behavioral competence of preschool and early school-age children. In J. Brooks-Gunn, G. Duncan & J. L. Aber (Eds.), *Neighborhood poverty: Context and consequences for children.* vol. 1 (pp. 79–118). New York: Russell Sage Foundation.

Chase-Lansdale, P. L., Mott, F. L., Brooks-Gunn, J. & Phillips, D. (1991). Children of the NLSY: A unique research opportunity. *Developmental Psychology, 17* (6), 918–931.

Clark, A. M. & Clarke, A. D. B. (1988). The adult outcome of early behavioral abnormalities. *International Journal of Behavioral Development, 11* (1), 3–19.

Coleman, J. S. (1988). Social capital in the creation of human capital. *American Journal of Sociology, 95,* S95–S120.

Conger, R. D., Conger, K. J. & Elder, G. H. (1997). Family economic hardship and adolescent adjustment: Mediating and moderating processes. In G. J. Duncan & J. Brooks-Gunn (Eds.), *Consequences of growing up poor.* New York: Russell Sage Foundation.

Conger, R. D., Conger, K. J., Elder, G. H., Lorenz, F. O., Simons, R. L. & Whitbeck, L. B. (1992). A family process model of economic hardship and adjustment of early adolescent boys. *Child Development, 63* (3), 526–541.

Conger, R. D., Conger, K. J., Elder, G. H., Lorenz, F. O., Simons, R. L., & Whitbeck, L. B. (1993). Family economic stress and adjustment of early adolescent girls. *Developmental Psychology, 29,* 206–219.

Crnic, K. A., Greenberg, M. T., Robinson, N. M. & Ragozin, A. S. (1984). Maternal stress and social support: Effects on the mother-infant relationship from birth to eighteen months. *American Journal of Orthopsychiatry, 54* (2), 224–235.

Crockenberg, S. G. (1981). Infant irritability, mother responsiveness, and social support influences on the security of infant-mother attachment. *Child Development, 52,* 857–865.

Doucette-Gates, A., Brooks-Gunn, J. & Chase-Lansdale, P. L. (in press). Adolescent research: The role of bias and equivalence In V. McLoyd & L. Steinberg (Eds.), *Studying minority adolescence.* Hillsdale, NJ: Erlbaum.

Duncan, G. & Brooks-Gunn, J. (Eds.) (1997). *Consequences of growing up poor.* New York: Russell Sage Foundation Press.

Duncan, G. J., Brooks-Gunn, J. & Klebanov, P. K. (1994). Economic deprivation and early-childhood development. *Child Development, 65,* 296–318.

Freeman, R. B. (1991). Employment and earnings of disadvantaged young men in a labor shortage economy. In C. Jencks & P. E. Peterson (Eds.), *The urban underclass.* Washington, DC: Brookings Institution.

Furstenberg, F. F., Jr., Brooks-Gunn, J. & Morgan, S. P. (1987). Adolescent mothers and their children in later life. *Family Planning Perspectives, 19,* 142–151.

Furstenberg, F. F., Jr. & Harris, K. M. (1993). When fathers matter/why fathers matter: The impact of paternal involvement on the offspring of adolescent mothers. In A. Lawson & D. L. Rhodes (Eds.), *The politics of pregnancy: Adolescent sexuality and public policy* (pp. 189–215). New Haven, CT: Yale University Press.

Furstenberg, F. F., Jr. & Hughes, M .E. (1997). The influence of neighborhoods on children's development: A theoretical perspective and research agenda. In J. Brooks-Gunn, G. Duncan & J. L. Aber (Eds.), *Neighborhood poverty: Policy implications in studying neighborhoods,* Vol. 2 (pp. 23–47). New York: Russell Sage Foundation.

Furstenberg, F. F., Jr., Levine, J. A. & Brooks-Gunn, J. (1990). The daughters of teenage mothers: Patterns of early childbearing in two generations. *Family Planning Perspectives, 22* (2), 54–61.

García Coll, C. T. (1989). The consequences of teenage childbearing in traditional Puerto Rican culture. In J. K. Nugent, B. M. Lester & T. B. Brazelton (Eds.), *The cultural context of infancy,* Vol. 1 (pp. 111–132). Norwood, NJ: Ablex.

García Coll, C. T. (1990). Developmental outcome of minority infants: A process-oriented look into our beginnings. *Child Development, 61,* 270–289.

García Coll, C. T., Escobar, M., Cebollero, P. & Valcarcel, M. (1989). Adolescent pregnancy and childbearing: Psychosocial consequences during the postpartum period. In C. T. García Coll & M. De Lourdes Mattei (Eds.), *The psychosocial development of Puerto Rican women* (pp. 84–114). New York: Praeger.

García Coll, C. T., Lamberty, G., Jenkins, R., McAdoo, H. P., Crnic, K., Wasik, H. & Vazquez Garcia, H. (1997). An integrative model for the study of developmental competencies in minority children. *Child Development, 67* (5), 1891–1914.

García Coll, C. T. & Magnuson, K. (in press). Cultural influences in child development: Are we ready for a paradigm shift? In C. Nelson & A. Masten (Eds.), *Minnesota symposium on child psychology,* Vol. 29. Minneapolis: University of Minnesota Press.

Goodyer, I. M. (1990). Family relationships, life events and childhood psychopathology. *Journal of Child Psychology and Psychiatry, 31* (1), 161–192.

Guo, G., Brooks-Gunn, J. & Harris, K. M. (1996). Parental labor-force attachment and grade retention among urban black children. *Sociology of Education, 69,* 217–236.

Helms, J. E. (1992). Why is there no study of cultural equivalence in standardized cognitive ability testing? *American Psychologist, 47* (9), 1083–1101.

Hess, R. & Shipman, V. (1965). Early experience and the socialization of cognitive modes in children. *Child Development, 36,* 869–886.

Hetherington, E. M. & Clingempeel, G. (1987). *Global coding manual.* Charlottesville: University of Virginia.

Hughes, D. & DuMont, K. (1993). Using focus groups to facilitate culturally anchored research. *American Journal of Community Psychology, 21* (6), 775–806.

Hughes, D., Seidman, E. & Williams, N. (1993). Cultural phenomena and the research enterprise: Toward a culturally anchored methodology. *American Journal of Community Psychology, 21* (6), 687–703.

Huston, A. C. (Ed.) (1991). *Children in poverty: Child development and public policy* (pp. 51–78). Cambridge, MA: Cambridge University Press.

Infant Health and Development Program (1990). Enhancing the outcomes of low-birth-weight, premature infants. *Journal of American Medical Association, 263,* 3035–3042.

Jarrett, R. L. (1995). Growing up poor: The family experiences of socially mobile youth in low income African-American neighborhoods. *Journal of Adolescent Research, 10* (1), 111–135.

Klebanov, P. K., Brooks-Gunn, J., Chase-Lansdale, L. & Gordon, R. (1997). Are neighborhood effects on young children mediated by features of the home environment? In J. Brooks-Gunn, G. Duncan & J. L. Aber (Eds.), *Neighborhood poverty: Context and consequences for children,* Vol. 1 (pp. 119–145). New York: Russell Sage Foundation.

Klebanov, P. K., Brooks-Gunn, J. & Duncan, G. J. (1994). Does neighborhood and family poverty affect mothers' parenting, mental health, and social support? *Journal of Marriage and the Family, 56* (2), 441–455.

Klebanov, P. K., Brooks-Gunn, J., McCarton, C. & McCormick, M. M. (in press). The contribution of neighborhood and family income upon developmental test scores over the first three years of life. *Child Development.*

Kohen, D. & Brooks-Gunn, J. (in press). Socio-economic characteristics: Mediators of parenting behavior. In L. Burton & P. L. Chase-Lansdale (Eds)., *Diversity and family processes.* Hillsdale, NJ: Erlbaum.

Korbin, J. E. (1994). Sociocultural factors in child maltreatment. In G. B. Melton & F. D. Barry (Eds.), *Protecting children from abuse and neglect: Foundations for a new strategy* (pp. 182– 223). New York: Guilford Press.

Korbin, J. E. & Coulton, C. J. (1997). Understanding the neighborhood context for children and families: Combining epidemiological and ethnographic approaches. In J. Brooks-Gunn, G. Duncan & J. L. Aber (Eds.), *Neighborhood poverty: Policy implications in studying neighborhoods,* Vol. 2 (pp. 65–79). New York: Russell Sage Foundation .

Lancaster, J. B. & Hamburg, B. A. (Eds.) (1986). *School-age pregnancy and parenthood: Biosocial dimensions.* New York: Aldine-DeGruyter.

Leadbeater, B. J. & Christman, J. M. (1989). It's a boy! It's a girl! It's a mistake. Or is it? Review of adolescent mothers in later life. *New Ideas in Psychology, 7* (3), 347–354.

Levine, L., García Coll, C. T. & Oh, W. (1985). Determinants of mother-infant interaction in adolescent mothers. *Pediatrics, 75* (1), 23–29.

Lewin-Epstein, N. (1986). Effects of residential segregation and neighborhood opportunity structure on the employment of black and white youth. *The Sociological Quarterly, 27* (4), 559–570.

Liaw, F. & Brooks-Gunn, J. (1994). Cumulative familial risks and low birth weight children's cognitive and behavioral development. *Journal of Clinical Child Psychology, 23* (4), 360–372.

Maccoby, E. E. & Martin, J. A. (1983). Socialization in the context of the family: Parent-child interaction. In P. H. Mussen & E. M. Hetherington (Eds.), *Handbook of child psychology: Socialization, personality, and social development.* New York: Wiley.

Marin, G., Sabogal, F., VanOss-Marin, B., Otero-Sabogal, R. & Perez-Stable, E. J. (1987). Development of a short acculturation scale for Hispanics. *Hispanic Journal of the Behavioral Sciences, 9* (2), 183–205.

McCarton, C. C., Brooks-Gunn, J. & Tonascia, J. (1994). The cognitive, behavioral and health status of mainland Puerto Rican children in the Infant Health and Development Program. In C. García Coll & G. Lamberty (Eds.), *Puerto Rican women and children: Issues in health, growth, and development* (pp. 161–189). New York: Plenum.

McCormick, M. C. & Brooks-Gunn, J. (1989). Health care for children and adolescents. In H. Freeman & S. Levine (Eds.), *Handbook of medical sociology* (pp. 347–380). Englewood Cliffs, NJ: Prentice-Hall.

McLanahan, S. L., Garfinkel, I., Brooks-Gunn, J. & Zhao, H. (1998, April). *Unwed fathers and fragile families*. Paper presented at the Population Association of America annual meeting, Chicago, April 2–4, 1998.

McLanahan, S. & Sandefur, G. (1994). *Growing up with a single parent: What hurts, what helps*. Cambridge: Harvard University Press.

McLoyd, V. C. (1990). The impact of economic hardship on black families and development. *Child Development, 61*, 311–346.

McLoyd, V. C., Jayaratne-Epstein, T., Ceballo, R. & Borquez, J. (1994). Unemployment and work interruption among African American single mothers: Effects on parenting and adolescent socioemotional functioning. *Child Development, 65* (2), 562–589.

Moos, R. H. & Billings, A. G. (1982). Conceptualizing and measuring coping resources and processes. In L. Goldberger & S. Breznitz (Eds.), *Handbook of stress: Theoretical and clinical aspects* (pp. 212–230). New York: Free Press.

Parker, L., Greer, S., & Zuckerman, B. (1988). Double jeopardy: The impact of poverty on early child development. *Pediatric Clinics of North America, 35* (6), 1227–1240.

Petersen, A. C., Compas, B., Brooks-Gunn, J., Stemmler, M., Ely, S. & Grant, K. (1993). Depression in adolescence. *American Psychologist, 48* (2), 155–168.

Rauh, V. A., Wasserman, G. A. & Brunelli, S. A. (1990). Determinants of maternal child-rearing attitudes. *American Academy of Child and Adolescent Psychiatry, 29* (3), 375–381.

Sampson, R. J. & Morenoff, J. (1997). Ecological perspectives on the neighborhood context of urban poverty: Past and present. In J. Brooks-Gunn, G. J. Duncan & J. L. Aber (Eds.), *Neighborhood poverty: Policy implications in studying neighborhoods*, Vol. 2 (pp. 1–22). New York: Russell Sage Foundation.

Sampson R. J., Raudenbush, S.W. & Earls, F. (1997). Neighborhoods and violent crime: A multilevel study of collective efficacy. *Science, 277*, 918–924.

Sigel, I. E. (1986). *Parent belief systems: The psychological consequences for children*. Hillsdale, NJ: Erlbaum.

Sigel, I. E., McGillicuddy-DeLisi, A. V. & Goodnow, J. J. (Eds.) (1992). *Parent belief systems: The psychological consequences for children*, 2nd ed. Hillsdale, NJ: Erlbaum.

Slaughter-Defoe, D.T., Nakagawa, K., Takanishi, R. & Johnson, D. J. (1990). Toward cultural/ecological perspectives on schooling and achievement in African- and Asian-American children. *Child Development, 61*, 363–383.

Smith, J. R., Brooks-Gunn, J. & Klebanov, P. K. (1997). The consequences of living in poverty for young children's cognitive and verbal ability and early school achievement. In G. J. Duncan & J. Brooks-Gunn (Eds.), *Consequences of growing up poor* (pp. 132–189). New York: Russell Sage Foundation

Spencer, M. B., Brookins, G. K. & Allen, W. R. (1985). *Beginnings: The social and affective development of black children*. Hillsdale, NJ: Erlbaum.

Spencer, M. B. & Markstrom-Adams, C. (1990). Identity processes among racial and ethnic minority children in America. *Child Development, 61*, 290–310.

Spiker, D., Ferguson, J. & Brooks-Gunn, J. (1993). Enhancing maternal interactive behavior and child social competence in low-birth-weight, premature infants. *Child Development, 64* (3), 754–768.

Stack, C. B. (1974). *All our kin: Strategies for survival in a black urban community*. New York: Harper & Row.

Steinberg, L., Dornbusch, S. M. & Brown, B. B. (1992). Ethnic differences in adolescent achievement: An ecological perspective. *American Psychologist, 47* (6), 723–729.

Steinberg, L., Mounts, N. S., Lamborn, S. D. & Dornbusch, S. M. (1991). Authoritative parenting and adolescent adjustment across varied ecological niches. *Journal of Research on Adolescence, 1* (1), 19–36.

Sugland, B. W., Zaslow, M., Smith, J. R., Brooks-Gunn, J., Coates, D., Blumenthal, C., Moore, K. A., Griffin, T. & Bradley, R. (1995). The Early Childhood HOME inventory and HOME-Short Form in differing racial/ethnic groups: Are there differences in underlying structure, internal consistency of subscales, and patterns of prediction? *Journal of Family Issues, 16,* 632–663.

Thompson, L. & Walker, A. J. (1989). Women and men in marriage, work, and parenthood. *Journal of Marriage and the Family, 5,* 845–871.

Vazquez Garcia, H. A., García Coll, C., Erkut, S., Alarcon, O. & Tropp, L. A. (in press). Family values of Latino adolescents. In F. A. Villarruel (Ed.), *Latino adolescents: Building upon Latino diversity.* New York: Garland.

Wasserman, G. A., Rauh, V. A., Brunelli, S. A., Garcia-Castro, M., et al. (1990). Psychosocial attributes and life experiences of disadvantaged minority mothers: Age and ethnic variations. *Child Development, 61* (2), 566–580.

Waters, M. C. (1991). *The intersection of race, ethnicity, and class: Second generation West Indians in the United States.* Unpublished manuscript.

Wilson, W. J. (1987). *The truly disadvantaged.* Chicago: The University of Chicago.

Wilson, W. J. (1991a). Studying inner-city social dislocations: The challenge of public agenda research. *American Sociological Review, 56* (11), 1–14.

Wilson, W. J. (1991b). Public policy research and the truly disadvantaged. In C. Jencks & P. E. Peterson (Eds.), *The urban underclass* (pp. 460–481). Washington, DC: Brookings Institution.

# 3 DEVELOPMENTAL AND CULTURAL CONTEXT CONSIDERATIONS FOR RESEARCH ON AFRICAN AMERICAN ADOLESCENTS

*Dena Phillips Swanson*
*Margaret Beale Spencer*

Societal forces often limit the opportunities and optimal development of African American children and youth. Chronic conditions associated with this group's lack of status, political power, and economic opportunity are associated with particularly patterned outcomes frequently labeled as deviant by majority group cultural norms. As they approach adolescence, children's social experiences broaden progressively into the larger society. Along with the normative transition, black children face high-risk conditions, unusual challenges, and stressful experiences specific to social status, ethnicity, color, and race—all highly identifiable self-characteristics that require a virtual responsive "state of readiness." Like their white counterparts, black children are expected to address and cope appropriately and competently with unavoidable physiological changes, complex social conditions, and other explicitly and symbolically expressed concerns and expectations traditionally associated with the adolescent period. Normal cognitive maturation makes one's awareness of these expectations and symbolic communications unavoidable. Black youth, in addition, are burdened with emotional and cognitive dissonance producing messages about race, ethnicity, and color that become progressively complex with age. Their preparedness to handle the diverse sources of tension varies as a function of the psychohistorical period and the child-rearing context of the family (e.g., parental child-rearing requirements in the 1960s American South), unique physiognomy (e.g., skin color), maturational status (e.g., being a large, early-maturing black boy), physical characteristics (e.g., endomorphic vs. ectomorphic body type), and majority group normed standards of beauty (e.g., hair color and type for girls). These sources of difference from the nonminority norm make the transition into adolescence and its associated coping requirements significantly different and difficult. Required are diverse resources to offset stress, and effective coping skills and abilities for use in managing unexpected assaults to the multiple levels of the self (e.g., context and situation-specific selves).

Accordingly, at the minimum, it is necessary to address concerns regarding life-course processes and outcomes for African American youth from a psychodynamic, developmentally sensitive, and contextually linked theoretical perspective. Such an approach, on the one hand, affords a useful conceptual frame of reference, provides opportunities for differentiated and precise plans of support for maximizing resiliency, and informs programs of prevention, intervention, and treatment for decreasing vulnerability. On the other side, the consideration of a more inclusive and dynamic framework provides specificity for models of service delivery and teacher training programs and increases the probability of youth resiliency and decreased rates of vulnerability. In general, conceptually dynamic, developmentally sensitive, multidimensional, and contextually linked theoretical perspectives can serve to diminish adverse social, policy, and educational impacts. In general, inclusive perspectives facilitate better understanding of patterns, processes, and outcomes of individual changes associated with development and related life-course transitions; in fact, irrespective of ethnicity, race, gender, social status, and color, they provide more valid and reliable interpretations of human behavior.

A better understanding of the additional support required for decreasing stress and enhancing life-course competence formation should be particularly helpful and instructive when applied to the adolescent period—an unusually rapid period of growth and development. Adaptive strategies are especially important for minority status individuals independent of developmental stage: Living within contexts of risk often associated with visible undervalued characteristics is a daily source of stress across the life-course. It is particularly during the adolescent period that mature, diverse, and effective adaptive strategies are needed for effective coping and, in fact, survival if the available statistics on minority males are to be taken seriously (e.g., Gibbs, 1988). Independent of ethnicity, social status, and race-relevant stresses, which serve only to exacerbate the normative developmental tensions specific to a particular developmental stage, the adolescent period in and of itself is loaded with myriad coping opportunities.

While there has been a growing literature related to African American adolescents (e.g., Spencer & Dornbusch, 1990; Swanson & Spencer, 1991), there are several concerns related to the focus of research generally, to the questions formulated, and to suggested solutions that might contribute to informative interpretations of youths' life experiences and options. One concern is the general lack of a theoretical approach (except for theoretical assumptions of pathology and deviancy). Relative to cultural and ethnic minorities, research has not been theoretically driven but, in fact, has frequently borrowed from mainstream literature, which, for the most part, has not included questions regarding children of color and their unique experiences. Second, research has not been developmentally sensitive when considering the experiences of minority youth. Somehow "normal" developmental processes have not been integrated into interpretations of how minority youth respond to their unique American experiences as they strive to accrue competence within multiple social ecologies that provide particularly stratified cultural contexts.

Third, a more thoughtful conceptualization and representation of context is needed that considers the diverse impacts that contexts can have on development for similar-appearing minority youth that share particular contexts. That is, it is important to also include an individual's *interpretation* of social experiences and inferred expectations for self. For example, expressed in different ways across the life-course, there are multiple pathways through which economic disadvantage can significantly wield its affect. Exploring the influences of decaying neighborhoods; strained parental resources; marginalized and underserviced neighborhoods; underfunded, crowded classrooms; and low academic expectations represent important methods for understanding adolescent behavioral responses. It is critical to identify how socioeconomic status burdens family functioning and relationships between parents and adolescents, and how the interpretation of these contextual experiences as adolescent social cognitions affect adolescents' expectations, motivations, emotional expression and regulation, and behavioral responses. There is a tremendous need to use interactive models and to initiate explicit and careful assessments of context at multiple levels. The added information provides a framework for interpreting diverse behavioral outcomes from similarly appearing youth. The strategy aids the explanation of findings and affords a more accurate use of data for informing program design and policy initiatives. In essence, there is a need for a theoretical framework that will drive the empirical work on minority youth and their families. This chapter presents considerations for empirical investigations when addressing minority group children and adolescents. We address general adolescent issues that are commonly investigated. One anticipated outcome of this chapter is to expand the conceptual and interpretative framework from which African American youths' behaviors are addressed.

THEORETICAL CONSIDERATIONS

The context in which adolescents develop has important implications for psychological functioning (Bronfenbrenner, 1979; Garbarino, 1982). Ecological factors such as cultural stereotypes, family composition, neighborhood characteristics, school experiences, and peer relations play a major role in the interpretation of developmental processes and related behavioral outcomes. A Phenomenological Variant of Ecological Systems Theory (PVEST) (Spencer, 1995) introduces a conceptual framework that is concerned with risk, vulnerability, and resiliency of urban youth growing up in high-risk environments. This framework provides an identity-focused cultural ecological (ICE) developmental perspective and illustrates the association of context variables with developmental processes and outcomes. From this perspective developmental processes are linked to risk conditions, stress encountered, coping methods employed, adaptive identity processes utilized, and patterned outcomes, especially for visible minority group members (Spencer, 1995). Undergirding diverse conditions of risk are self-appraisal processes that provide an interpretive frame for assessing degree of stress, and coping requirements.

Researchers have identified modes of coping that enable African American youth to adapt to impoverished contexts, problematic lifestyles, and oppressive conditions, but are maladaptive for success in mainstream society (*see* Gibbs, 1988). In response to the uncertainties of their environment, many African American adolescents have developed a number of coping skills and adaptive behaviors that compensate for their marginal minority status. Like other youths, anxiety may be triggered by academic problems, family conflict, community violence, interpersonal relationships, stressors, employment concerns, and career issues. The difference in experience more often is due to factors of chronicity, depth, and intensity. Behaviors such as hyperactivity, acting out, and aggression in younger adolescents may be clues to anxiety, while delinquent activity, substance abuse, and sexual promiscuity may be responses to underlying anxiety or depression in older adolescents (Gibbs, 1995). The presence of coping skills, social supports, and positive self-characteristics have been found to offset the risk of emotional upheaval and social problems posed by high stress and/or physical vulnerability particularly in children and adolescents. Less positive and fewer coping resources increase the likelihood that emotional or behavioral disorders will occur even under conditions of moderate stress (Albee, 1982).

## SPENCER'S PHENOMENOLOGICAL VARIANT OF ECOLOGICAL SYSTEMS THEORY

We believe that adolescent development for African American youth is, objectively speaking, no different from that of other youth. The physical and social realities that are fundamentally different are specific to the situation of people of color in the United States and are a function of their racial group membership (e.g., developmentally instigative traits) and historical status (e.g., intergenerational poverty) in the United States. Between-group differences and treatment determine particular situational experiences that can lead to contrasting developmental outcomes. Heretofore, there have been few models of development that demonstrate the dynamism between particular characteristics of the context and of the individual (particularly those of color) along with intervening developmental specific processes dynamically interacting and unfolding over time.

Spencer's Phenomenological Variant of Ecological Systems Theory (PVEST) (Spencer, 1995; Spencer, Cunningham & Swanson, 1995; Spencer, Dupree & Hartmann, 1997) affords a constructive response to Comer and Hill's (1985) challenge concerning the need for better conceptual frameworks. They lamented that "many psychiatric programs do not provide trainees with a conceptual framework which enables them to understand how economic, educational, health care quality and availability, housing, racism, and other major environmental conditions—past and present—affect social network, family and child functioning" (p. 180). The theory represents an incorporation and a synthesis of prior frameworks along with initial and current research findings from our empirical research activities to date (*see* Figure 3–1). Although somewhat cumbersome, the term "phenomenological" underscores and emphasizes the individual's unique perception of an experience. As indicated in prior theoretical statements (e.g., Spencer, 1985), generally missed is the individual's unique meaning-making process of an experience. The process is inherently and unavoidably social cognitive in that one's perception of an experience can influence coping responses (e.g., one perceives that a coping response is needed).

Coping is conceptualized both as expressed strategies (e.g., skills and abilities) and as a coping outcome (e.g., physical and mental health or competence). Coping strategies can be of a reactive variety and, thus, can be appropriate or constructive (e.g., seeking out a network of support) or maladaptive (e.g., aggressive responses to perceptions of risk). Coping strategies can also represent more stable identity-linked psychosocial processes that may show some consistency across situations and time (e.g., sex-role identity). On the other hand, coping products are the result of effective or ineffective coping strategies. The situation may arouse a maladaptive coping strategy, although a productive coping outcome may still occur if the maladaptive strategy is balanced by positive psychosocial identity processes. In contrast to other theories that seek to explain child development and resiliency by including factors such as socioeconomic status, self-esteem, and aggressive tendencies, PVEST is more dynamic in its concern with process.

The framework encourages an analysis of processes by which critical factors (including social address variables such as female headship) actually have an impact on or interact with coping responses. The dynamism of the theory is due to its focus on both the actual features of and the specific psychodynamic activities that take place in myriad contexts, which the various social address variables merely describe.

The assessment of contextual factors that contribute to responses to impoverished conditions can occur simultaneously on multiple levels and may be represented by any one or a combination of context-assessing scales: census variables (e.g., tract level), crime statistics (e.g., block-level statistics), neighborhood assessments (including objective drive-thru [windshield] measures), relationships among neighbors that address parental monitoring support, and household income. Contextual characteristics (e.g., crowding) are frequently recognized as significant sources of psychological risk but are seldom explicitly incorporated and investigated as important contributors to developmental outcomes. These various risk conditions are, in essence, linked to experiences of stress, which are then associated with varying methods of coping: reactive mechanisms for survival that may be maladaptive (e.g., a bravado or hypermasculinity orientation) or adaptive (e.g., identifying and utilizing mentors or social organizations). Experiencing adverse conditions requires coping responses that, over time, become incorporated into (more environmentally stable) psychosocial (identity) processes and are reinforcing of either supportive or nonproductive life-course outcomes.

Due to its heavy emphasis on identity processes, Spencer's Phenomenological Variant of Ecological Systems Theory provides an identity-focused cultural ecological (ICE) perspective. Within the ICE perspective, phenomenological processes (an individual's perception of an experience) are as crucial to the interpretation of behavior and explanation for it as the actual experience. To illustrate, Cunningham (1994) examined African American adolescent males' perceptions of their context. His findings indicate that perceiving an inadequate fit between self and the context significantly influenced reactive (i.e., negative) coping responses, while negative environmental experiences (i.e., stress) predicted exaggerated male bravado attitudes. Spencer, Cunningham, and Swanson (1995) have linked these reactive coping responses to identity development.

An ICE perspective serves as a basis "for capturing the individual's intersubjectivity . . . [which] is especially relevant given the unique status of adolescent thought processes, which allow a degree of recursive thinking unavailable at earlier periods in development" (Spencer, 1995, p. 49). Furthermore, the ICE perspective is useful in explaining how development-re-

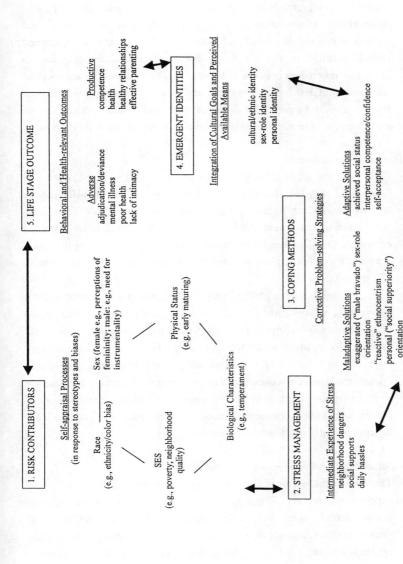

*Figure 3–1. A phenomenological variant of ecological systems theory (PVEST).*

lated stressors (e.g., negotiating greater independence) can be mediated by family dynamics and environmental stimuli. Parental supervision of adolescents living in hostile environments may conflict with adolescent expectations for increased independence and may be perceived as family hassles from the youths' perspective. However, such monitoring of activities may be necessary in high-risk environments. Thus, particularly for underrepresented and minimally researched groups and individuals who reside in complex and embedded situations, the ICE perspective affords significant utility for examining relationships between self (both singularly and within groups) and contexts. An ICE perspective is intrinsically and extrinsically linked to context but also, in keeping with Bronfenbrenner and Crouter (1983), affords a person-process-context analysis of continuous psychological processes.

## DEVELOPMENT AND CONTEXT

Contextual and social influences are not unique to adolescence. The role and significance of these influences vary with development across the life course. As a method of demonstrating the efficacy of the PVEST, this section provides illustrative examples from the literature. We illustrate and examine adolescent issues and stresses in areas of racial- and gender-identity processes, academic experiences, physical development, and family influences from an ICE perspective.

To highlight interactions between development and context and for interpreting psychological processes and specific outcomes, a brief review of racial attitude findings during early childhood is presented prior to addressing identity processes during adolescence. The purpose of first addressing an earlier psychosocial developmental period is to provide demonstrating use of a historical accounting of empirical research findings to document how a perspective that considers the interaction between development and contextually linked experiences provides a more accurate framework for interpreting later psychosocial outcomes.

### Childhood and Cultural Membership: A Brief Review

The view of the self or identity as a cognitive construction of one's social experiences is not new. The acquisition of societal meaning is an important developmental process. Knowledge concerning self and others develops simultaneously in response to social interactions and normal cognitive maturation. Racial attitude research during the first half of the twentieth century that assumed Eurocentric racial attitudes (i.e., valuing all things white as positive) among African American children also suggested negative self-esteem. What was not addressed when interpreting the Eurocentric attitudes was the role of developmental processes, specifically cognitive maturation. As African American children develop awareness of self and other objects, general knowledge of their group and their world also increases (*see* Spencer, 1984).

It would appear that for young children, the interaction between early social experiences, cognitive development, and identity processes produces significantly different developmental outcomes as a consequence of the status of the group. Further, within racial groups, lower-income children are exposed to more discordant information than their middle-income cohorts. For youth of color, the existence and reinforcement of European values concerning class, color, and caste require a reinterpretation (i.e., psychological intervention) or modification (i.e., sociocultural intervention) of existing information to insure that positive identity elements are incorporated into the self system.

Psychosocial development during the preschool years proceeds in parallel fashion with the child's cognitive construction of the world. Thus, an expected developmental course of identity formation for young black egocentric children, given their unique experiences, is toward identity imbalance unless intervention occurs (Spencer, 1985). The imbalance is due to the pattern of findings which suggests that African American preschoolers can have a positive personal identity (i.e., self-esteem) although generally reporting Eurocentric preferences and attitudes (Spencer, 1982, 1984). Developmental transition from a state of identity imbalance (between personal and group identity) to a more mature view of the self requires a cognitive shift from an egocentric or self-centered perspective to a more objective, less stereotypic view of culture and one's group identity. One's understanding of, exposure to, and knowledge about cultural practices, beliefs, and values may be characterized as cultural cognition (Spencer, 1985). Previous research indicates that cultural cognition for young preoperational children is developmentally linked to more general cognitive functioning (Spencer, 1982, 1984). The relationship suggests that with increasing awareness and conceptual differentiation, young children learn about racial stereotypes in the same manner that one obtains information about the world of objects. Personal (self-concept) and group identity (racial stereotyping) appear to represent two independent conceptual categories about the self during the preoperational period (i.e., years 2–7) of cognitive egocentrism. The critical insight from research findings obtained during the previous two decades is that negative own-group racial stereotyping may be observed for minority group children during the preoperational period (Spencer, 1982, 1984, 1985). However, the observation does not necessarily mean that egocentric children actually internalize negative attributes to their personal identity. During the early cognitive egocentric period, own-group negative racial stereotyping in these children must be viewed as objectively held information about the environment and not as reflections of personal identity. This objectively held information about the world becomes integrated with knowledge of self-as-object through concrete operational thought during the early school years. As black children move into the larger society, they face additional risks if they have not been prepared to understand and take pride in their own culture. On the one hand, as critical socialization agents, parents play an important racial socialization role in the inculcation of positive cultural values (Spencer, 1983, 1990). On the other hand, in addition to the traditional developmental tasks described by Havighurst (1973), a critical developmental task of minority-status children is the acquisition and internalization of positive cultural values and identity elements, that is, recognition and valuing of cultural capital. The parental socialization role and the child's developmental identity task are assumed to occur within a supportive, reinforcing context, although these processes occur in a nonminority-preferenced society.

## Adolescence and Cultural Membership

During adolescence, when identity formation becomes one of the most prominent developmental tasks (Erikson, 1968; Havighurst, 1973), navigating through this process requires an integration of information from one's past, present, and anticipated future ability to achieve desired goals. It involves personal reflection and observation of oneself in relation to others. Interactions with the outside world increase, allowing further integration of cognitive skills, social skills (i.e., behavior), and emotions. Erikson (1968) emphasizes the role of social and cultural factors for development. By adolescence, minority youth are well aware of the values of the majority culture and its standards of performance, achievement, and beauty. Therefore, adapting to the developmental demands also requires balancing aspects of the self with the social environment (Compas, 1987; Kagan, 1983). For McCandless and Evans (1973), this process further involves an integration of "selves or identifications" with perceptions of future development. As such, synthesizing prior experiences with future expectations represents a critical aspect of identity formation.

For African American adolescents, as with other visible minorities, complex ego-formation processes require an integration of their racial identity. Minority status represents an inextricable aspect of ego identity that contributes to a framework for defining parameters for life-course choices and opportunities. Cultural values not only represent an important aspect of accrued knowledge, but also provide youth with information necessary to interpret and proactively respond to environmental experiences and stereotypic messages concerning their minority status (Ogbu, 1986). In contrast to childhood, adolescents have a greater awareness of racial group membership and the expectations, privileges, restraints, and social responsibilities that accompany that membership (McCandless & Evans, 1973). This heightened awareness of group membership is accompanied by a heightened consciousness of gender-linked behaviors and expectations.

## Adolescence and Sex Role Considerations

Gender, like ethnicity, has been routinely promoted as an important factor in development. It has been addressed with respect to physical and physiological issues (Wingard, 1987); particular idiosyncrasies such as changes in achievement patterns for girls entering adolescence (Hare & Castenell, 1985); its relationship to parental characteristics, behaviors, and beliefs (Allen, 1985; Clark, 1983; Spencer, 1990); and various temporal patterns (e.g., years of schooling achieved, employment attained) (Gibbs, 1988). Similar relations have been drawn linking sex-role orientation to developmental concerns such as identity achievement status (Streitmatter, 1993) and adolescent relationships (see Maccoby, 1990). It has also been associated with problematic outcomes during adolescence (e.g., delinquency and teen parenting) (Hagan, Simpson & Gillis, 1987; Merrick, 1995).

Although the African American community is inundated with assumptions concerning the experiences of its youths, there are, for example, few studies available that specifically link, from within a developmental framework, sex-role socialization and contextual characteristics (see Cunningham, 1994; Spencer, Cunningham & Swanson, 1995, for assessments related to males). For example, dysfunctional and pathological relations have historically provided an interpretational frame for negative outcomes among African American males, particularly noticeable during adolescence. However, a close examination and careful review of the literature suggests that minority adolescents exhibiting problematic behaviors (e.g., aggressive acts, early engagement in sexual activity) are also more likely to be among those with the fewest economic resources and inadequate educational preparation.

For example, Jencks and Mayer (1990) reported that adolescents who are reared in affluent neighborhoods obtain more years of schooling than adolescents from similar family structures in poorer neighborhoods. For males, residing in predominantly welfare-dependent neighborhoods during childhood potentially reduces their chances of obtaining well-paid employment as adults. Such environments are sourly bereft of apprenticeship opportunities so critical to a productive resolution of the identity conflict (Erikson, 1968).

As suggested by Bandura (1978), self-system development is reciprocally determined from self/other appraisal processes. Accordingly, being either a male or a female requires unavoidable appraisal processes that consider the self in the context of expected sex roles. Historically, a well-adjusted male was expected to be independent and assertive while females were expected to be sensitive and nurturant. Within the self/other appraisal process, females must therefore consider various views concerning femininity. Males, on the other hand, must appraise instrumentality, given unavoidable sex-role stereotypes about the anticipated provider role assumed by men. For example, the role of "house husband," although existent, has not gained currency to the extent that it is viewed as generally desirable and valued by males.

Ladner's (1972) research on sex-role development suggests that positive characteristics of adulthood such as strength and independence are less sex-role differentiated among poor African American adolescents than their Anglo middle-class counterparts. Multiple gender roles have been a reality for African American women for generations. Historically, black women's identity has been defined to include multiple roles in addition to those of mother and wife; in contrast, an extended gender identity for white middle-class American women is a more recent phenomenon. Black women expect to maintain paying positions as adults, which influences their motivation toward educational and occupational attainments (*see* Hyde, 1991). Although this certainly speaks well of the employment potential for African American females, little remains known of what impact expectations regarding future employability and economic stability among males will have on their current motivation and behavior, particularly given the prevailing expectation of the male provider role.

In a study of gender-role orientation associated with problem behaviors among high school males, Pleck, Sonenstein, and Ku (1994) found that problem behaviors in adolescent males were associated with their attitudes toward masculinity. Adolescent males that reported traditional beliefs about masculinity (e.g., "A young man should be tough, even if he's not big," "It is essential for a guy to get respect from others," and "Men are always ready for sex") also were more likely to have school difficulties, engage in alcohol and drug use, participate in delinquent activities, and be sexually active. Although an understanding of identity processes is critical for interpreting both aversive and advantageous life-course experiences, it is also necessary to assess their interactions with contextual variables and characteristics.

Contributing factors relevant to identity formation include educational aspirations, expectations for the future, level of ego development, parental and other kin support, and cognitive maturity. However, as previously mentioned, the extent to which these constructs interact with exosystem-level contextual characteristics (e.g., educational and workplace decision making) remains largely unaddressed. To sum, contextual factors may contribute to or perpetuate risk conditions from which these identity processes evolve.

## Educational and Maturational Considerations

The extent to which adolescents experience competence in academic endeavors is critical for their preparation and success in future endeavors. Schools, theoretically, are a microcosm of the larger society; a sense of efficacy in this setting promotes constructive adaptations to adult role demands. During adolescence, academic achievements facilitate increased competence, purpose, and commitment. According to Bowman (1989), "intense student role conflicts [during adolescence] can seriously thwart a sense of personal competence, generate aimlessness, and erode social commitments" (p. 129). The role of psychosocial processes for academic competence is not only pivotal for navigating the difficult transition to gainful employment in adulthood but also serves as a resource for healthy/positive identity development during adolescence.

For minorities, educational preparation remains the cornerstone for future career consolidation. Despite advances in decreasing the high school dropout rates on a national level, blacks, particularly males, continue to lag far behind their counterparts in academic performance. This trend actually begins during the early primary school grades and continues throughout the later years of school (*see* Spencer, 1995). Many high school graduates are likely to be functionally illiterate and less likely to enter college; and the few who decide to enter college are less likely to graduate (*see* Bowman, 1989). Many youth continue to experience the consequences of institutional racism and individual prejudice embedded in schools, school systems, and regulating policies (Comer, 1988; Wilson, 1991). This is particularly salient because of incongruities between public policies (e.g., discrimination) and actual discriminatory practices (Chestang, 1972); the pattern continues throughout the life-span experiences of African Americans and other groups of color. When positive experiences prove to be elusive and social encouragement too weak, academic accomplishments and thus future job marketability are potentially compromised. The situation invites significant conflict particularly for those adolescents who are able to discern the disparities.

A study by Hirsh and Rapkin (1987) examined the psychological adjustment and transition to junior high. They assessed the self-esteem, quality of school life, and academic competence of 159 students (26% African American). They reported higher general self-esteem among more academically competent students, with girls reporting more satisfaction with the quality of school life than boys. Although they found no race differences on general self-esteem, they noted that on a short self-report symptom checklist, African American students reported greater distrust of the environment (e.g., feeling that most people cannot be trusted, others do not give you proper credit for your achievements) than they reported negative internal states such as depression or anxiety (e.g., feeling lonely or blue, feeling very self-conscious with others). The findings regarding general self-esteem for African American youth are consistent with other findings (Hare, 1977; Spencer, 1984; Taylor, 1976). The effect of distrusting the environment, although not appearing to affect self-esteem, remains a potential source of risk and subsequent stress that may have an impact on academic engagement and strategies used to cope with a perceived distrustful environment. For example, greater behavioral maturity is expected from early physically maturing adolescents (Peterson & Crockett, 1985). For early maturing African American males, greater physical maturity (e.g., increased height and muscular development) is often perceived as a source of potential threat.

Spencer et al. (1998) examined the relationships among physical status (e.g., height and weight relative to peers), perceived hassles related to desires for autonomy, and learning behaviors. For males, early adolescent maturational status (i.e., being above the mean for weight) was linked to a preference for independent learning in middle to late adolescence. The findings, although modest, suggest the need for greater understanding of the interaction among changes in physical status and contextual (i.e., social and academic) experiences of physically larger African American male adolescents.

A relationship was also found between pubertal status and stress for the youngest group of early adolescents: the larger they were, the fewer stressors noted. This finding indicates that the timing of physical maturation and pubertal status may have different influences on stress engagement for younger and older *early* adolescent males (i.e., 12- and 13-year-olds versus 11-year-olds). An additional finding showed that a negative attitude toward learning among middle to late adolescent males was predicted by early adolescent-experienced stress. The finding is in keeping with other theorizing for minority boys, which suggests that psychic stress interferes with more "productive" learning opportunities (Spencer, 1995).

On the other hand, for girls, early adolescent stresses that are linked to autonomy were associated with lower negative attitudes toward learning later on; it suggests that girls require different programs of support. Although maturation and pubertal status information is generally available and copious for nonminority group youth, little information is available on youth of color. More specifically, the findings by Spencer et al. (1998) suggests that programs which provide safe, appropriate, "monitored" opportunities for demonstrations of independence may keep girls more academically focused longer and offset, perhaps, views of early childbearing as "independence opportunities."

*Family Considerations*

Adolescence, as a transitional period, is frequently characterized by conflicting behaviors that may oscillate between immature, childlike behavior and mature, adultlike behavior. Parental relationships provide feedback and expectations congruent with increased maturation (i.e., more responsibility), whereas peer relationships provide feedback more consistent with physical development. The expectation of greater autonomy provides the potential for parent-child conflicts when behavior is inconsistent with parental expectations. Although negotiating the desire for greater autonomy and experiencing an increase in parental conflict, numerous studies have also confirmed the importance of the parent-child relationship in the formation of positive relationships, a confident sense of identity, and successful separation and autonomous functioning (Steinberg, 1987, 1988). The development of independence from parents is a critical psychosocial task that adolescents must achieve in becoming autonomous, self-sufficient, productive, and competent adults. Perceiving roles and boundaries as a challenge to autonomy is a characteristic adolescent response. However, the quality, type, and requirements for boundaries will vary depending upon the characteristics of the context. For example, specific expectations and requirements around an issue such as maintaining a curfew must be negotiated. Accordingly, parental responses to neighborhood police presence vary significantly as a function of the child's gender. Parents of African American adolescent boys viewed police presence negatively, while parents of African American females were more positive about the presence of police. The pattern of findings suggests a perception of police as a source of hassles for parents of males and a source of protection for parents of females (Spencer, Swanson & Glymph, 1996). While addressing perceptions of neighborhood resources, the finding also raises questions regarding how parents' perceptions of the context may affect differential male and female socialization practices.

Historically, parents have been recognized as providing different socialization experiences for males and females. Considerable emphasis, for example, has been given to how father-absence and female-headed homes affect identity. Males are encouraged to be physical and allowed more independence, while females are more likely to receive assistance rather than encouragement toward independent mastery. Fathers appear to encourage more gender-specific activities in their children, and both parents tend to be more attentive and controlling toward same-sex children. It is the effects of the latter finding which suggests that males and females may present differential outcomes to father-absence versus mother-absence (Ruble, 1988). It has been suggested, for example, that males who are reared in female-headed homes without a positive male figure lack identification with a male role model and therefore may overexaggerate a sense of masculinity by being excessively aggressive, assertive, and often antisocial (*see* Cunningham, 1993; Ketterlinus & Lamb, 1994).

In a sample of African American and white older female adolescents, Harris, Gold, and Henderson (1991) examined the influence of father-absence on gender-role orientation and achievement. Given prior findings indicating that fathers played an important role in forming more traditional traits in their daughters, the researchers expected females without fathers to exhibit greater masculine-linked attributes and have higher achievement motives during their development. They found that for their African American sample, there were significantly higher achievement needs and higher masculinity and androgynous attributes, although this was not supported for the overall sample. The extent to which this finding reflects a characteristic of female-headed (father "absence") outcomes or part of the cultural socialization experience associated with the multiple roles of African American females discussed earlier is a consideration for future investigations.

CONCLUSION

Patterns of developmental outcomes are linked to unavoidable cognitive, emotional, social, and biological processes; these patterns occur in multiple environments that vary in level of risk, represent an ongoing and sensitive integration of the past with current experiences, and illustrate necessary transitions between stages that may vary in severity (Spencer, 1995). The resolution of normative developmental tasks and issues undergird the quality of adult life; accordingly the self-appraisal processes for specific groups may be associated with unique strategies for addressing developmental tasks and normative themes, although under precarious contextual conditions.

What does this mean for the prediction of adolescent and young adult competence and confidence? A consistent finding apparent from the literature on identity, for example, is that for African American youth, personal identity development and cultural identity processes function independently of school or academic identity issues. An additional important school-based experience is simply how youth view the self as a learner (Irvine, 1990). Research findings indicate that as early as the preschool years there are differences in how youngsters perceive themselves as learners when compared against middle childhood perceptions (Spencer, Dobbs & Swanson, 1988), indicating clear developmental differences that have an impact on outcomes.

In general, research on African American children, adolescents, and young adults suggests that self processes are heavily linked to context characteristics, person characteristics, coping methods, and adaptive processes. More explicit research is needed that will provide an understanding of both adaptive and maladaptive outcomes for African American youth. As efforts are being made to provide a better understanding of psychological processes, simultaneous considerations must be made toward understanding the context as well as understanding the meanings youth assign to their experiences in those contexts. Future research that further explores these linkages will provide greater specificity that is required to facilitate use in policy, training, and the design of supportive programs of intervention and prevention. Such efforts need to be theoretically driven, developmentally sensitive, and multidimensional. The research reviewed and theoretical model presented serves as one starting point.

ACKNOWLEDGMENTS

The preparation of this report was supported by funds awarded to the second author from several sources: The Commonwealth Fund, Spencer Foundation, W. T. Grant Foundation, Social Science Research Council, and the Ford Foundation. In addition, the Annenberg Foundation provided supplemental funding.

REFERENCES

Albee, G. W. (1982). Preventing psychopathology and promoting human potential. *American Psychologist, 37,* 1043–1050.

Allen, W. R. (1985). Race, income and family dynamics: A study of adolescent male socialization processes and outcomes. In M. B. Spencer, W. R. Allen & G. K. Brookins (Eds.), *Beginnings: The social and affective development of black children* (pp. 273–292). Hillsdale, NJ: Erlbaum.

Bandura, A. (1978). The self system in reciprocal determinism. *American Psychologist, 33* (4), 344–358.

Bowman, P. (1989). Research perspectives on black men: Role strain and adaptation across the adult life cycle. In R. L. Jones (Ed.), *Black adult development and aging* (pp. 117–150). Berkeley, CA: Cobb & Henry.

Bronfenbrenner, U. (1979). *The ecology of human development: Experiments by nature and design.* Cambridge, MA: Harvard University Press.

Bronfenbrenner, U. & Crouter, A. C. (1983). The evolution of environmental models in developmental research. In P. H. Mussen (Ed.), *Handbook of child psychology: Vol. 1. History, theory and methods* (pp. 357–414). New York: Wiley.

Chestang, L. W. (1972). *Character development in a hostile environment.* Occasional Paper No. 3 (Series) (pp. 1–12). Chicago: University of Chicago Press.

Clark, R. (1983). *Family life and school achievement: Why poor black children succeed and fail.* Chicago: University of Chicago Press.

Comer, J. P. (1988). Educating poor minority children. *Scientific American, 259* (5), 42–48.

Comer, J. P. & Hill, H. (1985). Social policy and the mental health of black children. *Journal of the American Academy of Child Psychiatry, 24* (2), 175–181.

Compas, B. E. (1987). Coping with stress during childhood and adolescence. *Psychological Bulletin, 101,* 393–403.

Cunningham, M. (1993). Sex role influences on African Americans: A literature review. *Journal of African American Male Studies, 1,* 30–37.

Cunningham, M. (1994). *Expressions of manhood: Predictors of educational achievement and African American adolescent males.* Unpublished Ph.D. dissertation. Atlanta, GA., Emory University.

Cunningham, M. & Spencer, M. B. (1996). The black male experiences measure. In R. Jones (Ed.), *Handbook of tests and measurements for black populations.* Hampton, VA: Cobb and Henry Publishers.

Erikson, E. H. (1968). *Identity and crisis.* New York: Norton.

Garbarino, J. (1982). *Children and families in the social environment.* New York: Aldine.

Gibbs, J. T. (1988). *Young black and male in America: An endangered species.* Dover, MA: Auburn House.

Gibbs, J. T. (1995). Health and mental health of black adolescents. In R. L. Taylor (Ed.), *African American youth: Their social and economic status in the United States* (pp. 71–90). Westport, CT: Praeger.

Hagan, J., Simpson, J. & Gillis, A. R. (1987). Class in the household: A power-control theory of gender and delinquency. *American Journal of Sociology, 92* (4), 788–816.

Hare, B. R. (1977). Racial and socioeconomic variations in preadolescence: Area specific and general self esteem. *International Journal of Intercultural Relations, 1* (3), 31–51.

Hare, B. R. & Castenell, L. A. (1985). No place to run, no place to hide: Comparative status and future prospects of black boys. In M. B. Spencer, G. K. Brookins & W. R. Allen (Eds.), *Beginnings: The social and affective development of black children* (pp. 185–200). Hillsdale, NJ: Erlbaum.

Harris, S. M., Gold, S. R. & Henderson, B. B. (1991). Relationships between achievement and affiliation needs and sex-role orientation of college women whose fathers were absent from home. *Perceptual and Motor Skills, 72,* 1307–1315.

Havighurst, R. J. (1973). History of developmental psychology: Socialization and personality development through the life-span. In P. B. Baltes & K. W. Schaie (Eds.), *Life-span developmental psychology.* New York: Academic Press.

Hirsh, F. J. & Rapkin, B. D. (1987). The transition to junior high school: A longitudinal study of self-esteem, psychological symptomatology, school life, and social support. *Child Development, 58,* 1235–1243.

Hyde, J. S. (1991). *Half the human experience: The psychology of women* (4th ed). Lexington, MA: D.C. Heath.

Irvine, J. J. (1990). *Black students and school failure: Policies, practices, and prescription.* New York: Greenwood.

Jencks, C. & Meyer, S. (1990). The social consequences of growing up in a poor neighborhood. In L. E. Lynn, Jr. & M. G. H. McGeary (Eds.), *Inner city poverty in the United States* (pp. 111–186). Washington, DC: National Academy Press.

Kagan, J. (1983). Stress and coping in early development. In N. Garmezy & M. Rutter (Eds.), *Stress, coping and development in children* (pp. 191–216). New York: McGraw-Hill.

Ketterlinus, R. & Lamb, M. E. (Eds.) (1994). *Adolescent problem behaviors.* Hillsdale, NJ: Erlbaum.

Kochman, T. J. (1992). *The relationship between environmental characteristics and the psychological functioning of African American youth.* Unpublished bachelor's with honors thesis. Atlanta, GA., Emory University.

Ladner, J. A. (1972). *Tomorrow's tomorrow: The black woman.* New York: Doubleday.

Maccoby, E. E. (1990). Gender and relationships: A developmental account. *American Psychologist, 45* (4), 513–520.

McCandless, B. R. & Evans, F. D. (1973). *Children and youth: Psychosocial development.* Detroit: Dryden.

Merrick, E. N. (1995). Adolescent childbearing as career "choice": Perspective from an ecological context. *Journal of Counseling & Development, 73,* 288–295.

Ogbu, J. U. (1986). The consequences of the American caste system. In U. Neisser (Ed.), *The school achievement of minority children: New perspectives* (pp. 19–56). Hillsdale, NJ: Erlbaum.

Peterson, A. C. & Crockett, L. (1985). Pubertal timing and grade effects on adjustment. *Journal of Youth and Adolescence, 14,* 191–206.

Pleck, J. H., Sonenstein, F. L. & Ku, L. C. (1994). Problem behaviors and masculine ideology in adolescent males. In R. Ketterlinus and M. E. Lamb (Eds.), *Adolescent problem behaviors.* Hillsdale, NJ: Erlbaum.

Ruble, D. N. (1988). Sex-role development. In M. H. Bornstein and M. E. Lamb (Eds.), *Developmental psychology: An advanced textbook,* 2nd ed. (pp. 411–459). Hillsdale, NJ: Erlbaum.

Simmons, R. G., Burgeson, R., Carlton-Ford, S. & Blyth, D. A. (1987). The impact of cumulative change in early adolescence. *Child Development, 58,* 1220–1234.

Spencer, M. B. (1982). Preschool children's social cognition and cultural cognition: A cognitive developmental interpretation of race dissonance findings. *Journal of Psychology, 112,* 275–296.

Spencer, M. B. (1983). Children's cultural values and parental child rearing strategies. *Developmental Review, 4,* 351–370.

Spencer, M. B. (1984). Black children's race awareness, racial attitudes, and self-concept: A reinterpretation. *Journal of Child Psychology and Psychiatry, 25* (3), 433–441.

Spencer, M. B. (1985). Cultural cognition and social cognition as identity factors in black children's personal-social growth. In M. B. Spencer, G. K. Brookins & W. R. Allen (Eds.), *Beginnings: Social and affective development of black children* (pp. 215–230). Hillsdale, NJ: Erlbaum.

Spencer, M. B. (1990). Parental values transmission: Implications for black child development. In J. B. Stewart & H. Cheathan (Eds.), *Interdisciplinary perspectives on black families* (pp. 111–130). New Brunswick, NJ: Transaction Books.

Spencer, M. B. (1995). Old issues and new theorizing about African American youth: A phenomenological variant of ecological systems theory. In R. L. Taylor (Ed.), *Black youth: Perspectives on their status in the United States* (pp. 37–70). Westport, CT: Praeger.

Spencer, M. B., Cunningham, M. & Swanson, D. P. (1995). Identity as coping: Adolescent African American males' adaptive responses to high risk environments. In H. W. Harris, H. C. Blue & E. H. Griffith (Eds.), *Racial and ethnic identity* (pp. 31–52). New York: Routledge.

Spencer, M. B., Dobbs, B. & Swanson, D. P. (1988). Afro-American adolescents: Adaptational processes and socioeconomic diversity in behavioral outcomes. *Journal of Adolescence, 11* (2), 117–137.

Spencer, M. B. & Dornbusch, S. (1990). Challenges in studying minority youth.. In S.

Feldman & G. Elliot (Eds.), *At the threshold: The developing adolescent*. Cambridge, MA: Harvard University Press.

Spencer, M. B., Dupree, D. & Hartmann, T. (1997). A phenomenological variant of ecological systems theory (PVEST): A self-organization perspective in context. *Development and Psychopathology, 9,* 817–833.

Spencer, M. B., Dupree, D., Swanson, D. P. & Cunningham, M. (1998). The influence of physical maturation and hassles on African American adolescents' learning behaviors. *Journal of Comparative Family Studies* (special issue), *29* (1), 197–209.

Spencer, M. B. & Horowitz, F. D. (1973). Racial attitudes and color concept-attitude modification in black and Caucasion preschool children. *Developmental Psychology, 9,* 246–254.

Spencer, M. B., Swanson, D. P. & Glymph, A. (1996). The prediction of parental well-being: Influences of African American adolescent perceptions and experience of context. In C. D. Ryff & M. M. Seltzer (Eds.), *Mid-life parenting*. Chicago: University of Chicago Press.

Steinberg, L. (1987). Impact of puberty on family relations: Effects of pubertal status and pubertal timing. *Developmental Psychology, 23,* 451–460.

Steinberg, L. D. (1988). Reciprocal relation between parent-child distance and pubertal maturation. *Developmental Psychology, 24,* 122–128.

Streitmatter, J. (1993). Gender differences in identity development: An examination of longitudinal data. *Adolescence, 28* (109), 55–66.

Swanson, D. P. & Spencer, M. B. (1991). Youth policy, poverty, and African-Americans: Implications for resilience. *Education and Urban Society, 24* (1), 148–161.

Taylor, R. L. (1976). Psychological development among black children and youth: A re-examination. *American Journal of Orthopsychiatry, 46,* 4–19.

Wilson, W. J. (1991). Public policy research and the truly disadvantaged. In C. Jencks & P. E. Peterson (Eds.), *The urban underclass* (pp. 460–481). Washington, DC: The Brookings Institution.

Wingard, D. L. (1987). Sex differential in health and mortality. *Women and Health, 12,* 103–145.

# Cultural Context of Children's Development

*John U. Ogbu*

There are several reasons the development of minority children has been studied out of cultural context. One reason is the dominance of a Eurocentric, middle-class perspective that holds up the linguistic, motivational, and cognitive patterns of mainstream white Americans as the goal of all development. Thus, we go with instruments to measure the extent to which African American, Chinese American, or Native American children have developed mainstream white American forms of language (e.g., vocabulary, grammar). We make no allowance that black children growing up in a community that speaks Black English will acquire the black language pattern, not the mainstream white American pattern. Another reason is that we generally believe or assume that the mainstream white language, motivation, and cognition are the things that make children successful in school and make citizens succeed in the opportunity structure as adults. We forget that children who grow up in African villages, in Chinese or Korean communities in China and Korea, or in Latin American barrios, when they enter the public schools, can learn to speak and strive to achieve and think like mainstream white Americans do. They can succeed in the U.S. schools and adult opportunity structure through changes whereby they learn to become Americans in these domains.

A third barrier to the study of minority children's development in cultural context is our focus on problem children. For many reasons researchers rarely include normal minority children in their study. To complicate matters, researchers may generalize their findings to all children of the particular minority group they studied.

The fourth problem is that child development researchers, including minority child development researchers, lack adequate understanding of what culture is and how it influences behavior and development. Researchers are usually familiar with theories of development underlying the substantive issue or attribute they are studying (e.g., language, emotion), but they know very little about the culture in which they are studying that particular attribute and how it functions within. In language development studies, for example, an investigator in a black American community will generally be conversant with theories of language development in a universal sense but would not have a good intellectual understanding of Black English. The same can be said of students of language development among other minorities. This is not surprising because the guiding research paradigm in child development forces researchers to measure a given element out of cultural context. Emphasis is on instrumentation, correlation, and other methodological considerations. Data are collected with consent but minimum rapport. The investigator rarely spends more than the amount of time to get the responses to preconstructed questionnaires. He or she cannot claim to know the people they are studying more than just obtaining the information they think they need. We have good technicians who can conduct well-designed studies of language, motivation, cognition, and the like totally removed from their cultural context.

Cross-cultural studies suggest that language, motivation, cognition, emotion, and social relations differ from culture to culture because they are culturally constructed and required (Hymes, 1962; LeVine, 1967; Maquet, 1961). This is not to deny that there are individual differences in these attributes. There is even a case for a genetic basis of these attributes. But what the child develops is a culturally constructed attribute that varies from culture to culture; it is not generic. Therefore, if we are going to learn how children develop the attributes, we should begin by studying their culture and how that culture shapes and uses that attribute. The argument here is that those who study minority children's development should first become familiar with the culture of the population from which the children come. Accordingly, let us explore what is meant by culture.

## WHAT IS CULTURE?

There are many definitions of culture among anthropologists. The preferred definition of this author lies within the cultural-ecological school of anthropology. According to this school of thought, culture is a people's adaptive way of life. Following LeVine (1973), we can distinguish analytically six components of culture: (1) customary ways of behaving (e.g., making a living, eating, expressing affection, getting married, raising children, responding to illness or to death, getting ahead in society, dealing with the supernatural, going for a job interview, holding conferences); (2) codes or assumptions, expectations, and emotions underlying those customary behaviors; (3) artifacts—things that members of a population make or have made that have meanings for them (e.g., airports, cars, family homes, restaurants, supermarkets, televisions, traffic signs); (4) institutions—economic, political, religious, and social, what Cohen (1971) calls the imperatives of culture—which form a recognizable pattern requiring knowledge, beliefs, competencies or skills, and customary behaviors in a fairly predictable manner; (5) patterns of social relations; and (6) cultural frame of reference. The six components constitute a kind of cultural world in a given community. People create and change culture and pass it on to their children who, in turn, may change it. But their culture also shapes or influences them. For example, children in the United States are born into a culture with a free-enterprise economic system and are brought up to function in this free enterprise competitive economic system, not a socialist or other type of economic system (Ogbu, 1981, 1994; *see also* Cohen, 1971; Edgerton & Langness, 1968; LeVine, 1973; Spradley, 1979).

## CULTURE, BEHAVIOR, AND HUMAN ATTRIBUTES

The ways we talk (language), think (cognition), strive to achieve (motivation), feel (emotion), and relate to one another (sociability) depend partly on culture. Culture influences behavior because people learn, as they grow up, to speak, think, feel, and relate in the cultural world of their community. Each human population lives in a somewhat different cultural world, and consequently, members of different populations think, feel, and behave differently. Culture is the framework, or window, through which members of the population see the world around them, interpret events in that world, behave according to acceptable standards, and react to the perceived reality. To understand members of different populations it is necessary to understand their cultures (Edgerton & Langness, 1968; Spradley, 1979).

An example of a cultural or customary behavior in the United States is the ritual of caring for the mouth (Miner, 1956). The assumptions underlying this customary or cultural behavior lie in American people's belief that the body houses two dangerous elements, namely, debility and disease, which must be prevented. Consequently, every home in the United States contains a shrine for a daily mouth ritual (brushing of teeth), and occasionally Americans consult a "holy-mouth-man," or dentist, who is a specialist in the magical care of their mouths.

Another customary behavior limited to one segment of the United States is the "stylin' out" of the black preacher through a special "code talk." The preacher's code talk is specialized to facilitate in-group or community feeling and to conceal the aspirations and feelings of black Americans from the dominant white Americans. White Americans would have difficulty understanding the language and style of the preachers; thus, they may attend such a church service and not comprehend the preacher's message to his congregation about white Americans (Holt, 1972).

Other examples of customary behaviors in the United States that call for culturally patterned use of human attributes are baby showers, buying a home, celebrating the Fourth of July, dining out, employment interviews, grocery shopping, letters of recommendation, retirement, Thanksgiving dinners, and waiting in line. During these, Americans are expected to follow more or less rule-governed, learned ways of talking, thinking, feeling, and relating.

## CULTURAL DIFFERENCES IN BEHAVIOR AND ATTRIBUTES

Different populations—even populations within one society—may differ in culture (i.e., they differ in their adaptations) for several reasons. One is that communities may live in different physical or social environments requiring different adaptations. Furthermore, communities may have had different historical experiences that shaped the way they perceive, interpret, and respond to things, situations, and events within their environments, and within their relationships with one another and with outsiders. Thus, members of different communities may behave differently with different assumptions toward the same phenomenon. The essential point is that communities differ in culture because they live in different environments that differ in resources and opportunities or because they have had different historical experiences.

The influence of culture on behavior, and hence on human attributes, can be readily observed by comparing the solutions that different populations have developed for some common problems. Compare, for example, the way two populations make a living (economy and technology), govern themselves (polity), organize their domestic life for reproduction (family and raising children), manage their relationship with the supernatural (religion), communicate with one another (folk theory of speaking), and try to get ahead (status mobility strategy). Each version of these solutions both requires and promotes its own customary behaviors, knowledge, assumptions, and emotions that support the behaviors.

## SOME EXAMPLES OF CULTURAL BEHAVIORS

The influence of culture on behavior that in turn affects the nature of language, cognition, motivation, emotion, and other attributes children develop is most readily observed when comparing behaviors of people from different cultures trying to solve a similar problem, as shown by the following examples.

## Getting Ahead in Society and Achievement Motivation

Consider the solution to the problem of getting ahead in society. Different cultures prescribe and inculcate different strategies that affect attributes for getting ahead. Mainstream middle-class white American culture prescribes the strategy of individual competition. In this culture it is believed that social mobility, upward or downward, depends on an individual's ability or fate. In contrast, the culture of the Kanuri of northern Nigeria prescribes a different strategy for getting ahead. The aspirant is expected to achieve social mobility through a patron-client relationship. The person should attach him- or herself to and serve a patron who rewards him or her with the desired position or wealth after the aspirant has served the patron in a culturally approved manner and has demonstrated his or her trust by showing loyalty, obedience, servility, and compliance to the patron.

This way of getting ahead is also found among black Americans, although it was more common in the past. Through the experience of many generations, black Americans learned that one strategy prescribed for them by U.S. society for achieving self-betterment or social mobility in the wider society is through favoritism, not merit. They also learned that favoritism can be solicited by being dependent, compliant, and manipulative; as a result they tend to seek white Americans, both as individuals and as organizations, to serve as patrons to individual blacks and to black groups and black organizations. The federal government in particular has historically assumed the role of a patron, serving as an employer, a sponsor of educational and other training programs, an adviser and protector of civil rights, and as distributor of subsistence assistance, or welfare. This patron-client strategy became a part of black American culture. Blacks even encoded this strategy in their language as "uncle tomming."

## Cultural Variation in Vocabulary or Language Concept

Culture influences the vocabulary or concept in a language because it uses the language to codify its members' environment and their experiences. Therefore, the language spoken by people in different cultures who inhabit different environments and have different historical experiences will differ in particular content areas. This means that the languages of members of some cultures will have some concepts that are absent in the languages of members of other cultures. So, some concepts that people find natural in their own language are not necessarily universal or generic to the rest of human cultures. The reason those concepts are absent in another culture is not because members of that culture lack the biological structures or genes to develop them; it is not because parents in that culture cannot teach their children to acquire the "missing" concepts; and it is not because individuals in that culture are lagging in psychobiological development. Those concepts are "missing" in the second culture because they are not relevant to the cultural way of life and historical experience and so have not been encoded into the language.

In summarizing evidence in support of the Whorfian hypothesis, Fishman (1964) provides several examples of cultural differences in language codification of the environment. He shows how one culture may have several terms for a given phenomenon, while another culture has only one term for the same phenomenon, and still a third culture has no concept for it at all. Examples of instances of variation in the codification of a given phenomenon include the following: (1). *FLY:* English speakers have several terms for ideas and objects associated with flying, such as fly (noun), fly (verb), pilot, airplane. Hopi speakers, on the other hand, have only one term for the idea and object "fly." (2) *SNOW:* English speakers have two forms of the word "snow," as a noun and as a verb; Eskimos have several forms of the word "snow"; the Ibos of Nigeria have none. (3) *COLOR:* English speakers distinguish between blue and green but lump together shades of black to gray; Navajo speakers lump blue and green together and have no terms for different shades of black.

*Culture and Communication: The Social Meaning of Language*

Culture also influences the social meaning of language or communication—that is, what it means to "talk well" among members of a culture. Hymes (1971) introduced the notion of a "speech community," which allows us to better understand cultural influences on communication or what is regarded as appropriate ways to talk by members of a culture. A *speech community* is a population whose members share a common language (vocabulary, grammar, phonology, etc.) and a common theory of speaking—that is, a common understanding of what it means to be a good or bad speaker, an effective or ineffective speaker, in short, the meaning of "communicative competence." Within a speech community there are *speech situations*, or situations that are considered appropriate for certain types of speeches (e.g., speeches in connection with birthday parties, lovemaking, baby showers, election campaigns), and *speech events,* or events that are culturally defined, such as a conversation, a lecture, a debate, a confession, or a job interview. According to Hymes, a speech event is governed by cultural rules that are learned and known to members of a speech community. For example, the speech event of a private conversation can take place at a wedding reception, a memorial service, a campaign rally, or during grocery shopping, but in each case it is governed by cultural rules. The speech community also employs other *communicative codes* besides verbal ones, including gestures, facial expressions, postures, paralinguistic sounds like intonation, voices, loudness, distance maintained from others in interaction, clothing, deodorants, and scents, and has *communication channels,* such as verbal channel, kinesics and body movement, and proxemics or culturally patterned use of space.

Hymes (1971) defines competence in communication within a speech community as knowing when it is appropriate to speak and to remain silent, which communicative code to use, where and when to use it, and for whom it is appropriate. Thus, communicative competence or ability to talk well in a speech community involves not only the ability to convey information in one or more available channels, but also the ability to match channel, form, content, and style to specific contexts and situations—that is, to use communicative skills appropriately.

In a pluralistic society like that in the United States, there are several speech communities among speakers of the English language (*see* Figure 4–1 for some examples). Communication in these speech communities is influenced by the different ways in which their cultures define "good talk," or by their theories of speaking. The different definitions mean that the cultures have different requirements for being a competent speaker. These differences in theories of speaking and in competencies for being a competent speaker often result in cross-cultural miscommunication among populations in the United States (*see* Becknell, 1987; Kochman, 1982). The different speech communities in the United States have different formulas for learning and teaching how to be a "good talker."

### Cultural Context of Mathematical Knowledge and Skills

Studies of mathematical knowledge and behaviors in different cultures provide examples of their cultural context. Such differences exist between the United States and the Kpelle of Liberia in West Africa as described by Gay and Cole (1967). Both the Kpelle and Americans have some mathematical ideas in common, since people in both cultures count, add, subtract, multiply, and divide. But unlike Americans the Kpelle do not carry out the activities of adding, subtracting, multiplying, or dividing explicitly. Nor do the Kpelle have concepts for these abstract operations, namely, addition, subtraction, multiplication, and division, even though they add, subtract, multiply, and divide. Another difference is that the Kpelle do not have the concepts of "zero" and "number."

There are other human attributes or skills where cultural context is important for understanding differences among populations. Edward Hall (1959, 1966) has, for example, shown the importance of cultural context in differences in time orientation and spatial orientation. As summarized by Brislin (1993), for mainstream white Americans, punctuality is important. This value is readily observed at a scheduled meeting, say at 9:30 A.M. People attending the meeting expect that the meeting will start at 9:30 A.M. promptly, or at least before 9:45 A.M. If it does not start by 9:50 A.M., some people might say that the meeting should start because some of them have other appointments at 10:30 A.M. or some other specific time. This time awareness contrasts sharply with how people in some other countries view the concept. For example, a meeting in Brazil scheduled for 9.30 A.M. may start at 10:45 A.M., 11:00 A.M., or even later. Latin American cultures clearly place different values on time. While mainstream white Americans place more emphasis on "clock time," Latin Americans and other peoples place more emphasis on "event time" (Brislin, 1993).

As for spatial orientation, mainstream white Americans differ from Latin Americans in use of space during social interaction. At informal social interactions, mainstream white Americans tend to maintain a distance of approximately the length of a tall man's arm (about three feet) between two people. If the distance is closer, one or both parties may begin to feel uncomfortable; if the interacting parties are male and female, a closer distance may be interpreted as a sexual advance. In Latin America, the distance between two people in an informal interaction may be closer, about two and a half feet. Cultural conflict will arise if the distance is closer, especially if the interacting parties are a male and a female, as both parties may begin to feel uncomfortable. On the other hand, if the distance is more than two and a half feet, the intentions of the interacting parties may be questioned and the integrating parties may feel uncomfortable (Brislin, 1993).

## Cultural Frame of Reference and Cultural Context of Behavior

The sixth component of culture, cultural frame of reference, is totally missing in conventional studies of child development and, therefore, deserves some elaboration. A cultural frame of reference refers to the correct or ideal way to behave within a culture—that is, different attitudes, beliefs, preferences, and practices are considered appropriate by members of different cultures or populations. A population's cultural frame of reference may be oppositional or ambivalent to the cultural frame of reference of another population, depending on the relationship between the two populations. When cultural frames of reference are not in opposition, interacting parties from different populations usually interpret the cultural/language differences between them as barriers to be overcome.

They also usually consciously strive to overcome these initial cultural differences by crossing cultural boundaries. In contrast, when cultural frames of reference are in opposition, the interacting parties tend to perceive the cultural/language differences between them as boundary-maintaining markers of group or community identity. They are less motivated to overcome the initial cultural differences and thus have greater difficulty crossing cultural boundaries.

The influence of cultural frame of reference can be observed in the interaction between members of subordinate or minority groups and members of the dominant groups in plural societies. In the United States the cultural frames of reference of some nonwhite immigrant minority groups, such as the Chinese (ARC, 1984) and the Punjabis (Gibson, 1988), were formed prior to their emigration. Their cultural frames of reference are different from, but are not necessarily oppositional to, the cultural frame of reference of mainstream white Americans. These minorities often consider not knowing how to behave according to the mainstream white American cultural frame of reference in certain situations to be barriers to the attainment of the goals of their emigration. Therefore, they are willing to learn how to behave according to the cultural frame of reference of mainstream white Americans in the selected domains. The immigrants do not see crossing cultural and language boundaries as compromising their ethnic identity.

In contrast, the cultural frames of reference of some other nonwhite minorities were formed after these groups had been forced into continuous contact with mainstream white Americans through slavery, conquest, and colonization. Such was the case in the formation of the cultural frames of reference among black Americans (Luster, 1992; Ogbu, 1988) and Native Americans (Kramer, 1991). The cultural frames of reference of these involuntary or nonimmigrant minorities appear to have developed as oppositional or ambivalent responses to subordination by mainstream white Americans. Furthermore, involuntary minorities do not usually think that the reason for their poor economic and social well-being is that they do not know how to talk or behave like mainstream white Americans in school and the workplace. In addition, they tend to interpret the cultural differences as symbols of their group identity; behaving like mainstream white Americans could result in a loss of their minority cultural identity.

Such an unwillingness or inability to cross cultural boundaries occurs in other situations that do not involve minority-majority relations. It can be found in the interactions between the Walloons and the Flemings in Belgium

(Irving, 1980; Lijphart, 1981) and between the Tewa and the Hopi of the American Southwest (Dozier, 1951). Edward Spicer (1966, 1971) has reviewed cases of cultural persistence or opposition involving the Jews, the Irish, the Welsh, the Catalans, the Mayas, the Yaquis, the Senecas, the Cherokees, and the Navajos (*see also* Castile & Kushner, 1981).

Culture is a concept that enables us to understand people's behavior. It is, as Bohannan (1992) notes, a phenomenon both inside the minds of the members of a population and in their environment as acts, artifacts, and institutions. People behave in cultural ways because their culture provides for them to be brought up in their cultural worlds. The language, cognition, motivation, emotion, and other attributes they develop are understandable within their cultural context. Cultural frame of reference governs the behavior of its members.

## HUMAN DEVELOPMENT IN CULTURAL CONTEXT
### *What Is Human Development?*

Human development, as applied to children, is the child's acquisition, as he or she matures, of his or her society's or group's customary behaviors and attributes—that is, the language, thoughts, emotions, motivation, and so on that accompany and support the customary behaviors. There are no correct or generic ways of expressing customary behaviors, languages or communications, thoughts, emotions, and motivations which children in all cultures acquire or develop as they grow up. When children are born into a society or culture, they do not yet possess the customary behaviors, language, beliefs and thoughts, emotions, and motivations characteristic of that society or culture (*see* Figure 4–1). But as they develop or reach different stages of development, children learn appropriate phases and types of their society's customary behaviors and culturally valued attributes.

### *What Children Develop*

Culture, cultural differences, and cultural frames of reference are what children develop or learn as they grow up. The customary behaviors and attributes that children in different cultures develop or learn may be different because the children grow up and participate in different cultural worlds whose contents and frames of reference are different and define competence differently. In general, competence may be defined as the capacity and the quality that enable a person to get things done in a manner considered appropriate by members of his or her culture (Connolly & Bruner, 1974). An example is the ability of a member of the inner-city black community in Chicago to speak Black English vernacular in a manner considered appro-

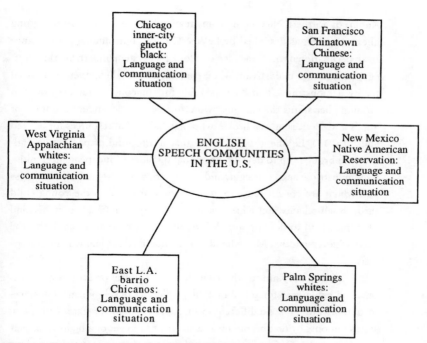

Figure 1. Speech communities of the English langugage in the U.S.

priate by members of his or her speech community. From this perspective we can define human development as a child's acquisition of the cognitive, communicative, motivational, social-emotional or affective competence as defined by members of his or her particular culture or social group.

As pointed out earlier, children born into a particular society or culture do not yet possess the customary behaviors, language, beliefs and thoughts, emotions, and motivations characteristic of that culture but they will need to learn these attributes in order to achieve the social and economic status of adulthood. These attributes—communicative, cognitive, motivational, and social-emotional—are cultural products that have been constructed out of the people's social histories. Although these cultural products may differ from culture to culture, children in every culture are born with human capacities and predispositions to learn them, no matter how the attributes are expressed.

## Some Examples of Culturally Valued or Functional Attributes

### ACHIEVEMENT MOTIVATION

Consider the differences in the achievement motivation and strategies for getting ahead in mainstream white American culture and the culture of the

Kanuri of northern Nigeria. In mainstream white American culture, getting ahead requires, as described by LeVine (1967), "outstanding performance in an occupational role"; the ideology (or belief system underlying this strategy) asserts, and mainstream white Americans' actual experience or social reality demonstrates, that "it is possible for someone of humble origin to attain higher status through his own effort as an independent producer of goods and services or as a broker who marshals social resources for desired ends" (p. 17). LeVine goes on to say that in this kind of population children are brought up to develop "personal qualities of independence, initiative, industriousness, foresight, and some daring which will lead to success and which are considered important virtues to instill in the young child through self-reliance and achievement training" (p. 18). Children in this kind of culture tend to develop a high level of need achievement similar to the need achievement that McClelland (1961) described for mainstream Americans.

Among the Kanuri, who have different cultural prescriptions, ideology, and experience for social mobility, children's development of achievement motivation takes a different form. A person of lower status can rise in status but only by first becoming a subservient follower of a high-status person (Cohen, 1965). The aspirant will then start showing him- or herself to be utterly loyal, obedient, and useful to his patron, who will eventually reward the lackey with riches, positions, and power. The qualities that are valued in Kanuri culture include obedience, compliance, deference, and servility, and the importance of these qualities is stressed in the upbringing of children.

LANGUAGE CODIFICATION OF ENVIRONMENT AND EXPERIENCE

From our earlier discussion of the influence of culture on the vocabulary of a language, it should be clear that the vocabulary or concepts children acquire about a particular domain of life depends on how their culture codifies the language. Absence, presence, or elaboration of coding of concepts does not depend merely on what parents teach their children. The concepts must be functional or based on experience.

But language development goes beyond the acquisition of vocabulary and grammar. Children are socialized to acquire social meanings of language in order to become competent speakers in their speech community. According to Hymes (1971), as children grow older or develop, they learn the language (i.e., vocabulary and grammar) of their speech community as well as their community's theory of speaking. That is, they learn both their language and the habits, attitudes, and rules associated with the value and use of that

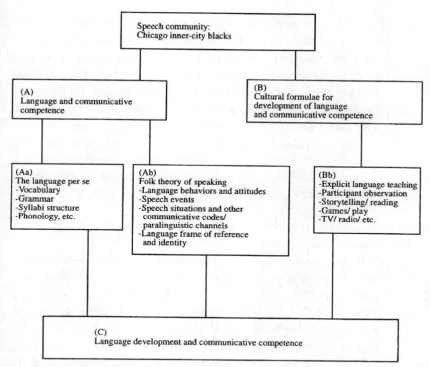

*Figure 4–2. Language development in a cultural context.*

language. Every normal child usually successfully learns both the language and the theory of speaking of his or her speech community.

## THE CHALLENGE TO RESEARCH IN CHILD DEVELOPMENT

We now turn to the study of child development in cultural context, illustrated by the study of language development. Earlier it was argued that there are two levels of language in a culture and therefore two levels of development: Children must develop linguistically in terms of (1) acquiring the language per se (vocabulary or concepts and grammar) of their population and (2) acquiring the communicative competence or ability to speak well according to members of the culture. Figure 4–2 represents these two levels in a hypothetical Black English–speaking inner-city Chicago. Box A shows the language form (Aa) and practice or communicative competence (Ab). Box B covers the area of language development achieved through cultural formulae in the population (Bb), dealing with the transmission and acquisition of the language and communicative competence by maturing children.

How does one study language development in the context of the culture of the Chicago inner-city black community? The study of language development in this cultural context poses two challenges to the researcher. First, it calls for the researcher to become fully knowledgeable in language forms and communicative competence that black children in inner-city Chicago will acquire to be competent speakers in their speech community (Box A in Figure 4–2); second, it calls for the researcher to acquire a general knowledge of the formulae that exist in this speech community for transmission and acquisition of its language forms and communicative competence (Box B in Figure 4–2). Additionally, the researcher can study language development in his or her selected sample of children (Box C in Figure 4–2).

## First Prerequisite: What the Researcher Needs to Know About Children's Language Development

To become competent speakers of their language, Chicago inner-city black children have to acquire the form of English spoken in their community, namely, Black English vernacular. This includes vocabulary, grammar, and phonology (Labov, 1972). But knowledge of the language alone does not make a child in the Chicago inner-city black community a competent speaker of his or her language. The black child in this community must also acquire the social meanings of Black English vernacular and the appropriate language behaviors associated with speaking well in inner-city Chicago (Hymes, 1962). Therefore, the researcher must also study the social meanings of Black English vernacular as well as the language behaviors in the culture. To study language development in cultural context, then, a researcher's information background must include knowledge of the language form as well as the knowledge of the social meanings of the language form. A researcher who is studying language development of black children in inner-city Chicago should study how the children develop the language that actually exists and is practiced in the population or culture in which the black children live and are growing up. The research should not be directed toward investigating their development of some generic English or the kind of English that is spoken in another speech community (e.g., Standard English of, say, mainstream white residents of Palm Springs). Many researchers commit the error of assuming that black inner-city children develop or should develop the kind of English spoken by mainstream white Americans. How could they develop a language if it is not spoken around them?

During our recent study of sociolinguistic factors in a black neighborhood in Oakland, California, many parents and grandparents gave unreasonable explanations of why their children and grandchildren talk the way they talk. First, they said that the way they talk is a part of their black identity and that the way white people talk is a part of their white identity. Furthermore, they went on to explain that their children speak their "regular [Black] English" because it is the language they hear in their environment, or speech community. But if their children or grandchildren live in a white speech community, they will talk like white children (i.e., speak Standard English) and not talk like people in the ghetto. The difference between the way a black child in the ghetto speaks and the way a black child in a white community speaks is not simply due to the fact that the black ghetto parent is unable to teach his or her child how to speak Standard English. The reason the black child in a white community talks like white children is not because his or her parents taught him or her to talk like white people. In both cases the black children learn and speak the way people in their respective speech community speaks. This point is brought out in one grandmother's explanation as to why her grandchildren living in a white suburb talk like white children (Ogdu, n.d.).

**Grandmother:** Well, sometimes they [children] change. They start talking like other races. 'Cuz I have some grandchildren out in the southern part of California and they don't talk like us, they talk like whites.

**Interviewer:** Okay. So, sometimes . . .

**Grandmother:** . . . . environment has a lot to do with it. More white users, school with more whites, than with blacks, they change.

What this grandmother means by "environment" is the speech community, not to be confused with the pathological or nonpathological environment or home characteristics that inner-city students use in language development.

In contrast, researchers commit the error because they believe that inner-city black children need to develop Standard English in order to do well in school. They forget that children who speak different languages (e.g., Black English vernacular) learn to speak their different languages at home and then learn to speak Standard English when they go to public school. This is the way inner-city black parents think it should be. If inner-city black children do not make this transition, the reason does not lie in their language development but in the nature of the relationship between Black English vernacular and Standard English (Ogbu, 1995). A researcher who is knowledgeable in Black English vernacular and is studying language development among black children in cultural context will usually come to the conclusion that black children develop Black English vernacular normally just like mainstream white children develop Standard English normally.

*Second Prerequisite: Familiarity with the Cultural Formulae for Transmitting and*
   *Acquiring Language and Communication Patterns*

Other background knowledge that a researcher has to have in order to study language development in cultural context is the knowledge of the formulae that exist in the culture (e.g., Chicago inner-city black speech community) for transmitting and acquiring Black English vernacular and communicative competence in the community (*see* Figure 4–2, Box B). There is not just one correct way of teaching children the English language and its social meanings and associated behaviors in their speech communities in the United States. Nor is there just one correct way by which children themselves in the different speech communities learn the version of the English language as well as its associated social meanings and behaviors. There are different formulae for the transmission and acquisition of language and communicative competence in the speech communities represented in Figure 4–1. Different speech communities of the English language have different formulae for teaching children their version of English and how to talk well. They also have different ways whereby their children acquire competence in speaking.

Researchers studying language development out of cultural context usually commit the error of assuming that there is one correct or generic way to teach children language development. They usually have in mind the method of mainstream white Americans. It is suggested that researchers study how language and communicative competence are actually transmitted and acquired by members of the speech community and how their methods or formulae enable them to teach and acquire their language and talk successfully. Parents in Chicago inner-city black communities will not use the techniques of parents in mainstream white American communities to teach their children how to speak Black English vernacular, just as one would not expect the latter to use the methods of Chicago inner-city blacks to teach their children how to speak Standard English. Each speech community—Chicago inner-city blacks and mainstream whites—has its own way of language development. One is not necessarily better than the other, but each needs to be appreciated and studied in terms of how language development functions within the respective culture.

CONCLUSION

The conventional approach to the study of child development, particularly minority child development, is unsatisfactory because it is based on wrong assumptions. For example, it is based on the false assumption that there is one correct way of speaking a language, which is lacking among black children and other minorities. It is also based on the false assumption that there is one correct way by which children, including minority children, learn language and how to talk correctly.

However, the study of children's development in cultural context is likely to be difficult, time-consuming, and expensive. It will require more time and resources than the conventional approach. It requires more time and resources to understand the language and practice of language as they exist in the children's culture or speech community; it requires time and resources to gain a good knowledge of the formulae that exist in a culture for the transmission and acquisition of the population's language or other attributes.

Researchers studying black children's development out of cultural context have often concluded that the differences between blacks and whites are due to black poverty. That does not mean that poverty does not affect the language development of inner-city black children, as even poor blacks have developed functional and meaningful language and communicative patterns that should be studied in their own right. Generally, researchers' conclusions are based on lack of adequate knowledge of black culture, even among black researchers. Furthermore, besides adapting to poverty, black Americans have also made cultural adaptations based on their involuntary or nonimmigrant minority status in the United States (Ogbu, 1995a). This adaptation includes more than inner-city blacks and has consequences for black language, cognition, motivation, and social-emotional attributes of black Americans.

A word about comparative study of child development: Although this author favors a comparative approach to research in child development (Ogbu, 1981), the type of comparisons one often finds in conventional research on minority children may be problematic. The latter often compares minorities negatively with the dominant group. In a true comparative study there is nothing wrong with comparing development among minority children with development among mainstream white children. However, the comparison should explain the differences or similarities in terms of the cultural context of each group; it should not explain the differences in terms of the cultural context of mainstream white children's development.

Similarly, children's development in different minority populations should be compared. But the findings should be explained in terms of the cultural context of the development of each group. The labels we use for various minority populations do not always capture the differences within the groups. For example, there are many subgroups of the Hispanic population, and it is important to distinguish among the subgroups. For example, in our current research on minority education in Oakland, California, we distinguish Mexican Americans, Mexicanos, and Latinos among the Hispanic sample. Among the Chinese we focus on Cantonese-speaking Chinese. Even among the latter we find other subgroup differences.

It is only through comparative research that we can develop a true theory of human development. When we have studied development of the children in their different cultural contexts we can sort out things that are similar and things that are different in development within different groups. We then could try to explain the reasons for the differences and similarities and arrive at some general understanding, without viewing any particular group as the model toward which all children's development should be directed.

## ACKNOWLEDGMENTS

The preparation of this chapter was supported by the University of California faculty research funds and by grants from the Carnegie Corporation of New York, the W. T. Grant Foundation, the MacArthur Foundation, the Russell Sage Foundation, and the Spencer Foundation. This chapter is based on a paper given at a preconference roundtable, "Children of Color: Research, Health, and Public Policy Issues," March 28–29, 1995, held prior to the biennial meeting of the Society for Research in Child Development.

## REFERENCES

ARC (1984). *Bilingual education in a Chinese population: Final research report.* Contract No. 400–80– 0013, National Institute of Education, Washington, DC.

Becknell, C. E. (1987). *Blacks in the workforce: A black manager's perspective.* Albuquerque, NM: Horizon Communications.

Bohannan, P. (1957). *Justice and judgement among the Tiv.* London: Oxford University Press.

Bohannan, P. (1992). *We, the people: An introduction to cultural anthropology.* Prospect Heights, IL: Westview Press.

Brislin, R. (1993). *Understanding culture's influences on behavior.* New York: Harcourt Brace.

Bruner, J. S. (1974). Nature and the uses of immaturity. In K. J. Connolly & J. S. Bruner (Eds.), *The growth of competence* (pp. 11–48). New York: Academic Press.

Castile, G. P. & Kushner, G. (Eds.) (1981). *Persistent peoples: Cultural enclaves in perspective.* Tucson: University of Arizona Press.

Cohen, R. (1965). "Some aspects of institutionalized exchange: A Kanuri example. *Cahiers D'Etudes Africaine, 5,* 353–369.

Cohen, Y. A. (1971). "The shaping of men's minds: Adaptations to the imperatives of culture." In M. L. Wax, S. Diamond & F. O. Gearing (Eds.), *Anthropological perspectives on education* (pp. 19–50). New York: Basic Books.

Connolly, K. J., & Bruner, J. S. (1984). Introduction. In K. J. Connolly and J. S. Bruner (Eds.), *The growth of competence* (pp. 3–7). London: Academic Press.

Dasen, P. (1972). Cross-cultural Piagetian research: A summary. *Journal of Cross-Cultural Psychology, 3,* 23–39.

Dasen, P. (1977). Introduction. In P. Dasen (Ed.), *Piagetian psychology: Cross-cultural contributions* (pp. 1–25). New York: Gardner Press.

Dozier, E. (1951). Resistance to acculturation and assimilation in an Indian pueblo. *American Anthropologist, 53,* 56–66.

Edgerton, R. B. & Langness, L.L. (1968). *Methods and style in the study of culture.* San Francisco: Chandler & Sharp.

Fishman, J. A. (1964). A systematization of the Whorfian hypothesis. In G. G. Sampson

(Ed.), *Approaches, contexts, and problems of social psychology* (pp. 27–43). Englewood Cliffs, NJ: Prentice-Hall.

Gay, J. & Cole, M. (1967). *The new mathematics and an old culture: Learning among the Kpelle of Liberia.* New York: Holt.

Gibson, M. A. (1988). *Accommodation without assimilation: Punjabi Sikhs in an American high school and population.* Ithaca, NY: Cornell University Press.

Ginsburg, H. & Opper, S. (1979). *Piaget's theory of intellectual development: An introduction.* Englewood Cliffs, NJ: Prentice-Hall.

Hall, E. T. (1959). *The silent language.* Garden City, NY: Doubleday.

Hall, E. T. (1966). *The hidden dimension.* Garden City, NY: Doubleday.

Hansen, J. F. (1979). *Sociocultural perspectives on human learning: An introduction to educational anthropology.* Englewood Cliffs, NJ: Prentice-Hall.

Haymes, D. (1964). The ethnography of speaking. In T. Gladwin & W. S. Sturtevant (Eds.), *Anthropology and human behavior* (pp. 15–53). Washington, DC: Anthropological Society of Washington.

Holt, G. S. (1972). Stylin' outta the black pulpit. In T. Kochman (Ed.), *Rappin' and stylin' out: Communication in urban black America* (pp. 189–204). Urbana, IL: University of Illinois Press.

Hymes, D. (1964). The ethnography of speaking. In T. Gladwin & W. S. Sturtevant (Eds.), *Anthropology and human behavior* (pp 15–53). Washington, DC: Anthropological Society of Washington.

Hymes, D. (1971). On linguistic theory, communicative competence, and the education of disadvantaged children. In M. L. Wax, S. Diamond & F. O. Gearing (Eds.), *Anthropological perspectives on education.* New York: Basic Books.

Irving, R. E. M. (1980). *The Flemings and Walloons of Belgium* (Report #46). London: Minority Rights Group.

Kochman, T. (1982). *Black and white styles in conflict.* Chicago: University of Chicago Press.

Kramer, B. J. (1991). Education and American Indians: The experience of the Ute Indian tribe. In M. A. Gibson & J. U. Ogbu (Eds.), *Minority status and schooling* (pp. 287–326). New York: Garland.

Labov, W. (1972). *Language in the inner city: studies in the Black English vernacular.* Philadelphia: University of Pennsylvania Press.

LeVine, R. A. (1967). *Dreams and deeds: Achievement motivation in Nigeria.* Chicago: University of Chicago Press.

LeVine, R. A. (1973). *Culture, behavior and personality.* Chicago: Aldine.

Lijphart, A. (Ed.) (1981). *Conflict and coexistence in Belgium: The dynamics of a culturally divided society.* Berkeley: University of California Press.

Luster, L. (1992). *Schooling, survival, and struggle: Black women and the GED.* Unpublished Ph. D. dissertation, School of Education, Stanford University.

Maquet, J. (1961). *The premise of inequality.* London: Oxford University Press.

McClelland, D. C. (1961). *The achieving society.* Princeton: Van Nostrand.

Miner, H. (1956). Body ritual among the Nacirema. *American Anthropologist, 58,* 503–507.

Ogbu, J. U. (1981). Origins of human competence: A cultural-ecological perspective. *Child Development, 52,* 413–429.

Ogbu, J. U. (1988). Diversity and equity in public education: Community forces and minority school adjustment and performance. In R. Haskins & D. McRae (Eds.), *Policies for America's public schools: Teachers, equity, and indicators.* Norwood, NJ: Ablex.

Ogbu, J. U. (1994). Minority status, cultural frame of reference, and schooling. In D. Keller-Cohen (Ed.), *Literacy: Interdisciplinary conversations* (pp. 361–384). Creskill, NJ: Hampton Press.

Ogbu, J. U. (1995a). Cultural problems in minority education: Their interpretations and consequences—part two: Case studies. *Urban Review, 27.*

Ogbu, J. U. (1995b). The influences of culture on learning and behavior. In J. H. Falk & L. D. Dierking (Eds.), *Public institutions for personal learning* (pp. 79–95). Washington, DC: Museum Association for Technical Information.

Ogbu, J. U. (1997). *Beyond language: Ebonics, proper English, and identity in a black American speech community.* Department of Anthropology, University of California, Berkeley.

Spicer, E. H. (1966). The process of enslavement in middle America. *36th Congress of International de Americanistas Seville, 3,* 267–279.

Spicer, E. H. (1971). Persistent cultural systems: A comparative study of identity systems that can adapt to contrasting environments. *Science, 174,* 795–800.

Spradley, J. P. (1979). The concept of culture. In J. P. Spradley (Ed.), *Ethnographic interviews* (pp.7–9). New York: Holt.

# SECTION 11
# HEALTH CARE ISSUES

# 5   CHILDREN IN CRISIS

## THE MENTAL HEALTH STATUS OF
## IMMIGRANT AND MIGRANT HISPANIC CHILDREN

*Mary Lou de Leon Siantz*

With a constant stream of new immigrants who bring the beliefs, values, and practices of their home cultures, the United States has become a society of unparalleled diversity. Yet, American history has always been one of immigration and diversity. Eight nationalities were represented on Columbus's first voyage to America's shores. They were greeted by a variety of Native Americans who had migrated across Siberia and over the Bering Strait to Alaska (Takaki, 1993). Columbus's "later children" came from Europe in large numbers at the turn of the twentieth century. In 1940, 70% of immigrants to the United States came from Europe and 37% from Asia. During the 1970s and 1980s, 17 million immigrants entered, doubling the number that had arrived during the four preceding decades (Fix & Passel, 1994). By 1992, 15% of immigrants were from Europe, 37% from Asia, and 44% from Latin America and the Caribbean. In 1993, more than one million immigrants arrived. Among the fastest growing segment of children age 15 and under are first- and second-generation immigrant children. According to Haney (1987), the total number of immigrant school-age children 5 to 18 years ranges from 2.1 million to 2.7 million. Immigrant children are, therefore, becoming a very important part of our communities and schools. Most of the immigrant children and their families who arrive in the United States today come from Mexico, Central and South America, and Asia. Today hostility is directed mainly toward Hispanics and to a lesser extent Asians (Fix & Passel, 1994).

According to the Immigration and Naturalization Service (INS, 1996), only about three in ten newcomers are "undocumented aliens." Even so, immigration experts say they are the main source of a rising national hostility toward all immigrants legal and illegal, as effects of immigration on labor and public expenditures are publicly debated with malice and intolerance (Loh, 1994). Immigrants, whether documented or undocumented, are assumed to contribute little to the American economy, to drain its social resources, and to occupy jobs for lower wages than most Americans would accept. If immigrants are poor and economic times challenging, the mixture is especially volatile. Yet it is shortsighted to ignore the needs of immigrant children and their parents and the barriers they face in becoming contributing members of our society.

Immigrant children and families in the United States face conflicting social and cultural demands while trying to acculturate to a new country. The relationship between immigrant status and mental health is complex and is influenced by a range of factors. Loss, separation, traumatic events, and eventual adaptation to new and evolving life circumstances are experiences that most immigrants experience across the life span. The community of origin, the circumstances of the migration, and the characteristics of the resettlement are factors that affect families and children as they adapt to a new cultural, linguistic, social, and climatic environment (Laosa, 1990). In view of the stressors that immigrant children encounter, it is becoming increasingly important for researchers and practitioners to learn about their mental health needs in order to understand how to help these children and their families. The purpose of this chapter is to consider factors that affect the mental health of immigrant and migrant Hispanic children as they grow and develop. A theoretical model of resilience to help visualize these factors will be presented.

## HISPANIC IMMIGRANT POPULATION

The 1990 census counted 2.1 million foreign-born children in the United States. Adding second-generation immigrants increases the number of children to more than 5 million as of 1990 (Fix & Passel, 1994). In 1995 more than 10% of the total U.S. population (nearly 27 million) was of Hispanic origin (U.S. Bureau of the Census, 1995). This group included persons whose birth or family originated in Mexico, Central or South America, Puerto Rico, Cuba, or other parts of the Caribbean. Over 40% of the 27 million Hispanics were either foreign-born or born in Puerto Rico. The single largest group within the foreign-born population was Mexican (6.7 million). In general, the rate of growth in the Hispanic community is about seven times larger than among non-Hispanics, with 25% of Americans from Hispanic origin projected by 2050 (U.S. Bureau of the Census, 1996).

As the next century approaches, such population trends in the United States suggest that Hispanic youth are and will continue to be a significant portion of the nation's population. By the year 2000 it is projected that 2,496,000 Hispanic children will be under 5 years of age, and 6,207,000

Table 5–1. Parental Profile of the Hispanic Health and Nutrition
Examination Survey

| | Mexican American | Cuban American | Puerto Rican |
|---|---|---|---|
| Mother's age (years) | 24.4 | 26.9 | 24.1 |
| Father's age (years) | 27.2 | 30.2 | 27.4 |
| Head of household, years in school | 9.2 | 11.03 | 10.06 |
| Family income | $14,900 | $16,800 | $11,600 |
| Family size | 5.16 | 4.4 | 4.7 |

will be 5 to12 years of age. By 2040, Hispanics will constitute one-quarter (24.8%) of all preschool children in the United States (COSSMHO, 1993).

However, Hispanics are not a homogeneous group, despite the fact that they share a common language. The Hispanic community is a rich mosaic of racial and ethnic populations (U.S. Bureau of the Census, 1995). Variance exists among families according to the Hispanic Health and Nutrition Examination Survey (Haney, 1987), conducted by the National Center for Health Statistics in response to the need for detailed health information about Hispanics. Among the children and parents sampled for this survey, it was found that mothers' ages ranged from 24.1 to 26.9 years with the Puerto Rican mothers being the youngest, as Table 5–1 illustrates. Fathers of children sampled were somewhat older. Paternal age ranged from 27.2 years (Mexican American) to 30.2 years (Cuban American). The number of years in school for head of the household varied from 9.2 years to 11.03 years. Mexican American heads of household were the least educated. Family income also varied, with the Puerto Rican household reporting the least income ($11,600).

Such information helps to tailor research, intervention, and policies that respond to the particular experiences of a Hispanic subgroup in order to empower families and promote child competence. Oftentimes, the term "Hispanic" is simplistically used and broadly refers to all populations with ancestral ties to Spain, Latin America, or the Spanish-speaking Caribbean. Such uncritical ethnic labeling may obscure the diversity of social histories and cultural identities that characterize these populations. By identifying subgroups based on national origin, such as Mexican American, Puerto Rican, Cuban, or Central or South American, a more specific level of categorization is provided. Poorly defined groupings can result in research, programs, and policies that are not responsive to the culture and its actual needs (Novello, 1991).

Adaptation among immigrant children and their families needs to be considered in a continuum that ranges from adaptation to maladjustment. Disparate findings have shown both increased and decreased rates of psychiatric disorder among immigrant children compared to nonimmigrant children (Munroe-Blum et al., 1989; Board on Children and Families, 1995). Some studies have indicated that many immigrant children are able to overcome the hardships they encounter in immigrating and acculturating to their new surroundings at home and at school and are not maladjusted (Weinberg, 1979). Others have found that second-generation Hispanic children are at higher risk for mental disorders because they often feel trapped between two cultures (Martinez & Valdez, 1992). According to Aronowitz (1984), when mental health problems appear, they appear as behavioral disorders or identity disorders in adolescence. Current knowledge indicates that acute psychiatric disorders are infrequent among immigrant children (Sam, 1994). However, there have been no systematic investigations of the rate of psychiatric disorder, mental health status, and adjustment of immigrant children in the United States.

## THEORETICAL FRAMEWORK
### Risk and Resilience

Why do some immigrant children successfully adapt to their new environment, in spite of unusually challenging circumstances, and excel beyond the academic and social norms of U.S. natives, while others do not adapt? Among Hispanics the prevalence of educational and mental health problems rise as a function of their length of time in the United States. (Baral, 1979; Borjas & Tienda, 1985; Canino, Earley & Rogler, 1980; Valdez, 1986). Evidence suggests that Hispanics widely vary in their coping strategies, adjustment, development, and adaptation (Laosa, 1990; London, 1990). Their vulnerability to the events and processes associated with their immigration and settlement experiences also varies.

Figure 5–1 presents an analytic model of the joint influences hypothesized to predict child outcomes. It is not an inclusive model, but rather provides a framework for the consideration of the joint influences that have an impact on child outcomes. Represented within this figure are the key concepts of resilience theory: risk and protective factors, and child outcomes. The model builds on a stress and resilience framework (Garmezy, 1985; Laosa, 1990), and has been extended to include concepts relevant to successful outcomes among immigrant and migrant children. The model attempts to identify characteristics and processes that predict a range of child outcomes that can potentially occur among immigrant children. In this

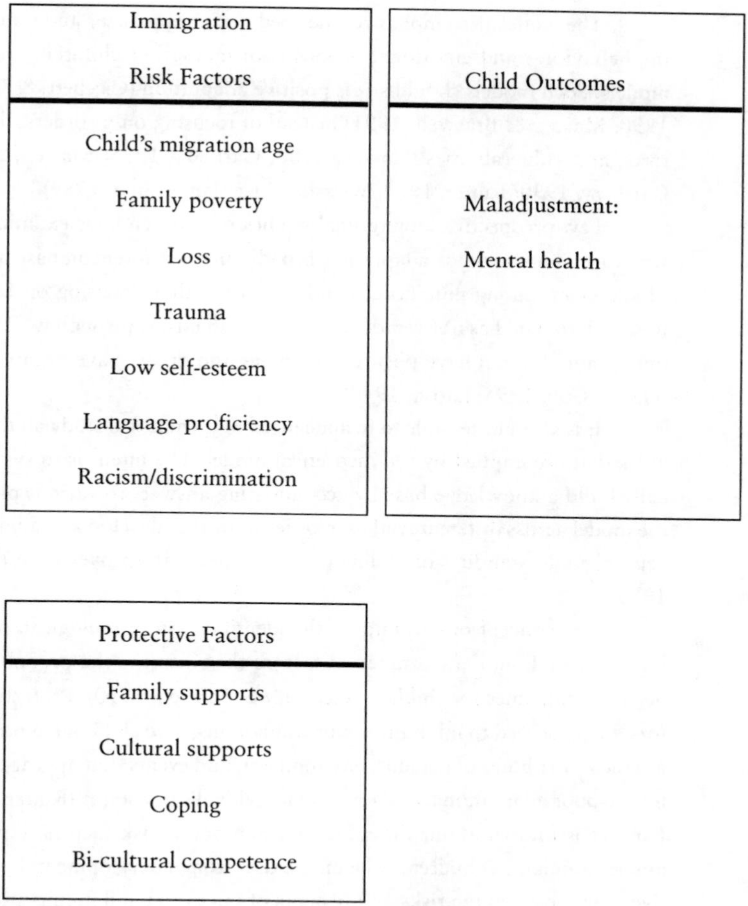

| Immigration Risk Factors | Child Outcomes |
|---|---|
| Child's migration age | |
| Family poverty | Maladjustment: |
| Loss | Mental health |
| Trauma | |
| Low self-esteem | |
| Language proficiency | |
| Racism/discrimination | |

| Protective Factors |
|---|
| Family supports |
| Cultural supports |
| Coping |
| Bi-cultural competence |

*Figure 5–1: Adaptation Model of Risk and Resilience.*

model, differences in environmental family stress (risk factors) are mediated by parent and child characteristics (protective factors) that shape a child outcome (adaptation level). This process is a dynamic one with opportunities for life changes to be handled in such a way that risks may or may not have a negative impact on the child's outcome. The model emphasizes the joint importance of environmental, parent, and child characteristics on child outcomes. Outcomes include not only mental health but also academic performance and social adjustment. Another characteristic of this model is its emphasis on reciprocal influences and adaptation as ongoing processes over time.

The model also emphasizes the need to conceptualize, study, and treat the behavioral and emotional problems of immigrant children with new models. Such models should stress positive adaptation (Cicchetti & Cohen, 1990; Masten & Braswell, 1991) instead of focusing on disorders, deficits, risks, and vulnerabilities (Cowen, 1988; Garmezy, 1985; Masten, Best & Garmezy, 1990; Rutter, 1990; Weissberg, Caplan & Sivo, 1989).

Few prospective longitudinal studies of children have examined the structure and course of adaptation broadly defined to encompass a range of successes among immigrant children, rather than focusing on failures. Research to date has not yet identified the mechanisms through which some immigrant children have positive outcomes and others have negative ones (García Coll, 1995; Laosa, 1990).

It is also not feasible to include in a single empirical study all the variables that are implied by the theoretical model. The intent is to systematically build a knowledge base by accumulating answers to various pieces of the model across different studies in order to further develop and adjust conceptual understanding of resilience in this population over time (Laosa, 1990).

The concept of risk implies the identification of biological, psychological, social, and environmental factors that increase the probability of negative outcomes for children (Garmezy & Masten, 1990). Protective factors are presumed to inhibit the expression of negative child outcomes. They are those attributes of persons, environment, and events that appear to ameliorate poor adaptation based upon an individual's risk status (Rutter, 1990). Far less is known about these factors than about risk factors, especially among immigrant children. A lacunae exists from a developmental perspective that considers the risks and benefits of migration and immigration and its impact on a child's adaptive outcomes (mental health, academic achievement, and social adjustment). Risk factors that should be considered include the impact of prejudice and discrimination as immigrant children grow and develop as well as the impact of acculturation on a child's adaptive outcomes. Protective factors that need further study include: child characteristics such as age at migration, problem-solving ability, perceived social competence, and coping patterns; family characteristics; and the availability and use of external support systems both by parents and by children.

## Migration Risks: A Family Perspective

The mental health and development of today's Hispanic immigrant children and adolescents cannot be understood apart from their family's immigrant experience. They are part of a family. Family structure and dynamics, and parental mental health and behavior, have a direct impact on a child's well-being (Board on Children and Families, 1995; Siantz de Leon, 1990). Historically, the family has been the means for cultural transmission, providing a natural atmosphere for traditions to be passed from generation to generation in order to keep culture and traditions alive. Such traditions have provided families with a sense of stability and support that provides comfort, guidance, and a means of coping with daily life (McCubbin et al., 1993).

In order to understand how migration is a risk that can affect an immigrant child's mental health, it is first necessary to understand the importance of the family and the cultural values that provide the framework for children's socialization. Among Hispanics, these values include familism, respect, and gender roles. Such values need to be integrated into a multicultural society (Greenfield, 1994) to support families.

## Familism

The family is one of the most important aspects of life among Hispanic immigrants. Familism is a cultural value that involves strong individual identification with an attachment to the nuclear and extended families, as well as strong feelings of loyalty, reciprocity, and solidarity among members of the same family (Triandis et al., 1982; Siantz de Leon, 1994). In addition to emotional support, the extended family (*la familia*) is the primary source of financial assistance, exchange of work, and advice and help in solving personal problems. Immigrant children learn that their family has familial and religious rituals that bind them together to build a strong sense of community (Cervantes & Ramirez, 1992). Hispanic immigrants especially value their families and prize their children, a tradition that has helped the family survive in spite of difficult circumstances (Zuniga, 1992). Yet little is known about these families and the effects of parental characteristics on the mental health of immigrant children. For mental health researchers, this implies a need to consider the family in planning their research. For service providers, the consequences of behavior change on the family must be considered (Marin et al., 1990).

Research on the Hispanic family has focused on traditional family structure and values often resulting in a nonvalidated stereotypic image of the Hispanic family. According to this view, the Hispanic family is a patriarchal structure characterized by the absolute authority of the father and the mother's self-sacrifice (Falicov, 1982). Children are expected to be submissive and obedient with their father and other authority figures. Descriptions of the family have been normative and moralistic, with the belief that assimilation would not only change but improve family functioning (Zuniga, 1992).

The benefits of assimilation have been assumed with few studies that have examined the process of sociocultural change to the Euro-American mainstream and its benefits. The assumption that Hispanic families are static and homogeneous has caused many social scientists to consider the Mexican American and other Hispanic families resistant to change. Factors such as immigration, length of U.S. residence, generation, and women's labor force participation have been given little attention (Zambrana & Silva-Palacios, 1989).

Mexican immigrants are a highly self-selected group with many psychological and cultural characteristics that contribute toward success in the United States. These traits include: (1) completion of more years in school than the national average of that country, (2) skilled or semiskilled occupational preparation, (3) deferred gratification, and (4) risk taking. This background enables them to save money that is needed to cross the border (Buriel, 1994). Research in Mexico has found that immigrants are among the most psychologically well-adjusted members of the Mexican population (Buriel, 1994). Mexican immigrants represent that portion of the Mexican population that wants to achieve middle-class standing through hard work and perseverance.

## Respect

*Respeto* is a cultural value that dictates deferential behavior toward others, particularly strangers (Marin & Van Oss Marin, 1991; Siantz de Leon, 1994). Behaviors that promote smooth and pleasant relationships with empathy toward the feelings of other people are emphasized. Interpersonal conflict is avoided, with positive behaviors emphasized and negative behaviors in conflicting situations deemphasized. The implication for mental health research and intervention is that families and children must be respected. Furthermore, there must be an opportunity for face-saving in the disclosure of personal information.

## Gender Roles

Gender roles must also be considered (Siantz de Leon, 1990, 1994). Men have traditionally had power and authority outside the family, while women have been responsible for the daily affairs of the family. However, these sex-role traditions have changed as families have acculturated with both parents working (Levine, 1980; Marin & Van Oss Marin, 1991). Both have power and authority within their separate family roles. One implication for mental health intervention and research is that the importance of the male head of the household must be recognized, including the power he may have to facilitate or prevent an intervention, or change of behavior that may affect the family (Siantz de Leon, 1994).

## Parent-Child Conflict

Immigrant parents may resist the acculturation and assimilation of their children, since the marked differences between the host country's values and those from the home country can precipitate parent-child conflict (Canino & Spurlock, 1994). When children acculturate at a faster rate than their parents, intergenerational conflicts often occur. Assertiveness, competitiveness, and independence, while highly valued in the United States, contradict the core values of many Hispanic immigrant parents. Acculturated children may become too assertive for their parents and may lose respect for their elders. Conflict can also occur between parents and their adolescent children when they have been forced to immigrate with the family and leave their friends behind (Esquivel & Keitel, 1990). Immigrant parents therefore frequently experience depression and isolation, and may turn to their oldest children for comfort and assistance, as is common among Hispanic immigrant families. Sons may be expected to work. Daughters are expected to care for younger siblings, cook, and care for the home, especially if both parents must work to support the family. While some may feel that such behaviors take away from more age-appropriate experiences, many Hispanic parents believe that such responsibilities serve to enhance their children's adulthood.

## Poverty

Children of immigrant parents come from various socioeconomic backgrounds. While Hispanic immigrants are poor in general, Mexican immigrants are the poorest, with 36% living in poverty, in contrast to only 14% of native-born U.S. residents. The majority of Mexican immigrants come to the United States to improve their economic status, so they may be more open to some forms of sociocultural change in order to fulfill their economic aspiration. Such change may be expressed by adding new cultural competencies to existing ethnic competencies (biculturalism) instead of replacing them with new ones (assimilation) (Buriel, 1994).

In spite of high economic goals, at least one out of every three Hispanic children live in poverty (U.S. Bureau of Census, 1995). While Hispanic children constitute 11.6% of all children, they make up 21.5% of all children living in poverty. During the past decade Hispanic children accounted for half of the total growth of poor children in the United States, with children under age three the largest proportion (Zambrana, Dorrington & Hayes-Bautista, 1996).

The number of female-headed households is increasing. About 56% of these families, as well as 26.5% of families with both parents, live below the federal poverty line (COSSMHO, 1993). Increasing poverty among Hispanics continues in spite of increasing labor force participation, time at work, and educational levels. Underemployment, which includes working below one's ability or in part-time employment without health benefits, is prevalent among Hispanic families. There are twice as many underemployed Mexican males compared to white males and 1.6 as many underemployed Mexican females compared to white females (COSSMHO, 1993).

The effects of poverty on families and children are well documented, indicated by poor housing, inadequate schooling, and poor health. Among Puerto Rican children living in poor urban areas, researchers have documented the existence of low self-esteem, depression, aggression, and academic problems (Canino, Earley & Rogler, 1980). Mexican American migrant farmworker parents are at high risk for depression (Siantz de Leon, 1990). Poverty produces hopelessness for the future, so there is a need to understand and to be empathic about realistic social constraints that a child faces, especially when parents have few resources for child rearing and nurturing socialization (Brookins, 1993). Poor immigrant children are thus unprepared for the demands of school, including kindergarten and first grade (Hamburg, 1992), and teachers are less motivated to support and encourage such students to do their best (Kozol, 1991).

## Migration Risks: The Child's Perspective

### Age

A child's reaction to the loss of home, family, friends, and their possessions is influenced by his or her age. A very young child regards a friend as a playmate rather than a source of emotional support (Maccoby, 1983). He or she is more likely to comply with their parents' decision to migrate and less likely to resent leaving with their parents than an adolescent child.

A recent study of the adaptation of migrant Mexican American preschool children has highlighted the importance of parental social support for very young children. Preliminary results show that these preschool children consider their parents to be their greatest source of overall support and their siblings to be their second source of support. Boys identified their mothers as their primary source of emotional, instrumental, and informational support and companionship. Girls identified their mothers as their greatest source of emotional, instrumental, and informational support. At this age, little parental conflict was identified by both girls and boys (Siantz de Leon, 1994). The majority of mothers (69%) and fathers (72.4%) were born in Mexico and had been living in the United States for 19.07 years (mothers) and 19.55 years (fathers). The language of preference was mostly Spanish.

## Loss

One source of stress for immigrant children is the severance of extended family ties, loss of a substitute parent, friends, and supports during a time that they are adjusting to a new culture. These problems are even more stressful for children who have experienced political unrest in their native countries (Laosa, 1990; Pynoos & Eth, 1985). Inadequate family or community support is particularly challenging when immigrant children do not have access to the supports that they need to help them cope with their new surroundings (Athey & Ahearn, 1991; Maccoby, 1983; Munroe-Blum et al., 1989).

Loss of familiar routines along with loss of their home can also be extremely trying for an immigrant child, especially if the child does not feel protected by his or her parents (Coelho & Ahmed, 1980). Many very young immigrant children are left with one parent or a substitute caretaker while one or both parents migrate for economic reasons, promising to reunite the family as soon as circumstances permit. Having spent their early years with a substitute caretaker, these children undergo a second loss when reunited with their parent or parents and leaving behind the only caretaker they have known.

Children under ten years of age have not developed the capacity to recognize, understand, and resolve a loss. Consequently, they are not likely to make correct assumptions about the loss they have experienced. Their dependent role and inability to remove themselves from difficult situations makes them more vulnerable to developing mental health problems. Very young children, in particular, do not easily limit their feelings of helplessness or resolve their grief, especially if their family has been involved (Osterweis, Solomon & Green, 1984). Childhood bereavement has both short- and long-term consequences that may include neurosis, depression, academic and social impairment, delinquency, as well as adult mental illness (Coelho & Ahmed, 1980; Robertson & Robertson, 1989; Van Eerdewegh et al., 1982).

## Trauma

Immigrant refugee children sometimes experience events that are perceived as life threatening, terrifying, and outside the range of normal life experience. Some may witness the infliction of injury, mutilation, or the murder of a family member. These events constitute a psychic trauma for the child that can result in posttraumatic stress disorder (PTSD) (de Monchy, 1991). The manner in which a child experiences and internalizes a trauma is related to their age and developmental stage. Preschoolers are dependent on their parents, and may exhibit anxious attachment behavior (Bowlby, 1980). School-age children may radically change and become irritable, rude, and argumentative or complain of somatic problems (Pynoos & Eth, 1985). Adolescents, like adults, might engage in antisocial acts or lose impulse control. They may fear being ostracized because of the event and become pessimistic about the future (Pynoos & Eth, 1985).

The symptoms and severity of PTSD are also associated with the degree of violence, presence or absence of personal injury, and access to family support (Espino, 1991). Children who remain with their biological family are less psychologically disturbed because of the strong family bonds that develop from the crisis the entire family has shared (Ressler, Boothby & Steinbock, 1988). Researchers have found that the plight of many of these refugee children does not often significantly improve in their new host country because they continue to live in poverty with high conflict in their homes. They also experience educational delays, lower self-esteem, and depression. All converge on their ability to adapt and assimilate into their host country. Research in the mental health of refugee children who have been traumatized and who experience PTSD remains understudied, particularly among Hispanic refugee children.

Immigrant refugee children from Guatemala and El Salvador are at higher risk for experiencing traumatic events because of the political instability that these countries have more recently experienced. While refugee children from Central America are more likely to suffer from PTSD because of the traumatic events they have experienced, they are also more likely to be overlooked. This is due to the fact that these children cannot speak for themselves and the problems manifested by adult refugees are more quickly attended (Eisenbruch, 1988).

*Low Self-esteem*

In a society that does not value cultural differences among its citizens, the immigration experience can also negatively affect the self-esteem of children. For example, researchers have found that parent-child conflict among immigrant children not only increases, but is also associated with lower self-esteem and higher depression. This is particularly true for girls (Rumbaut, 1994). Lower self-esteem is associated with second-generation status (being U.S.-born). Recency of arrival to the United States as well as the family's economic situation are also associated with lower self-esteem. The unemployment of the father as well as his absence from the home are related to depression and decreased self-esteem. Depression and self-esteem may worsen if there is no one available to help with homework and if children are ashamed of their parents.

*Language Proficiency*

Self-esteem also decreases if a child is assigned to classes for limited-English-proficient (LEP) students. There are about six million Hispanic students, among fifty million students registered in K–12 in the United States (U.S. Department of Education, 1994). Close to two million of these students speak Spanish as their primary language and are not fluent in English (Fleischman & Hopsock, 1993; National Clearing House for Bilingual Education, 1995). The number of students with limited English-speaking ability has dramatically grown during the past 20 years and continues to grow. Limited English proficient is a frequent designation for most non-English-speaking immigrant children upon beginning their studies at school. Higher English proficiency and good grades are associated with a higher self-esteem among Hispanic immigrant students (Buriel, 1994).

The general view of students from Spanish-speaking backgrounds is not good. These children tend to do poorly in U.S. schools, having lower levels of achievement and higher dropout rates than their white counterparts (Valencia, 1991). Poverty and lower levels of parental education place these children at risk for educational underachievement regardless of language of instruction.

Behavior directly or indirectly related to a lack of linguistic proficiency constitute the most frequent reason for psychiatric referral of students whose primary language is not English (Canino & Spurlock, 1994; Oritiz & Maldonado-Colon, 1986). Many of the problems that teachers identify are characteristic of students who are in the process of acquiring a second language. When immigrant students are beginning to develop the linguistic abilities they need to handle the complex language their teacher uses and the instructional materials they are given, their achievement is challenged. Such children are frequently referred to special education. They become further alienated when they feel that their linguistic style is inferior to Standard English. Hakuta and Garcia (1989) have found that when a second language is added and where bilingualism is not a stigma, bilingualism is associated with higher levels of cognitive achievement. Even critics of bilingual education contend that LEP children should not be considered a burden; they should be viewed as an opportunity to develop bilingual adults (Rossell & Baker, 1996).

## Racism and Discrimination

Ethnic prejudice and racism have been viewed as antipathy that is based on a faulty and inflexible generalization that is directed toward a group or an individual because of their membership in that group (Allport, 1954). The group or person who becomes the object of prejudice is often in a position of disadvantage. Racism thwarts the character and spirit of the disparaged group (Brookins, 1993). The potential for experiencing the stress of prejudice and racism exists for most immigrant/minority children, especially as they move into society at large when relocating into a predominantly nonminority community (Spurlock, 1986; Canino & Spurlock, 1994). These experiences of prejudice and foreclosed options often contribute to a variety of problems and antisocial behavior, such as loss of academic potential, early engagement in sexual intercourse, childbearing, gang involvement, delinquency, and drug use (Brookins, 1993; Laosa, 1990). Immigrant children are likely to be subjected to social policies that are at times unwittingly designed to undermine their optimal growth and development (Kozol, 1991). Hispanics have experienced a long history of racism and discrimination, particularly in the Southwest (Carter, 1970; McWilliams, 1968). While the historical circumstances of Hispanics and African Americans is different, both share the common history of exclusion and isolation from the U.S. social, economic, and educational mainstream. Such experiences are relevant to their position in U.S. society at present (Goldenberg, 1996; Laosa, 1984).

Like Native Americans, Hispanic Americans "were here first," a fact that has led some to refer to these two groups as "territorial minorities" (de la Garza, Kruszewski & Arciniega, 1973). The Southwest has been filled with ethnic claims and counterclaims that include the American Indian, the Spanish European, the Mexican American, and the Anglo American present. From the standpoint of the American non-Latino population, it has been difficult to separate current attitudes toward recent Latino immigration from racist attitudes of the past toward Hispanics who were native to the United States or even whose families lived here before the American Southwest became part of the United States.

Even within the Hispanic population, responses toward new immigrants have developed new tensions. While antagonism toward immigrants has been strongest among non-Latinos, many immigrant rights groups have found that anti-immigration sentiment is not simply masked racial discrimination. Resentment over the influx of new Latino immigrants has also been strong among many second-, third-, and fourth-generation families in Latino enclaves such as East Los Angeles (Nazario, 1996). For example, almost one-third of California's Latinos supported Proposition 187, the statewide initiative that proposed to terminate all services to illegal immigrants (Navario, 1996).

The impact of discrimination on Hispanic immigrant children has been hard to measure. In one study, ethnically diverse adolescents were shown negative or threatening information about their ethnic group. It was reported that the videotaped information had an effect on the subject's overall rating of their group, but did not affect their ethnic identification (Phinney, Chavira & Tate, 1993). Subjects were able to discriminate between themselves and the ethnic group, acknowledging that the negative traits in their group did not need to reflect on its members. How immigrant children and adolescents experience discrimination, learn to cope with it, and adapt to their host culture needs further investigation (García-Coll, 1995).

## PROTECTIVE FACTORS
### Family Supports

No children, including immigrant children, can be assessed apart from the families in which they are embedded. Family structure and dynamics, and parental mental health and behavior have a direct impact on a child's well-being (Board on Children and Families, 1995; Siantz, 1990). Parenting that is sensitive to a child's personality, abilities, and the developmental tasks they face encourages a variety of positive outcomes that include social competence, intellectual achievement, and emotional security (Baldwin, Cole & Baldwin, 1990; Belsky, 1984; Rutter, 1990). A family's ability to provide support to their children protects them from stress and has an important role in their child's positive development and adaptation.

The availability of social supports to both parents and children positively influences their mental health. During the first ten years following immigration, it is not uncommon for immigrants and their children to live in an extended household that includes relatives and other nonfamily members (Golding & Burnam, 1990). In time, living arrangements change because of economic, social, and cultural reasons. However, as immigrants move out of extended households, they prefer to remain in the surrounding area in order to maintain some of the social support of family and friends (Golding & Burnam, 1990). The longer immigrants live in the United States, the more their family networks grow through marriage, births, and the continued immigration of other family members. As individual family members become acculturated, their extended family grows with second- and third-generation Mexican Americans having larger and more integrated extended families than immigrants (Buriel, 1994).

Family members maintain their involvement through visits and exchanges of services. The extended family assumes an idealized role among Mexican Americans. Close relationships are not limited to the nuclear family. Such relationships may include aunts, uncles, grandparents, cousins, in-laws, and even godparents, or "compadres." Those who can be relied on for support is in fact a large group. The perception of support from family is high even among immigrants with fewer family members, and it remains high as more family members are added across generations (Sabogal et al., 1987). The family can thus be viewed as an adapting entity with its own developmental processes, and this adapting entity transcends the development of individual members. Researchers have found that internal family attitudes such as cohesion, expressiveness, conflict, organization, and control do not change from one generation to the next. External family variables such as independence, achievement, intellectual orientation, and recreational orientation are modified across generations in response to extrafamilial pressures (Rueschenberg & Buriel, 1989).

Some individuals have criticized familism as a deterrent to mobility because it reinforces attachment to people, places, and things. For Mexican Americans of lower socioeconomic status, the family is often the primary source of support, a force that helps and sustains family members in achieving goals that might be difficult for an individual (Siantz de Leon, 1994). For example, among migrant farmworkers, aunts or grandmothers might help with child care while the rest of the family members pool their resources to work in the field and maximize their financial potential during the harvest season. This pool of financial resources can include school-age children who can contribute to the family income from their labor in the fields.

Among migrant farmworker mothers, access to support from spouse, partner, family, and friends is vital to their mental health and parenting (Siantz, 1990). Having access to a selection of supportive persons to whom one may turn in time of need may be better than having only one person available. With greater choice, more resources for solving problems may be available (Vega & Kolody, 1985). A mother's access to a variety of supportive persons while enduring the stress of being a migrant farmworker parent may be an important factor influencing her mental health and response to her children (Siantz, 1990b).

Satisfaction with emotional support is associated with positive mother-child communication (Weintraub & Wolf, 1983). This in turn may increase the mother's ability to give effective directions to the child, helping the child to conform to rules (Weintraub & Wolf, 1983). A child who has the opportunity to learn and master verbal and nonverbal strategies may be more likely to develop and maintain positive peer interaction (McLoyd, 1990). Without access to supportive relationships, including child care, the mother may feel abandoned with no one to turn to in time of need, which increases her risk for depression (Siantz, 1990a).

Migrant farmworker fathers have also reported a need for social support, though they often seek it outside the home. It may be that these fathers also perceive an inconsistency between the family's expectations of their involvement and the ridicule and stigma from friends and members of their peer group for being active in family work (Siantz, 1994). Effort expended in home life may be considered energy taken from their primary role as the breadwinner and an indicator of failure as the provider and head of the family (Zuniga, 1992).

## Cultural Supports

Helping Hispanic children to understand their cultural roots facilitates pride not only in themselves, but also in their ancestral group. It is a major step toward helping children develop positive bicultural identities and increase their self-esteem and developmental potential in a new host society. Understanding how ethnic identity develops is therefore important in supporting a bicultural ethnic identity.

## Ethnic Identity

A child's perceptions and concepts about racial differences follow a developmental sequence similar to that of other perceptions and concepts about other factors (Bernal et al., 1990). Developmental sequencing of ethnic identity may be expected to parallel gender identity components (Aboud, 1987; Katz, 1983). The use of ethnic behaviors, like gender behaviors, may be initially determined by the child's family instead of the child and may begin early in life. While most children can classify and label their own gender by age 2.5 to 3 years, ethnic identification probably occurs later because the physical and social markers for ethnicity are less clear than those for gender. Children lack understanding of ethnic labels or the ability to classify by ethnic group prior to that time (Aboud, 1987). Understanding that one's own ethnicity is constant may be expected to develop around eight to ten years of age (Aboud & Skerry, 1983; Semaj, 1980).

Others have found that ethnic self-identification, knowledge, preferences, and use of ethnic role behaviors are associated with a child's Spanish-language utilization at home. For example, Mexican American children who speak Spanish are more likely to know about their Mexican identity and background, and to display and prefer ethnic behavior (Knight et al., 1990).

## Bicultural Competence

While immigrant children in the past have been considered polarized—in two worlds—a more recent concept of biculturalism emphasizes the point that persons can effectively function in two or more cultures without negative effects. What this means is that children can live in two cultures by becoming competent in the cultural beliefs and values of both cultures, developing culturally acceptable behaviors, effective relationships, communications skills, and a sense of acceptance in both cultures (LaFromboise, Coleman & Gerton, 1993). Individuals are biculturally competent when they can navigate between two cultures that each have distinct characteristics, tasks, beliefs, and norms. It requires that a person embrace one culture while acknowledging the other's norms and developmental tasks as standards for effective functioning within the broader context of society (Brookins, 1993).

## Coping

Coping has been defined as the behavior that protects an individual from internal and external stresses (Rutter, 1983). Research suggests that the manner in which a person cognitively appraises his or her life events strongly influences how he or she responds to them. Wide variation should also be expected among Hispanic immigrants' cognitive appraisal of the events surrounding their losses, dislocation, and life in a new environment. Where some will see opportunities and challenges, others will see unwanted circumstances to be resisted or passively endured (Laosa, 1990). Little is known about how immigrant families' coping responses ultimately affect their psychological and social well-being, parenting style, and their child's development.

## ADAPTATION

### Mental Health

Immigrant children and their families face conflicting social and cultural demands while trying to adapt to a new host country whose hospitality can range from inviting to hostile, unfamiliar, and even discriminatory. Both children and parents must deal with loss, separation, and family disruption in addition to the migration itself. The relationship between immigrant status and mental health is complex. The psychiatric well-being of a particular immigrant group is determined by the interaction of a host of risk and protective factors. These include the circumstances of the migration, the age of the child, and the characteristics of the resettlement (García-Coll, 1995; Laosa, 1990). In spite of growing interest in the mental health of immigrant groups, there has been little systematic research concerning the mental health, psychiatric, or social adjustment of immigrant children. Difficulties in conducting and interpreting studies of the psychiatric adjustment of immigrant children have resulted from discrepancies in the definition of immigrant status, sampling limitations, variable diagnostic approaches, and the lack of epidemiologic studies (Blum et al., 1989).

While there have been important clinical advances in the consideration of cultural and ethnic minority issues for a wide range of psychotherapies, treatment research has not kept up with these developments (Canino & Spurlock, 1994). Treatment outcome research is almost nonexistent with immigrant children and adolescents (Constantino, Malgady & Rogler, 1994). One study with Puerto Rican youth demonstrated that culturally sensitive interventions that integrate cultural context and content reduced symptoms of anxiety and increased self-esteem, social judgment, and ethnic identity (Malgady, Rogler & Constantino, 1986). In this study "cuento" therapy mimicked traditional Puerto Rican storytelling and used traditions, values, and normative behavior, as well as ethnic identity development as a therapeutic tool. It significantly reduced children's trait anxiety relative to traditional therapy or no intervention. A need exists to develop, adapt, and test mental health treatment approaches that show empirical promise with immigrant populations, especially children and adolescents (Baruth & Manning, 1992; García-Coll, 1995).

*Mental Health Research Implications*

Immigrant children need to be studied in their own right, without regard for the view that a control group is needed for adequate interpretation. More research is needed to determine to what extent the health and social needs of immigrant children differ on the basis of culture of origin and the conditions of the resettlement process.

As this population continues to grow, it has become clearer that most mental health professionals who serve them do not have adequate information, applicable training, or appropriate resources to address their clients' problems and needs. This gap is acute in large urban areas as well as rural areas. Especially needed are studies that focus on the prevention of mental health problems. Both risk and protective factors need to be considered, especially those factors that mediate or moderate stress, that predict a child's psychological adjustment to a new country, and that strengthen the child's mental health throughout his or her development. The focus should be not only on the negative experiences and pathological effects but also on identifying factors that contribute to positive outcomes (García-Coll, 1995; Rutter, 1990). Research on factors that influence Hispanic immigrant children's adaptation is in its infancy (Laosa, 1990).

*Research Partnerships*

Building research partnerships is important to successful research in the Hispanic community. The process should begin during the planning stage of the study and continue through completion. Communication with leaders who are trusted by the community is crucial to gaining entry for data collection. Identifying the benefits of participating in the research to the community at large as well as to individual participants is equally important. Early discussions can prevent problems that may arise from improper instrumentation or inclusion of sensitive topics that could bias results, cause high rates of refusal, cause dropouts from the study, or produce difficulty in accessing specific respondents (Marin & VanOss-Marin, 1991). That research may not be a priority for most of these families also needs to be recognized. Communication can occur through large meetings where key individuals learn about the project and volunteer their ideas for the project's successful implementation. Communication can also occur through community or project newletters and flyers in Spanish and/or English, or by word of mouth. Researchers can also share their expertise with the community by providing training and technical assistance as needed by local community projects. Sharing such expertise not only benefits the participants but also serves to enhance the researcher's credibility and build trust (Siantz, 1994).

*Policy Implications*

It is shortsighted to ignore the needs of Hispanic immigrant children, their parents, and the barriers they face in becoming constructive members of American society. Policies and interventions that will ensure their well-being, mental health, and developmental potential must build on their identified strengths. It is time for a new vision of a multicultural society, one that builds partnerships among mental health professionals, researchers, policymakers, and immigrant communities; one that helps to develop new and innovative research models, strategies, and intervention; one that helps to build programs that will not only benefit the mental health of immigrant children and families, but also expand the diverse human resource potential of the United States. Policies should empower an immigrant child's ability to construct a knowledgeable, confident self-identity and to become a competent American citizen. Culturally competent, accessible, comprehensive preschool programs, like Migrant Head Start, that now serve children of many Mexican immigrant farmworkers, need to be supported and replicated. Such programs have long understood the plight of the immigrant child and family as well as their cultural strengths. Migrant Head Start has empowered these children and their families to become successful additions to their host country and has thus begun to strengthen the diversity of American society.

## Conclusion

Americans have been ambivalent about immigration since the nation's beginning. Benjamin Franklin, before he signed the Declaration of Independence, complained about immigrants. Germans, he groused, were being allowed to "swarm into our settlements and by herding together, establish their language and manners to the exclusion of ours" (Loh, 1994).

We are at a crossroads. We can either say to these newcomers, "We accept you provisionally to the extent that you can re-create yourselves into a standard American mold," or, "we welcome you as full members of our nation and accept that we as a people have a new richness and diversity." This will require new forms of public institutions to celebrate and support that diversity while at the same time unite us as a nation. On the other hand, we can leave it to chance whether or not immigrant children feel good about themselves, adapt, and develop the skills and language needed to enhance the social and economic future of the United States.

## References

Aboud, F. E. (1987). Self and ethnic concepts in relation to ethnic constancy. *Canadian Journal of Behavioral Sciences, 15,* 14–26.

Aronowitz, M. (1984). The social and emotional adjustment of immigrant children: A review of the literature. *International Review of Migration, 18* (2), 237–257.

Athey, J. & Ahearn, F. (1991). The mental health of refugee children: An overview. In F. Ahearn & J. Athey (Eds.), *Refugee children: Theory, research, and services* (pp. 3–19). Baltimore, MD: Johns Hopkins University Press.

Baldwin, A. L., Cole, R. E. & Baldwin, C. P. (1990). Parental pathology, family interaction, and the competence of the child in school. *Monographs of the Society for Research in Child Development, 47* (197).

Baral, D. P. (1979). Academic achievement of recent immigrants from Mexico. *Journal of the National Association of Bilingual Education, 3* (13), 1–13.

Baruth, L. G. & Manning, M. L. (1992). Understanding and counseling Hispanic American children. *Elementary School Guidance & Counseling, 27,* 113–122.

Belsky, D. (1984). The determinants of parenting: A process model. *Child Development, 55,* 83–96.

Board on Children and Families, Commission on Behavioral and Social Sciences and Education, National Research Council, Institute of Medicine (1995). Immigrant children and their families: Issues for research and policy. *The Future of Children, 5* (2), 72–89.

Borjas, G. & Tienda, M. (Eds.) (1985). *Hispanics in the U.S. economy.* New York: Academic Press.

Brookins, G. K. (1993). Culture, ethnicity, and bicultural competence: Implications for children with chronic illness and disability. *Pediatrics, 91* (5), 1056–1062.

Bowlby, J. (1980). *Attachment and loss,* vol. 3, *Loss.* New York: Basic Books.

Buriel, R. (1994). Acculturation, respect for cultural differences, and biculturalism among three generations of Mexican-American and European-American school children. *Journal of Genetic Psychology, 154,* 531–543.

Canino, I. A., Earley, B. F. & Rogler, L. H. (1980). *The Puerto Rican child in New York City: Stress and mental health.* New York: Hispanic Research Center, Fordham University.

Canino, I. A. & Spurlock, J. (1994). *Culturally diverse children and adolescents: Assessment, diagnosis, and treatment.* New York: Guilford.

Cicchetti, D. & Cohen, D. (1990). Perspectives on developmental psychopathology. In D. Cicchetti & D. J. Cohen (Eds.), *Developmental psychopathology* (pp. 3–20). New York: Wiley.

Cicchetti, D. & Garmezy, N. (1993). Prospects and promises in the study of resilience. *Development and Psychopathology, 5,* 497–502.

Coelho, G. V. & Ahmed, P. I. (Eds.) (1980). *Uprooting and development: Dilemmas of coping with modernization.* New York: Plenum.

Constantino, G., Malgady, R. G. & Rogler, L. H. (1986). Cuento therapy: A culturally sensitive modality for Puerto Rican children. *Journal of Consulting and Clinical Psychology, 54,* 639–645.

Constantino, G., Malgady, R. G. & Rogler, L. H. (1994). Storytelling through pictures: Culturally sensitive psychotherapy for Hispanic children and adolescents. *Journal of Clinical Child Psychology, 23* (1), 13–20.

COSSMHO: The National Coalition of Hispanic Health and Human Service Organizations (1993). *Growing up Hispanic.* Washington, DC: Author.

De la Garza, R., Kruszewski, Z. A. & Arciniega, T. A. (Eds.) (1973). *Chicanos and Native Americans: The territorial minorities.* Englewood Cliffs, NJ: Prentice-Hall.

de Monchy, M. L. (1991). Recovery and rebuilding: The challenge for refugee children and service providers. In F. Ahearn & J. Athey (Eds.), *Refugee children: Theory, research, and services* (pp. 163–180). Baltimore, MD: Johns Hopkins University Press.

Eisenbruck, M. (1988). The mental health of refugee children and their cultural development. *International Migration Review, 22* (2), 282–300.

Espino, C. (1991). Trauma and adaptation: The case of Central American children. In F. Ahearn & J. Athey (Eds.), *Refugee children: Theory, research, and services* (pp. 106–124). Baltimore, MD: Johns Hopkins University Press.

Esquivel, G. & Keitel, M. (1990). Counseling immigrant children in the schools. *Elementary School Guidance & Counseling, 24,* 213–221.

Eth, S. & Pynoos, R. S. (1985). Interaction of trauma and grief in childhood. In S. Eth & R. S. Pynoos (Eds.), *Post traumatic stress disorder in children* (pp. 168–186]. Washington, DC: American Psychiatric Press.

Falicov, D. (1982). Mexican families. In M. McGoldrick & J. K. Giordano (Eds.), *Ethnicity and family therapy.* New York: Guilford.

Fix, M. & Passel, J. S. (1994). *Immigration and immigrants: Setting the record straight.* Washington, DC: Urban Institute.

García-Coll, C. (1995). *The effect of migration on child development.* National Symposium on "International migration and family change: The experience of U.S. immigrants." Pennsylvania State University, November 2–3, 1995.

Garmezy, N. (1985). Stress resistant children: The search for protective factors. In J. E. Stevenson (Ed.), *Recent research in developmental psychopathology* (pp. 213–233). Oxford: Pergamon Press. [Book supplemental to the *Journal of Child Psychology and Psychiatry.* No. 4.]

Garmezy, N. & Masten, A. (1990). Assessing, preventing, and reaching childhood. In L. Eugene Arnold (Ed.), *Childhood stress* (pp. 459–474). New York: Wiley.

Goldenberg, C. (1996). Latin American immigration and U.S. schools. *Social Policy Report, Society for Research in Child Development, 10* (1), 1–31.

Golding, J. M. & Burnam, A. (1990). Immigration, stress, and depressive symptoms in a Mexican American community. *The Journal of Nervous and Mental Disease, 178* (3), 161–171.

Greenfield, P. M. (1994). Independence and interdependence as developmental scripts: Implications for theory, research, and practice. In P. M. Greenfield & R. Cocking (Eds.), *Cross-cultural roots of minority child development* (pp. 1–40). Hillsdale, NJ: Erlbaum.

Hakuta, K. & Garcia, E. (1989). Bilingualism and education. *American Psychologist, 44* (2), 373–379.

Hamburg, D. A. (1992). *Today's children: Creating a future for a generation in crisis.* New York: Times Books.

Haney, W. (1987). An estimation of immigrant and immigrant student populations in the United States as of October 1986. Background paper for immigrant student project. Boston College. *Hispanic Health and Nutrition Examination Survey* (HHANES) (1988).

Immigration and Naturalization Service (1996). Numbers, criminals, sanctions. *Migration News, 3* (6).

Kozol, J. (1991). *Savage inequalities: Children in America's schools.* New York: Crown.

LaFromboise, T., Coleman, H. L. K. & Gerton, J. (1993). Psychological impact of biculturalism: Evidence and theory. *Psychological Bulletin, 114* (3), 395–412.

Laosa, L. (1984). Social policies toward children of diverse ethnic, racial, and language groups in the United States. In H. W. Stevenson & A. E. Siegel (Eds.), *Child development research and social policy* (pp. 1–109). Chicago: University of Chicago Press.

Laosa, L. (1990). Psychosocial stress, coping, and development of Hispanic immigrant children. In F. C. Serafica, A. I. Schwebel, R. K. Fussell, P. D. Isaac & L. B. Myers (Eds.), *Mental health of ethnic minorities* (pp. 39–65). New York: Praeger.

Loh, J. (1994, July 3). Ambivalence about immigrants. *Louisville, Kentucky Courier-Journal.*

London, C. (1990). Educating young new immigrants: How can the United States cope? *International Journal of Adolescence and Youth, 2,* 81–100.

Maccoby, E. E. (1983). Socio-emotional development and response to stressors. In N. Garmezy & M. Rutter (Eds.), *Stress, coping, and development in children* (pp. 217–234). New York: McGraw-Hill.

Marin, G., Marin, B. V., Perez-Stable, E. J., Sabogal, F. & Otero-Sabogal, R. (1990). The role of acculturation on the attitudes, norms, and expectancies of Hispanic smokers. *Journal of Cross-Cultural Psychology, 20,* 399–415.

Martinez, K. J. & Valdez, D. (1992). Cultural considerations in play therapy with Hispanic children. In L. Vargas & J. D. Koss-Chioino (Eds.), *Working with culture, psychotherapeutic interventions with ethnic minority children and adolescents* (pp. 85–102). San Francisco: Jossey-Bass.

Masten, A.S. & Braswell, L. (1991). Developmental psychopathology: An integrative framework for understanding behavior problems in children and adolescents. In P. R. Martin (Ed.), *Handbook of behavior therapy and psychological science: An integrative approach.* New York: Pergamon.

McCubbin, H., Thompson, E. A., Thompson, A. I., McCubbin, M. A. & Kaston, A. (1993). Culture, ethnicity, and the family: Critical factors in childhood chronic illnesses and disabilities. *Pediatrics, 91* (5), 1063–1070.

McLoyd, V. & Wilson, L. (1991). The strain of living poor: Parenting, social support, and child mental health. In A. C. Huston (Ed.), *Children in poverty* (pp. 105–135). Cambridge, Eng.: Cambridge University Press.

Munroe-Blum, H., Boyle, M., Offord, D. & Kates, N. (1989). Immigrant children: Psychiatric disorder, school performance, and service utilization. *American Journal of Orthopsychiatry, 59* (4), 510–519.

Nazario, S. (1996, March 4). Tensions on Hereford Drive. *Los Angeles Times,* pp. A1, A14.

Novello, A. (1991). Hispanic health: Time for data, time for action. *Journal of American Medical Association, 265* (2), 253–255.

Ortiz, A. & Maldonado-Colon, E. (1986). Recognizing learning disabilities in bilingual children: How to lessen inappropriate referrals of language minority students to special education. *Journal of Reading, Writing, and Learning Disabilities International, 2* (1), 43–56.

Osterweis, M., Solomon, F. & Green, M. (1984). *Bereavement, reactions, consequences, and care.* Washington, DC: Institute of Medicine, National Academy of Sciences.

Phinney, J. S., Chavira, V. & Tate, J. D. (1993). The effect of ethnic threat on ethnic self concept and own-group ratings. *Journal of Social Psychology, 133* (4), 469–478.

Pynoos, R. S. & Eth, S. (1985). Children traumatized by witnessing acts of personal violence: Homicide, rape, or suicide behavior. In S. Eth & R. S. Pynoos (Eds.), *Post traumatic stress disorder in children* (pp. 17–43). Washington, DC: American Psychiatric Press.

Raphael, B. (1983). *The anatomy of bereavement.* New York: Basic Books.

Ressler, E. M., Boothby, N. & Steinbock, D. J. (1988). *Unaccompanied children.* New York: Oxford University Press.

Robert Wood Johnson Foundation (1987). *Access to health care in the United States: Results of a 1986 survey* (Special report, Whole No. 2). Princeton, NJ: Author.

Robertson, J. & Robertson, J. (1989). *Separation and the very young.* London: Free Association Books.

Rodriguez, O. (1987). *Hispanics and human services: Help-seeking in the inner city* (Monograph No. 14). New York: Fordham University, Hispanic Research Center.

Rossell, C. & Baker, K. (1996). The educational effectiveness of bilingual education. *Research in the Teaching of English, 30,* 1–68.

Rueschenberg, E. & Buriel, R. (1989). Mexican American family functioning and acculturation: A family systems perspective. *Hispanic Journal of Behavioral Sciences, 11,* 232–244.

Rumbaut, R. G. (1994). The crucible within: Ethnic identity, self esteem, and the segmented assimilation among children of immigrants. *International Migration Review, 28,* 748–794.

Rutter, M. (1983). Stress, coping and development: Some issues and some questions. In N. Garmezy & M. Rutter (Eds.), *Stress, coping, and development in children* (pp. 1–41). New York: McGraw-Hill.

Rutter, M. (1990). Psychosocial resilience and protective mechanisms. In J. Rolf, A. S. Masten, D. Cicchetti, K. H. Nuechterlein & S. Weintraub (Eds.), *Risk and protective factors in the development of psychopathology* (pp. 181–214). Cambridge, Eng.: Cambridge University Press.

Sabogal, F., Marin, G., Otero-Sabogal, R., Marin, B. V. & Perez-Stable, E. J. (1987). Hispanic familialism and acculturation: What changes and what doesn't. *Hispanic Journal of Behavioral Science, 5* (9), 397–412.

Sam, D. L. (1994). The psychological adjustment of young immigrants in Norway. *Scandinavian Journal of Psychology, 35,* 240–253.

Semaj, L. (1980). The development of racial evaluation and preference: A cognitive approach. *Journal of Black Psychology, 6,* 59–79.

Siantz, M. L. de Leon (1990). Maternal acceptance/rejection of Mexican-American migrant mothers. *Psychology of Women Quarterly, 2* (14), 245–254.

Siantz, M. L. de Leon (1994). Parental factors correlated with developmental outcome in the migrant Head Start child. *Early Childhood Research Quarterly, 9* (3), 481–504.

Spurlock, J. (1986). Development of self concept in Afro-American children. *Hospital and community psychiatry, 37* (1), 66–70.

Takaki, R. (1993). *A different mirror: A history of multicultural America*. Boston: Little, Brown.

Triandis, H. C., Marin, G., Betancourt, H., Lisansky, J. & Chang, B. (1982). *Dimensions of familism among Hispanic and mainstream Navy recruits*. Chicago: University of Illinois Press.

U.S. Bureau of the Census (1995). *March 1994 current population survey, Hispanic data*. Washington, DC: U.S. Government Printing Office.

U.S. Bureau of the Census (1996). Population projections of the United States by age, sex, race, and Hispanic origin: 1995 to 2050. *Current Population Reports*, Series P25–1130. Washington, DC: U.S. Government Printing Office.

U.S. Department of Education (1994). *Mini-digest of educational statistics* (NCES 94–131). Washington, DC. U.S. Government Printing Office.

Valdez, R. B. (1986, February). *A framework for policy development for the Latino population*. Testimony prepared for the 2nd Annual California Hispanic Legislative Conference.

Valencia, R. (Ed.) (1991). *Chicano school failure and success: Research and policy agendas for the 1990's*. New York: Falmer.

Van Eerdewegh, M., Bieri, M., Parilla, R. & Clayton, P. (1982). The bereaved child. *British Journal of Psychiatry, 140*, 23–20.

Vega, W. & Kolody, B. (1985). The meaning of social support and the mediation of stress across cultures. In W. Vega & M. Miranda (Eds.), *Stress and Hispanic mental health: Relating research to service delivery* (pp. 48–75). Rockville, MD: National Institute of Mental Health.

Weinberg, A. (1979). Mental health aspects of voluntary migration. In C. Zwingman & M. Pfister-Ammende (Eds.), *Uprooting and after* (pp. 110–120). New York: Springer-Verlag.

Weissberg, R. P., Caplan, M. & Sivo, P. J. (1989). A new conceptual framework for establishing school-based social competence promotion programs. In L. A. Bond & B. E. Compas (Eds.), *Primary prevention and promotion in schools* (pp. 255–296). Newbury Park, CA: Sage.

Zambrana, R. E., Dorrington, C. & Hayes-Bautista, D. (1996). Family and child health, a neglected vision. In R. E. Zambrana (Ed.), *Understanding Latino families: Scholarship, policy, and practice* (pp. 157–177). Thousand Oaks, CA: Sage.

Zambrana, R. E. & Silva-Palacios, V. (1989). Gender differences in stress among Mexican immigrant adolescents in Los Angeles, California. *Journal of Adolescent Research, 4* (4), 426–442.

Zuniga, S. (1992). Families with Latino roots. In E. Lynch & M. H. Hanson (Eds.), *Developing cross cultural competence* (pp. 151–179). Baltimore: Brookes.

# 6 HEALTH BEHAVIORS OF MEXICAN AMERICAN FAMILIES

## MYTHS AND REALITIES

*Norma Olvera*
*Jennifer H. Hays*
*Thomas G. Power*
*Claudia Yañez*

Increasing interest in the health status of Hispanics in the United States has arisen due to the extraordinary growth of this group. During the past decade, the Hispanic population has increased at a rate of 39% as compared to less than an 8% increase in non-Hispanic whites. By the year 2000, the U.S. Hispanic population is expected to reach 31 million, which will make Hispanics the largest ethnic group in the country (U.S. Bureau of the Census, 1990). High birthrates and immigration account for the rapid Hispanic population growth in the United States. Compared with the fertility rate of the general population (65 births per 1,000 females), Hispanics have a higher fertility rate (97 births per 1,000 females), give birth to children at younger ages, and have more children (COSSMHO, 1988). Despite the rapid growth of the Hispanic population, limited epidemiological data exist on this ethnic group. Most epidemiological data on Hispanics have been compiled primarily from the 1982–1984 Hispanic Health and Nutrition Examination Survey (HHANES) of the National Center for Health Statistics.

Before discussing health status and sociocultural correlates of Hispanics, a brief discussion of the term " Hispanic" will be presented to highlight the underlying diversity of the Hispanic population. The chapter will also discuss the study Al Bienestar del Niño (For the well-being of the child), which examines the effects of sociocultural factors on maternal socialization strategies that promote children's health knowledge, and identifies strategies used by Mexican American mothers to promote healthful practices in their preschool and school-aged children. Finally, conclusions about future research interventions are drawn.

## AN EXPLANATION OF THE TERM "HISPANIC"

The term "Hispanic" was used by the U.S. Bureau of the Census in 1980 to identify and group individuals who have a Spanish surname or who were born in a Spanish-speaking country or are Spanish speaking. However, this term is misleading because Hispanics, perhaps more than any other ethnic group in the United States, constitute a significantly heterogeneous group of individuals. Differences exist among the Hispanic subgroups in their place of origin, their number of years in the United States and immigrant status, their levels of acculturation, their levels of education, their degree of English proficiency and reliance on the Spanish language for communication, their geographical distribution, and their level of economic and political power (Poma & Park, 1988). For instance, some Hispanics are native-born U.S. citizens whose ancestors lived in California, Texas, Arizona, Colorado, or New Mexico years before the Pilgrims arrived at Plymouth, Massachusetts, in 1620. Others are more recent arrivals who are considered either documented or undocumented permanent residents, or who are documented political-economic refugees (Cuellar, 1990). Ethnically, Hispanic subgroups are also different from one another. Some Hispanic subgroups identify themselves more as descendants of the *indios* who have lived in North America since precolonial times rather than as descendants of the Spaniards who conquered them. Others consider themselves *negros,* descendants of the Africans brought as slaves to Central and South America and the Caribbean. Others identify themselves as *mestizos,* a combination of Spaniards and *indios,* or as *mulatos,* a combination of Spaniards and *negros.* Yet others consider themselves Americans (Cuellar, 1990).

Of the 19.4 million Hispanics in the United States, 62% are of Mexican origin, 18% are Puerto Rican, 5% are Cuban, 11% are Central or South American, and 8% are of other Hispanic origin. Subgroups tend to concentrate in diverse geographic areas, with Mexicans in California and Texas, Puerto Ricans in New York, and Cubans in Florida (Hispanic Health Council, 1991). There is great variability of health status among the various Hispanic groups. Thus, the indiscriminate use of the Hispanic rubric without further ethnic qualifiers creates problems for interpretations, applicability of generalizations, and recommendations yielded from one subgroup to another (Cuellar, 1990). Researchers must expect more heterogeneity than homogeneity when addressing the prevailing and the future health needs of this diverse population.

## Health Status

### MORTALITY

Precise estimates of Hispanic death rates are impossible to determine because until 1988, the national death certificates did not include Hispanic identifiers (COSSMHO, 1988). However, a review of death certificates with Hispanic surnames and 1979–1981 mortality data tapes from the National Center for Health Statistics indicates that Hispanics die of the major national killers: heart disease, cancer, and stroke (Hispanic Health Council, 1991). Although the overall death rates due to these major killers appear to be lower for Hispanics than those for non-Hispanic whites (even after controlling for annual family income), these findings may be deceptive (Sorlie et al., 1993). Within Hispanic subgroups there exists a great variation in death rates due to heart disease, cancer, and stroke, and in some cases the death rates from these ailments are similar or higher than those experienced by non-Hispanic whites. For instance, Puerto Rican-born males had a 20% higher rate of heart disease than the other Hispanic groups. This rate is closer to the rate for non-Hispanic whites. Puerto Rican males' mortality rate from chronic liver disease and cirrhosis is twice that of Mexican Americans and approximately three times that of Cubans (Cuellar, 1990). Compared to non-Hispanic whites, death due to stomach cancer is twice as high for Hispanics as for whites.

Violent deaths are responsible for high mortality rates among male adolescents and young adults of Mexican American, Puerto Rican, and Cuban origin. All Hispanic male subgroups have higher death rates due to homicide than white males. Suicide rates for Cuban and Puerto Rican males exceeds rates for white males (Cuellar, 1990; Shai & Rosenwaike, 1988). Furthermore, differences in mortality rates exist between Hispanic U.S.-born and foreign-born members of the same ancestral group. Foreign-born Hispanics, particularly Mexican Americans, have a very low relative risk of death compared with native-born persons (Sorlie et al., 1993). However, a "healthy migrant effect" appears to exist wherein foreign-born persons from both Hispanic and non-Hispanic groups show lower mortality rates than native-born persons.

## Morbidity

Hispanics, when compared with their non-Hispanic white counterparts, are at an increased risk for obesity, diabetes, hypertension, tuberculosis, human immunodeficiency virus infection, and certain types of cancer (Hispanic Health Council, 1991). Growing evidence indicates that these risk factors for morbidity vary greatly among the Hispanic subgroups. For instance, Mexican Americans and Puerto Ricans are three times more likely to have type II diabetes than the general population (Stern & Hattner, 1990). Obesity and diet are largely associated with diabetes in Hispanics. Based on the HHANES data, 26% of Puerto Ricans, 24% of Mexican Americans, and 16% of Cubans aged 45–74 years have diabetes. Furthermore, two out of five Mexican American or Puerto Rican females are likely to be overweight, whereas approximately one out of four Mexican American or Puerto Rican males are overweight (Centers for Disease Control, 1989).

Puerto Rican women are at disproportionately high risk for breast and cervical cancer (Munoz, 1988). Mexican American women have a higher incidence of gall bladder cancer than whites (Diehl & Stern, 1989). Increases in cigarette smoking have resulted in a doubling of the rate of lung cancer among Hispanic women (Novello, Wise & Kleinman, 1991). Based on data from the HHANES study, 44% of Mexican American men smoked, compared with 42% of Cuban men, and 41% of Puerto Rican men. Overall, of the three major subgroups of Hispanics, Puerto Ricans have the worst health status. They have the highest incidence of acute medical conditions and chronic health problems (Hispanic Health Council, 1991).

Low-income Hispanics exhibit a higher risk for unrecognized and untreated hypertension (Kumanyika et al., 1989) than whites, and hypertension is more prevalent among Hispanics than whites (COSSMHO, 1988). The incidence of tuberculosis is 4.3 times greater for Hispanics than whites (Rieder et al., 1989). In addition, new threats to the health of the Hispanic population in the United States are emerging. The impact of the AIDS epidemic in certain Hispanic subgroups, such as Puerto Ricans, has been alarming. Even though Hispanics represent only 8% of the total U.S. population, they constitute approximately 15% of all reported cases of AIDS in the United States (Poma & Park, 1988; Novello, Wise & Kleinman, 1991).

## Sociocultural Factors Influencing Hispanic Health Status

The health status of the diverse Hispanic subgroups in the United States is influenced by varied economic, cultural, and social factors (Hispanic Health Council, 1991; Ginzburg, 1991; Sorlie et al., 1993). Low income and lack of health insurance limit Hispanic access to primary health care. Compared with the United States population in general, Hispanics are more likely to be underemployed or employed part-time, or to have blue-collar jobs with no insurance benefits. Hispanics are less likely to have a college or high school education, which negatively influences their families' income and access to health insurance. Of the Hispanic subgroups, Cuban Americans have the highest income, while Puerto Ricans have the lowest (Hispanic Health Council, 1991; Poma & Park, 1988).

Hispanics also face language and cultural barriers that hinder their access to health care in the United States. Recent arrivals often have limited English proficiency, which restricts their health care choices or makes them feel estranged from the complicated U.S. health care system. Differences in health behaviors and health status also exist between U.S.-born and foreign-born Hispanics. As Hispanics become more acculturated to the mainstream society, their health status worsens. They consume a less healthful diet and increase their use of tobacco (Hispanic Health Council, 1991). Less acculturated Mexican Americans have a significantly lower likelihood of seeking outpatient care for physical or emotional problems than those who are more acculturated. Furthermore, less acculturated patients with Medicaid use inpatient services four times less than the more acculturated patients with Medicaid, even after controlling for need (Wells et al., 1989). Cultural beliefs such as fatalism often have been associated with the health status of Hispanic ethnic groups. Golden and colleagues (1983) report that Hispanic families with more external orientation are less likely to feel in control of their health and are less likely to utilize health care services.

Although a variety of health needs and deficiencies are associated with the Hispanic community, the population also exhibits strengths that need to be further examined. For instance, despite a relatively low income, lack of health care coverage, lack of English proficiency, and low utilization of prenatal care among Hispanics, the rates of infant mortality and low birthweight newborns are quite low compared with those of non-Hispanic whites and African Americans (Mendoza, 1994; see Chapter 7 this volume). This epidemiological paradox is believed to be a result of social and cultural characteristics that promote health among the Hispanic population (Sorlie et al., 1993). Thus, research examining the protective factors associated with the health of the Hispanic population can provide valuable insight into pathways to sound health.

## Al Bienestar del Niño Study

Al Bienestar del Niño (For the Well-Being of the Child) was developed to identify pathways to health by focusing attention on the needs of Hispanic children and the strategies that Hispanic parents use to help children acquire healthy lifestyle practices. This is even more relevant given that Hispanics are a youthful population, with an average age of 23 years, compared to 31 years for non-Hispanic whites (Poma & Park, 1988). Most of the research of children's health behaviors consists of descriptive studies of children's knowledge, attitudes, or practices at a particular age rather than research that has been approached from a developmental perspective. The purpose of the Al Bienestar del Niño study was to examine the development of health behaviors in Mexican American children. The specific objectives of this study were to: assess the effects of sociocultural factors on maternal socialization strategies that promote children's health knowledge, and to identify strategies used by Mexican American mothers to promote healthful practices in their preschool and school-aged children.

## THE INTERNALIZATION MODEL

The research on internalization serves as a useful theoretical basis for studying the influence of child-rearing strategies on the development of health behaviors (Grusec, 1983; Hoffman, 1983; Lepper, 1983; Perry & Perry, 1983). Internalization refers to the process of acquiring social and cultural customs and norms, and using them to guide behavior in the absence of adult supervision. Internalization differs from compliance in that in compliance, children are motivated by external rewards and punishments, whereas in internalization, the motivation is internal, such as self-induced pleasure or guilt. In the Al Bienestar del Niño study, we have taken the concept of internalization from its original context of moral development, and applied it to the process of acquiring attitudes and behaviors that are associated with maintaining health and preventing injury.

Power and Manire (1993) propose a developmental model of internalization to explain the influence of parenting practices on the acquisition of cultural values and beliefs. Based on Ogbu's (1981) cultural-ecological approach to child rearing, the model incorporates many of the social-psychological constructs employed in contemporary theories of socialization. The model proposes that three processes are required for internalization: (1) an understanding of the rules of appropriate behavior in various contexts; (2) the ability to exercise sufficient impulse control and self-regulation to follow rules; and (3) the development of an internal rather than an external motivation to comply with these rules.

Parenting practices that minimize the use of external controls and maximize the child's understanding of and participation in the behavior are expected to lead to children internalizing the desired behavior. According to the internalization model, to promote understanding of parental rules, parents need to use age-appropriate explanations of rules in various contexts and provide opportunities to observe others following rules (modeling). To promote self-regulation, parents need to offer clear expectations about the behavior and appropriate consequences for the behavior. To foster the development of internal motivation, parents need to use both child-oriented rationales (e.g., "carrots make your teeth strong") and nonpower assertive strategies that are minimally sufficient to elicit compliance (e.g., suggestions, hints, questions), and allow the child opportunities for independent decision making. Thus, the child can participate more actively in the behavior rather than simply complying with the situation.

The participants in the Al Bienestar del Niño study were eighty low-income Mexican American mothers and their children who were aged four to eight ($M$ = 6 years, 6 months; $SD$ = 1 year, 3 months) at the beginning of the study. Study families were followed for four years. Forty-two (53%) of the target children were boys. All children lived in intact families, and the majority of families had three or four children. The mothers were predominantly first-generation immigrants from Mexico (91%) with a few years of formal education. Most mothers were homemakers, and fathers were employed (mainly part-time) almost exclusively in blue-collar jobs. Ninety percent of mothers reported speaking mostly Spanish. Families were recruited through Catholic churches, neighborhood canvassing, and referrals from an inner-city neighborhood densely populated by Hispanics, particularly Mexican Americans.

Data were collected through in-home observations of mothers and children, a structured play situation in a laboratory (children only), and questionnaires administered by an interviewer at home and in a laboratory. Detailed descriptions of the methodology have been reported elsewhere (Cousins, Power & Olvera-Ezzell, 1993; Olvera-Ezzell et al., 1994). Data were collected in three sessions. During the first session, bilingual Hispanic research assistants visited study families in their homes to discuss the purpose of the study, and upon receiving maternal signed consent, proceeded to conduct structured interviews to assess demographic characteristics and acculturation levels of mothers (Hazuda, Stern & Haffner, 1988). For the second visit, two bilingual research assistants visited the homes for an observation session that lasted from dinnertime to the target child's bedtime. After dinner, mothers were interviewed about their health beliefs (e.g., using the Multidimensional Health Locus of Control Scales developed by Wallston, Wallston & DeVellis, 1978), and family health practices (e.g., using the Eating Habits Socialization Interview developed by Olvera-Ezzell, Power & Cousins, 1990). Maternal behaviors coded during the dinnertime interactions included modeling, forcing compliance, threats/bribes, punishments, helping eating, and serving. The directiveness of maternal verbalizations—both in terms of the syntax employed and the types of semantic softeners and aggravators used—was coded using a system developed by Becker (1984) (*see* Table 6–1).

For the third session, target children's health knowledge about nutrition, hygiene, and safety was assessed individually in a structured play situation in a university laboratory that had been furnished as a playhouse. Target children were interviewed in their preferred language (English or Spanish) by a bilingual female Mexican American research assistant. Most of the child

TABLE 6–1. Maternal Directiveness Coding Categories

I.  *Syntactic Directiveness.* Categories are listed from the least to most directive.

    A.  *Hints.* Statements of condition (e.g., "There is more meat left.")

    B.  Question Directives. Information question form (e.g., "Do you want more milk?")

    C.  Permission Directives. Asks child's permission (e.g., "May I have it?")

    D.  *Embedded Imperatives.* Want or need stated as an imperative (e.g., "Can you give it to me?")

    E.  Need Statements. Want or need stated as an imperative (e.g., "I need you to finish eating.")

    F.  *Imperatives.* Direct imperatives toward child (e.g., "Take some more tortillas.")

II. *Semantic Directiveness*

    A.  *Semantic Softeners.*

        1.  *Minimization.* Diminishes task (e.g., "*Just* eat a couple.")

        2.  Convenience. Time open (e.g., "Take some more when you get a *chance.*")

        3.  Justfication. Reasoning or other justification (e.g., "You need to stop eating so much *so you won't gain weight.*")

        4.  *Bargaining.* Promises to reward (e.g., "If you finish your vegetables, *I'll get you some dessert.*")

        5.  *Permission.* Asks permission, also includes "please" (e.g., "Would you let me get you some more beans, *please?*")

        6.  *Affection.* Verbally expresses affection (e.g., "*Honey,* are you through eating yet?")

        7.  Communal Orientation. Use of the "royal we" (e.g., Why don't *we* try some of this?")

        8.  *Praise.* Praises child (e.g., "That's a *good boy.*")

        9.  *Tag Question.* Elicits agreement (e.g., "Try some of these, *O.K.?*")

        10. *Diminutive.* Uses diminutive (-ita or -ito) form (e.g., "Eat a *little bit* of your meat.")

    B.  *Semantic Aggravators.*

        1.  Threats. Threatens to punish (e.g., "If you don't stop fooling around, *you're going to your room.*")

        2.  *Immediacy.* Time limited or constrained (e.g., "Finish your dinner, *right now.*")

        3.  *Definiteness.* No choice allowed (e.g., "You *have* to eat them.")

        4.  *Impersonalization.* (e.g., "*Young lady,* act your age.")

        5.  *Repeats/Draws Attention.* (e.g., "Hey. Cut that out. *Cut that out.*")

Source: Cousins, Power & Olvera-Ezzell, 1993, Table 2.

interviews (81%) were conducted in Spanish. The interview protocol was originally written in English, and was translated, pilot-tested, and revised by a team of bilingual and bicultural Mexican Americans (including the first author of this chapter). The protocol was thoroughly pilot-tested with eight Mexican American families not participating in the study. Revisions to the protocol were made as needed to ensure its intelligibility.

Following a brief free-play period, the experimenter initiated the structured play situation by indicating that she wanted to "play house" and that she would pretend to be the "child," while the target child was asked to pretend to be "mommy" or "daddy." Using a standardized child's play protocol, the experimenter guided the child through the playhouse, asking questions, probing, and engaging in predetermined daily activities to elicit the child's knowledge of and rationales about the appropriateness of various health behaviors. For instance, the experimenter would ask, "Mommy, can I just have french fries for dinner?" Then, the child was asked "why" or "why not" to elicit rationales for the response.

In the area of nutrition, children's knowledge was assessed concerning the healthfulness of: (1) smoking, drinking coffee, and drinking alcohol; (2) consuming high-sugar or high-fat foods versus low-sugar or low-fat foods; and (3) other eating habits, in particular, continuing to eat despite feeling full, eating a limited variety of foods, and eating cookies before bedtime. In the realm of hygiene, three general areas were assessed: (1) personal grooming; (2) food contamination; and (3) contagious and noncontagious illness transmission, and illness prevention. In the realm of safety, five areas were assessed: (1) dealing with dangerous objects; (2) avoiding poisoning; (3) safety behaviors while playing indoors; (4) safety behaviors while playing outdoors; and (5) automobile and pedestrian safety. (For specific examples of each category see Olvera-Ezzell et al., 1994.)

Children's rationales for their responses across the health areas were coded based on a hierarchically organized coding scheme reflecting a predicted rise in conceptual organization with increasing age: from undifferentiated to concrete to abstract understanding. This coding scheme is consistent with those used to examine the relationship between general cognitive developmental stages and knowledge of illness causation (e.g., Bibace & Walsh, 1980, 1981; Perrin & Gerrity, 1981; Robinson, 1987). Children's rationales were coded according to five levels of complexity: (1) no rationales, (2) unelaborated rationales, (3) rationales involving references to immediate consequences, (4) references to delayed consequences, and (5) references to processes. Each level includes several subcategories (see Table 6–2).

TABLE 6-2. Child's Play Coding Scheme

| Rationale | Description | Examples |
|---|---|---|
| **I. No Rationale** | | |
| None | Child fails or refuses to answer the question or responds with clearly inappropriate or irrelevant content. | "Hey, this puppet looks like Miss Piggy." "I don't know." |
| **II. Unelaborated Rationales** | | |
| Magical/imminent justice | Responses dominated by magical or fantasy connotations. | "You can't drink coffee because it makes animals hot." "Don't play outside after dark because of the monsters." |
| Circular/routine | Responses in which answer is merely a paraphrase of the question. No articulation of the causal link between an event and its consequences. | "Brush your teeth because you are going to school." "Wash your hands because you are going to eat." |
| Personal preference | Explanations characterized by references to personal likes/dislikes or whim. | "I want to." "I like it." "I never tasted it." "I say so." |
| Punishment/authority | Explanations that involve notions of conformity to an authority. | "The police will take you to jail if you don't wear your seat belt." "My mom lets me do it." "My parents let me." |

| Rationale | Description | Examples |
|---|---|---|
| Status | Explanations are based on the status of an individual's age or gender. | "No, you can't smoke because you are a little girl." "Fathers can because they are men." |
| Good/bad | Explanations refer to quality of an object or action as merely "good" or "bad" for the body. If given with a more elaborated rationale, the good/bad rationale is overridden. | "Eat it because it's good for you." "It's healthy or unhealthy." "It's a drug." "It's natural." "It is junk food." "It is nutritious." |
| Functional | Includes explanations which pertain to an object serving a particular purpose. | "Don't jump on the bed because it's for sleeping." |

### III. References to Immediate Consequences

| Rationale | Description | Examples |
|---|---|---|
| Appearance/looks | Explanations that focus on physical appearance. This type of explanation also includes references to cleanliness or neatness. | "Brush your teeth so they will look nice." "You stink or smell bad." "Your hair will turn white." "Your body will get black." "Wash your hands because they are dirty." |
| Pain/injury/pain | Explanations based on characteristics of object that may cause pain or injury to a person physically or mentally. | "Don't play with knives because you can cut yourself." "It's dangerous; it's poisonous." "It's hot." "It's sharp." "You might have an accident." "I'm hungry; I'm thirsty." |

*(continued on next page)*

TABLE 6–2. *(Continued)*

| | *Rationale* | *Description* | *Examples* |
|---|---|---|---|
| **III. References to Immediate Consequences**—*(continued)* | | | |
| | Harm to objects | Explanations that refer to inducing physical damage to objects. | "Don't play with the ball. You might break something." |
| | Death | Explanations that imply death connotations as a consequence. | "Don't stick your finger in the outlet. You will die." |
| **IV. References to Delayed Consequences** | | | |
| | Sickness/health | Explanations that include references to physical growth, strength, or physical wellness or weakness. | "Don't eat too much or you will get sick." "Your teeth will fall out or you will get cavities." "Eat vegetables and fruit if you want to be strong." |
| | Weight | Explanations that pertain to weight loss or gain. | "Don't eat bread because you will get fat." "Eat only carrots so you will get skinnier." |
| **V. References to Processes** | | | |
| | Conditional | Explanations implying that an action can be conducted only if a specific condition is met. | "You can play with a ball in the house, but only if the ball is small." "Only if _____ then you can do _____." |

| Rationale | Description | Examples |
|---|---|---|
| Contagion | Explanations implying that the child can get ill from objects or people who are proximate to, but not touching, the child. | "You will get a toothache if you sit next to her." "I get sick by sitting next to you." |
| Undifferentiated germs | Explanations that included a general reference to "germs" or "bugs" as the cause of illness. | "Don't eat it because it has germs." "Don't eat that because it has little animals in it." |
| Germs disease transmission | Explanations in which germs are clearly connected to the process of disease transmission. | "Don't share food with her because you will get her germs and then you will get sick." |
| Food components | Explanations pertaining to contents of food (e.g., fat, salt, sugar, vitamins) | "Don't eat candy because it has too much sugar." |

Source: Olvera-Ezzell, Power, Cousins, Guerra & Trujillo, 1994, table 2.

In situations where children offered playful or fantastical responses, a series of probes was used after the short responses were given. Thus, if the child initially gave an "incorrect" response, or an "I do not know" response, the probes were immediately employed (e.g., "Are you sure? Remember, you are my mommy."). This type of questioning helped determine whether a child's response was correct before or after prompting, and explored the child's highest level of reasoning. The average length of the structured play situation was 40 minutes.

PREDICTORS OF SOCIALIZATION STRATEGIES

Cousins, Power, and Olvera-Ezzell (1993) examined the degree to which maternal education, acculturation, and health locus of control predicted maternal socialization strategies using a series of hierarchical multiple regressions analyses. In these regressions, child age was entered in the first step as a control variable, followed by the three health locus of control scales of the Wallston, Wallston, and De Vellis (1978) measure at step two. These were attribution of health outcomes to *change*, or to *internal* factors, or to behaviors of *powerful* others. At step three either education or the two acculturation variables from Hazuda, Stern, and Haffner (1988)—functional integration into the mainstream society (e.g., language use, social networks) and traditionality of attitudes—were added to see if they increased prediction over and above the contribution of health locus of control. As shown in Table 6–3, the significant beta weights (p < 0.05) indicated several effects of external health locus of control (HLOC), but none involving the internal factor. Mothers who thought that their health was governed by luck or fate were less likely to accurately discuss the healthfulness of foods with their children and more likely to use semantic aggravators in directing child behavior at the dinner table. Moreover, mothers who reported reliance on medical professionals used more directive techniques ( i.e., imperatives versus questions) at the dinner table (*see* Table 6–3).

The unique effects of maternal education were very limited. As shown in Table 6–3, once health locus of control was controlled for, only one beta weight for education, discouraging eating, was significant. Better educated mothers were more likely to discourage the child from overeating at the table. Finally, in contrast to education, several of the acculturation effects were significant after controlling for health locus of control. The only significant effects, however, were for nontraditionality, not for the measure of functional integration. Mothers with the most acculturated attitudes used the most forceful child-rearing techniques (imperatives and semantic aggravators), and fewer nondirective techniques such as questions.

TABLE 6–3. Significant Beta Weights from Hierarchical Regressions Predicting Socialization Behaviors

| | Step 1 Child Age | Step 2 HLOC | Step 3 Education or Acculturation | |
|---|---|---|---|---|
| **Interviews** | | | | |
| Pushes food | (−0.39***) | ns | ns | ns |
| Explains healthfulness | ns | (−0.30*)Chance | ns | ns |
| **Observations** | | | | |
| Encourage eating | (−0.44***) | ns | ns | ns |
| Discourage eating | ns | ns | (0.38**) | ns |
| Hints | ns | ns | ns | ns |
| Questions | ns | (−0.35**)PO | ns | (−0.34**) Non-traditional |
| Commands | ns | (0.29*)PO | ns | (0.31**) Non-traditional |
| Softeners | ns | ns | ns | ns |
| Aggravators | ns | (0.27*)Chance | ns | (0.23*) Non-traditional |

*$p$ <0.05, **$p$ <0.01, ***$p$ <0.001
PO = Powerful Others
ns = nonsignificant
Source: Adapted from Cousins, Power & Olvera-Ezzell, 1993, table 5.

PARENTING SOCIALIZATION STRATEGIES
AND CHILDREN'S NUTRITION KNOWLEDGE

Hays, Power and Olvera (1998) examined the relationship between maternal socialization strategies and children's nutrition knowledge. In order to do so, variables for the dinnertime observation and the Eating Habits Socialization Interview were used to predict outcomes from the child's play assessment including the proportion of nutrition items where the child gave the correct answer before prompting, the proportion of nutrition items where the child continued to give the wrong answer after prompting, and the proportion of explanations to nutrition items that correspond to the following categories: unelaborated, physical appearance/weight, discomfort/sickness/

health, and food components. Regressions showed that consistent with the internalization model, children most likely to give discomfort/sickness/health explanations had mothers who were the least directive during the dinnertime observations (i.e., they rarely used commands and frequently used semantic softeners).

Children's physical appearance/weight explanations were also predicted by mothers' behavior at dinner. Specifically, children who were most likely to give physical appearance/weight explanations during the child's play assessment had mothers who were most likely to discourage eating, were least likely to encourage eating, and tended to use more rationales during the home observations. Children's references to food components were predicted by maternal responses to the Eating Habits Socialization Interview. Children using these explanations had mothers who reported employing nondirective strategies for introducing a new food (i.e., the "provide opportunities" variable). Finally, the proportion of incorrect answers after prompting in the child's play assessment was predicted by responses to the Eating Habits Socialization Interview and Acculturation measure as well. Children who gave the most wrong answers had mothers who reported using fewer rationales, and giving their children fewer opportunities to make their own food choices. Most acculturated mothers (those more integrated into the majority culture) had children who gave fewer incorrect answers to the nutrition items.

## CONCLUSION

The specific objectives of this study were to assess the effects of the sociocultural factors on maternal socialization strategies that promote children's health knowledge, and to identify strategies used by Mexican American mothers to promote healthful practices in their preschool and school-aged children. Maternal health locus of control beliefs and acculturation levels were found to be predictors of socialization strategies. Mothers who held a more external orientation toward health (especially those who saw health as due to chance factors beyond their control, i.e., fatalism) used fewer socialization techniques that would promote the internalization of health habits in their children. For example, in an analysis of the nutrition socialization practices, it was found that more externally oriented mothers were more likely to use forceful, directive techniques to achieve compliance.

Maternal acculturation was also found to be a predictor of child-rearing practices. The most acculturated mothers (in terms of those who held less traditional values) tended to use more directive techniques (i.e., commands and aggravators), and fewer techniques that foster internalization, including asking questions, providing opportunities, and reasoning with the child. Results also revealed that the most acculturated mothers (those more integrated to the majority culture) had children who gave more correct answers to the nutrition items. These findings indicate that two aspects of acculturation showed opposite relationships with children's nutrition knowledge. Mothers who have high levels of contact with the majority culture but who maintain their traditional values may have children who exhibit the greatest level of nutrition knowledge. These results suggest that the relationship between maternal acculturation and children's health knowledge is a complex and multiply-determined one. Furthermore, these results are consistent with findings indicating that acculturation consists of multidimensional domains, each of which may have unique effects on a specific behavior. Felix-Ortiz and Newcomb (1995) reported that for certain types of drug use, different aspects of acculturation interact and are differently related to drug use. It is interesting to note that, although the range of acculturation was limited in this sample of first-generation immigrants, an effect of maternal acculturation on socialization strategies was determined when acculturation was viewed as a multiple domain (i.e., holding traditional values and being functionally integrated into the mainstream culture).

Results of this study also identify strategies used by Mexican American mothers to influence their child's health knowledge and support the applicability of the internalization model to the development of health and nutrition knowledge. During the dinnertime observations, most of the mothers who were characterized as nondirective (those who used fewer commands and more semantic softeners) had children who gave more sophisticated explanations regarding their food choices (i.e., discomfort/sickness/health and food components) during a later structured play situation. Mothers' observed use of reasoning was positively associated with the use of sophisticated child explanations (i.e., references to physical appearance/weight). In contrast, mothers who reported little use of reasoning had children who were likely to give more wrong answers to questions than children of mothers who reported influencing their child's behavior through reasoning. The interview data also confirmed our predictions. Mothers' reported use of nondirective techniques (i.e., provides opportunities) was positively associated with children's references to food components and negatively associated with incorrect answers to the nutrition items.

In summary, mothers who encouraged their children's nutrition understanding through reasoning and explanation, and who used minimal external pressure to elicit child compliance, had children who showed the greatest level of knowledge. These results are consistent with the theory that children are more likely to internalize parental values and are more likely to be motivated to comply when parents provide children with rationales and opportunities to respond on their own, rather than using more controlling tactics (Power & Manire, 1993).

There are protective factors associated with the health of Hispanics (e.g., family support), and the present study demonstrates the importance of one of them—parenting practices. Although the sample in the present study was a small and relatively homogeneous convenience sample, maternal socialization strategies that promote healthful habits in Mexican American children were identified. This type of research is critical for the development of educational and behavioral interventions. Preventive interventions should be designed to reinforce protective factors and counteract risk factors in order to disrupt processes that contribute to dysfunctionality (Coie et al., 1993). These interventions are more likely to be effective if they are based on a thorough understanding of the child-rearing norms, beliefs, and practices characteristic of a particular ethnic group. Because insufficient information is available on the protective factors of the Mexican American population, results from this study will be valuable in guiding program developers in the design and implementation of health-related interventions for this population.

ACKNOWLEDGMENTS

This research was supported by grant no. HD 23991 from the National Institute of Child Health and Human Development. Requests for reprints should be sent to the first author at Center for Immigration Research, College of Social Sciences, 492 PGH, University of Houston, Houston, TX 77204–3474.

REFERENCES

Becker, J. A. (1984, April). *Adult beliefs about the acquisition of pragmatic skills.* Paper presented at the Southwestern Conference on Human Development, Athens, GA.

Bibace, R. & Walsh, M. E. (1980). Development of children's concept of illness. *Pediatrics, 66,* 912–917.

Bibace, R. & Walsh, M. E. (1981). Children's conceptions of illness. In R. Bibace & M. E. Walsh (Eds.), *Children's conceptions of health, illness, and bodily functions* (pp. 30–48). San Francisco: Jossey-Bass.

Centers for Disease Control (1989). Prevalence of overweight for Hispanics—United States 1982–1984. *Morbity and Mortality Weekly Report, 38,* 838–843.

Coie, J. D., Watt, N. F., West, S. G., Hawkins, J. D., Asarnow, J. R., Markman, H. J., Ramey, S. L., Shure, M. B. & Long, B. (1993). The science of prevention: A conceptual framework and some directions for a national research program. *American Psychologist, 48* (10), 1013–1022.

COSSMHO (National Coalition of Hispanic Helath and Human Services Organizations) (1988). *Delivering preventative health care to Hispanics: A manual for providers.* Washington, DC: National Coaltion of Hispanic Health and Human Services Organizations.

Cousins, J. H., Power, T. G. & Olvera-Ezzell, N. (1993). Mexican-American mothers' socialization strategies: Effects of education, acculturation, and health locus of control. *Journal of Experimental Child Psychology, 55,* 258–276.

Cuellar, J. (1990). Hispanic American aging: Geriatric education curriculum development for selected health professionals. In *Minority aging: Essential curricula content for selected health and allied health professionals* (DHHS Publication No. HRSPDV 901). Washington, DC: U.S. Department of Health and Human Services.

Diehl, A. K. & Stern, M. P. (1989). Special health problems of Mexican-Americans: Obesity, gallbladder disease, diabetes mellitus, and cardiovascular disease. *Advances in Internal Medicine, 34,* 73–96.

Felix-Ortiz, M. & Newcomb, M. D. (1995). In G. B. Botvin, S. Schinke & M. A. Orlandi (Eds.), *Drug abuse prevention with multiethnic youth* (pp. 147–165). Thousand Oaks, CA: Sage.

Ginzburg, E. (1991). Access to health care for Hispanics. *Journal of the American Medical Association, 265,* 238–241.

Golden, M. P., Saltzer, E. B., DePaul-Snyder, L. & Reiff, M. I. (1983). Obesity and socioeconomic class in children and their mothers. *Journal of Developmental and Behavioral Pediatrics, 4,* 113–118.

Grusec, J. E. (1983). The internalization of altruistic disposition: A cognitive analysis. In E. T. Higgins, D. N. Ruble & W. W. Hartup (Eds.), *Social cognition and social development: A sociocultural perspective* (pp. 275–293). Cambridge, Eng.: Cambridge University Press.

Hays, J. H., Power, T. G. & Olvera, N. (1998). *Effects of maternal socialization strategies on children's nutrition knowledge and behavior.* Manuscript under review.

Hazuda, H. P., Stern, M. P. & Haffner, S. M. (1988). Acculturation and assimilation among Mexican-Americans: Scales and population-based data. *Social Science Quarterly, 69,* 687–706.

Hispanic Health Council on Scientific Affairs (1991). Hispanic health in the United States. *Journal of the American Medical Association, 265,* 248–252.

Hoffman, M. L. (1983). Affective and cognitive processes in moral internalization. In E. T. Higgins, D. N. Ruble & W. W. Hartup (Eds.), *Social cognition and social development: A sociocultural perspective* (pp. 236–274). Cambridge, Eng.: Cambridge University Press.

Kumanyika, S., Savage, D. D., Ramirez, A. G. & Hutchinson, J. (1989). Beliefs about high blood pressure prevention in a survey of blacks and Hispanics. *American Journal of Preventive Medicine, 5,* 21–26.

Lepper, M. R. (1983). Social-control processes and the internalization of altruistic dispositions: An attributional perspective. In E. T. Higgins, D. N. Ruble & W. W. Hartup (Eds.), *Social cognition and social development: A sociocultural perspective* (pp. 294–330). Cambridge, Eng.: Cambridge University Press.

Mendoza, F. S. (1994). The health of Latino children in the United States. *The Future of Children: Critical Health Issues for Children and Youth, 4,* 43–72.

Munoz, E. (1988). Care for the Hispanic poor: A growing segment of American society. *Journal of the American Medical Association, 260,* 2711–2712.

Nelson, K. (1986). *Event knowledge: Structure and function in development.* Hillsdale, NJ: Erlbaum.

Novello, A. C., Wise, P. H. & Kleinman, D. V. (1991). Hispanic health: Time for data, time for action. *Journal of the American Medical Association, 265,* 253–255.

Ogbu, J. U. (1981). Origins of human competence: A cultural-ecological perspective. *Child Development, 52,* 413–429.

Olvera-Ezzell, N., Power, T. G. & Cousins, J. H. (1990). Maternal socialization of children's eating habits: Strategies used by obese Mexican-American mothers. *Child Development, 61,* 395–400.

Olvera-Ezzell, N., Power, T. G., Cousins, J. H., Guerra, A. M. & Trujillo, M. (1994). The development of health knowledge in low-income Mexican-American children. *Child Development, 65,* 416–427.

Perrin, E. C. & Gerrity, P. S. (1981). There's a demon in your belly: Children's understanding of concepts regarding illness. *Pediatrics, 67,* 841–849.

Perry, A. G. & Perry, L. C. (1983). Social learning, causal attribution, and moral internalization. In J. Bisanz, G. L. Bisanz & R. Kail (Eds.), *Learning in children: Progress in cognitive development research* (pp. 105–136). New York: Springer-Verlag.

Poma, P. A. & Park, M. (1988). The Hispanic health challenge. *Journal of the National Medical Association, 80,* 1275–1277.

Power, T. G. & Manire, S. H. (1993). Childrearing and internalization: A developmental perspective. In J. Janssens & J. Gerris (Eds.), *Childrearing, moral and prosocial development.* The Netherlands: Swets & Zeitlinger B. V.

Rieder, H. L., Cauthen, G. M., Kelly, G. D., Bloch, A. B. & Snider, D. E., Jr. (1989). Tuberculosis in the United States. *Journal of the American Medical Association, 262,* 385–389.

Robinson, C. A. (1987). Preschool children's conceptualizations of health and illness. *Children's Health Care, 16,* 89–96.

Shai, D. & Rosenwaike, I. (1988). Violent deaths among Mexican-, Puerto Rican- and Cuban-born migrants in the United States. *Social Science & Medicine, 26,* 269–276.

Sorlie, P. D., Backlund, E., Johnson, N. J. & Rogot, E. (1993). Mortality by Hispanic status in the United States. *Journal of the American Medical Association, 270,* 2464–2468.

Stern, M. P. & Hattner, S. M. (1990). Type II diabetes and its complications in Mexican Americans. *Diabetes & Metabolism Review, 6,* 29–35.

U.S. Bureau of the Census (1990). *The Hispanic population in the United States. Current Population Reports.* Series P-20, No. 444. Washington, DC: U.S. Government Printing Office.

Wallston, K. A., Wallston, B. S. & DeVellis, R. (1978). Development of the multidimensional health locus of control scales. *Health Education Monographs, 6,* 160–170.

Wells, K. B., Golding, J. M., Hough, R. L., Burnam, M. A. & Karno, M. (1989). Acculturation and the probability of use of health services by Mexican Americans. *Health Service Research, 24,* 237–257.

# HEALTH ISSUES OF IMMIGRANT CHILDREN OF COLOR

*Fernando Mendoza*
*Noel Rosales*

In this chapter we will discuss selected health issues of immigrant children of color, and will include a demographic overview of the number and types of immigrant children and a description of the social factors that differentiate them from each other and from other children. As will be seen, the limited data on these children provide only an incomplete picture of their health. The chapter ends with some recommendations for further research in this area.

## DEMOGRAPHIC CHANGES

The demographic characteristics of this population of children is described in other chapters, but will be expanded here as it relates to the health issues of these children. Since the 1980s, immigration to the United States has increased and its primary countries of origin have changed. Significant increased immigration has come from Latin America and the Pacific Rim. Table 7–1 shows a comparison of the 1980 and 1990 census data with respect to overall changes in the population of the United States. These figures show the tremendous growth in the population of color in the United States, particularly in Hispanic and Asian Americans. The increase in the Hispanic population from 1980 to 1990 was 53%, and for Asian Americans, 107%. During the sample period, the non-Hispanic population increased only 4%, or by 8 million people. In contrast, during this same period Hispanics also increased by 8 million persons—a one-to-one increase of Hispanics to non-Hispanic whites.

Figure 7–1 shows how the increase in the population has occurred, and includes increases by fertility and immigration. These data show that for Hispanics, the net increase by fertility was 21 per 1,000 population, while by immigration the increase was 17 per 1,000 (Lewit & Baker, 1994). Thus, almost half of the increase in the Hispanic population since 1980 is from immigration. An examination of the Asian American population shows that the

TABLE 7–1. Demographic Changes, 1980–1990

| Group | Percent of 1990 U.S. population | Percent change 1980–90 | Increase (Millions) | 1990 Population ( Millions) |
|---|---|---|---|---|
| Non-Hispanic white | 80.3 | 4.4 | 8.0 | 199.7 |
| African American | 12.1 | 13.2 | 3.5 | 30.0 |
| Hispanic American | 9.0 | 53.0 | 7.8 | 22.3 |
| Asian American | 2.9 | 107.8 | 3.8 | 7.3 |
| Native American | 0.8 | 37.9 | 0.5 | 2.0 |

Source: 1990 Census: United States Department of Commerce

change is even more dramatic. Asian Americans increased their population by 20 per 1,000 by fertility and 46 per 1,000 by immigration. Thus, two-thirds of the growth of the Asian American population comes from immigration.

IMMIGRANT CHILDREN

What proportion of these new immigrants are children and how many come from Latin America and Asia? The most recent census survey, the 1994 Current Population Survey, shows that among noncitizens 14.2% are under 18 years old, and among those who have been naturalized 3.9% are children (Current Population Survey, 1994). Immigrant children (noncitizen and naturalized citizen) make up 3.6% of all U.S. children. Hispanic children make up 58% and Asian children make up 18% of noncitizen children. Among the naturalized-citizen child population, 37% are Hispanics and 39% are Asians. Furthermore, among naturalized children, Hispanics make up 82% of those under age 5, 28% of those between ages 5 and 15, and 40% of those between ages 16 and 17. In contrast, Asian children make up a greater portion of naturalized school-age children, comprising 14% of naturalized children under age 5, 45% of those aged 5 to 15 years, and 32% of those aged 16 to 17. Therefore, three-fourths of all nonnative children are children of color.

At present about one-third of all children in the United States are children of color: African American, Hispanic, Native American, or Asian. In states where immigration is high and children of color have been previously a significant segment of the population, this proportion is even higher. In states like California, children of color outnumber non-Hispanic white children. In fact, before the turn of the century, Hispanic children will comprise a greater percentage of California's children than non-Hispanic white children. What does this mean for the United States in general, and for states

*Figure 7–1. Average Annual Rate of Natural Increase and Net Immigration, 1981–1991*

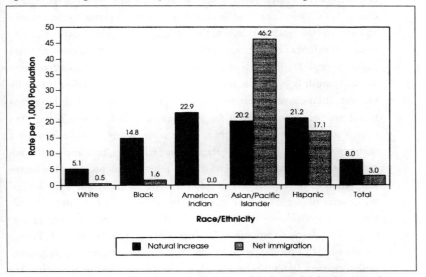

Both natural increase and immigration contribute to the growth and the changing ethnic mix of the population. Natural increase is the difference between the birth and death rates for each group. Net immigration includes both legal and estimated illegal immigration. All groups shown (except Hispanics) exclude Hispanic origin populations, and American Indian includes Eskimos and Aleuts.

- Rates of natural increase are two to three times lower for non-Hispanic whites than for other groups.
- Even if immigration were to cease completely, the proportion of the U.S. population that is non-Hispanic white would continue to decrease.
- The different rates of natural increase are important factors in the increasing diversity of the child population.

Source: Hollman, F. W. *U.S. population estimates by age, sex, race, and Hispanic origin: 1981 to 1991.* Current Population Reports, Series P–25, No. 1095. Washington, DC: US Government Printing Office: February 1993, pp. 30–31, Table 2.

that have large populations of children of color, both immigrant and native-born? It is always difficult to predict the future, but perhaps by examining the situation in California, we can begin to understand what might lie ahead. It will be important to learn from the California experience, and to prepare ourselves for the health, education, and quality-of-life issues these children will face during childhood.

## THE CALIFORNIA EXPERIENCE

Children in California's schools are predominantly children of color. California Tomorrow has estimated that by the year 2000 less than 45% of these children will be non-Hispanic white (Olsen & Chen, 1988). The increase in diversity of California's schoolchildren is even better displayed by the remarkable statistic that each year among the entering class of kindergartners, more than 100 different dialects are spoken. While the great majority of these children speak English, it is clear that other languages are being spoken at home. Spanish is by far the most common, followed to a lesser extent by Chinese. If language is a proxy for culture, then clearly these children represent multiple cultures. Such diversity has never before been seen in the United States. Yet even among those of the same culture, there are processes occurring that will differentiate them from each other, the processes of acculturation and assimilation. The former refers to the process of selective adaptation of the new country's culture, while the latter infers the loss of the country of origin's culture and the adaptation of the new country's culture. Thus, even though all Hispanic children are lumped into one group, they can be clearly differentiated by their country of origin (Mexico, Puerto Rico, Cuba, El Salvador, etc.); by whether they are new immigrants, naturalized citizens, or native- born; and by whether they and their families are acculturated or assimilated into American culture. This diverse group of California children will challenge the various institutions involved in maintaining children's well-being.

As with other populations of children, one of the key factors in determining the risk to their health and educational success is their family's socioeconomic status. Although African American children as a group have one of the highest levels of poverty in the United States, 50% or greater, immigrant children and Hispanic immigrant children in particular also suffer extremely high rates of poverty. Immigrant children from Mexico and Central American countries have poverty rates higher than those of African American children. In addition, among Mexican and Central American immigrant families, parental education is low, usually ninth grade or less. Both of these factors have a direct impact on these children's health and educational profiles. However, unlike most impoverished children in the United States, immigrant children are further differentiated by their immigration status, that is, whether they are legal residents of the United States. This one factor will determine whether they have a safety net of social and health services available to them. It will decide whether they will have some buffer from the environment of poverty. The availability of public services to immigrant children is an issue that continues to get media and policy attention. We are likely to see various changes in public policy toward more restrictive legislation in this area. We have already begun to see this in California. Unfortunately, we have also seen increases in poverty among children.

But are all immigrant children the same? What are some of the factors that may differentiate immigrant children of color from nonimmigrant children? In a California Tomorrow study of immigrant children and their families, several factors determined whether children and families were adapting well to their new environments (Olsen & Chen, 1988). First, those factors associated with the immigration. It is important to know the family's country of origin, their immigration status, and their reason for coming to the United States. These factors include whether families have immigrant communities from which they can seek support; their security and stability in the new country; and whether their immigration was planned or the result of a crisis. For example, a Puerto Rican child might come to the United States because his or her parents are seeking better jobs. Since Puerto Rico is a U.S. territory, the child and the parents are U.S. citizens entitled to the rights of citizenship. Unobstructed travel between the United States and Puerto Rico allows the family to maintain familial ties. This unobstructed migration has resulted in large mainland communities of Puerto Ricans, such as in New York City, and allows families to maintain cultural ties, including their language. This makes the move to a new country less disruptive to a child. In comparison, a child coming from Mexico to the United States because the parents are seeking a better economic life, may or may not be U.S. citizens or legal residents. If they are legal residents, then they will have similar experiences as Puerto Rican families. If they are not legal, then their lives will be focused on day-to-day survival and the threat of deportation. This chronic stressor in the family can affect various aspects of children's life, including their health, both physical and mental, as well as their educational performance (Olsen & Chen, 1988). However, a flow to and from Mexico is usually achievable for these families, and therefore, familial ties and social supports can be maintained. Moreover, the large Mexican and Mexican American communities provide the cultural and social supports that can lessen some of the uncertainties caused by the family's immigration status. In contrast, although Hispanic children from countries in Central America who have fled war may have similar residential status issues as children from Mexico, they may also have to deal with posttraumatic stress and their inability to return to their home countries because of the threat of violence. These children and families may be at higher risk for poor health and developmental and social outcomes as a result of chronic stress and disruption of familial ties.

Similarly, the California Tomorrow study found evidence which suggests that the country of origin and the reason for immigration were also significant factors in the successful integration of Asian children. For each country of origin (China, South Korea, Hong Kong, Vietnam, Cambodia, Laos, Japan, or the Philippines) there are different political, social, and economic reasons why people immigrate to the United States (Olsen & Chen, 1988). Moreover, immigrants can be classified as legal, others as illegal, and still others as refugees. Similar to Hispanics, classification of Asian families has significant implications for their children's health and well-being, as well as the family's ability to maintain itself intact and to assimilate into American society. Therefore, the future of an immigrant child in the United States can be one of hope and opportunity or one clouded by the uncertainty of their political status.

Another important factor in the adjustment of immigrant children is the age of the child at the time of immigration. Younger children have more flexibility to adjust to new conditions. One would expect that preschool-age children would find it much easier to adjust to a new environment than adolescents. However, that adjustment can be further enhanced if the immigrant child or adolescent is coming from a similar educational system. Therefore, immigrant children coming from schooling systems that are comparable to the U.S. system usually do better than those coming from less-educated backgrounds. Furthermore, if the immigrant parents have the economic resources to help buffer this transition into a new society, then their transition can be somewhat easier. Unfortunately, most immigrants are not economically well established. In fact, the major driving force for immigration is economic opportunities. On the nightly news shows, fathers and mothers are often shown crossing the border with their children, frequently at great physical risk, seeking a better life.

The increased animosity to this immigration has also been captured by the news media, showing the border patrols chasing people, walls being built along the borders, and the politicians calling for soldiers to man the borders. In California, the recently passed Proposition 187, a state initiative to stop immigrants from accessing public school, social and health services, is symptomatic of the overall attitude of the American public toward immigration. The immigrant then becomes the classic scapegoat for societal ills. For children and adolescents seeking a sense of self, family, and community, this environment can create conflict, lack of self-worth, and loss of well-being.

## Health Measures of Immigrant Children

What do we know about the health of immigrant children? Since there is no single measure of overall health status, we must examine a variety of health measures. Moreover, since health problems can vary with age, it is also important to assess health throughout childhood. Therefore, this discussion will cover specific health issues relevant to the period of infancy, early childhood, school age, and adolescence. Although limited, the data provide an outline of some of the important health issues for immigrant children.

*Infancy*

The three primary measures of health during infancy are the prevalence of low-birth-weight infants (the percentage of infants weighing less than $5\frac{1}{2}$ pounds at birth), the percentage of preterm infants (those born before 37 weeks of gestation), and infant mortality (the number of infant deaths during the first year of life per 1,000 live births). Each of these parameters has been strongly correlated with poverty, low parental education, and lack of access to health-care services. However, these areas of health have been mostly positive for new immigrants. Indeed, they have been so good, that the term "the immigrant paradox" has been coined to describe how immigrants with high rates of poverty, low parental education, and lack of access to health care still have very low levels of these adverse infant outcomes.

The prevalence of low-birth-weight infants is a general measure of a population's overall health and its ability to have healthy babies. Because infants born with a lower-than-average birth weight are much more likely to have health and developmental problems, this measure has significant implications for children's health. One would expect that if immigrant mothers have poor nutritional and health status, along with a lack of prenatal care, then they should have a high prevalence of low-birth-weight infants. In the United States, 5.6% of non-Hispanic white infants have a low birth weight, compared to 12.9% for African American infants (Mendoza et al., 1991), whose mothers are generally poorer, less well educated, and frequently do not receive prenatal care.

Yet, for the past two decades immigrants have had a consistently low prevalence of low birth weight. Studies show that immigrant Hispanic mothers have a 5.5% prevalence of low birth weight overall (by subgroup: Mexican immigrants, 5.0%; Mainland Puerto Ricans, 8.7%; and Cuban immigrants, 5.7%) (Mendoza et al., 1991). As noted earlier, immigrant legal status greatly affects access to health care. Mexican immigrants, who have some of the poorest social indicators, would be expected to have the worst outcome, but they do not. In fact, even with late or no prenatal care, their rate of low birth weight is 7.2%, compared to 9.5% for non-Hispanic whites in the same situation (Mendoza et al., 1991). This may be attributable to some protective aspect of Mexican culture or behavior, since U.S.-born Mexican American women tend to have higher rates of low-birth-weight babies.

This phenomenon is also seen in other immigrant groups as well. Singh and Yu (1996) report lower low-birth-weight prevalences for African, Mexican, Cuban, and Chinese immigrants than their U.S.-born ethnic counterparts. Alexander et al. (1996) found that foreign-born and U.S.-born Japanese mothers also have lower prevalence of low-birth-weight infants. Cobas et al. (1996) suggested that acculturation to American society increases the risk of low birth weight due to the likelihood that the mother smokes and eats a less traditional diet. However, this study also suggests that other factors in the acculturation process may have direct effects. For example, cultural behaviors associated with pregnancy may be protective factors. This phenomenon has been noted in Quebec, Canada, among immigrant mothers (Hyamn & Dussault, 1996). Unfortunately, this immigrant protective factor seems to decrease over time. Guendelman and English (1995) found that in a group of 1,114 immigrant Mexican women, those who had been in the United States for more than five years had highter rates of low-birth-weight infants

Obstetrical problems often result in a preterm birth. Since many immigrant women, particularly Hispanics, do not have access to prenatal care, they are at increased risk for preterm infants, who, like low-birth-weight infants, are likely to have medical and developmental problems. Although immigrant women may have a lower risk for low-birth-weight infants, their risk for preterm infants may be slightly higher if they do not have access to prenatal care.

Infant mortality, which refers to the death of an infant during the first year of life, is another measure of a population's health. Infant mortality can be broken down into two categories: neonatal (death during the first 28 days of life) and postneonatal (death during day 28 to 365 days). The neonatal mortality is usually due to major congenital anomalies, prematurity, or respiratory problems. Deaths after 28 days can be from any cause, but are most frequently from infectious diseases, trauma, or problems from the neonatal period. Although mortality rates can also be classified by the birth weight, the overall infant mortality rate provides an overview of the health status of infants. Again, as with low birth weight, infant mortality is better than expected for infants born to immigrant mothers compared to U.S.-born mothers of the same ethnic group (Becerra et al., 1991). Infant mortality rates for non-Hispanic white and African American infants are 8.3 and 17.2 per 1,000 live births, respectively. Overall, for Hispanics, it is 8.7 per 1,000 live births, though there is variability among the Hispanic subgroups: Mexican American, 8.3 per 1,000; Mainland Puerto Rican, 11.6 per 1,000; and Cuban American, 7.0 per 1,000. Mexican-born mothers have a lower rate for infant mortality (7.6 per 1,000), compared to U.S.-born Mexican American

mothers, whose infants have a rate of 9.0 per 1,000. In fact, this phenomenon is seen in all infants of foreign-born mothers (Becerra et al., 1991).
Weeks and Rumbaut (1991) evaluated infant mortality data of Indochinese
refugees from Vietnam, Laos, and Cambodia, as well as Hispanics, non-Hispanic whites, and African Americans, and found a much lower than expected
infant mortality among the Indochinese refugees and Hispanics.

Unfortunately, the protective factors of immigrant children are not
always long-lasting. Guendelman, English, and Chavez (1995) examined a
cross-sectional sample of 708 infants of Mexican immigrant mothers between
the ages of 6 to 18 months, and found 25% to have had a serious infection
since birth. This worsening health status of Hispanic immigrant children is
partly the result of lack of health-care access, and it is likely to get worse
because of legislative changes in health-care access for immigrants. Prior to
this legislation, approximately one-third of Mexican Americans did not have
health insurance (Mendoza, 1994). This was probably higher among immigrant children. In 1990, the Children and Youth Policy Project documented
that only 34.6% of U.S.-Hispanic children were completely immunized by
age two, compared to 47.2% for non-Hispanic white children. Although
African American children had an even lower immunization rate of 20%,
immigrant children had the lowest rate at 11.8%. Furthermore, among those
Hispanic children eligible for WIC (Women, Infants, and Children Program:
a U.S. nutritional program), many of whom are immigrants, only 49% had
received the benefits of this program (Mendoza, 1994).

In summary, immigrant infants seem to have factors that positively
affect their prevalence of low birthweight and infant mortality. However,
because of their immigrant status and their frequent lower socioeconomic
status that limit access to health care, some of these children may be at risk
for infectious diseases. Furthermore, if the parents become acculturated, they
are at an increased risk for poor health outcomes.

*Preschool Children*

During the preschool years children grow and develop rapidly. Children begin to interact with other children, and some enter preschool for their first
contact with institutions outside of their homes. Key health measures during
this time are measures of anthropometry (measures of physical growth), developmental attainment, prevalences of chronic illness, and rates of infectious
diseases. Unfortunately, the information on immigrant children of color is
somewhat sparse in this area, but we can extrapolate from the Mexican American experience, as it is one of the populations with the largest proportion of
immigrants.

Physical growth is a good proxy measure of overall health. Children who maintain an appropriate growth rate, particularly in height, are generally healthy and well nourished. In contrast, children who fail to maintain their physical growth, that is, that fall off their growth curve and are stunted, are highly likely to have either poor nutrition, a chronic illness, or recurrent illnesses. Although genetic potential can have an impact on the height of an individual child, a population of children usually has enough variability that one population can be compared to another if socioeconomic status is taken into account (Martorell, Mendoza & Castillo, 1988). Martorell, Mendoza, and Castillo examined the stature of Mexican American and Puerto Rican children assessed in the Hispanic Health and Nutrition Examination Survey (HHANES), 1982–1984. Although not evaluated by immigrant status, Mexican American preschooler stature was only slightly shorter than the U.S. norm, and their shorter stature was accounted for by the children's socioeconomic status (Martorell, Mendoza & Castillo, 1989). Puerto Rican preschoolers were of similar height to the U.S. norm (Martorell et al., 1994). When Mexican American children were compared with children in Mexico City, Mexican American children were taller, suggesting that changes in the health and nutritional environments had improved the growth of these children. A similar pattern of improvement has been seen among Asian refugee children under five years of age in the United States, reaffirming that the short stature usually seen in young immigrant children is usually due to nutritional and health problems rather than genetic potential (Yip et al., 1992).

The HHANES suggests that Mexican American preschool children have high dietary intakes of fats and sugars, and low intakes of fruits and vegetables (Murphy et al., 1990). However, the prevalence of iron-deficiency anemia was low at only 0.5%. At present, the U.S. average is less than 2%. Nonetheless, borderline dietary intake is a problem in rural populations of Mexican American children. In a California survey one in eight children in the Central Valley were experiencing hunger (True, 1992). From the anthropometric information, however, it appears that if given the appropriate nutrition, immigrant children can grow normally. Unfortunately, issues of poverty and lack of access to state and federal nutritional programs may limit improvement. Moreover, with the new legislation limiting programs to immigrant children, we may see even fewer gains in growth for immigrant children.

Developmental issues are difficult to assess for any population and even more so for immigrant populations because of the limited information about these populations. From the HHANES, parental reports showed that 0.2% of Mexican American and Puerto Rican children aged 6 months to 4 years were reported to have mental retardation (Mendoza, 1994). The severity of the mental retardation was not reported. Among U.S. children, 3% have some degree of mental retardation and 0.15% have severe mental retardation. Other findings of the HHANES were that 2.3% of Mexican American and 1.3% of Puerto Rican children had speech problems. The problem with the HHANES data is that the developmental problems were determined by parental report, and therefore are likely to underestimate the prevalence of these problems. At present, therefore, we have limited information to determine whether immigrant preschool children have more developmental problems than nonimmigrant children.

Chronic disease among preschool immigrant children does not appear to be higher than among nonimmigrant children. Again, because of the limited data in this area, we must rely on the HHANES and the analysis of the Mexican American and Puerto Rican samples. These data showed that for preschool children, only 2.3% of Mexican Americans and 7.4% of Mainland Puerto Ricans had a chronic illness. The Mexican American sample was clearly at or below what is usually seen as the national rate of 3% to 5%. However, the Puerto Rican sample was higher because of a higher rate of asthma. In fact, 62% of all Mainland Puerto Rican children with a chronic illness have asthma (Mendoza, Takata & Martorell, 1994). A similar high rate of asthma is also seen on the island of Puerto Rico. If one were to eliminate the asthma cases, then Mainland Puerto Rican children would have a similar rate of chronic medical conditions as Mexican Americans. Nevertheless, caution must be taken about making any assumptions about the prevalence of chronic illness among immigrants, since these data do not specifically identify immigrants among these Hispanic groups and also do not include other immigrants of color.

Unlike chronic illness, infectious diseases do seem to be higher among immigrants, and some, such as tuberculosis, parasitic infections, and HIV, can be life threatening. Tuberculosis has become a greater problem among immigrants. This infection has been spread because of the poor housing of immigrants and, in some cases, their reluctance to seek medical care because of immigration issues. This has also limited immigrant children's rate of immunization, as noted earlier. In cities like Los Angeles, this had resulted in outbreaks of measles among unimmunized children. In 1988 the risk of measles among Latino children was more than 12 times that of non-Hispanic white children (Sumaya, 1992). AIDS has been a major problem among both Puerto Rican and Mainland Puerto Rican children (Zorrilla, et al., 1994). Preschool children usually acquire AIDS perinatally, but with lack of access to care, identification may not occur until the preschool years. As only limited health care is available to immigrant children, infectious diseases may again become the epidemics they once were.

As mentioned previously, healthcare access for immigrant children is dependent on the child's as well as the parents' residential status. Clearly those that are not legal citizens will have difficulty getting health care unless their parents have the financial resources or health insurance to pay for health care. However, even those who are born in the United States and thereby should be entitled to public health care, may not receive the care to which they are entitled as citizens. In a study by Halfon et al. (1997) of 817 inner-city Latino children, 12 to 36 months old, of whom 96% were born in the United States, it was found that almost 40% had either episodic or no health care coverage. Thus, even when health care is available, accessibility may be inhibited by factors related to parents' immigration status. The authors of this article suggest that this may worsen with the current anti-immigrant sentiment in the country.

### School-Age Children

Health issues of school-age children are continuous with those identified in the preschool period. These include issues of growth, development, and chronic and infectious diseases. Health information on immigrant school-age children is limited. For Hispanic immigrants, as defined by the Mexican American sample in the HHANES, poverty is a major factor affecting children's growth, primarily their stature. To get somewhat closer to the question of whether immigrants have different growth patterns than nonimmigrants, language preference was used in regression analyses as a proxy for acculturation. It was found that language did not affect growth, and that among school-age children poverty was still the major determinant (Martorell, Mendoza & Castillo, 1989). Therefore, as before, the growth of immigrant children, both preschool and school-age, seems to be primarily determined by socioeconomic status. Given a good dietary environment, some studies suggest that catch-up growth is possible in this age group. It is during the school years though that among Mexican American children obesity becomes a problem (Kaplowitz, Martorell & Mendoza, 1989). Even among the poor, the prevalence of obesity is high. This suggests that with an increase in weight greater than height, Mexican American children have a body mass index greater than average, further implying obesity. Twenty percent of the population of children are over the ninetieth percentile for weight. If these trends continue over the years, these children will be at risk for diabetes and cardiovascular disease. To what degree obesity is a problem with newly arrived immigrants is not clearly known. One could postulate that immigrant families prior to improving their economic status consume cheaper and calorically dense foods, such as foods with a high fat content. Once they improve their economic status, they continue this type of diet, which may be calorically dense and nutrient poor. This increases weight over height. This hypothesis, however, remains unproven.

With respect to chronic illness and infectious diseases, school-age immigrant Hispanic children appear to be similar to preschoolers. Except for asthma, immigrant and nonimmigrant children have similar rates of chronic illness. When home language is used to assess those less acculturated and thereby more likely to be immigrant children, the rates of chronic illness for both English- and Spanish-speaking children are the same. This suggests that immigrant school-age children have rates of chronic illness similar to nonimmigrants. In contrast, they appear to have somewhat higher rates of infectious diseases, particularly among the newcomers. Recommendations have been made to assess immigrant children for tuberculosis and parasitic infections especially if they come from less-developed areas (Weissman, 1994). Similar recommendations have been made for immigrant children from other parts of the world where health care has been problematic. Once in the United States, all immigrant children need to be appropriately immunized to avoid outbreaks of childhood illnesses such as measles.

The developmental issues of school-age children of color will be addressed in other chapters. But, one should consider the mental health of school-age children as a separate issue from development, particularly since immigrant children may be reacting differently to their environment either because of past experiences or because of different cultural perspectives. Immigrant children from war-torn areas need to have their mental health needs met. Locke et al. (1996) examined 22 Central American mother-child pairs who had experienced political violence. Among children aged 5 to 13 years, 18 had a chronic illness, 13 showed mental health symptoms, and 2 had posttraumatic stress disorder. In the HHANES, school-age children wer asked to rate their health status, and the results showed that among Mex can American school-age children 11% rated their health to be either f or poor (Mendoza, 1994). Among Mainland Puerto Rican children the was 15%. This compares to 5% or less for most U.S. children. Both of proportions for Mexican American and Mainland Puerto Rican chi were significantly higher for Spanish-speaking children, 25% and 27 spectively. When the mothers of these children were asked to asse children's health, 17% of Mexican American mothers and 23% c land Puerto Rican mothers thought their children's health was eith poor. In contrast, among all school-age children in the HHANES

1% were determined to be in either fair or poor health by the survey physicians. This difference suggests that culture might have a significant impact on the perception of what "good" health is. Furthermore, immigrant children (i.e., Spanish-speaking children from the HHANES) appear to have significant concerns about their health even when physicians say they are in good health. It will be interesting to see if other immigrant children exhibit similar problems. This finding also speaks to the issues of developing an understanding of the cultural perspective of health in order to better address the health-care needs of immigrant children.

## Adolescents

In contrast to the younger age groups, Mexican American and Puerto Rican adolescents in the HHANES have significantly lower stature than the national mean (Martorell, 1994). Whether this is genetic, a result of persistent poverty, or a cohort effect has not been determined. Furthermore, since the adolescent growth spurt occurs early in adolescence, once this is past, catch-up growth is relatively minimal. Nonetheless, some growth does continue in the form of obesity. This starts in the school-age years and continues into adolescence. Although the HHANES data is cross-sectional, it suggests that obesity developing during the school years will continue into adolescence. To what degree this will hold true for other new immigrants still needs to be examined, but obesity clearly is becoming epidemic among all children.

Chronic illness rates among Hispanic adolescents from the HHANES was similar to school-age children, about 5%. When this rate is examined by the adolescent's language preference, for the Mexican American adolescents sampled, English-speaking adolescents have a somewhat higher rate f chronic medical conditions (5.2%), Spanish-speaking adolescents having lowest rate (1.8%) and bilingual adolescents being intermediate (3.7%). may imply that adolescents with chronic illnesses may be less likely to ate because of health conditions. Bilingual Mainland Puerto Rican its had the highest rate of chronic illness with 6.4% (Mendoza et Since there is limited data on other immigrant adolescents, these Hispanic adolescents can be viewed only as specific for Mexi- and Mainland Puerto Ricans. Whether these findings hold rant Hispanic adolescents such as those from Central to be determined.

on the health behaviors and rates of infectious diseases lescents is limited, we use studies on Mexican Ameri- ies for immigrant adolescents. A survey of sexual ws that they have fewer partners, but have sexual

153

intercourse more often than whites (Leyva, 1993). In a study by Reynoso, Felice, and Shragg (1993) immigrant Mexican pregnant teens were usually older than their U.S.-born counterparts, had less schooling, but were usually married to someone older and usually Mexican. It is important to understand the social context of the teen pregnancy, since it can be a different experience for immigrant teens.

Sexually active adolescents are also at risk for AIDS and STDs. Latino teens have a higher than expected rate for AIDS, particularly among Mainland Puerto Ricans. They also have higher rates of STDs than non-Hispanic whites. Although improving, the rates of STDs are still high among Hispanic adolescents. As with other infectious diseases, limited access to health care is one of the problems Hispanic immigrant adolescents need to overcome in order for these rates to improve. While adolescents are difficult to study and to involve in interventions, immigrant adolescents, particularly in the current political environment, may be very difficult to affect. However, because of their high risk they should receive high priority.

The other behaviors that have had significant health implications are those associated with violence and substance abuse. Examining the area of violence is particularly problematic because immigration status is usually not assessed in mortality data, and violence data is in itself difficult to obtain if not specifically addressed. Nonetheless, violence, particularly in the poor areas of inner cities, is quite prevalent. Recent data suggest that Latino male teens are three times more likely to die from a homicide than non-Hispanic white male teens (State of Hispanic Health, 1992). The data on immigrant drug use are sparse, but there is some suggestion that it is about the same as that of non-Hispanic white teens (Mendoza, 1994). Again, these data need further confirmation from other studies.

Last, as with school-age children, adolescents perceive their health to be worse than average. Mexican American and Mainland Puerto Rican adolescents reported their health to be fair or poor, 19% and 17%, respectively. Remarkably, among those adolescents sampled in the HHANES that were Mexican American and were Spanish-speaking, 33% reported that they had either fair or poor health. In stark contrast, survey physicians determined that only 1% of Mexican American adolescents were in fair or poor health. If health perception is a proxy measure of overall health or functional health, then it would seem that immigrant adolescents need significant attention given to their health concerns, at least to determine the cause of this high prevalence of perceived poor health. That one-third of Mexican American adolescents lack health insurance suggests that these two pieces of data may have some association.

## Conclusion

The first recommendation directed at improving the health of immigrant children and adolescents would be to develop a health data system that does not make these children invisible. For example, although the HHANES was the first ethnic-specific survey done on Hispanics, immigration status was not obtained. Although this is now a more politically problematic issue, in order to provide fair treatment of immigrant children we need to understand their health and social issues. Making policy and treatment decisions based on partial data and biases is neither just nor effective management of this issue. It will be important in the political discussions to keep in mind that immigrant children of color are not independent individuals and, therefore, should not be put at risk because of the immigration status of their parents.

Second, once in the United States children and adolescents should receive adequate health care. It is good public health policy and a just social policy. Moreover, as described earlier, many immigrant children, with preventive care and access to timely acute care, could maintain their health and would put only limited stress on the health-care system. It is imperative that we improve our understanding of the cultural aspects of health, including mental health, specifically as it applies to immigrant children of color. First, it could afford us a cost-effective way to maintain these children in good health if we could support and strengthen their already positive cultural factors. Furthermore, if we can better understand the immigrant children's perception of their health and illness as well as that of their family, then we would be closer to targeting the "real health problem" and make better use of our health-care system. Moreover, it would also make compliance with recommended "western" therapies more likely to occur.

Last, the demographics of our country indicate that diversity is the future, and immigrants of color as well as native children of color are a major part of that future. In order for this society to integrate each of these groups and make them productive individuals will take the collaborative efforts of various disciplines and groups: health, education, social sciences, government, and individual communities of color, themselves. It will take this type of concerted effort to address the health issues of the immigrant children of color.

## References

Alexander, G. R., Mor, J. M., Kogan, M. D., Leland, N. L. & Kieffer, E. (1996). Pregnancy outcome of U.S.-born and foreign-born Japanese-Americans. *American Journal of Public Health, 86,* 820–824.

Bezerra, J. E., Hogue, C. J., Atrash, H. K. & Perez, N. (1991). Infant mortality among Hispanics: A portrait of heterogeneity. *Journal of American Medical Association.*

Cobas, J. A., et al. (1996). Acculturation and low-birth-weight infants among Latino women: A reanalysis of HHANES data with structural equation models. *American Journal of Public Health, 86*, 394–396.

Current Population Survey (1994). *Current Population Reports,* Series P20–486.

Guendelman, S. & English, P. B. (1995). Effect of United States residence on birth outcomes among Mexican immigrants: An exploratory study. *American Journal of Epidemiology, 142*, 830–838.

Guendelman, S., English, P. & Chavez, G. (1995). Infants of Mexican immigrants: Health status of an emerging population. *Medical Care, 33*, 41–52.

Halfon, N., et al. (1997). Medicaid enrollment and health services access by Latino children. *Journal of the American Medical Association, 277*, 636–641.

Hyamn, I. & Dussault, G. (1996). The effect of acculturation on low birthweight immigrant women. *Canadian Journal of Public Health, 87*, 58–62.

Kaplowitz, H., Martorell, R. & Mendoza, F. (1989). Fatness and fat distribution in Mexican-American children and youths from the Hispanic Health and Nutrition Examination Survey. *American Journal of Human Biology, 1*, 631–648.

Lewit, E. M. & Baker, L. G. (1994). Race and ethnicity-changes for children. *Future of Children: Critical Health Issues for Children and Youth, 4* (3), 134–144.

Leyva, M. (1993). *Adolescents and HIV/STD: National Council of La Raza, Center for Health Promotion fact sheet.* Washington, DC: National Council of La Raza.

Locke, C., et al. (1996). The psychological and medical sequelae of war in Central American refugee mothers and children. *Archives of Pediatrics and Adolescent Medicine, 150*, 822–828.

Martorell, R., Mendoza, F. & Castillo, R. (1988). Poverty and stature in children. In J. C. Waterlow (Ed.), *Linear growth retardation in less developed countries. Nutrition workshop series, Vol. 14* (pp. 57–73). New York: Raven Press.

Martorell, R., Mendoza, F. & Castillo, R. (1989). Genetic and environmental determinants of growth in Mexican Americans. *Pediatrics, 84*, 864–871.

Martorell, R., et al. (1994). Physical growth, sexual maturation, and obesity in Puerto Rican children. In G. Lamberty and C. García Coll (Eds.), *Puerto Rican women and children: Issues in health, growth, and development* (pp. 119–135). New York: Plenum.

Mendoza, F. (1994). The health of Latino children in the United States. *Future of Children: Critical Health Issues for Children and Youth, 4*, 43–72.

Mendoza, F., et al. (1991). Selected measures of health status for Mexican American, Mainland Puerto Rican, and Cuban American children. *Journal of the American Medical Association, 265*, 227–232.

Mendoza, F., Takata, G. & Martorell, R. (1994). Health status and health care assessment for Mainland Puerto Rican children: Results from the Hispanic Health and Nutrition Examination Survey. In G. Lamberty and C. García Coll (Eds.), *Puerto Rican women and children: Issues in health, growth, and development* (pp. 211–227). New York: Plenum.

Murphy, S., et al. (1990). An evaluation of four food group intakes by Mexican American children. *Journal of the American Dietetic Association, 90*, 388–393.

Olsen, L. & Chen, M. T. (1988). Immigrant students and the California public schools: Crossing the schoolhouse border. *California Tomorrow Policy Research Report,* 12–30.

Olvera-Ezzell, N., Power, T. G., Cousins, J. H., Guerra, A. M. & Trujillo, M. (1994). The development of health knowledge in low-income Mexican-American children. *Child Development, 65*, 416–427.

Reynoso, T., Felice, M. & Shragg, G. (1993). Does American acculturation affect outcomes of Mexican American teenage pregnancy? *Journal of Adolescent Health, 14*, 257–261.

Singh, G. K. & Yu, S. M. (1996). Adverse pregnancy outcomes: Differences between

U.S. and foreign-born women in major U.S. racial and ethnic groups. *American Journal of Public Health, 86,* 837–843.

State of Hispanic Health (1992). Washington, DC: National Coalition of Hispanic Health and Human Services Organization.

Sumaya, C. (1992). Major infectious diseases causing excess morbidity in the Hispanic population. In A. Furino (Ed.), *Health policy and the Hispanic* (pp. 76–96). Boulder, CO: Westview.

True, L. (1992). Hunger in the balance: The impact of proposed AFDC cuts on childhood hunger in California. California Rural Legal Assistance Foundation, March 1992.

Weeks, J. & Rumbaut, R. (1991). Infant mortality among ethnic immigrant groups. *Social Science Medicine, 33,* 327–334.

Weissman, A. (1994). Preventive health care and screening of Latin American immigrants in the United States. *Journal of the American Board of Family Practice, 7,* 310–323.

Yip, R., et al. (1992). Improving growth status of Asian refugee children in the United States. *Journal of the American Medical Association, 267,* 937–940.

Zorrilla, C., Diaz, C., Romaguera, J. & Martin, M. (1994). Acquired immune deficiency syndrome (AIDS) in women and children in Puerto Rico. In G. Lamberty & C. García Coll (Eds.), *Puerto Rican women and children: Issues in health, growth, and development* (pp. 55–70). New York: Plenum.

# 8 CHILDREN OF IMMIGRANTS

## IS AMERICANIZATION HAZARDOUS TO INFANT HEALTH?

*Rubén G. Rumbaut*
*John R. Weeks*

The United States, that "permanently unfinished" society, has again become a nation of immigrants. The approximately 20 million foreign-born persons counted in the 1990 United States census formed the largest immigrant population in the world—indeed, in world history. Over two-thirds of that total had arrived only in the previous two decades, mostly from Asia and Latin America, especially Mexico, and fully one-third of that total was concentrated in one state, California, where today nearly a quarter of its huge population is foreign-born. Today's new immigration, which rivals the historic European flows of the pre–World War I era, is extraordinary in its diversity of color and class and national origins. In terms of color, most new immigrants self-reported as nonwhite in the 1990 census. The proportion of white immigrants declined from 88% of those who arrived before 1960 to 38% of those coming in the 1980s. This racial-ethnic makeup will change in still more complex ways due to rapidly increasing rates of ethnic intermarriage. In terms of class, today's immigrants include by far the most educated groups (Asian Indians, Taiwanese) and the least educated groups (Mexicans, Salvadorans) in American society, as well as the groups with the lowest poverty rates in the United States (Filipinos) and with the highest (Laotians and Cambodians)—a reflection of polar-opposite types of migrations. They also differ greatly in their English language skills, age/sex structures, patterns of fertility, and forms of family organization. These trends have accelerated further during the 1990s as a result of increasing legal and illegal immigration as well as refugee admissions, ushering in a decade of racial-ethnic diversification and stratification unprecedented in U.S. history—along with accompanying alarms about their adaptation to American society (Portes & Rumbaut, 1996; Rumbaut, 1994).

The folk wisdom on the adaptation of immigrants has conceived of their acculturation and assimilation—or Americanization—as a more or less linear process of progressive improvement and adjustment to American life. The general assumption here is guided by an implicit and ethnocentric deficit model: to get ahead immigrants need to learn how to "become American," to overcome their deficits with respect to the new language and culture, the new health care and educational system, the new economy and society. As they shed the old and acquire the new over time, they surmount those obstacles and make their way more successfully—a process of acculturation more or less completed by the second or third generation. Since today's immigration is largely composed of newcomers from developing nations in Asia and Latin America, concerns have been expressed about the speed and degree to which they can become assimilated—and hence about the social costs of the new immigrants—before they begin to produce net benefits to the new society. Recent research findings, however, especially in the area of immigrant health, raise significant questions about such ethnocentric assumptions. In fact, the findings often run precisely in the opposite direction of what might be expected from traditional perspectives on acculturation and assimilation. A few of those findings on the effects of Americanization, broadly conceived, on maternal risk factors and infant health outcomes are worth highlighting.

## IS AMERICANIZATION HAZARDOUS TO INFANT HEALTH?

The research literature has pointed to an infant health paradox among new immigrants to the United States. High-risk groups, particularly low-income immigrants from Mexico and Southeast Asia, show unexpectedly favorable perinatal outcomes and seem to be "superior health achievers" (cf. Caldwell, 1986). When these findings came to light, particularly with reference to Hispanics, there was a tendency to dismiss them as being a result of migration selectivity or incomplete data. After all, lower socioeconomic status immigrants, such as refugees from Vietnam, Cambodia, and Laos, and undocumented migrants from Mexico, El Salvador, and Guatemala, generally combine high fertility rates with high poverty rates, and face formidable barriers in accessing health-care and prenatal-care services (Rumbaut 1995; Rumbaut et al., 1988). Conventional wisdom would dictate that these least Americanized groups of disadvantaged newcomers may be expected to constitute a high-risk population exhibiting worse than average health outcomes. Nonetheless, it has become clear that the enigmatic results cannot be explained away by special circumstances or bad data. For example, Williams and his colleagues (1986) analyzed data for California for 1981 from the state's matched birth-death cohort file for four groups: non-Hispanic whites, blacks, U.S.-born Hispanics (mostly of Mexican descent), and Mexican immigrants. In terms of maternal risk factors, the Mexican-born women had less education, more children, shorter birth spacing, and a later start to prenatal care than any of the other three groups. Yet, in terms of perinatal outcomes, the Mexican-born women had the lowest percentage of low-birth-weight babies, the lowest post-neonatal infant mortality rates, and neonatal and total infant mortality rates that just matched the lower-risk white mothers. African Americans had the highest rates in these categories, followed by U.S.-born Hispanics and whites. The authors could not explain why the Mexican immigrants, despite their adverse socioeconomic circumstances and higher risk factors, produced such positive outcomes, but they speculated that it could be "the result of better nutrition, lower rates of smoking and alcohol consumption, or a higher regard for parental roles . . . [or that] migration has selected out healthier individuals among newly arrived Latinos" (Williams et al., 1986, p. 390).

We reported similar evidence in a study of linked live birth and infant death records in San Diego County for the period 1978–1985, covering some 270,000 live births (Rumbaut and Weeks, 1989). As sketched in more detail in Table 8–1, the data showed that the infant mortality rate was lowest for Southeast Asians (6.6 per 1,000), followed by other Asians (7.0), Hispanics (7.3), non-Hispanic whites (8.0), and African Americans (16.3). In fact, among the Southeast Asians, the lowest infant death rates in the county were found for the Vietnamese (5.5) and the Cambodians (5.8). These highly positive outcomes were all the more remarkable because the Indochinese refugee groups (including the Vietnamese) had significantly higher rates of poverty, unemployment, welfare dependency, fertility, prior infant mortality (before arrival in the United States), and late use of prenatal care services than any other racial-ethnic groups in the San Diego area, and because a high proportion of refugee mothers came from rural backgrounds with little or no prior education or literacy, proficiency in English, or readily transferable occupational skills.

It turns out that these findings were not unique to the San Diego metropolitan area, but were reflected statewide. In 1985 the state of California began publishing data on live births and infant deaths for more detailed ethnic groupings, including Vietnamese and Cambodians, using mother's place of birth as the principal criterion for ethnic identification. We compiled these statewide data and confirmed that during the late 1980s the Cambodians and Vietnamese had infant mortality rates of 5.2 and 7.5, compared to 7.7 for Mexican-born women and 8.5 for non-Hispanic whites (Weeks and Rumbaut, 1991). These differences were statistically significant. But just what was it that explained these differences could not be determined on the basis of the available vital statistics.

TABLE 8-1. Infant Mortality Rates and Selected Risk Factors of Pregnancy by Ethnic Groups in San Diego County, 1978–1985. (N live births = 269,252; N [linked] infant deaths = 2,281).

| Ethnic Group | Total Live Births (N)* | Infant Mortality | | | | Risk Factors | | |
|---|---|---|---|---|---|---|---|---|
| | | Infant Mortality Rate | Early Neonatal Death Rate | Post-Early Neonatal Deaths | % Late or No Prenatal Care | % Teenaged Mothers | % Unmarried Mothers |
| *Asian* | | | | | | | | |
| All Indochinese | 4,841 | 6.6 | 3.5 | 3.1 | 13.4 | 8.5 | 14.2 |
| Vietnamese | 2,187 | 5.5 | 3.7 | 1.8 | 9.9 | 5.1 | 14.4 |
| Cambodian | 687 | 5.8 | 4.4 | 1.5 | 15.2 | 5.2 | 20.2 |
| Lao | 977 | 7.2 | 3.1 | 4.1 | 13.1 | 10.5 | 12.5 |
| Hmong | 990 | 9.1 | 3.0 | 6.1 | 20.3 | 16.5 | 11.4 |
| Japanese | 2,253 | 6.2 | 3.1 | 3.1 | 2.4 | 8.7 | 11.5 |
| Chinese | 1,455 | 6.9 | 4.1 | 2.8 | 3.0 | 2.6 | 7.1 |
| Filipino | 12,445 | 7.2 | 4.2 | 3.0 | 3.4 | 5.6 | 7.9 |
| Hispanic | 71,641 | 7.3 | 4.1 | 3.2 | 6.6 | 15.4 | 23.5 |
| White (non-Hispanic) | 143,779 | 8.0 | 4.5 | 3.5 | 2.6 | 8.9 | 11.1 |
| Black (non-Hispanic) | 22,090 | 16.3 | 8.9 | 7.4 | 4.6 | 19.0 | 45.8 |
| Total | 269,252 | 8.5 | 4.7 | 3.7 | 4.2 | 11.6 | 18.0 |

\*$N$ = number of live births in San Diego County during 1978–85, on which the infant mortality rates are based.

Infant Mortality Rate = number of (linked) deaths of infants under 1 year old, per 1,000 live births.

Early Neonatal Mortality Rate = number of deaths of infants under 7 days old, per 1,000 live births.

Post-Early Neonatal Mortality Rate = number of deaths of infants 7–365 days old, per 1,000 live births.

Late Prenatal Care = cases where prenatal care was begun in the third trimester (7th to 9th month), or not at all.

Teenaged mothers = cases where mother was 19 years old or younger at the time of the baby's birth.

Unmarried mothers = cases where mother was single, separated, divorced, widowed, or unknown marital status.

In the public domain and adapted from: R. G. Rumbaut & J. R. Weeks (1989). Infant health among Indochinese refugees: Patterns of infant mortality, birthweight and prenatal care in comparative perspective. *Research in the Sociology of Health Care, 8*, 137–196.

Another study found that Chinese Americans had lower fetal, neo-natal, and postneonatal mortality rates than whites and other major ethnic-racial groups, and the superior health profile of Chinese infants was observed at every level of maternal education and for all maternal ages (Yu, 1982). Again, the available vital statistics lacked data with which to measure possible explanatory factors. Indeed, vital records and other related data sets are often incomplete—national-level data in particular typically lack information on nativity or immigration status—and where available the data are often aggregated into Procrustean, one-size-fits-all racial or panethnic categories that conceal the wide diversity among Asian, black, Hispanic, and white subgroups. Still, in a recent review of the literature, Eberstein (1991) cites research indicating that among blacks and Hispanics nationally, pregnancy outcomes (birth weight, infant mortality) are better for babies born to immigrants than to mothers born in the United States. Among Hispanics, an analysis of the 1983 and 1984 national data sets confirmed that infant mortality and low-birth-weight rates were lower for babies born to foreign-born versus U.S.-born Mexican and Cuban mothers, and for island-born versus mainland-born Puerto Rican mothers, again despite a lack of correspondence between the socioeconomic profiles of these Hispanic groups and their health outcomes (Bezerra et al., 1991).

In Illinois, similarly, Collins and Shay (1994) discovered that foreign-born Mexican and Central American mothers residing in very-low-income census tracts had much better pregnancy outcomes than either Puerto Rican or other U.S.-born Hispanics. In Massachusetts, a study of low-income black women served by Boston City Hospital found significant differences in health behaviors and birth outcomes between natives and immigrants—the latter mostly from Haiti, Jamaica, and other Caribbean and African countries (Cabral et al., 1990). Compared to the U.S.-born, the foreign-born women had better pre-pregnancy nutrition; were far less likely to use cigarettes, marijuana, alcohol, cocaine, or opiates during pregnancy; and gave birth to babies that were larger in head circumference and significantly less likely to be of low birth weight or premature—health advantages that remained even after controlling for many of the factors suspected to influence fetal growth.

Using data from the 1982–1984 Hispanic Health and Nutrition Examination Survey (HHANES), with a very large regional sample, Guendelman et al. (1990) found that low-birth-weight (LBW) rates were significantly higher for (more acculturated) second-generation U.S.-born women of Mexican descent compared with (less acculturated) first-generation Mexico-born women, despite the fact that the latter had lower socioeconomic status, a higher percentage of mothers over 35 years of age, and less adequate prenatal care. The risk of LBW was about four times higher for second- than first-generation primiparous women, and double for second- than first-generation multiparous women. Other studies based on the HHANES have also observed this association between greater acculturation and low birth weight (Scribner & Dwyer, 1989).

More recently, Guendelman and Abrams (1995) found that first-generation Mexican women, despite their socioeconomic disadvantages, had a lower risk of eating a poor diet than second-generation Mexican American women, whose nutrient intake resembled that of non-Hispanic white native women. For the immigrants, food choices actually deteriorated as income increased and as the degree of acculturation increased (as indicated in this study by generational status). The investigators speculated that such generational differences in nutrition may help explain the differences in low birth weight reported in the studies noted earlier—that is, that the Americanization of their diet may in turn be associated with a deterioration of the health of their babies. However, because HHANES did not follow women through their pregnancies, they were unable to test the hypothesis directly.

Findings from the HHANES, however, have shown a link between increasing acculturation and health-risk behaviors (Marks, Garcia & Solig, 1990) and drug use (Amaro et al., 1990; see also Vega et al., 1993a, 1993b). Adverse effects of acculturation have also been reported among Mexican Americans with respect to alcohol consumption patterns (Gilbert, 1989) and psychological distress (Kaplan & Marks, 1990). Indeed, intriguing questions have been raised by recent research on the mental health of ethnic minorities in the United States, including immigrants and refugees. A recently completed review of prevalence rates reported in the most important research studies conducted over the past two decades suggests that rapid acculturation does not necessarily lead to conventionally anticipated outcomes (Vega & Rumbaut, 1991).

Instead, these studies suggest that Americanization can itself be a traumatic process rather than a simple solution to the traumas of immigration. For example, results from the HHANES (Moscicki et al., 1989) indicate low symptom levels for Mexican Americans in the southwestern United States, and still lower rates of depressive symptoms and major depression for Cubans in Miami compared to all other Hispanic groups. The Los Angeles ECA study (one of five Epidemiological Catchment Area projects—the most comprehensive field surveys of their kind in the United States) also reported lower rates of major depression for Mexican Americans than for non-Hispanic whites. Significantly, among Mexican Americans, immigrants had lower rates of lifetime major depression than did U.S.-born persons of Mexican descent, and among Mexican immigrants, the higher the level of acculturation, the higher was the prevalence of various types of psychiatric disorders. Furthermore, U.S.-born Mexican Americans and non-Hispanic whites were much more likely than immigrants to be drug abusers (Burnam et al., 1987; *see also* Vega & Amaro, 1994).

## DATA, METHODS, AND STUDY POPULATION

In an attempt to sort out the reasons for the paradox of sociodemographically high-risk groups having better than average perinatal health outcomes, we examined an in-depth data set drawn from the Comprehensive Perinatal Program (CPP) of the University of California, San Diego (UCSD) Medical Center. From 1980 until 1991, when the program was suddenly phased out, the CPP provided a program of prenatal assessment, education, and health care to low-income women in San Diego County. Most of the pregnant women receiving CPP prenatal services and delivering their babies at the UCSD Medical Center were immigrants from Mexico, as well as Vietnam, Laos, and Cambodia. The CPP data set consists of nearly 500 variables per case (including most of the variables listed in the research literature as likely determinants of pregnancy outcomes) for a large sample of both foreign-born and U.S.-born women. In the search for explanations of racial-ethnic and nativity differences in pregnancy outcomes, the study thus permitted a detailed multivariate analysis of biomedical and sociocultural maternal risk factors in their association with the immediate outcome of the pregnancy. Biomedical factors include health history, pregravid weight and weight gain during pregnancy, the age of the woman and her reproductive history (including previous pregnancies and the outcome of those pregnancies). Sociocultural variables include such things as smoking, drug and alcohol abuse, nutritional intake, social support, severe psychosocial stressors, religion, ethnicity and nativity, English-language proficiency, educational attainment, employment, and the financial and other resources available to the woman during her pregnancy.

Our research did not involve the actual collection of new data, but rather the abstracting, coding (in consultation with a staff physician), and computer entry of data extant in CPP files. The CPP data consisted of discrete medical, nutritional, and psychosocial assessments and reassessments, including complete histories, physical exams, and laboratory tests, done by a professional staff of physicians, nurse practitioners, licensed nutritionists, and social workers, as well as extensive demographic information collected at the preliminary screening of patients. For non-English-speaking mothers, all interviews were conducted with the help of trained bilingual/bicultural interpreters. The CPP data set in effect already controls for the fact that participating mothers all lived in the same urban area and shared a common situation of economic disadvantage (to be eligible they had to meet low-income criteria), as well as the same type of prenatal-care services and hospital setting of delivery. Thus, differences among groups of women cannot be assumed to be due to differences in access to or the quality of the medical environment; in effect, our study controls for tertiary risk factors.

Finally, we also collected maternal data on all deliveries at the UCSD Medical Center, including medical diagnoses and information on complications of pregnancy, labor, and delivery. And from separate hospital records, an infant outcome form was developed for each baby delivered at the medical center, providing a variety of outcome measures (or dependent variables), including birth weight, gestational age, head circumference, Coombs index (a measure of hemolytic disease), APGAR scores, diagnoses at birth, complications, and the length of hospitalization of the baby. All of these infant outcome variables were coded and entered into computer files, and then matched with the mothers' data file to produce a final data set for analysis and hypothesis testing.

Data were collected for a total of 2,320 pregnancies occurring to women seen at CPP during fiscal years 1989 to 1991. Among these were 1,464 records for babies delivered at the UCSD Medical Center, for which we also were able to match hospital outcome data. We will focus here on this latter group of 1,464 pregnancies, for which the greatest amount of information is available. Of the 1,464 women included in our data set, 253 (almost 20%) were born in the United States, and the remaining 1,211 (80%) were born outside the United States, predominantly in Mexico or Asia, reflecting patterns of contemporary immigration and concentration in California. More specifically, of the 1,101 foreign-born Hispanic women, 1,070 were born in Mexico and the rest in Central America. Of the 74 foreign-born Asian women, 50 were Indochinese refugees born in Vietnam, Laos, or Cambodia, and nearly all of the rest were born in the Philippines, Korea, Taiwan, or China. As expected, most non-Hispanic white and black women were U.S.-born. The foreign-born whites came mainly from Europe, Canada, and the Middle East; foreign-born blacks were mainly from sub-Saharan Africa. The women ranged in age from 13 to 42; their average age was 25.

## FINDINGS

With so many independent variables and dependent variables available for analysis, it is of course impossible to review here all of the details yielded so far by our still ongoing and expanding study (but see Rumbaut and Weeks, 1996, for a more detailed exposition). However, given our focus in this chap-

TABLE 8–2. Maternal Risk Factors: Socioeconomic Status, Marital Status, and Social Support, by Race-Ethnicity and Nativity of Low-Income Women Receiving CPP Prenatal Care Services. All Women were U.S.-born Immigrants. (San Diego Comprehensive Perinatal Program 1989–1991 Sample, $N = 1,464$.)

| Maternal Characteristics | Nativity | Hispanic (1,150) | Asian (79) | White (201) | Black (34) | p¹ | Total (1,464) | p² |
|---|---|---|---|---|---|---|---|---|
| *Socioeconomic Status* | | | | | | | | |
| % high school graduate | U.S.-born | 63.8 | 80.0 | 81.3 | 75.0 | ** | 77.2 | ** |
| | immigrant | 27.0 | 34.7 | 86.2 | 33.3 | | 29.0 | |
| % English is primary language | U.S.-born | 36.7 | 100.0 | 95.9 | 96.4 | ** | 84.1 | ** |
| | immigrant | 0.8 | 8.1 | 63.3 | 66.7 | | 3.1 | |
| % in the labor force (pregnant) | U.S.-born | 26.5 | 40.0 | 47.6 | 35.8 | ** | 42.0 | ** |
| | immigrant | 25.3 | 16.7 | 25.0 | 16.7 | | 24.7 | |
| monthly income per person ($) | U.S.-born | 279 | 187 | 316 | 189 | ** | 293 | ** |
| | immigrant | 194 | 236 | 252 | 195 | | 198 | |
| *Marital Status and Social Support* | | | | | | | | |
| % married | U.S.-born | 55.1 | 60.0 | 56.1 | 42.9 | * | 54.5 | * |
| | immigrant | 59.9 | 73.0 | 60.0 | 83.3 | | 60.8 | |
| % size of family-household is 4+ | U.S.-born | 34.7 | 20.0 | 43.9 | 32.1 | | 40.3 | |
| | immigrant | 48.4 | 58.1 | 40.0 | 50.0 | | 48.8 | |
| % stressful relationship with father of the baby | U.S.-born | 29.8 | 0.0 | 22.3 | 37.0 | * | 24.9 | ** |
| | immigrant | 15.6 | 11.1 | 13.8 | 0.0 | | 15.2 | |
| % stressful relationship with family and parents | U.S.-born | 25.5 | 20.0 | 31.3 | 17.9 | ** | 28.5 | ** |
| | immigrant | 6.2 | 8.3 | 6.9 | 0.0 | | 6.3 | |

[1] Statistical significance of difference between racial/ethnic groups: ** $p < 0.0001$; * $p < 0.05$.
[2] Statistical significance of difference between natives and immigrants: ** $p < 0.0001$; * $p < 0.05$

ter on nativity and ethnicity differentials—that is, on examining the differences between the foreign-born and the native-born within each of the four main race-ethnic categories—we have summarized our findings in four data tables. Each table breaks down selected information on maternal risk factors and infant health outcomes by nativity (U.S.-born or immigrant) and race-ethnicity (Hispanic, Asian, white, black). In the discussion that follows, as appropriate, more detailed information will be added to highlight within-group differences as well (among immigrants, e.g., between the Indochinese and other Asians, or between Mexican and Central American Hispanics, or between European, Canadian, and Middle Eastern whites). We begin by documenting differences in the maternal risk profiles of the women in the CPP sample. We will then shift our focus to differences in and determinants of infant health outcomes.

*Maternal Risk Factors*

Table 8–2 provides data on social and economic characteristics of the women in the CPP sample. All differences between natives and immigrants, and between racial-ethnic groups, are significant beyond the 0.0001 level. As expected, U.S.-born women had higher levels of education, English proficiency, employment, and per capita income than immigrant women. Over one-third (36%) of the immigrants had only an elementary-level education or less, compared to none of the natives; conversely, over three-fourths (77%) of the natives were high school graduates, compared to only 29% of the foreign-born. Among Asian immigrants (not shown in Table 8–2), the Indochinese were by far the least educated (61% had a sixth grade education or less); they were followed by immigrant mothers from Mexico and Central America. By contrast, among white immigrants, Middle Easteners and Europeans were actually more highly educated than native whites and any of the other ethnic groups. English language primacy—a proxy for Americanization—generally mirrors those educational differentials, except that Hispanic immigrant women rank at the bottom on that indicator. As Table 8–2 shows, less than 1% of the Hispanic immigrant women use English as their primary language, as do only 8% of the Asian-born; but about two-thirds of both white and black immigrants speak English primarily, indicative of their much greater level of linguistic and cultural assimilation. Native-born women are almost entirely anglicized, with the notable exception of U.S.-born Hispanic women (who are overwhelmingly of Mexican origin): only 36.7% of them report using English as their primary language, a fact that may reflect in part the unique location of San Diego along the Mexican border and the continuing vitality of Spanish in that context.

Immigrant women overall were much less likely than the native-born to be in the labor force during their pregnancies: less than a quarter (24.7%), compared to 42% of tne U.S.-born. Among the immigrants, this was especially the case among the Indochinese refugees, while Central American immigrant women were more likely to be in the job market than any other foreign-born group. Among the natives, non-Hispanic white women had the highest rate of labor force participation (with almost half of them reporting holding a job during their pregnancy). Although to be eligible for the CPP all women had to meet low-income threshholds, there was still substantial variability in incomes: native women report per capita monthly incomes of $293 from all sources, compared to only $198 per person for immigrant families. However, among the U.S.-born, Anglos ($316) greatly exceeded the per person average of $189 among African Americans.

The bottom section of Table 8–2 shows significant differences in marital status and levels of social support between immigrants and natives. Immigrant women are more likely to be married and in larger families than native-born women, and significantly less likely to live alone. Native-born women are significantly more likely than immigrants to have stressful relationships with the father of the baby and with her own parents and family—and also to have had a history of child abuse or neglect as a child, to have had a history of psychological problems, and to be assessed by the psychosocial worker to be excessively depressed or moody. These patterns are present for virtually all of these variables (not all of which are shown in Table 8–2) across all racial-ethnic groups.

Table 8–3 presents data on physical characteristics and pregnancy and health histories. There are no statistically significant differences in the age of the mothers by nativity, including the proportion of teen mothers. Immigrant women are significantly shorter on average (the Indochinese are the shortest, at 4'11" in average height), weigh less, and had gained less weight between prenatal assessments than native-born women. While there were no statistically significant differences in the proportion of mothers who had had a previous live or preterm birth, the Indochinese were far more likely to be multiparous and to report previous pregnancies that ended in prematurity (second only to African Americans) or a perinatal death (second only to U.S.-born Hispanics). By contrast, except for the European and Canadian immigrants, U.S.-born women across ethnic-racial categories were far more likely to report one or multiple abortions (induced or spontaneous). A medical diagnosis of a surgically scarred uterus was most likely for native white women and least likely for Asians, especially the Indochinese (in logistic regressions we found that it is most strongly associated with a previous cesarean section, and

TABLE 8–3. Maternal Risk Factors: Anthropometry, Pregnancy and Health History, by Race-Ethnicity and Nativity of Low-Income Women Receiving CPP Prenatal Care Services. (San Diego Comprehensive Perinatal Program 1989–1991 Sample, $N = 1,464$.)

| Maternal Characteristics | Nativity | Hispanic (1,150) | Asian (79) | White (201) | Black (34) | $p^1$ | Total (1,464) | $p^2$ |
|---|---|---|---|---|---|---|---|---|
| **Age, Height, and Weight** | | | | | | | | |
| mean age (years) | U.S.-born | 23.0 | 23.4 | 26.1 | 24.2 | * | 25.2 | |
| | immigrant | 25.2 | 27.2 | 26.7 | 27.3 | | 25.4 | |
| % teen mothers (age 13–19) | U.S.-born | 24.5 | 20.0 | 16.4 | 25.0 | * | 19.0 | |
| | immigrant | 17.0 | 14.9 | 13.3 | 16.7 | | 16.8 | |
| mean height (inches) | U.S.-born | 63 | 63 | 65 | 65 | ** | 64 | ** |
| | immigrant | 61 | 60 | 63 | 62 | | 61 | |
| pregravid weight (pounds) | U.S.-born | 144 | 114 | 134 | 136 | ** | 136 | ** |
| | immigrant | 128 | 118 | 131 | 149 | | 129 | |
| **Pregnancy and Health History** | | | | | | | | |
| % previous live birth | U.S.-born | 61.2 | 20.0 | 55.0 | 50.0 | | 54.9 | |
| | immigrant | 56.5 | 70.3 | 53.3 | 50.0 | | 57.2 | |
| % previous perinatal death | U.S.-born | 8.2 | 0.0 | 3.5 | 0.0 | * | 4.0 | |
| | immigrant | 3.8 | 5.4 | 0.0 | 0.0 | | 3.8 | |
| % 2+ abortions (spont./induced) | U.S.-born | 12.2 | 20.0 | 21.6 | 14.8 | ** | 19.0 | ** |
| | immigrant | 4.6 | 5.6 | 10.7 | 16.7 | | 4.9 | |
| $M$ # of medical conditions in Hx | U.S.-born | 2.3 | 2.2 | 3.3 | 2.5 | ** | 3.0 | ** |
| | immigrant | 1.3 | 0.8 | 1.8 | 1.7 | | 1.3 | |

[1] Statistical significance of difference between racial/ethnic groups: ** $p < 0.0001$; * $p < 0.05$.
[2] Statistical significance of difference between natives and immigrants: ** $p < 0.0001$; * $p < 0.05$.

to a lesser extent with venereal diasease and endocrine disorders reported in the medical history, and with use of an IUD as a contraceptive).

Upon entering the Comprehensive Perinatal Program each pregnant woman underwent an initial physical exam, including a pelvic examination, and completed a battery of medical assessments, including a health history to serve as an index of biomedical factors that could raise the risk of a poor perinatal outcome. The medical history was in the form of a checklist that indicated the presence or absence of conditions such as congenital anomalies, genetic diseases, multiple births, diabetes mellitus, malignancies, hypertension, heart disease, rheumatic fever, pulmonary disease, gastrointestinal problems, renal disease, genitourinary tract problems, abnormal uterine bleeding, infertility, venereal disease, phlebitis or varicosities, neurologic disorders, metabolic or endocrine disorders, anemia or hemoglobinopathy, blood disorders, infectious diseases, operations or accidents, allergies or medicinal allergies, blood transfusions, and other hospitalizations. The last row of Table 8–3 provides a summed index of the total of medical conditions that were checked in the health history: native-born women reported an average of 3.0, compared to 1.3 among the foreign-born. More specifically, U.S.-born women were far more likely than immigrant women to report gastrointestinal and genitourinary problems, abnormal uterine bleeding, venereal disease, pulmonary disease, allergies, operations and accidents, and also relatively more likely to report congenital anomalies, heart disease, and anemia. By ethnicity, Asian-origin women reported the least medical conditions, followed by Hispanics, African Americans, and then native Anglos, who reported the most.

Table 8–4 presents data on health-related risk behaviors (smoking, drug and alcohol use, risk of exposure to AIDS). The data show clearly that a much higher fraction of U.S.-born women have a history of smoking than do foreign-born women, and this is true for every ethnic category. Overall, women born in the United States are more than three times more likely to have ever smoked (26.1%) than immigrant women (6.8%); moreover, among those who smoke, the native-born smoke more cigarettes per day than immigrant women who are current smokers. However, European and Canadian immigrant women were more likely than any group to smoke, and to smoke more heavily. The data on alcohol intake (not shown) revealed that a very small fraction of women were admitting to using alcohol at the time of entrance into CPP. Only 4% of women indicated any alcohol use, although women born in the United States were more than three times as likely (11%) to be using alcohol as women born outside of the United States (3%). By race-ethnicity, the data show that 3% of both Asian and Hispanic women

TABLE 8–4. Maternal Risk Factors : Health-Related Risk Behaviors and Conditions, by Race-Ethnicity and Nativity of Low-Income Women Receiving CPP Prenatal Care Services. (San Diego Comprehensive Perinatal Program 1989–1991 Sample, $N = 1,464$.)

| Maternal Characteristics | Nativity | Hispanic (1,150) | Asian (79) | White (201) | Black (34) | $p^1$ | Total (1,464) | $p^2$ |
|---|---|---|---|---|---|---|---|---|
| *Health Related Risk Behaviors* | | | | | | | | |
| % history of smoking | U.S.-born | 14.3 | 40.0 | 29.8 | 21.3 | ** | 26.1 | ** |
| | immigrant | 6.6 | 2.7 | 26.7 | 0.0 | | 6.8 | |
| present # cigarettes per day | U.S.-born | 1.6 | 5.2 | 3.3 | 2.3 | ** | 2.3 | ** |
| | immigrant | 0.4 | 0.6 | 2.6 | 0.0 | | 0.5 | |
| % history of alcohol/drug abuse | U.S.-born | 25.5 | 60.0 | 33.1 | 22.2 | ** | 31.0 | ** |
| | immigrant | 1.8 | 4.2 | 13.8 | 0.0 | | 2.2 | |
| % present alcohol/drug abuse | U.S.-born | 10.2 | 20.0 | 11.7 | 17.9 | ** | 12.3 | ** |
| | immigrant | 0.8 | 0.0 | 6.7 | 0.0 | | 0.9 | |
| % at risk for AIDS | U.S.-born | 6.7 | 0.0 | 5.5 | 4.0 | ** | 5.5 | ** |
| | immigrant | 0.7 | 0.0 | 0.0 | 0.0 | | 0.7 | |
| % CPP high-risk index[3] | U.S.-born | 18.4 | 40.0 | 20.5 | 28.6 | ** | 21.4 | ** |
| | immigrant | 8.3 | 12.7 | 7.1 | 16.7 | | 8.5 | |

[1] Statistical significance of difference between racial/ethnic groups: ** $p < 0.0001$; * $p < 0.05$.

[2] Statistical significance of difference between natives and immigrants: ** $p < 0.0001$; * $p < 0.05$.

[3] Indicates a pregnant woman who was over age 40 or who had one or more of the following conditions: diabetes mellitus, hypertension, cardiac disease (Class II or IV), chronic renal disease, congenital/chromosomal anomalies, hemoglobinopathies, isoimmunization (Rh), alcohol or drug abuse, habitual abortions, incompetent cervix, prior fetal or neonatal death, prior neurologically damaged infant, or significant social problems.

indicated some alcohol use, compared with 12% of Anglo and African American women. Although smoking and drinking often go together, we found that most smokers (82%) did not admit to using alcohol, although smokers were still six times more likely to use alcohol than nonsmokers.

The CPP data collection procedure asked two key questions about the prior and current use of drugs and/or alcohol, and then followed up with questions asking about each one separately. Among women born in the United States, 31% had a history of drug or alcohol abuse, compared to a miniscule 2% of women born outside of the United States. As can be seen in Table 8–4, these differences prevail for each of the ethnic groups. A similar story can be told for present alcohol or drug abusers. Only 1% of the foreign-born women fell into this category, compared to 12.3% of U.S.-born women. Again, this pattern was exhibited by each ethnic group (*see* Table 8–4). Overall, native Anglos had a higher proportion of mothers reporting a history of drug or alcohol abuse, African Americans were more likely to be present drug or alcohol users, and U.S.-born Hispanics were more likely to be at risk for AIDS.

A related risk index produced by staff of CPP had a combined biomedical/sociocultural component. In the collection of health history information, CPP staff noted if the pregnant woman was over age 40 or had a history of one or more of the following conditions: diabetes mellitus, hypertension, cardiac disease (class III or IV), chronic renal disease, congenital/chromosomal anomalies, hemoglobinopathies, isoimmunization (Rh), alcohol or drug abuse, habitual abortions, incompetent cervix, prior fetal or neonatal death, prior neurologically damaged infant, or significant social problems. A check next to any one of these conditions meant that the woman was at high risk. According to this index overall 21% of the native-born were noted as being at high risk—nearly three times the fraction of the foreign-born (8%). This immigrant advantage held across all racial-ethnic groups. Grouped together by race-ethnicity, 9% of Hispanic women, 14% of Asians, 19% of whites, and 26% of black women were checked as being at high risk on this index.

*Infant Health Outcomes*

The foregoing has documented significant differences in a wide range of maternal risk factors by nativity and ethnicity for the pregnant women in the CPP sample. How were these differences reflected in the actual health of the babies they went on to deliver at the UCSD Medical Center? We now shift the focus of our analysis from maternal risk factors to two measures of infant health outcomes: the proportion of low-birth-weight babies delivered—that is, of babies who weighed in at less than 2,500 grams at birth—and an "optimum infant health outcome score" we constructed from the data available from hospital records. Table 8–5 presents a breakdown of those two outcome measures by nativity and ethnicity.

The perinatal outcome identified in the literature as being most closely associated with neonatal death is birth weight. This variable can be used as a continuous measure (grams at birth) or grouped into discrete categories (typically "very low weight," "low weight," and "above low weight"). The usual break points define low weight as less than 2,500 grams, and very low weight as less than 1,500 grams. In our analysis we have used both of these ways of measuring birth weight—as a continuous measurement, and as a set of discrete categories using the standard birth weight criteria. There is essentially no difference overall between U.S.-born and foreign-born women with respect to the mean weight in grams of their babies. There are, however, clear ethnic differences in the average size of babies. Anglo mothers gave birth to the largest infants on average, followed by Hispanics, Asians, and then African Americans. This is exactly the same rank ordering as has been found elsewhere. However, birth weight per se is not a particularly good indicator of birth outcome, since U.S.-born African American women and immigrant Asian women gave birth to the smallest babies on average, despite the fact that our earlier research indicates that these two groups represent the extremes with respect to infant mortality. Looking more specifically at the percentage of babies that are low birth weight (LBW), the data in Table 8–5 show that nearly twice as many infants of U.S.-born women weighed in at less than 2,500 grams than was true for immigrant women. This difference was statistically significant at the .05 level. Furthermore, the relationship was in the expected direction (the U.S.-born woman was more likely to bear a low weight child) for each of the four racial-ethnic groups under consideration. Consistent with the previously observed pattern of infant mortality, the incidence of low birth weight was highest among babies born to African American women, and lowest among Asians.

The "optimum infant health outcome score" measure presented in Table 8–5 requires a brief explanation. We systematically examined each of the infant health outcome variables in the data set, and experimented with a variety of overall indices of outcome, combining variables by means of factor analysis. Four variables that clustered together to form a single factor emerged from this inspection: (1) babies born weighing less than 2,500 grams (low birthweight); (2) babies delivered by cesarean section; (3) babies with one or more diagnoses noted at delivery (such as sepsis, hyperbilirubinemia, and anemia); and (4) the number of days the infant stayed in the hospital. These four were combined to form a single outcome scale. Because a simple additive scale is more easily interpretable and amenable to practical policy recommendations, we have used it as our principal measure of outcome (the dependent variable) in regression analyses. Specifically, we formed this scale by adding 1 if an infant weighed more than 2,500 grams (the positive outcome); adding 1 if the baby was delivered vaginally and not by C-section (the positive outcome); adding 1 if no diagnoses were noted at birth (the positive outcome); and adding 1 if the number of days in the hospital was less than 3 (the positive outcome). This produced a scale ranging from zero (the lowest quality outcome) to 4 (the optimum outcome). We then divided this score by 4 to produce an outcome index ranging from zero to 1, where 1 is the optimum outcome.

Table 8–5 shows the percentage of babies who achieved the optimum infant health score of 1. By nativity, a higher proportion of the babies born to immigrant women (61.3%) achieved an optimum health outcome score of 1 than did the babies of nonimmigrant mothers (54.1%). By race-ethnicity, interestingly, the results replicated the same ethnic pattern of infant mortality rates we reported at the outset—that is, Asian babies have the most positive health outcome scores, followed by Hispanics, then white Anglos, and finally African Americans. These differences were significant beyond the 0.01 level. One can infer from this that our scale incorporates a set of morbidity indicators that may be most closely associated with infant mortality—particularly with early neonatal mortality, which almost always occurs within the hospital setting. In any event, we have used that measure as a principal dependent variable in order to examine the effects of a wide range of likely determinants, including the set of maternal risk factors discussed earlier.

## Determinants of Infant Health Outcomes

We dichotomized the dependent variable into those women who had none of the negative outcomes that comprised our score and those who had one or more. Thus a woman with an optimum infant health outcome had a baby weighing more than 2,500 grams, with a vaginal delivery, zero diagnoses at birth, and the baby stayed in the hospital fewer than three days. Anything else was considered a less than optimum outcome. A maximum-likelihood logistic regression analysis on this dichotomized dependent variable identified ten variables as significant determinants of infant health outcomes. Specifically, the odds of an optimum infant health outcome increased if the mother had had a previous live birth (more pregnancies were associated with more positive outcome scores) and if the baby was a girl; the odds were sig-

TABLE 8-5. Maternal Risk Factors: Low Birthweight Births and Infant Health Outcome Scores, by Race-Ethnicity and Nativity of Low-Income Women Receiving CPP Prenatal Care Services. (San Diego Comprehensive Perinatal Program 1989–1991 Sample, $N = 1,464$.)

| Infant Health Outcomes | Nativity | Hispanic (1,150) | Asian (79) | White (201) | Black (34) | $p^1$ | Total (1,464) | $p^2$ |
|---|---|---|---|---|---|---|---|---|
| *Infant Health Outcomes* | | | | | | | | |
| % low birthweight (< 2,500 grams) | U.S.-born | 4.1 | 20.0 | 2.3 | 3.6 | * | 3.2 | * |
| | immigrant | 1.9 | 0.0 | 0.0 | 0.0 | | 1.7 | |
| % optimum health outcome score[3] | U.S.-born | 53.1 | 60.0 | 56.1 | 42.9 | * | 54.1 | * |
| | immigrant | 61.2 | 71.6 | 43.3 | 50.0 | | 61.3 | |

[1] Statistical significance of difference between racial/ethnic groups: ** $p < 0.0001$; * $p < 0.05$.
[2] Statistical significance of difference between natives and immigrants: ** $p < 0.0001$; * $p < 0.05$.
[3] Optimal score on a 4-point scale; indicates a spontaneous vaginal delivery of a normal birthweight baby (> 2,500 grams), with no diagnoses noted at birth, who stayed in the hospital only one or two days.

nificantly lowered if the mother was older (the younger the woman, the better the outcome), had a surgically scarred uterus (which is strongly associated with negative outcomes), had a higher than average weight gain and a higher than average intake of protein in her diet during her pregnancy (the greater the daily protein consumption, the worse the outcome), had inadequate financial resources (relative to others in this sample of already low-income women), had abused drugs or alcohol during her pregnancy, and had a CPP high-risk score. Recall (*see* Table 8–4) that this latter score is a composite index that indicates whether the mother had had a prior fetal or infant death, a history of alcohol or drug abuse, habitual abortions, significant social problems, and/or various specific medical conditions. With these variables entered, and of particular interest for our study, immigration status washed out of the regression equation, as did all major ethnicities—and all other predictor variables, for that matter. The sole exception is the curious persistence of Middle Eastern ethnicity in all models (although that should be interpreted cautiously, given the very small sample of only eight women).

We repeated the logistic regression analysis separately for multiparous and primiparous women, separately for each of the four racial-ethnic groups, and separately for each of the components of the outcome scale (low birth weight, number of diagnoses at birth, length of hospitalization, and C-section). It is beyond our scope here to elaborate each of these separate analyses, except that they help to further refine and confirm the predictive import of several of the selected variables—and their limitations. Again, with the same ten predictor variables controlled, all other factors washed out of the equation, including the key nativity and race-ethnicity variables. These findings appear to explain some of the key biomedical and sociocultural reasons why low socioeconomic-status immigrants are superior health achievers. On the other hand, despite the vast number of variables we examined, we were only moderately successful in predicting a positive or negative outcome. This is partly because the underlying variables influencing outcome do appear to differ from one ethnocultural group to another. These conclusions suggest that we must delve further into the lives of women to deepen our understanding of some of the processes and the contexts that shape perinatal outcomes.

But they also raise other questions about the meaning, complexity, and implications of those findings. For example, the finding that high protein intake is associated with poorer reproductive outcomes carries potentially important policy implications and bears more systematic scrutiny—though it supports several different research studies which have found that high-protein supplements in the diets of pregnant women were associated with fetal growth retardation, an excess of premature deliveries, and lower-birth-weight babies (*see* especially Rush, Stein & Susser, 1980).

Other variables amenable to service provider intervention include weight gain during pregnancy, drug and alcohol abuse, and inadequate financial resources (which even in this sample which already controlled for low-income women remains a significant predictor of poorer perinatal health). Although we cannot elaborate this further here, a close examination of each of the other risk factors that emerged in the logistic regression as significant predictors of optimum infant health scores would introduce considerable complexity to the story here told.

## Conclusion

One main implication of our study is that it challenges us to desimplify and deconstruct conventional notions about social class, race and ethnicity, and about the meaning of the Americanization of immigrants. Our study cautions us from jumping too quickly to conclusions based solely on racial classifications or nativity status. For instance, it turns out that the best infant health outcomes were observed for an Asian immigrant group (the Indochinese, who were also the least educated of all), but the worst outcomes for a white immigrant group (the Middle Easteners, who were also the most educated of all). And while immigrants do indeed do better than natives overall, the most assimilated immigrants (white Europeans and Canadians) do worse than U.S.-born Asians, Hispanics, and blacks.

Still, given these caveats, the following general picture emerges quite clearly from our findings: Asians and Hispanics (who are mostly foreign-born) clearly had superior outcomes relative to Anglos and African Americans (who are mostly U.S.-born); and within racial-ethnic groups, outcomes were better for immigrants than for natives. Specifically, U.S.-born women (who in this sample are mainly Anglos) were significantly more likely than immigrant women (who in this sample are mainly Mexicans and Indochinese) to: (1) have higher levels of education, employment, and per capita income; (2) be taller, heavier, and gain more weight during their pregnancies; (3) have had fewer live births and more abortions; (4) have diets lower in fruits and cereals and higher in fats and milk products; (5) report more medical conditions, especially venereal disease and genitourinary problems; (6) smoke, abuse drugs and alcohol, and be at risk for AIDS; (7) have a personal history of significant psychosocial problems, including having been a victim of child abuse and now of spousal abuse, and having currently stressful relationships both with the father of the baby and with their own family and parents; (8) be depressed, considered at risk psychosocially, and referred to a social worker; and (9) have generally poorer pregnancy outcomes—which is why infant health outcomes seem to worsen as the levels of education, English literacy, and general assimilation, or Americanization, of the mother increase. In this context, then, part of the puzzle, or "infant health paradox," discussed in the research literature begins to clear up: that is, relative to the foreign-born in this sample of low-income women, the comparative socioeconomic advantages of the U.S.-born appear to be overwhelmed by biomedical, nutritional, and psychosocial disadvantages.

In that sense, our data point to the conclusion that immigrant women are indeed superior health achievers, and that accounts for at least some part of their more-positive-than-expected perinatal outcomes. At the same time, it is also true that immigrant women will be more likely to have social support for the pregnancy, even if economic resources are deficient, and they are very unlikely to smoke, drink alcohol, or use drugs. Their diet, even if calorically deficient, tends to emphasize carbohydrates and vegetables rather than fats, oils, and sweets. Overall, our data tend to confirm the idea that Americanization is bad for pregnant low-income women if and to the extent that it is associated with getting pregnant without family support, with few sanctions for smoking or abusing alcohol or drugs, and with an emphasis on "fast" and "junk" foods that may be low in nutritional content. Our findings accentuate the theme that service providers must be prepared to evaluate and appropriately deal with differences in the ethnocultural background of their clients. Women from different cultural origins bring a host of varying backgrounds and behaviors to each pregnancy. Some of these factors interact positively with the high-technology biomedical environment in which birthing occurs in the United States, while others do not. Our research reinforces the literature that suggests that lack of smoking, lack of drug use, lack of alcohol, and a low-fat diet all appear to contribute to better pregnancy outcomes. It also reinforces the finding that problem pregnancies lead to recidivism, reinforcing the need for closer monitoring of women who have a history of anything but normal spontaneous vaginal deliveries.

Although we have analyzed a rich data set, there are some important limitations. The geographic restriction, as well as the potential selectivity of program participants, puts a limit on the generalizability of results. Moreover, the lack of a large pool of African American women in the program minimizes our ability to make comparisons with the group having the ethnically most distinct pattern of birth weight and infant mortality. We were also limited in the number of American-born women of Asian origin in the sample. Only now are the young women born in the United States of Southeast Asian parents coming of reproductive age. How they compare with their foreign-born sisters and cousins is a question to be answered in the future—and will need to be addressed by future research. Despite such limitations, our study offers important insights into a question that is increasingly a focus of national debate and controversy: controlling for socioeconomic status, what specifically explains racial and ethnic differences in infant health and mortality?

As a final word, it must be emphasized that despite the richness of our data set, and the reasonable size of our sample of women investigated, in the end there were only ten variables that emerged as having a statistically significant effect on perinatal outcome—when all other variables were taken into account—and together those ten variables accounted for only a small amount of the variation in perinatal outcomes. The relatively low levels of association between the independent variables and our measure of outcome might well be due to things that were unmeasured or unmeasurable, namely, ways of thinking about the world, organizing life, and conducting everyday activities—and the situational context or structure of these activities—that may differ in important ways from one ethnic group to another. Most of the variation remains locked up in the black box of social and cultural variability, and future research must continue to enrich our understanding of the processes that seem differentially to allow some groups to experience healthier reproductive outcomes.

## ACKNOWLEDGMENTS

The research on which this paper is based was supported by grant MCJ-060595 from the Maternal and Child Health Research Program of the Bureau of Maternal and Child Health and Resources Development, U.S. Department of Health and Human Services, for the project "Perinatal Risks and Outcomes Among Low-Income Immigrants."

## REFERENCES

Amaro, H., Whitaker, R., Coffman, J. & Heeren, T. (1990). Acculturation and marijuana and cocaine use: Findings from HHANES, 1982–84. *American Journal of Public Health, 80* (supplement), 54–60.

Bezerra, J. E., Hogue, C., Atrash, H. K. & Perez, N. (1991). Infant mortality among Hispanics: A portrait of heterogeneity. *Journal of the American Medical Association, 265* (2), 217–221.

Burnam, A., Hough, R. L., Kamo, M., Escobar, J. & Telles, C. (1987). Acculturation and lifetime prevalence of psychiatric disorders among Mexican Americans in Los Angeles. *Journal of Health and Social Behavior, 28,* 89–102.

Cabral, H., Fried, L. E., Levenson, S., Amaro, H. & Zuckerman, B. (1990). Foreign-born and U.S.-born black women: Differences in health behaviors and birth outcomes. *American Journal of Public Health, 80* (1), 70–72.

Caldwell, J. (1986). Routes to low mortality in poor countries. *Population and Development Review, 12* (2), 171–220.

Collins, J.W., Jr. & Shay, D. K. (1994). Prevalence of low birth weight among Hispanic infants with United States-born and foreign-born mothers: The effect of urban poverty. *American Journal of Epidemiology, 139* (2), 184–192.

Eberstein, I. W. (1991). Race/ethnicity and infant mortality. Paper presented at the annual meeting of the American Sociological Association, Cincinnati.

Gilbert, M. (1989). Alcohol consumption patterns in immigrant and later generation Mexican American women. *Hispanic Journal of Behavioral Sciences, 9,* 299–313.

Guendelman, S. & Abrams, B. (1995). Dietary intake among Mexican American women: Generational differences and a comparison with white non-Hispanic women. *American Journal of Public Health, 85* (1), 20–25.

Guendelman, S., Gould, J., Hudcs, M. & Eskanazi, B. (1990). Generational differences in perinatal health among the Mexican American population: Findings from HHANES, 1982–84. *American Journal of Public Health, 80* (supplement), 61–65.

Kaplan, M. & Marks, G. (1990). Adverse effects of acculturation: Psychological distress among Mexican American young adults. *Social Science and Medicine, 31* (12), 1313–1319.

Marks, G., García, M. & Solis, J. (1990). Health risk behaviors in Hispanics in the United States: Findings from HHANES, 1982–84. *American Journal of Public Health, 80* (supplement), 20–26.

Moscicki, E. K., et al. (1989). Depressive symptoms among Mexican Americans: The Hispanic Health and Nutrition Examination Survey. *American Journal of Epidemiology, 130,* 348–360.

Portes, A. & Rumbaut, R,G. (1996). *Immigrant America: A portrait,* (2nd ed.). Berkeley: University of California Press.

Rumbaut, R. G. (1994). Origins and destinies: Immigration to the United States since World War II. *Sociological Forum, 9* (4), 583–621.

———. (1995). Vietnamese, Laotian, and Cambodian Americans. In P. G. Min (Ed.), *Asian Americans: Contemporary trends and issues* (pp. 232–270). Thousand Oaks, CA: Sage.

Rumbaut, R.G., Chavez, L., Moser, R., Pickwell, S. & Wishik, S. (1988). The politics of migrant health care: A comparative study of Mexican immigrants and Indochinese refugees. *Research in the Sociology of Health Care, 7,* 148–202.

Rumbaut, R. G. & Weeks, J. R. (1989). Infant health among Indochinese refugees: Patterns of infant mortality, birth weight and prenatal care in comparative perspective. *Research in the Sociology of Health Care, 8,* 137–196.

———. (1996). Unraveling a public health enigma: Why do immigrants experience superior perinatal health outcomes? *Research in the Sociology of Health Care, 13B,* 337–391.

Rush, D., Stein, Z. & Susser, M. (1980). A randomized controlled trial of prenatal nutritional supplementation in New York City. *Pediatrics, 65* (4), 683–697.

Samuels, B. (1986). Infant mortality and low birth weight among minority groups in the United States: A review of the literature. In U.S. DHHS, *Report of the Secretary's Task Force on Black and Minority Health,* Volume VI, *Infant mortality and low birth weight.* Bethesda, MD: National Institutes of Health.

Scribner, R. & Dwyer, J. (1989). Acculturation and low birth weight among Latinos in the Hispanic HANES. *American Journal of Public Health, 79,* 1263–1267.

Vega, W. A. & Amaro, H. (1994). Latino outlook: Good health, uncertain prognosis. *Annual Review of Public Health, 15,* 39–67.

Vega, W. A., Kolody, B., Noble, A. & Hwang, J. et al. (1993a). *Profile of alcohol and drug use during pregnancy in California, 1992.* Scientific Report to the State of California Department of Alcohol and Drug Programs, Office of Perinatal Substance Abuse.

Vega, W. A., Kolody, B., Hwang, J. & Noble, A. (1993b). Prevalence and magnitude of perinatal substance exposures in California. *New England Journal of Medicine, 329* (12), 850–854.

Vega, W. A. & Rumbaut, R. G. (1991). Ethnic minorities and mental health. *Annual Review of Sociology, 17,* 351–383.

Weeks, J. R. & Rumbaut, R. G. (1991). Infant mortality among ethnic immigrant groups. *Social Science and Medicine, 33* (3), 327–334.

Williams, R. L., Chen, P. M., Binkin, N. & Clingman, E. (1986). Pregnancy outcomes among Spanish surname women in California. *American Journal of Public Health, 76,* 387–391.

Yu, E. (1982). The low mortality rates of Chinese infants: Some plausible explanations. *Social Science and Medicine, 16,* 253–265.

# Section III
# Public Policy Issues

# 9 UNITED STATES IMMIGRATION POLICY AND CHINESE CHILDREN AND FAMILIES

*Rowena Fong, Colette Browne*

To the average white middle-class American, the word "immigrant" conjures up visions of Haitians in sinking rafts making for the Florida shore, the holds of rusty Chinese freighters packed with people fleeing the People's Republic, and Mexicans coming across the border to clean houses and tend lawns in San Diego suburbs—all of them coming to take jobs away from those other Americans who were here first. The Clinton administration has justified the North American Free Trade Agreement and the bailout of the Mexican peso in terms of "getting control of our borders," by which it means keeping out what it regards as hordes of pigmented foreigners. California's Proposition 187 was directed toward the same end: making nonwhite immigrants go away by refusing them and their children services such as public hospitals and public schools.

Despite America's proud self-definition as a nation of immigrants, and despite nearly 150 years of Chinese immigration, the United States is still not adequately prepared to meet the needs of the hundreds of thousands of Chinese children and their families who live in this country. In fact, current immigration policy initiatives will almost certainly make life significantly more difficult for them. This difficulty stems from a lack of integrating cultural norms and values in policy formulation and implementation.

American immigration policy has been acting on Chinese people for over a century, beginning with the Chinese Exclusion Act of 1882, which banned the entry of Chinese laborers into the United States. A thoroughgoing revision of American immigration policy occurred in 1965, with the Immigration and Nationality Act. Since that time about 20,000 Chinese immigrants have come to the United States each year, with additional numbers of ethnic Chinese coming from Hong Kong, Singapore, Vietnam, and other countries. The main principle guiding U.S. screening has been a preference for reuniting families. Other significant groups of Chinese have been post-Tiananmen students, ethnic Chinese refugees from Vietnam, and a small number of wealthy immigrants from Hong Kong who have, in effect, bought the right to enter the United States. The total number of Chinese in America in 1990 was 1,645,472, making the Chinese the largest Asian group in the United States (U.S. Bureau of the Census, 1991). However, family reunification has not always been without costs to the Chinese immigrant or refugee child and family.

This chapter reviews American immigration policy, specifically focusing on policies that have an impact on Chinese children and families. It describes the several different kinds of Chinese children and families in the United States, discusses the core values that all Chinese Americans share, presents some of the problems Chinese immigrant children and families have had in the United States, discusses how the immigration policies have had an impact upon the problems of Chinese parents and children, and proposes future recommendations to address these problems.

VARIETIES OF CHINESE AMERICANS

The Chinese are one of America's fastest-growing ethnic minority populations and represent the largest group in the Asian American population at 22.6% (U.S. Bureau of the Census, 1991; Uba, 1994). There are several different kinds of Chinese Americans, depending on place of birth or origin, level of acculturation, political ideology, and settlement status. There are American-born Chinese; there are immigrants from Hong Kong and other countries; and refugees from Vietnam and the People's Republic of China. These different kinds of families face different child developmental concerns. For example, Chinese American families that were born and raised in the United States are affected by generational conflicts between grandparent, parent, and child because of different levels of acculturation. Chinese who have immigrated from the People's Republic of China (PRC) before 1979 typically have several children. More recent immigrants from the PRC, since the advent of the single-child policy in 1979, usually have just one child. Thus nuclear and extended family dynamics are different, and spoiling may be an issue in single-child families from the PRC (Fong, 1990). Other Chinese families may come from non-Communist countries, such as Hong Kong, Taiwan, or Singapore, and have to deal with some of the same immigrant problems as the PRC-driven Chinese, such as bilingualism and academic achievement pressure for children and youth, but not the single-child family dynamics. Despite the differences in social and political environment backgrounds, there are commonalities in cultural values and beliefs held by all these types of Chinese children and families. But there are also differences in their child-rearing patterns and behaviors because of distinct cultural and social environments.

There is not just one kind of Chinese child in America. There is enormous diversity and complexity within the population called Chinese American. A significant minority are the American-born children of American-born parents, or of immigrants who have been here for many years. Some but not all of these children are from families that have reached the middle class in the last generation, and almost all have good English-language skills and are receiving American educations. The issues for this group, such as identity crises and communication gaps, are likely to be more like the issues that exist for other working-class and middle-class American-born children than are the issues for Chinese immigrant children.

According to Longres (1990), immigrants "take up stakes, more or less voluntarily, in one national society and migrate to another land, where they become part of a new national society" (p. 101). By contrast, refugees have been defined as people who have no choice and leave their homelands involuntarily under coercion with no guarantee of ethnic or cultural survival (Ryan, 1992; Trueba, Jacobs & Kirton, 1990). This distinction is important, because what people have experienced before coming to America and under what circumstances they have come greatly affect their adjustment to their new social environment. Immigrants have experienced many sorts of difficulty, but generally have plans and hopes that compensate for their pains. Refugees may have to deal with extremely stressful issues—such as being separated from and trying to locate family members—related to the trauma they endured when leaving their country, in addition to settling into a new life (Ahearn & Athey, 1991; Huang, 1990; Ryan, 1992). Immigrant and refugee family concerns differ from those of American-born Chinese families. Immigrant and refugee families tend to bring with them and rely on the traditional values of their culture, although they may have to struggle with maintaining their identity in the face of American values and practices.

Recent Chinese immigrants from Hong Kong are different from American-born Chinese. More of them speak at least some English, because of a century and a half of British colonialism. Many Hong Kong immigrants have come to America to avoid the chaos they anticipate will overtake their homeland since it reverted to rule by the People's Republic in 1997. These immigrants may be very rich, middle-class, or poor. Many of them have relatives in the United States and can form successful extended family relationships easily. They speak primarily Cantonese and can connect with the institutional support systems of the Chinatowns and satellite suburban communities that exist in most American cities (Loo, 1991).

That is less likely to be the case for immigrants from the People's Republic of China (PRC), Singapore, Taiwan, or Malaysia. Some of these children are members of educated middle-class families; others are extremely poor. Some have relatives in the United States, but others may not. Some speak Cantonese; others speak Fujianese, Mandarin, or another Chinese dialect. Some speak excellent English; most do not. They may have less access to the support systems of Chinese American institutions. Some of the PRC immigrants share with many of the ethnic Chinese who come from Vietnam the experience of being refugees. Refugee experiences vary enormously. For some such families, there has been a harrowing journey replete with bribes, violence, and leaky boats, sometimes even with the loss of family members along the way. Others' papers label them as refugees, but they came on jumbo jets and their parents attended U.S. graduate schools and now earn substantial incomes.

Even among those who come from the People's Republic of China, Chinese people are very different from one another. China is as large in land area as Europe, is much larger in population, and possesses a similar variety of peoples. While China's government has for many centuries tried to blend the country's many peoples, the blending has not been complete (Fong & Spickard, 1994; Gladney, 1991). Almost all Chinese citizens use a common written language, but there are many distinct regional dialects. Similarly there are lots of regional variations on national patterns of child socialization. There is a strong Chinese national identity, but regional and ethnic subidentities are also strong (Honig, 1992; Wu, 1991).

Cultural, linguistic, and social heterogeneity among the Chinese people in China is pronounced, but most people outside of China do not understand it. In modern China (including Taiwan) both the government and intellectuals have spent a great deal of time and energy trying to forge an image of a unified, homogenous Chinese people (race and culture) and nation-state (Wu, 1991). In fact, ethnic prejudice and discrimination by one Chinese group against another are common practices in Chinese social life, especially in major cities, where migrant communities, such as merchant groups or craftspeople, are formed.

In recent times Guangzhou, Fujian, Shanghai, and other coastal urban centers have experienced a superheated economy and a virtual end to socialism, increasing inequities of wealth and social status—and all the social disruptions that go along with the early stages of capitalist development. Immigrants from such places bring with them a legacy of social striving and instability. And most recent PRC immigrants have come from such rapidly changing places. By contrast, immigrants who come in much smaller numbers from provinces like Hubei and Yunnan are less likely to be skilled in the highly competitive ways of capitalist economies, and their families are more likely to approximate traditional norms.

## COMMON CHINESE CULTURAL VALUES

It is essential that those who live and work with Chinese Americans understand distinctions such as these: between native-born and immigrant, between immigrant and refugee, between immigrant from Hong Kong and newcomer from the PRC, between people from different parts of the PRC and other parts of the world. However, despite the diversity among the different kinds of Chinese Americans, there are certain commonalities based on Chinese cultural values, beliefs, and norms applicable to all Chinese American children and families: (a) the upholding of filial piety; (b) the predominant emphasis on roles and sibling order; (c) the importance of the extended family and avoidance of loss of face; and (d) the context of self embedded in family and community.

Some of the traditional values whose roots are grounded in Confucianism revolve around two major principles or cultural concepts: filial piety and loss of face. Filial piety, originally a Chinese cultural principle that has spread to other Asian cultures, refers to traditional patterns of social relations that emphasize respect for male authority and the elderly, dictate sharply defined roles for men and women, and demand duty and obligation to the family from all of its members (Ho, 1987; Huang, 1991; Sue, Sue & Sue, 1982).

Eldest sons in traditional Chinese families are obligated to take care of the elders, carry on the family name, and meet all the obligations of family leadership. Women, however, are obligated to be submissive wives. Their roles are determined partly by the husband's sibling order in the family. For example, greater expectations and duties would be given the wife of the eldest son than to the wife of the third son. Such hierarchal role expectations also apply to children. Hirayama and Cetingok (1988) describe the family structure of immigrants when they first arrive as a "hierarchy of parent-child relationships." They state that "parents, particularly the father, maintain ultimate authority over most family affairs. Children are to assume dependent roles and be obedient to their parents" (p. 45). The principle of respecting one's parents and elders is instilled as a major value of the system of filial piety.

The belief that the family comes first is implicit in filial piety. Individual identity and desires—for the adult or the child—are subsumed under obligation to the family (Lum, 1992). Duty and obligation are primary values of traditional Chinese families, and affect the Chinese Americans who seem in other respects to be nontraditional.

The behavior of the Chinese extended family members reflects certain strengths—resilience, patience, respect for authority, and sense of duty toward family and community (Sue & Morishima, 1990; Hirayama & Cetingok, 1988). Duty toward family and community are implicit in the Chinese avoidance of losing face. Chinese individuals guard their behaviors to avoid acting in ways that would bring shame to the family or allow the family name to be dishonored. Although the concept of loss of face can be applied to an individual, it more commonly applies to the group or extended family and is effective in promoting conformity (Kitano & Daniels, 1988; Shon & Ja, 1982).

When problems do happen within the Chinese family, the family, for fear of loss of face, will keep the problem within the nuclear family. In some instances, the nuclear family will take its problem to the extended family. Thus extended family members are an acceptable resource from whom to seek support, help with problem solving, and guidance. Going to an outsider—a nonfamily member—for help or allowing someone outside the family to become aware of family problems will most likely be perceived as shameful and threatening loss of face. Having an outsider actually take part in dealing with a family problem may cause the family, especially the father, who is the major authority figure, to suffer humiliation.

The predominance of family and the value placed on avoiding loss of face applies to the Chinese children as well as the adults. These values are embedded in the perspective that the individual child is a part of the family and community and that the environment of the community and family play an influential role in the socialization process of Chinese children (Fong, 1997).

Chinese people in each of the backgrounds discussed earlier place a high value on children and put great burdens and expectations regarding the family on each individual. And each Chinese society and culture has always placed a high value on the nuclear and extended family system and the need for children to perpetuate the family line and bring honor to its name. Thus children are highly valued in Chinese culture. In most locations, sons are still more highly valued than daughters.

Son or daughter, in Chinese families the functioning of the individual is in the context of the family. In a Chinese family to single out an individual—adult or child—may cause discomfort (Ho, 1992; Shon & Ja, 1982; Sung, 1987). Although the family, not the individual, is the proper focus, the expectation of obligation to the family can be a burden to the individual. Yet, in return, the family serves as a protector from outside threats and a source of wisdom for problem solving. Lee (1982) cites the Chinese family as of "central importance in providing the necessary resources for growth and the definition of social expectations and responsibilities"(p. 536). Responsibilities take the form of also fulfilling obligations: child to parent, wife to husband, daughter-in-law to mother-in-law. Obligation is a cultural value upheld within the family and outside the family.

## U.S. IMMIGRATION POLICY AND CHINESE AMERICANS

Immigration policy has shaped the lives of Chinese Americans powerfully and for several generations. It has affected their places of residence, their employment and income, their gender ratio, and their social and political lives. A succession of immigration policies reaching back more than a century has had an impact upon the Chinese in America. These policies include the 1868 Burlingame Treaty; the 1882 Chinese Exclusion Act; the 1953 Refugee Relief Act; the 1965 Immigration and Nationality Act (with amendments); the 1986 Immigration Reform and Control Act; and the Immigration Act of 1990. The impact of these policies on Chinese immigrant and refugee families was felt throughout the history of Chinese immigration to the United States.

In the mid-1800s the first Asian group to come to the United States as immigrants were the Chinese (Fong, 1992). They came at first mostly as single men in the 1850s and 1860s, and found jobs on sugar plantations in Hawaii, in gold mines in California, and on railroads spanning the western part of the United States. However, the chief reactions the Chinese received from other Americans were not friendly. Resentment swelled against these "coolie" laborers, and discriminatory practices began: laws restricting residence and occupation, discriminatory taxes, even physical violence (Brown, 1993).

In 1868 China and the United States signed the Burlingame Treaty, which was an agreement for reciprocal immigration, travel, and trade. But there were no provisions for citizenship for foreign-born Chinese. The only way a Chinese could be an American citizen was by virtue of birth in the United States (Daniels, 1988). In 1882 Congress finally knuckled under to an anti-Chinese lobby and passed the Chinese Exclusion Act, which effectively halted Chinese immigration by barring the entry of Chinese laborers. Exemptions were made for merchants, students, teachers, diplomats, and travelers who showed certificates signed by the Chinese government and the U.S. consul in China (Chan, 1991).

This Chinese Exclusion Act was passed in a burst of racial agitation and stayed in effect till 1943. The targets were not Chinese children but the single men who came to work in the American West, leaving their families home in China (Nee & Nee, 1973; Sandmeyer, 1973). That ban held through World War II, and only a small number of Chinese American families with children were established in that period, often by circumventing the exclusion laws (Chan, 1991; Wong, 1995). The exclusion was relaxed minutely in 1943, again slightly more in 1952 under the Immigration and Naturalization Act, which set up a quota system based upon the 1950 census (Bennett, 1963).

This act applied to immigrants. Legislation for refugees, the Refugee Relief Act, was passed in 1953. It was "the first major breach in the numerical restrictions of the Act of 1952 and the national origins formula" (Bennett, 1963, p. 195). It offered relief to those individuals who were persecuted for their political beliefs and responded to the demands of special-interest, private, religious, and nationality groups who wanted enlarged quotas (Bennett, 1963).

In the 1960s the Kennedy and Johnson administrations achieved a thorough revision of the American immigration policy with the establishment of the new Immigration Act of 1965. Several reforms were made, mostly due to a commitment to racial equality, an intentional parallel to the Civil Rights Act of 1964 (Muller, 1993). The reforms did away with quotas and, according to Muller, "constrained immigration to no more than 20,000 from any nation, with an aggregate global limit" (p. 48). This change opened a way for a surge of immigrants from Asia, increasing from about 150,000 in 1950 to more than 2.7 million in the 1980s. The priority goal was on family reunification; the act allowed a large number of visas and less-stringent visa requirements in the family categories (Hing, 1993b). Preferences were given to immediate family members of U.S. citizens and permanent residents. Skilled workers and professionals were also given limited preference if need was demonstrated for their occupation or training.

According to Stanford immigrant law professor Bill Hing (1993b) the 1965 reforms categorized immigrants as either immediate relatives of U.S. citizens or under the preference system. Immediate relatives—parents of adult citizens, spouses, and minors, unmarried children of citizens—were not counted against the country's quota. The quota immigrants came under a preference system, which had seven categories (Hing 1993b, p. 129):

1. adult, unmarried sons and daughters of citizens
2. spouses, and unmarried sons and daughters of lawful permanent resident aliens
3. members of professions or those workers with exceptional ability in the arts or sciences

4. married sons and daughters of citizens
5. siblings of adult citizens
6. skilled or unskilled workers, where there was a shortage of employable and willing workers in the United States
7. persons fleeing from a Communist-dominated country, country of the Middle East, or people uprooted because of a natural catastrophe.

As reforms were being made for immigrants, some were also being made for refugees. The 1980 Refugee Act "for the first time established admission guidelines and separated refugee entry from the normal quota system" (Muller, 1993, p. 307).

The 1980s saw the beginnings of a backlash against immigrants of all sorts, Chinese included, culminating in the Immigration Reform and Control Act (IRCA) of 1986. Although the IRCA was an attempt to curtail immigration, it did offer legalization to immigrants who had earlier entered the United States illegally (Finch, 1990; Gelfand & Bialik-Gilad, 1989). IRCA had six provisions (Le-Doux & Stephens, 1992, p. 34–35): "legalized amnesty program for undocumented immigrants; program for H-2 temporary foreign and seasonal workers; employer sanctions; antidiscrimination employment provisions; increased enforcement capabilities of the Immigration and Naturalization Service; and State Legalization Impact Assistant Grants." These grants allowed a mechanism whereby states and local governments could ask for reimbursement for the costs incurred from helping immigrants adjust to having a documented rather than an undocumented status.

The IRCA of 1986 "did not substantially reduce illegal entry but it appeared to signal a less permissive attitude toward aliens than has been the case in recent decades," states Muller (1993, p. 11). This anti-immigrant attitude, compounded by elements within the conservative political movement, manifests itself in the form of "fears associated with the social consequences of nonwhite immigration" (Muller, 1993, p. 11).

These fears were evident to a further degree in the Immigration Act of 1990. The priority of the act was to protect American workers, and yet there was an admission of need for workers from other nations. Under the 1990 reforms, there were two preference systems, one for family and the other for employment, operating independently in parallel. The family preference still had the immediate relative category for parents, spouses, and unmarried children. There were some changes in the family preference categories compared to the 1965 reforms. Under the 1990 reforms the family preferences and employment preferences had broader categories (Table 9–1).

TABLE 9–1. Immigration Preference Features, Acts of 1965 and 1990

| Preference Rank | 1965 Act | 1990 Act | |
|---|---|---|---|
| | | Family Preferences | Employment Preferences |
| First | Unmarried sons and daughters | Unmarried sons and daughters | Immigrants with extraordinary ability, outstanding researchers, executives, professors |
| Second | Spouses, unmarried sons and daughters or lawful permanent residents | A) Spouses and children (unmarried under 21 years)<br>B) Unmarried sons and daughters over 21 years | Professors holding advanced degrees or exceptional ability |
| Third | Members of professions or those with exceptional ability in arts or sciences | Married sons and daughters of U.S. citizens | Skilled workers, professionals |
| Fourth | Married sons and daughters of citizens | Brothers and sisters of adult citizens | Special Immigrants |
| Fifth | Siblings of adult workers | | |
| Sixth | Skilled or unskilled workers | | Investors who create at least 10 new jobs |
| Seventh | Persons fleeing Communist or Middle East or catastrophe-torn countries | | |

*Source:* Table based on information written by Bill Hing, *Making and Remaking Asian Pacific America: Immigration Policy.* In LEAP, *The State of Asian Pacific America: Policy issues to the year 2000* (pp. 127–139). Los Angeles: LEAP and UCLA Asian American Studies Center.

Alongside the family preferences there was a system of economic preferences: job skills or dollars to invest placed an aspiring immigrant high on the preference list as being a close family member of an American citizen. The economic incentive under the 1990 act allows admission to "diversity immigrants" or "investor immigrants" (Briggs & Moore, 1994) who come from countries in which immigration has been low since 1965.

In summary, the 1965 act was good for Chinese American children and families in that its preference system was built around reuniting families who had been separated. The racial purity goals of the previous immigration acts were replaced by the concept of family reunification regardless of race (Briggs & Moore, 1994). The act did provide for a modest increase in overall immigration, expanded the definition of "immediate family," and took out the racial discrimination that had previously existed (Briggs & Moore, 1994).

In contrast, the 1990 act was somewhat less good for families. It still allowed family members to come to the United States on the basis of family-oriented preferences. But alongside the family preference system was a system of preference with economic motivations. This tended to divide families: one family member with money or skill would leave Hong Kong or China and go to America, often leaving behind the rest of the family with the intention of bringing them over later. In an era of stable quotas (by now roughly 25,000 maximum per country per annum), this meant fewer families were being united and more families were being split. There currently is talk in Congress of reducing immigration quotas. If quotas decrease, there will be even more pressure on the core of Chinese American culture and society, the family.

## PROBLEMS FOR CHINESE AMERICAN CHILDREN

Sue and Chin (1983) summarize some major issues for Chinese immigrant children (cf. Brislin et al., 1973). They see four crucial mental health issues for Chinese children in their development: achievement, power, affiliation, and independence.

The achievement issue is the pressure that Chinese parents put on children to perform and excel in education. Sollenberger (1968) and Ou and McAdoo (1993) report that Chinese parents have a high level of expectation that their children must do well in school. The traditional value of excelling academically and bringing honor to the family is the way to mitigate or avoid bringing loss of face to the family.

The educational pressure may also reflect the power issue with which Chinese American children and parents struggle. The power issue relates to questions of the child's ability or inability to control his or her fate, to relate to authority figures, and so forth. Power struggles focus in areas of parents' strict control over children's behavior and activities, like school and peers. The power issue stems from the traditional value of filial piety, where children are to obey the parents and parents have strict role expectations, raising the children to be respectful, dutiful, and obedient.

The affiliation issue speaks of the child's ability or inability to form bonds of intimacy and group belonging. This group belonging is a major factor in the development of self-identity during adolescence. The result of this inability to form group belonging may result in a variety of behaviors, including teenage suicide attempts. Liu et. al. (1990) report an increase between 1970 and 1980 in foreign-born immigrants aged 15 to 24. These foreign-born teenagers "have lived part of their lives abroad and may continue to speak a language other than English. They can be expected to have experienced culture shock and some amount of identity problems after their arrival in the United States. . . . The foreign-born suicide rate is higher than that found for native-born. . . . The rate for foreign-born Chinese is 7.1 per 100,000 compared with 5.2 for native-born youth" (Liu et al., 1990, p. 104). Although no conclusive findings are reported, Liu et al. (1990) do raise the question of whether the breakdown of the family structure and the transitional nature of the family in migration are contributing variables to immigrant adolescent suicide.

Besides suicide, gang involvement may be another coping mechanism for lack of affiliation that Chinese American youth turn to. Sung (1987) identified the length of absence of immigrant parents due to long work hours as a major stressor for New York Chinatown Chinese American youth. She concludes that the way some foreign-born youth cope with familial and kinship network loss is gang involvement.

The independence issues focus on the tensions within immigrant American families consisting of foreign-born parents and American-born children and the conflict of control and independence (Ho, 1987). The conflict comes between younger members, who are often acculturated and Americanized (assertive, independent, and individualistic), and the parents, who are traditional in their thinking (stressing family first, obedience to parents, and avoidance of behaviors causing loss of face).

The independence issue is also reflected in the struggle between youth, parents, and grandparents where there are generational conflicts with parents and grandparents. The immigrant parents and grandparents who are expecting the younger generation to remain respectful, dutiful, and obedient have difficulty with the acculturated youth who struggle to be assertive, independent, and individualistic—values espoused in the United States.

This struggle for independence is compounded by psychological issues related to losses and the process of immigrating—loss of home, friends, stable sense of place. The cognitive reaction of children and youth to the new environment may mask emotional distress and anxiety (Ho, 1992). One common denominator for Chinese immigrant and refugee children and families is that they are likely to have spent a substantial part of their childhood separated from one or the other parent, causing related problems of individual emotional functioning and family relationship adjustment. Even those who have experienced intact nuclear families throughout their lives have had to endure being uprooted from their homes and losing friends and extended family.

Although there have been conflicts in the Chinese American family because of the amount of control it exerts over its members, the traditional and rigid family roles have tended to promote stability and security (Shon & Ja, 1982). Despite interpersonal conflicts between generational members, the extended family system in Chinese culture has shaped the needs and expectations of immigrant children and families in general positive ways that promote stability. The Chinese American family, however, has been affected adversely in recent years by new immigration policies that have reduced the ability of Chinese to produce that kind of family in America. Because of limited quotas and policy stipulations, that economic considerations are taking equal priority with family preference, Chinese American children and families suffer the difficulty of maintaining extended family systems that offer structure and support. Under current immigration policies, it is harder for many Chinese immigrants to produce a meaningful family web in the United States. The results of this are likely to be additional psychological and social problems arising for Chinese children and families.

Other pressures for Chinese immigrant children and families are likely to arise given the negative mood of the country regarding immigration in general. Those who serve immigrant communities note increasing problems about:

1. lack of access for immigrants to even basic social services, such as education and health care. This is reflected in the Proposition 187 mood, which cut off services to illegal immigrants in California and, more recently, to legal immigrants as well;

2. exacerbation of the current problem of obtaining quality and equality of education;

3. exacerbation of the already strong Chinese American tendency to underuse mental health resources; and

4. potential for the rise of various kinds of discrimination.

If the public discourse continues in the direction of sanctioning abuse of immigrants and discrimination against their children, then other problems that exist for Chinese American children and families can only get worse (Lindsay, 1985).

## CONCLUSION

Current trends in U.S. immigration policy are tending to weaken the Chinese American immigrant family web. Therefore, it is necessary to go back to an immigration policy that unambiguously supports the reunification of Chinese American families. As Francis Fukuyama (1994), author of "Immigrants and Family Values," states:

> These problems [that immigrants face] can be tackled with specific changes in public policy. But the central issue raised by the immigration question is indeed a cultural one, and as such less susceptible to policy manipulation. The problem here is not the foreign culture that immigrants bring with them from the Third World, but the contemporary elite culture of Americans. (p. 167)

Other concerns are possible smaller limits on Chinese immigrant numbers and the selecting of immigrants for cash or skills rather than for family reunification, as immigration policy is supposed to uphold. Borjas (1990) describes the dilemma an individual and family face in deciding whether to pursue the status of "diversity immigrants or investor immigrants":

> In particular, single or unattached persons decide to immigrate by comparing their own economic opportunities among potential countries of residence. Families make the immigration decision by comparing the family's economic welfare among the various countries. The family must also determine the placement of its members in the immigration chain (who goes first?). Finally, all members of the family unit must decide whether to go along with the family's immigration decision or to break away from the family altogether and do what is personally best for them. In the end, persons immigrating as part of a family unit, whether they came at the same time or in sequence, will differ from persons who moved on their own. (p. 178)

This decision to move alone, to move within the family decision-made priority order, or to move with the pressure of providing for the rest of the family's economic well-being puts a lot of pressure on the individual and the family, challenging and potentially damaging the traditional cultural values of family first, respect for elders, and obedience to parents—which are fundamental to Chinese family functioning. Stressors for Chinese immigrants to the United States may also interfere with filial relations, as Lin and Liu (1993b, p. 271) report in the areas of "absence of structural and institutional support, generational differences in the pace of assimilation, and the cultural differences between the Chinese and American society."

California's Proposition 187 is just one sign of a backlash that is sure to have negative effects on Chinese children and families. "The 1990 reforms put into place the concept of a ceiling on preference visas, which could be extended to the immediate relative category given strong xenophobia or nativism" (Hing 1993b, p. 128). Anti-immigration feeling could slow or even halt the reunification of Chinese American families (as it did in 1882) with deleterious effects on Chinese American children.

What has been missing from the formulation of U.S. immigration policy has been systematic attention to the needs and cultural patterns of particular immigrant groups. In an article on "The Mental Health of Chinese-American Children," Sue and Chin (1983) describe certain long-term and systematic social stressors that act negatively on Chinese American children: conflict between ancestral and host culture, personal and institutional racism, and rapid social change. In dealing with such stressors, they find that Chinese American children have significant personal and community resources that aid mental health. But by far the most important resource for Chinese American children is the family, both nuclear and extended.

It is the suggestion of this chapter that if immigration policy is in any way to serve the needs of Chinese American children, it must take these factors into account. In particular, it must acknowledge the central importance of the extended family and act to support and strengthen it. It must maintain the goal of family reunification, including strong preference for not only nuclear but extended family members. It must not give in to the xenophobic trends of our time by cutting the number of immigrants who can come, nor replace family preferences with economic ones. Rather, immigration policy should seek to serve the interests of Chinese Americans, and indeed other immigrant children and their families.

REFERENCES

Ahearn, Jr., F. & Athey, J. (Eds.) (1991). *Refugee children: Theory, research, and services.* Baltimore: Johns Hopkins University Press.
Anzovin, S. (Ed.) (1985). *The problem of immigration.* New York: H. W. Wilson.
Bennett, M. (1963). *American immigration policies: A history.* Washington, DC: Public Affairs Press.

Borjas, G. (1990). *Friends or strangers: The impact of immigrants on the U.S. economy.* New York: Basic Books.

Briggs, Jr., V. & Moore, S. (1994). *Still an open door: U.S. immigration policy and the American economy.* Washington, DC: American University Press.

Brislin, R., Lonner, W. & Thorndike, R. (1973). *Cross cultural research methods.* New York: Wiley.

Brown, L. (1993). *Immigration: Cultural conflicts and social adjustments.* New York: Longmans, Green.

Chan, S. (1991). *Asian Americans: An interpretive history.* Boston: Twayne.

Daniels, R. (1988). *Asian Americans: Chinese and Japanese in the United States since 1850.* Seattle: University of Washington Press.

Finch, W. A., Jr. (1990). The Immigration Reform and Control Act of 1986: A preliminary assessment. *Social Service Review, 64,* 245–260.

Fong, R. (1990). *China's single child policy: The impact on family and schools.* Unpublished doctoral dissertation, Harvard University.

———. (1992). History of Asian Americans. In Sharlene Furuto et al. (Eds.), *Social work practice with Asian Americans* (pp. 3–26). Beverly Hills, CA: Sage.

———. (1997). Child welfare practice with Chinese families: Assessment issues for immigrants from the People's Republic of China. *Journal of Family Social Work, 2,* 33–48.

Fong, R. & Spickard, P. (1994). Ethnic relations in the People's Republic of China: Images and social distance. *Journal of Northeast Asian Studies, 13,* 26–48.

Fukuyama, F. (1994). Immigrants and family values. In N. Mills (Ed.), *Arguing immigration: The debate over the changing face of America* (pp. 151–168). New York: Simon & Schuster.

Gelfand, D. E. & Bialik-Gilad, R. (1989). Immigration reform and social work. *Social Work, 34,* 23–27.

Gladney, D. (1991). *Muslim Chinese: Ethnic nationalism in the People's Republic.* Cambridge, MA: Council on East Asian Studies, Harvard University.

Hing, B. (1993a). *Making and remaking Asian America through immigration policy, 1850–1990.* Stanford, CA: Stanford University Press.

———. 1993b. Immigration Policy. In LEAP, *The state of Asian Pacific America: Policy issues to the year 2000* (pp. 127–139). Los Angeles: LEAP and UCLA Asian American Studies Center.

Hirayama, H. & Cetingok, M. (1988). Empowerment: A social work approach for Asian immigrants. *Social Work Casework, 69,* 41–47.

Ho, M. K. (1987). *Family therapy with ethnic minorities.* Newbury Park, CA: Sage.

———. (1992). *Minority children and adolescents in therapy.* Newbury Park, CA: Sage.

Honig, E. (1992). *Creating Chinese ethnicity: Subei people in Shanghai, 1850–1980.* New Haven, CT: Yale University Press.

Huang, K. (1991). Chinese Americans. In N. Mokuau (Ed.), *Handbook of social services for Asian and Pacific Islanders* (pp. 79–96). New York: Greenwood Press.

Huang, L. (1990). Southeast Asian refugee children and adolescents. In J. T. Gibbs & L. N. Huang (Eds.), *Children of color: Psychological interventions with minority youth* (pp. 278–321). San Francisco: Jossey-Bass.

Huang, L. & Ying, Y. (1990). Chinese American children and adolescents. In J. T. Gibbs & L. N. Huang (Eds.), *Children of color: Psychological interventions with minority youth* (pp. 30–66). San Francisco: Jossey-Bass.

Kitano, H. & Daniels, R. (1988). *Asian Americans.* Englewood Cliffs, NJ: Prentice-Hall.

Le-Doux, C. & Stephens, K. (1992). Refugee and immigrant social service delivery: Critical management issues. In A. S. Ryan (Ed.), *Social work with immigrants and refugees.* (pp. 31–45). New York: Haworth Press.

Lee, E. (1982). A social systems approach to assessment and treatment for Chinese

American families. In M. McGoldrick, J. Pierce & J. Giordano (Eds.), *Ethnicity and family therapy* (pp. 527–551). New York: Guilford Press.

Lin, C. & Liu, W. (1993). Intergenerational relationships among Chinese immigrant families from Taiwan. In H. P. McAdoo (Ed.), *Family ethnicity: Strength in diversity* (pp. 271–286). Newbury Park, CA: Sage.

Lindsay, R. (1985). The new Asian immigrants. In S. Anzovin (Ed.), *The problem of immigration.* New York: H. W. Wilson.

Liu, W. T., Yu, E., Chang, C. & Fernandez, M. (1990). The mental health of Asian American teenagers: A research challenge. In A. R. Stiffman & L. E. Davis (Eds.), *Ethnic issues in adolescent mental health* (pp. 92–112). Newbury Park, CA: Sage.

Longres, J. (1990). *Human behavior in the social environment.* Itasca, IL: F. E. Peacock.

Loo, C. (1991). *Chinatown: Most time, hard time.* New York: Praeger.

Lum, D. (1992). *Social work practice and people of color: A process-stage approach.* Pacific Grove, CA: Brooks/Cole.

Muller, T. (1993). *Immigrants and the American city.* New York: New York University Press.

Nee, V. & Nee, B. (1973). *Longtime Californ'.* Boston: Houghton Mifflin.

Ou, Y. S. & McAdoo, H. (1993). Socialization of Chinese American children. In H. P. McAdoo (Ed.), *Family ethnicity: Strength in diversity* (pp. 245–270). Newbury Park, CA: Sage.

Ryan, A. (Ed.) (1992). *Social work with immigrants and refugees.* New York: Haworth Press.

Sandmeyer, E. (1973). *The Anti-Chinese movement in California,* 2nd ed. Urbana: University of Illinois Press.

Shon, S. P. & Ja, D. (1982). Asian families. In M. McGoldrick, J. Pearce & J. Giordano (Eds.), *Ethnicity and family therapy* (pp. 208–228). New York: Guilford.

Sollenberger, R. (1968). Chinese American child-rearing practices and juvenile delinquency. *Journal of Social Psychology, 74,* 13–23.

Sue, D., Sue, D. & Sue, D. (1982). Psychological development of Chinese-American children. In G. Powell (Ed.), *The psychosocial development of minority group children* (pp. 159–166). New York: Brunner/Mazel.

Sue, S. & Chin, R. (1983). The mental health of Chinese American children: Stressors and resources. In G. Powell (Ed.), *The psychosocial development of minority group children* (pp. 385–400). New York: Brunner/Mazel.

Sue, S. & Morishima, J. (1990). *The mental health of Asian Americans.* San Francisco: Jossey-Bass.

Sung, B. (1987). *The adjustment experience of Chinese immigrant children in New York City.* Staten Island, NY: Center for Migration Studies.

Trueba, H., Jacobs, L. & Kirton, E. (1990). *Cultural conflict and adaptation.* New York: Falmer.

Uba, L. (1994). *Asian Americans: Personality patterns, identity, and mental health.* New York: Guilford.

U.S. Bureau of the Census (1991). *Race and Hispanic origin. 1990 Census Profile.* Washington, D.C.: U.S. Bureau of the Census.

Wong, M. G. (1995). Chinese Americans. In. P. G. Min (Ed.), *Asian Americans: Contemporary trends and issues* (pp. 58–94). Newbury Park, CA: Sage.

Wu, D. (1991). The construction of Chinese and non-Chinese identities. *Daedalus: Journal of American Academy of Arts and Sciences, 20,* 159–180.

# 10 DIVERSE CHILDREN OF COLOR

## RESEARCH AND POLICY IMPLICATIONS

*Harriette Pipes McAdoo*

Children from families of color have become an increasing area of concern for those who are in positions of conducting research and formulating social policy. There are implications that will need to be studied and to be prepared for if we are going to be in positions to address the challenges that will come from a demographically diverse society. This chapter will explore the dynamics of changing demography of the United States. It will examine the type of policy that would be more supportive for diverse children and families and the programs that are most in jeopardy of being modified. Information will be given on sources of help for researchers and parents.

CONTEXTUAL DIVERSITY OF CHILDREN OF COLOR

Policy and research considerations of children of color will be discussed within the framework of an integrative model for the study of developmental competencies in children of color (García Coll et al., 1996). The social position and social stratification constructs are part of the core of a theoretical formulation of children's development. Variations in behaviors differ in large part because children develop in different developmental niches (MacPhee, Fritz & Miller-Heyl, 1996). Cochran, Larner, Rile, Gunnarsson & Henderson (1990) stated that structural forces in society constrain network membership by means of group identity, prejudice, and limited access to social capital that varies with cultural placements. The importance of the history of oppression, prejudice, and social and economic segregation in the policy formulations must not be overlooked.

The financial resources that are available for families of color are directly related to the economic isolation in which these families have been placed. The national trends of their available resources of all families have changed enormously in the past half-century and have had six demographic transformations (Hernandez, 1997). The first three were the shift to non-farm work, smaller family size, and increases in educational attainment. The second three had special significance for people of color: increased employment of mothers, the increase in single-mother families, and a substantial rise in childhood poverty. These changes occurred about ten years in advance for people of color before they occurred within families who were not of color (McAdoo, 1996a). Those children live in environments that differ in many ways from others in social organization, economic opportunities, and behaviors (Hernandez, 1997).

As these culturally diverse families are examined within the contexts of the family, school, and community, both the strengths and the weaknesses in the developmental processes will need to be considered (Boykin & Toms, 1985; García Coll & García, 1995; McAdoo, 1993a, 1995). The cultural sustaining roles of family and kin networks play a protective resource for children of color within the context of the family. These inhibiting and promoting environments influence the day-to-day interactions and experiences, interacting with the children's characteristics. However, McLoyd (1990) found out that ethnic groups consistently differed in measures of social stratification, but when these differences were co-varied in the pooled regressions, ethnicity did not explain variance in child-rearing practices. Therefore it is necessary to be sensitive to the conditions of the children and not to be driven by what may be conceptually in error, as we formulate policies that will address the issues that confront them.

## MAJOR INCREASES OF MULTICULTURAL FAMILIES

Few other countries have the proportion of ethnic families that the United States will soon have. As a country the United States is moving toward a complex level of multiculturalism. We will need to become more pluralistic in our orientations to address the multiple issues that will become of even · more concern in the immediate future. A fact of family life in America today is that families are composed of differing groups of individuals who have had many diverse experiences.

There are many different patterns of economic and social life that characterize families in North America (Hernandez, 1997; McAdoo, 1997). The growing diversities of economic and social experiences are increasing exponentially. The common element of being of descent of different cultures does not decide exactly what the life patterns of individuals will be. There are groups of color who have made major gains and are prospering; there are groups who are barely holding on to their gains; and there are groups of families who are sliding backward into economic chaos (McAdoo, 1995).

Our society is becoming more multicultural and multidimensional. Growing proportions of our society are coming from diverse families, both in natural increases in populations and from increases in immigration. Census projections have led to the prediction that by the year 2050 families of color will be over 50% of the families in North America (Marable, 1993). Whites of European descent will become a new minority group by then.

The increases have been the result of legal and illegal immigration and by natural increases. Immigration was an efficient way of managing when labor was needed for growing industrialization. However, immigration becomes less appealing when there are recessions, economic slowdowns, and fewer optimistic views of the future. Immigration is less desirable when this surplus labor comes in different colors, languages, family patterns, and diverse religions (McAdoo, 1995). Policies as a result are beginning to be changed to prevent further entry of people who are so different.

Our country has had a major influx of immigrants and births of those whose descent comes from countries that are non-European in origin. Drastic increases have been found in certain areas around the country. Persons whose descent is from China, Japan, and the Pacific Rim countries have increased from the 1980 to the 1990 census by 200%. Persons of Latino descent increased by 36%, while African Americans have increased by 26% (Frey, 1993). Native Americans have increased in selected areas due to selected migrations and reaffirmation of families. The proportion of families in North America from ethnic groups are no longer a minority of individuals within this country.

Immigration of groups of color has come at a time in which increases in the natural birthrates have also gone up. Persons of color tend to have larger families, because of the cultural patterns and often religious beliefs about not limiting family size. An additional factor is that these families of color are younger than those of the non-Hispanic white groups. They therefore will be in the age range of becoming parents far longer than most families. As a result, persons of color have more children per family, while nonethnic families have children at less than the replacement level. More children of color are being born, and fewer are born who are not of color.

These changes have caused each new generation of Americans to be more racially and ethnically diverse than its predecessor. The use of the term "minorities" has been questioned because of the demographic changes that are occurring in the United States. These children will no longer be minorities, but will become the numerical majority of persons in our society. Our own country will reflect the colors, the races, the diversities, and the languages of different groups who are now citizens.

Of the original baby boomers, 75% were non-Hispanic whites of European descent. In 1994, fewer than 66% of newborns were of non-Hispanic European descent. These new babies differ radically from each other in race, socioeconomic class, and in living arrangements. In addition, the next baby-boom generation, the children of the boomers, will be the first generation to question seriously all traditional racial categories. This is because so many of today's children are of mixed races. There has been an increase of interracial marriages, and there is one mixed-race child for every 35 members born in their cohort (Mitchell, 1995).

The predictions of a growing majority of persons of color already has taken place as these increases have occurred in states such as California, New York, and Florida. These groups will increase even more in the future. Legal and informal means have forced these groups of color even more into the narrow context of isolation. This environment is more difficult for these children to enter easily. These populations are here to stay, and we must therefore begin to examine our research and policy approaches to these families (McAdoo, 1996a).

## Resiliences of and Challenges Faced by Families of Color

Different social classes, divergent cultural groups, different ethnic group identities, and historical experiences in North America have resulted in family patterns and trends that may differ from those of families who are not of color. Ethnic families have been resilient and have overcome many overwhelming barriers (McAdoo, 1995; Wilkinson, 1997). These families, from all socioeconomic levels, should not be viewed only as persons who need help, but as groups who collectively are becoming one of the dominant groups in North America.

There have been attempts to focus on the large number of families of color who are in trouble. There is a tendency to overlook the families who are coping under less than ideal conditions and are rearing their children into competent adults under difficult situations.

It is important to understand that the common element of being of color does not decide exactly what the life patterns of individuals will be (McAdoo, 1995). It has, however, become more difficult to excel under the present environment.

## Sociocultural Challenges of American Families and Children

Different social classes, divergent cultural groups, different ethnic group identities, and historical experiences in North America have resulted in family patterns and trends that may differ from those of families who are not of color. The exchange of information between the racial-cultural group and the wider society is facilitated by the social networks of kin and friends (Wellman, 1990). The communication between the spheres of children's lives are crucial components of coping with differences that may exist.

When parents are in situations that may be marginal, the parents have difficulty responding to the developmental needs of their children. Even when sociocultural resources are more than adequate, children and families confront the damaging effects of devaluation, racism and isolation that can have an impact on self-efficacy (Harrison et al., 1995). The inability to effectively access the resources of the mainstream environment is one of the reasons that persons of color tend to rely on their extended family and friends. The social capital that is available from their social networks will play an important role in the ability of the parents and children to be able to obtain needed resources from the environment. Such assistance of the social networks buffers the negative effects of stress of being in a different social-cultural group, in an environment in which cultural differences are not readily accepted. Persons of cultural groups have developmental niches that are unique to each racial-ethnic group (MacPhee, Fritz & Miller-Heyl, 1996). These niches are elements that should be taken into consideration as research is designed and policies are implemented that would be supportive for people of color.

Child-rearing practices of some groups will be imparted by the ecological dimensions of class, ethnicity, and educational attainment level. Native Americans, for example, tend to emphasize communal values (Dehyle, 1992). Hispanic parents tend to value conformity and obedience, and are more inclined to be controlling and to use punishment (Knight, Verdin & Roosa, 1994; Martinez, 1993; Quintana, 1991). These attributes and values may put the children at a disadvantage when they enter into competition with the mainstream environment.

Researchers have recognized that factors beyond the structural makeup of the family may help to determine indirectly the disciplinary styles and practices of families (Erlanger, 1974; Portes, Dunham & Williams, 1986). However, when one examines the data, the factors of diverse racial groups being lower income and having lower socioeconomic status are often confounded. The designers of research efforts will need to be more articulate in the delineation of characteristics. They should attempt to avoid the misuse of only lower socioeconomic status samples for their research. Too often low-income groups are selected because they are more accessible, compliant, and unsophisticated. To be able to make observations about persons of color that accurately present generalizable data, it will be necessary for the wide range of groups within each ethnic group to be examined.

Middle-class, educated, urban persons will often present pictures of their family life and their children that contradicts many of the widely accepted beliefs, or stereotypes, about a particular group.

When one analyzes these groups for commonalities, one finds strong similarities. There are very similar family patterns in groups of color—Native American, Mexican American, African American, and Asian families. These are the common cultural patterns that have contributed to the resiliency of families of color. There are supportive social networks, flexible relationships within the family units, a strong sense of religiosity, extensive use of extended family helping arrangements, the adoption of fictive kin who become as family, and strong identification with their racial group (Allen, 1993; Boyd-Franklin, 1989; McAdoo, 1993b; Stack, 1974).

The extended families of African Americans is practically the same as "familism" in Mexican Americans, but they are often never discussed together or compared. The respect that is given the elderly in Asian families is similar to the central roles of the elderly in Native American families. All of these groups have culturally evolved in unique ways that reflect the country or origin, the culture, and the geographic location of their groups, yet are very similar in their family patterns. Elements of these behaviors are imbedded in a sense of obligation and are reciprocal in nature (Dodson, 1996; Keefe, Padilla & Carlos, 1979; Quintana, 1991; McAdoo, 1996b). The sense of connectedness and respect for family members is commonly found at all socioeconomic levels, even in groups with few resources. Cochran, et al. (1990) argued that structural forces in society constrain social network memberships that vary across cultures by means of prejudice, group identity, and limited access to social capital. Even when behaviors of some individuals are far from ideal, as one often finds in poor urban centers, one will find elements of care and respect for the kin and fictive kin.

These extended family arrangements were coupled with the extensive helping arrangements that were typical in many of the social supports of families (Aschenbrenner, 1975; Harjo, 1993; McAdoo, 1993a). These "webs of kinship" form cooperative relationships that cut across families and households (Fortes, 1949). However, the extended family helping arrangements have begun to be modified with the increase in limited family resources. These extended patterns of resiliency have continued to provide protective covers for entire families and communities. Family members have found themselves financially stretched and are often close to the breaking point because of economic survival issues. Younger persons are also growing up without the protection of the wider family networks and therefore are changing the family patterns. The extensive helping networks are slowly becoming erased because of the economic situations in which families find themselves.

Family patterns are changing in all families in the United States and probably will be unable to convert again to dual-parent homes. Younger persons are growing up without the protection of wider family networks and without both parents in the home. The majority of many groups have higher rates of children who are growing up without both parents. Economic uncertainty accounts for many of the family structures, but the overwhelming causal factor is the imbalance of the sex ratios in families of color (Bennet, Bloom & Craig, 1989; Cready & Fossett, 1997; Guttenberg & Secord, 1983; McLanahan, Garfinkel & Watson, 1988; Tucker & Mitchell-Kernan, 1991). There are simply not enough men available who would make good husbands. This fact causes marriages not to form or, when formed, to disintegrate because of stresses and strains that are inherent within the living situations of groups of color.

## RESEARCH IMPLICATIONS OF CHANGES IN AMERICAN FAMILIES

There is a growing awareness within the research and policy communities that culture plays an important and essential role within family life. Situations are now different for these children who are developing in ways that are different from those of their parents. We will need to document children's abilities of coping with stressful situations and the strengths of their particular culture. Policies should be examined in light of the group differences that may be problematic for these groups.

We will need to be aware of the policies and research approaches that will be more sensitive to these children who come from different experiences and cultures. Research approaches of design requirements, the race and culture of the persons who are in the design process, and doing the actual interviewing may be different from present arrangements considering the group that is being studied.

There is a need for a more realistic view of these diverse children and families, and avoidance of the use of stereotypes. Researchers need to explore the wide range of socioeconomic groups that are found in all ethnic groups. Misleading pictures are obtained when only the mean scores of groups are known. On all variables we need to get the distribution of the social class groups' educational levels.

The country of origin for children is a very important but too often overlooked design element. For example, too many studies use the term "Hispanic" and put anybody in it who speaks Spanish, regardless of the very different cultural groups and individual histories that are included. The term "Asian" is sometimes used, putting together Chinese, Japanese, East Asians, and other groups without regard for the significant cultural differences. Yet we know that there are different cultural norms, child-rearing approaches, and levels of acculturation of each of these groups.

When research projects are designed, it is necessary to be aware of the difficulties in analyzing the results of any study that used this approach. It is impossible to have a sample of 80% to 90% children of color without discussing the contextual cultural situation of these children. But our society is not open and accepting of change. We should be aware that the growing levels of conservatism did not happen overnight. There are groups within our society who are afraid of change. They are well financed and organized, and they are not concerned with being supportive of families and children who may be different. These are the opinions and attitudes with which we are faced in attempts to help children.

As researchers it is necessary to respond to new policies that are often not supportive of children. Politics plays a great part in where children and families are today. Family income, welfare, and resources are for the most part politically determined, especially for those of color. As the many changes are occurring in Congress, and in the state capitals of this country, it is often easy to overlook the political realities that are being played out within the lives of families.

## POLICY IMPLICATIONS OF GROWING MULTICULTURALISM

Policies are often based upon the commonly acknowledged beliefs about different groups of persons of color. However, one finds that research often has major faults that deny many of the facts that are presented in the literature. Changes in demography, the increases in families of color, and a growing awareness of the major part that culture, family of origin, and the continuing importance of race highlight the need for better research upon which the policies will be based.

The changing demographics have not been accepted with total grace by those who are in positions of authority. Persons of color are increasingly faced with problematic issues, including the devaluation of their institutions, persons, values, and artifacts that are related to their cultures. These devaluations are the result of insistence on the continuation of former research paradigms that are European American in orientation. The predominant cultural beliefs have been handed down for generations in the European context and has been continued into the Americas.

The use of these ideas has placed persons of descent of color into situations and institutions that are indeed inferior. As a consequence persons of all colors have found themselves isolated to an extent from the educational and economic mainstreams of American life. Devaluations of cultural attributes have had a profound impact on the development of persons of color. This isolation from the socioeconomic realities denies the elements that allow individuals access into the mainstream of American life.

There is a growing awareness within the research and policy communities that culture plays an important and essential role within family life. Situations are now different for these children who are developing in ways that will be different from those of their parents. We will need to document children's abilities of coping with stressful situations and the strengths of their particular culture. Policies should be examined in light of the group differences that may be problematic for these groups.

An awareness of the policies and research approaches that will be more sensitive to these children who come from different experiences and cultures is needed. Research approaches of design requirements, the race and culture of the persons who are in the design process, and doing the actual interviewing may be different from present arrangements considering the group that is being studied.

All areas related to children will have to develop research agendas. In the health arena, for example, the House Appropriations Committee has asked for such an agenda related to health care affecting quality and outcome measures. The Agency for Health Care Policy and Research (1997) has responded by presenting a report.

The goals of preventing or coping with poverty of children are in direct competition with the newer policies that are currently being considered. These new policies are aimed at concentrating wealth and power among a few well-endowed white males. The facts that we originally thought were true have been found to be wanting. The facts are rights of children, female empowerment, nondiscrimination, and the desire for a level playing field. We have found that they are tenuous and totally dependent on the whims of those who are in power at any one time.

Programs such as school lunches and welfare support are being threatened. Calls are being made for block grants. This is very reminiscent of earlier calls for state's rights, especially in the southern segregationist states. Racism is entering the process even more, as cognitive abilities are assailed in the "bell curve," as affirmative action is denigrated, and, increasingly, as policymakers are becoming more conservative in their orientations. Majors (1994) has stated that achieving racial justice is a long-term goal.

Research agenda for children and families of color will have to be focused on specific issues. In order to be effective in providing results based on empirical research, and in transferring what is known to persons who are making policy and implementing programs, it will be necessary to modify the approaches of working with policymakers and program administrators. Research can no longer be conducted as before. As researchers, money may not be available, but we do have the skills of designing studies and interpreting data results. The usual tactics of conducting studies and simply publishing the results in academic journals is no longer sufficient. Empirical research must provide succinct results. Suggestions of programs of implementation will have to be specific to the agency or department with which specific policies are related. Issues and monies are moving from the national to the state levels. Researchers had trouble keeping abreast of federal policies, and now it will be necessary to understand up to 50 different state levels of policies of important issues.

There is a need to become more vigilant and politically active and to conduct research that will document the impact of new policy changes that are sure to come. Research must be made accessible for advocacy groups. There is an important need for us to translate our findings into language that is understandable for advocacy groups, policy designers, and for congressional staffers. Testimonies will have to be refined for congressional hearings. It has been said that the research findings and our interpretations of concepts should be placed on two or at most three four-by-six bibliography cards. If there are any more than this it will not be read or remembered. To be useful, it is necessary for us to become educated and to pass on our knowledge to those who are formulating policies. Individual efforts will have to be augmented with the collective voices of our professional organizations, coupled with the skillful use of multimedia tools. We will need to become more sophisticated in the uses of media and publicity to allow the research findings to be heard by those who are in positions of formulating policies.

There are organizations and advocacy groups whose materials can be very helpful as we attempt to work to support policies that are supportive of families of color. The National Council of Family Relations' Public Policy Committee (1994) has produced a pamphlet titled *Action Alert: Critical Legislative Developments at Federal and State Levels Affecting Poor Families*. It condenses the most recent and relevant ideas of the Children's Defense Fund, the Child Welfare League, and the Center for Law and Social Policy. Foundations are becoming increasingly important in translating existing knowledge. The Packard Foundation (*The Future of Children*, 1995) is one example of a foundation attempting to provide objective analysis and evaluation of effective programs and policies. This book was presented to complement the technical analysis that is found in academic journals. It also attempts to give additional information to coverage given in the popular press and to augment the efforts of special-interest groups.

Marian Wright Edelman (1996) of the Children's Defense Fund has stated that we must formulate an action agenda for our children. Edelman has provided directions for useful policies affecting African American children, but these would be relevant for all persons of color, and for researchers who are sympathetic to the cause of influencing policies and programs that will be appropriate in the coming years. Edelman stated that it is necessary to (1) become an active and effective advocate for ethnic and poor children; (2) become well informed about the needs of children and families in your area and nationally; (3) not accept or give excuses for doing nothing; (4) understand that no one is going to give these children anything, especially if it seems it is taking away from the mainstream children; (5) recognize that the ground rules for achieving change are different now than they were five or ten years ago; (6) focus attention and energies; (7) expend energy on real issues and not on symbolic ones; (8) persist and dig in for a long fight; (9) use what you have to get what you must; and (10) confront and attack the right enemies and stand united. This action agenda for children and families focuses on specific goals to help children now and in the future. Two kinds of activities for researchers and advocacy workers are included in this agenda. Activities at the local level will need to be undertaken and often can entail the use of existing research and resources. At the state and national levels, the policies and practices will need to be changed at the institutional and governmental level. As we move into a period of time when there will be more persons of color in the labor market, and when they will form the majority of persons in this country, we are all dependent upon the futures of our families and children. They will need to draw even more on the traditional sources of support that have been found to be successful in the past.

Circumstances of the process whereby policies for children become a reality: Aldous (1997) has stated that in the future emphasis will be placed on coalition building and negotiations among leaders of interested groups. A variety of agencies and programs have the responsibility for the health, education, social and financial welfare, housing, and civil rights of America's children. These policies and programs will need to be monitored and changed to ensure the equitable treatment of all children. The future of all of us will be determined, to a great extent, by our abilities to take action and to improve the situations of America's children.

REFERENCES

Aldous, J. (1997). Making family policy in difficult times. *Journal of family issues, 18* (1), January, 4–6.

Allen, W. (1993). Black families: protectors of the realm. *Morehouse Research Institute Bulletin, 93* (3), 1–3.

Aschenbrenner, J. (1975). *Lifelines: Black families in Chicago.* New York: Holt, Rinehart & Winston.

Bennett, N., Bloom, D. & Craig, P. (1989). The divergence of black and white marriage patterns. *American Journal of Sociology, 95,* 692–722.

Boyd-Franklin, N. (1989). *Black families in therapy.* New York: Guilford Press.

Boykin, A. & Toms, F. (1985). Black child socialization: A conceptual framework. In H. McAdoo and J. McAdoo (Eds.), *Black children: Social, educational, and parental environments* (pp. 33–52). Newbury Park, CA: Sage.

Center for the Future of Children (Spring 1995). *The future of children.* Los Angeles: The David and Lucille Packard Foundation.

Child Health Services: Building a Research Agenda (1997). Report to the Committee on Appropriations, U.S. House of Representatives. Washington, DC: Department of Health and Human Services.

Cochran, M., Larner, M., Rile, D., Gunnarsson, L. & Henderson, C. (1990). *Extending families: The social networks of parents and their children.* Cambridge, UK: Cambridge University Press.

Cready, C. & Fossett, M. (1997). Mate availability and African American family structure in the U.S. nonmetropolitan south, 1960–1990. *Journal of Marriage and the Family, 59,* 192–203.

DeGenova, M. (1977). *Families in cultural context: Strengths and challenges in diversity.* Mountain View, CA: Mayfield Publishing.

Dehyle, D. (1992). Constructing failure and maintaining cultural identity: Navajo and Ute school leavers. *Journal of American Indian Education, 31,* 24–47.

Dodson, J. (1996). Conceptualizations of African American families. In H. McAdoo (Ed.), *Black Families,* 3rd ed. Thousand Oaks, CA: Sage.

Edelman, M. (1996). An advocacy agenda for black families and children. In H. McAdoo (Ed.), *Black Families,* 3rd ed. (pp. 323–332). Newbury Park, CA: Sage.

Erlanger, J. (1974). Social class and corporal punishment in childrearing: A reassessment. *American sociological review, 39,* 68–85.

Fortes, M. (1949). *The web of kinship.* London: Oxford University Press.

Frey, W. (1993). University of Michigan researcher sees patterns in census data. In J. Tilove & J. Hallinnan, A nation divided: A melting pot we're not. *Ann Arbor News* (Nov.).

García Coll, C. & García, H. A. V. (1995). Hispanic children and their families: On a differing track from the very beginning. In H. Fitzgerald, B. Lester & B. Zuckerman (Eds.), *Children of poverty: Research, health care, and policy issues* (pp. 57–83). New York: Garland.

García Coll, C., Lamberty, G., Jenkins, R., McAdoo, H., Crnic, K. & Wasik, B. (1996). An integrative model for the study of developmental competencies in minority children. *Child Development, 67,* 1891–1914.

Guttenberg, M. & Secord, P. (1983). *Too many women? The sex ratio question.* Beverly Hills, CA: Sage.

Harjo, S. (1993). The American Indian experience. In H. McAdoo (Ed.), *Family ethnicity: Strength in diversity.* Newbury Park, CA: Sage.

Harrison, A., Wilson, M., Pine, C., Chan, S. & Burie, R. (1990). Family ecologies of ethnic minority children. *Child Development, 61,* 347–362.

Hernandez, D. (1997). Child development and social demography of childhood. *Child Development, 68,* 149–169.

Jones, J. (1991). Racism: A cultural analysis of the problem. In R. Jones (Ed.), *Black psychology,* 3rd ed. (pp. 609–635). Berkeley, CA: Cobb & Henry.

Keefe, S., Padilla, A. & Carlos, M. (1979). The Mexican-American as an emotional support system. *Human Organization, 38,* 144–152.

Knight, G., Verdin, L. & Roosa, M. (1994). Socialization and family correlates of mental health outcomes among Hispanic and Anglo American children: Consideration of cross-ethnic scholar equivalence. *Child Development, 65,* 212–224.

MacPhee, D., Fritz, J. & Miller-Heyl, J. (1996). Ethnic variations in personal social networks. *Child Development, 67,* 3278–3295.

Majors, B. (1994, Sept./Oct.). General assembly news. *World: Journal of the Unitarian Univeralist Association,* pp. 47–53.

Marable, M. (1993, Sept./Oct.). Racism and multicultural democracy. *Poverty & Race.* (Poverty and Race Research Action Council) 2, 1–4, 12–13.

Martinez, E. (1993). Parenting young children in Mexican American/Hispanic families. In H. McAdoo (Ed.), *Family ethnicity: Strengths in diversity.* Newbury Park, CA: Sage.

McAdoo, H. (1993a). Family equality and ethnic diversity. In K. Altergott (Ed.), *One world, many families* (pp. 52–55). Minneapolis: National Council on Family Relations.

McAdoo, H. (1993b). The social cultural contexts of ecological developmental family models. In P. Boss, W. Doherty, R. LaRossa, W. Shumm & S. Steinmetz (Eds.), *Sourcebook of family theories and methods: A conceptual approach* (pp. 298–301). New York: Plenum.

McAdoo, H. (1995). African American families: Strength and realities. In H. McCubbin, E. Thompson, A. Thompson & J. Fromer (Eds.), *Resiliency in ethnic minority families: African American families.* University of Wisconsin Madison Press.

McAdoo, H. (Ed.) (1996a). *Family ethnicity: Strengths in diversity.* Newbury Park, CA: Sage.

McAdoo, H. (1996b). *Black families,* 3rd ed. Newbury Park, CA: Sage.

McAdoo, H. (1997). African American families. In C. Mendel, R. Habenstein & R. Wright (Eds.), *Ethnic families in America: Patterns and variations.* New York: Prentice-Hall.

McLanahan, S., Garfinkel, I. & Watson, D. (1988). Family structure, poverty, and the underclass. In M. McGeary & L. Lynn, Jr. (Eds.), *Urban change and poverty* (pp. 102–147. Washington, DC: National Academy Press.

McLoyd, V. C. (1990). Impact of economic hardship on black families and children: Psychological distress, parenting, and socioemotional development. *Child Development, 61,* 311–346.

Mindel, C., Habenstein, R. & Wright, R. (Eds.) (1980). *Ethic families in America: Patterns and variations.* New York: Elsevier.

Mitchell, S. (1995, October). The next baby boom. *American Demographics,* 22–31.

National Council of Family Relations (1994). *Action alert: Critical legislative developments at federal and state levels affecting poor families.* Minneapolis: National Council of Family Relations, 3989 Central Avenue NE, #550 (612–781–9331).

Portes, P., Dunham, R. & Williams, S. (1986). Assessing child-rearing styles in ecological settings: Its relations to culture, social class, early age intervention and scholastic achievement. *Adolescence, 21,* 723–735.

Quintana, F. (1991). *Pabladores: Hispanic Americans in the Ute frontier.* Notre Dame, IN: University of Notre Dame Press.

Stack, C. (1974). *All our kin: Strategies for survival in a black community.* New York: Harper & Row.

Tucker, B. & Mitchell-Kernan, C. (Eds.) (1991). *The decline of marriage among Afri-*

can Americans: Causes, consequences, and policy implications. New York: Russell-Sage.

Wellman, B. (1990). The place of kinfolk in personal community networks. *Marriage and family review, 15,* 195–225.

Wilkinson, D. (1996). Family ethnicity in America. In H. McAdoo (Ed.), *Family ethnicity: Strength in diversity.* Newbury Park, CA: Sage.

Wilkinson, D. (1997). American families of African descent. In M. DeGenova (Ed.), *Families in cultural context: Strengths and challenges in diversity* (pp. 335–360). London: Mayfield Publishing.

Yinger, M. (1976). Ethnicity in complex societies. In O. Larson & L. Coser (Eds.), *The uses of controversy in sociology* (pp. 197–216). New York: Free Press.

# 11 THEORY AND RESEARCH WITH CHILDREN OF COLOR

## IMPLICATIONS FOR SOCIAL POLICY

*Cynthia García Coll*
*Katherine Magnuson*

The purpose of this chapter is to draw some parallels between the theoretical and research underpinnings of the literature on children of color and the formulation of social policies that affect these children and their families. The irony of looking at social policies and children of color does not escape us in this task. Social policy for children of color for the most part does not exist; rather there are policies and there are children of color, and there are instances in which they intersect. In other words, most social policies that affect children and families of color are not specifically designed for these populations. However, because Native Americans, Hispanics, and African Americans are disproportionately represented in the lower socioeconomic strata of our nation, most social policy formulated by state and federal agencies targeting low-income families and their children tend to be applied to a large percentage of these populations (Washington, 1988). For example, in 1994 two-thirds of the children served by Head Start programs were nonwhite, 36% of the children served were black, and 24% were Hispanic (Head Start, 1995).

Historically, our nation has been concerned with the economic inequality among individuals and groups in our society (de Lone, 1979). In particular, we have been especially concerned with the needs of children who live in poverty, because we recognize that children born into poverty are disadvantaged by virtue of their birthplace in the social order. Our social programs over the past one hundred years have tried to address the needs of these children. To a certain extent, this has been based on our conceptualization of poverty as a self-perpetuating phenomenon. As de Lone (1979) described, we tend to see economic inequality as "at least partly the result of a vicious cycle that can best be broken by intervening in the victim's childhood—that poor children have poor parents who will rear them poorly to lead poor lives" (p. 21).

This understanding of poverty has created an impetus for intervening on the behalf of low-income children. It has enabled policymakers to make an explicit connection between providing services to poor children and our national hopes for creating a more egalitarian society. Consequently, most of our policies for children in poverty have been meant to provide them with experiences to enhance their social and intellectual development with the subsequent hope that they will lead improved lives. We have placed in these children and the programs that serve them the burden of decreasing the economic inequality present in our society (de Lone, 1979; Grubb & Lazerson, 1982).

However, the failure of our country and policies to ameliorate inequality is apparent in the context of current income statistics of different ethnic and racial groups. Programs to promote equality of opportunity or life chances have not proven to be effective equalizers, for either children or their families. Native Americans, blacks, and Hispanics have the lowest average incomes and the highest proportion of families with incomes below the official poverty line (Laosa, 1984). In 1991 according to the U.S. Bureau of the Census, 45.9% of African American and 40.4% of Hispanic origin children were living under the official poverty line. Between 1979 and 1992, the number of Latino families living in poverty increased by 127.2%, and the number of African American families increased by 41.4% (Enchautegui, 1995). Furthermore, African American and Puerto Rican children are more likely to be living in persistent poverty than white children (Duncan, 1991; Huston, McLoyd & García Coll, 1994). Native American children are often overlooked in poverty discussions, however; in 1986 Native Americans had a lower median income than either African Americans or white Americans, with the median income of Native Americans living on reservations amounting to only one-third of white median income (LaFromboise & Low, 1989).

The continuing economic disparity between groups within the United States is troublesome. It signifies the failure of our policies that intervene with children and families to remedy the uneven economic distribution and the vicious cycle of poverty. It warns us that we have not provided equal opportunities to all families and children. It highlights the continuing racism and discrimination in our society as well as the weaknesses in our structural economy (de Lone, 1979; Grubb & Lazerson, 1982). We know that children who live in poverty are at risk for a number of adverse behavioral and developmental outcomes (Huston, McLoyd & García Coll, 1994; Parker, Greer & Zuckerman, 1988), yet we continue to allow children to develop in dire circumstances. Even more alarming is that by failing to reduce economic inequality between racial and ethnic groups we are continuing to disproportionately place children of color at risk. Therefore, it is crucial that we examine the policies that have been targeted to help low-income families and children as well as our knowledge base about how these children develop.

## UNDERLYING PRINCIPLES OF CURRENT SOCIAL POLICIES

Most social policies that have been targeted to serve low-income families and children of color have been based on a compensation/remediation framework (Baratz & Baratz, 1970; Connell, 1994; Laosa, 1984). In order to provide poor children with better life chances, the majority of our social policies and programs seek to provide supplemental or corrective services in the form of individual assistance to these children and their parents. The term "compensation" refers to the notion that this assistance is intended to make up for previously insufficient experiences; "remediation" refers to the notion that these services are mainly corrective in purpose (Sameroff & Fiese, 1990).

There are several key principles underlying such an approach to social policy that warrant explicit recognition. The first assumption is that there exist demonstrated deficits (e.g., parenting or school readiness deficit) within certain populations (most frequently low-income populations of color) that inhibit or prevent the success of children in mainstream societal structures such as schools. The second assumption is that the most efficient way out of poverty is through education, as demonstrated by individual academic achievement (Halpern, 1990). Another assumption is that the deficiencies for which policies seek to compensate are found in comparison to a white mainstream or middle-class standard (Baratz & Baratz, 1970; Laosa, 1984).

This set of assumptions taken together form a compensation/remediation approach that attributes low-income children's "deficits" to their families' different patterns of behavior. In this paradigm, the parents of these children have failed to provide the core experiences that facilitate their children's achievement. Policies based on a compensation/remediation approach argue that by creating structures which provide the family or child with supplemental experiences that are more in line with middle-class mainstream white child rearing, the deficits can be corrected and the children will be enabled to transcend their disadvantaged backgrounds and succeed in mainstream schools.

These programs have sought to address specific problems of the populations they serve, without directly dealing with the underlying reasons for the problems that these families and children face: pervasive poverty and racism (deLone, 1979; Grubb & Lazerson, 1982; Siegal, 1983; Swadner & Lubeck, 1995). In other words, the programs structured for these children attribute most of their interpersonal or intrapersonal problems to the experiences in their family life. Following this reasoning, a poor mother is by definition inadequate: she creates through her low income the very situation that causes her child's failure (Siegal, 1983). Therefore, any causal factor located outside of the individual child or family, though possibly in passing considered a contributing factor, is not central to social policies or intervention efforts. Furthermore, the compensation/remediation paradigm relegates the disadvantaged minority to a permanent marginalized position outside of the mainstream, perpetuating the conceptualization that this minority needs intervention, and implying that everyone else is on the same footing (Connell, 1994).

Throughout the past 30 years the type of publicly funded interventions applied to families has changed, but the basic premise that these children demonstrate a deficit attributable to their early childhood experiences that will cause their failure if not corrected has not changed. In the 1960s a wave of new federally funded compensatory and remediative programs were enacted as part of President Lyndon Johnson's War on Poverty (Brown, 1985). Two types of these programs emerged: early childhood education and parenting classes. It is not our intent to suggest that all early childhood education programs or parenting programs are compensatory or remediative in nature. Programs such as child-care centers and nursery schools, or programs that primarily provide diagnostic and screening services, are not classified as compensatory (Baratz & Baratz, 1970).

## Early Childhood Education Programs

Early childhood compensation programs for low-income children became widespread after the desegregation and destratification of the American educational system. The ascendance of equal educational opportunity as a right of all children, including traditionally excluded minorities, led to more equal access to educational structures. However, equal access did not translate into equal achievement. Educators found that low-income and minority children performed less well on standard measures of academic achievement, and were more likely to be held back, drop out, and not continue on to college (Baratz & Baratz, 1970). Having put faith in education as the pathway out of poverty, the failure of certain segments of the population to succeed in equal proportions, despite more equal opportunity, was distressing and posed a challenge to the individualistic and egalitarian tenets of our society. Policymakers then turned their efforts toward improving the development of low-income children.

At this time it was assumed that low-income and minority children were entering classrooms without possessing the cognitive and linguistic skills that more successful mainstream students demonstrated. This difference in skill level was attributed to an experiential deficit in their early learning environments, more specifically, their home life. Policymakers focused on the perceived disorganization and lack of stimulation in these children's homes (Siegal, 1983). The solution was to provide these children with learning opportunities that would lead to the acquisition of the skills they were missing. Alternative early learning environments, centers and classrooms, were funded and created by policymakers and educators. In effect, these special settings, staffed by trained professionals, were created to provide the stimulation, individual attention, and socializing activities deemed necessary for future academic success. Therefore, low-income children prior to the age of school entry were removed from their homes during the day, and placed in classes specifically created to correct the perceived deficits. The intent was not to help low-income families get out of detrimental conditions in which they lived, but to help children survive the circumstances relatively unscathed, and to prepare them for future successes.

The programs, which still exist, vary greatly in design. For the most part, they target children's social and cognitive development, that is, the attitudes and aptitudes considered necessary for academic achievement. The classrooms usually center around a "developmentally appropriate curriculum" with structured activities taught by trained early childhood education professionals or paraprofessionals (Lubeck, 1994). Often the curriculums focus on linguistic and verbal skills that are related to school achievement. The method of teaching can vary greatly; some employ child-centered or child-initiated learning, while other classrooms are more teacher directed. Some stress academic skills, while others stress social skills. The programs vary as much in duration as they do in content.

Even with such heterogeneity in program designs, given that the primary concern of early childhood education has been the cognitive and intellectual development of the child, the evaluations used to measure the effectiveness of these programs have been based on children's performances on standard cognitive tests. Intelligence quotient (IQ) tests and school performance as manifested in such indicators as grade retention and special education placement are the most frequently examined outcomes. The efficacy of these programs has been determined by comparing these indicators with samples of children with similar backgrounds who remain at home until school entry. The programs have shown to have a modest impact on intellectual and cognitive development of the children who have participated (Barnett, 1995).

In making such a generalization about early childhood education programs, Head Start emerges as an exception. Head Start, one of the most successful programs for low-income children, was launched in 1965 as part of the massive community action program legislated by the Economic Opportunity Act of 1964. It was the first comprehensive preschool program created to reach the "whole child" and thus for the most part to recognize the power of contextual influences on child development (Laosa, 1984). The program, which continues today, includes health, social, and educational services for low-income preschool-age children.

Head Start was based on the notion that children develop within the context of their families and the philosophy of community action. Consequently, it was designed to facilitate the participation of parents in their children's learning, by involving them both in the classroom and in the decision-making process of the local programs. In this respect, Head Start has succeeded. Each Head Start center is required to have a parent coordinator, and nationally, 85% of parents volunteer in the classrooms yearly (Zigler & Styfoco, 1994). Head Start's emphasis on including and supporting the parent's role in their children's development addresses some of the contextual factors that promote and inhibit children's learning.

However, even with a recognition of the critical importance of families for the development of children, Head Start has at best made modest attempts in addressing the main inhibiting structural influences faced by the families it serves. Proponents argue that Head Start provides jobs for the population it seeks to serve by creating the opportunity for them to pursue positions and paraprofessional degrees in child care/development. In fact, Zigler and Styfoco (1994) report that 35% of Head Start employees are parents of current or former Head Start participants. This is not negligible. However, the extent to which the poor have been able to attain economic mobility because of Head Start is questionable. The salaries that Head Start workers receive are not even considerable enough to lift a single parent out of poverty (Ceglowski, 1994).

Other positive benefits from Head Start programs that might be present in the families and communities, such as increased adult literacy or employment, have not been adequately documented (Zigler, 1993). The majority of evaluation research that has been used to support the continued federal funding of Head Start still focuses on cognitive and educational gains of the child, rather than looking at children's life success, family or parental development, or other contextual variables (Lazar & Darlington, 1982; Zigler, 1993). Furthermore, these contextual results are incidental, because the programs are not intended, nor funded, to provide the parents with direct opportunities for self-improvement or long-term improved economic opportunities.

The children served by Head Start are still facing pervasive poverty and racism and thus the compounding risk factors associated with these conditions. As Sameroff (1993) pointed out:

> The fact that all children who experience Head Start do not go on to happy, healthy, productive lives is not surprising to those of us who have observed the living conditions and the school systems into which they graduate. . . . The Head Start experience is only one facet of the lives of these children, if the other facets are working against us, it is very difficult to make a major change in the life circumstances of these children. (p. 44)

## Parenting Education

Although recently revived, parent education and home visiting programs have an extensive history in the United States (Weiss, 1993). As Weiss (1993) describes, "there is a long history of setting up home visits as a silver bullet—the panacea for poverty—and of subsequent disappointment" (p. 115). These programs have been created and have operated on the premise that changing parents' and families' moral character and behavior, as opposed to just the child's, would eliminate poverty and other social ills that plague children's development. As Grubb and Lazerson (1982) explained, parenting education classes tend to hold up the old ideal of educated mother, thereby proposing a simple solution to complex societal problems.

The shift in policies from child-centered programs to parent-centered programs blossomed in the late 1970s (Grubb & Lazerson, 1982). This shift was based on the disappointing results of the evaluations of early childhood education programs (e.g., the Westinghouse Study; Cicirelli, Evans & Schiller, 1969). The evaluations of such programs found some lasting benefits for the participating children, but for the most part, it was demonstrated that early childhood education programs, which ran for a few months prior to school entrance, could not correct the perceived deficits of poor or minority children (Baratz & Baratz, 1970). This led to the notion that children were exhibiting fundamental deficits that could be mitigated only by an even more basic type of compensation/remediation than early childhood education programs could provide.

Parent education programs were further boosted by research that suggested low-income mothers had different communication and teaching styles than middle-class mothers (e.g., Hess & Shipman, 1965). This difference in mothering became the root of the hypothetical deficit demonstrated by low-income and minority children. Parenting education services were created to provide new competencies and knowledge to guide parents in raising their children. Consequently, the goal of the programs has been to modify the way that parents interact with their children and, in particular, to instruct mothers in development-enhancing behavior toward their children (Laosa, 1983, 1984). Proponents of parent education programs argued that because children spent the majority of their time in the company of their families, changing their parents' child-rearing patterns would in effect create a more intensive and individualized form of intervention in the lives of low-income children than child-centered programs (Florin & Dokecki, 1983). It was hoped that this intervention could in turn lead to improved educational outcomes.

Parent education programs vary considerably in the scope of competencies they hope to teach parents and in how they deliver services. Although all programs seek to foster the healthy development of young children, like early childhood education programs, they vary in goals, content, timing, and duration. However, the primary goal of most programs has been to improve the educational and parenting roles of parents. These programs concentrate on teaching parents desirable socialization and educational patterns (Laosa, 1983, 1984). In many programs, the education has a home visiting component in addition to a center- or group-based program. This has in part been an attempt to reach more isolated families that might face transportation or child-care barriers (Weiss, 1993).

By focusing on the parent-child relationship and the home environment, parent education programs create a dynamic whereby parents are "found responsible for any child or family problems" (Siegal, 1983). For the most part, this approach has overlooked the contribution of poverty or the stress and difficulties created by poor living conditions as a probable or even possible source of their poor parenting. Parents are held accountable for managing the daily difficulties as well as for interacting with their children according to standards of mainstream parental behavior that are believed to produce well-adjusted children (Laosa, 1984). The curricula are based primarily around the notion that these mothers need knowledge about how to interact with their children, rather than strategies to overcome or to cope with outside environmental demands that might be impinging upon their parenting abilities (Grubb & Lazerson, 1982; Laosa, 1984). Schorr (1992) described conventional parenting education as "quite irrelevant" to socially isolated and otherwise seriously disadvantaged parents (p. 271). She explained that these mothers are unlikely to find helpful the information they are given during these classes.

The varying scope of parenting programs has made an aggregate assessment or generalization of their impact on children's development difficult. In a review of caregiver focused interventions, Seitz and Provence (1990) point out that much less is known about these types of programs than other types of programs. This is particularly true given the wide range in the design of the programs and the targeted populations. For example, a review of home visiting programs for pregnant women and parents of young children found that the effectiveness of the programs varied with the characteristics and risk status of the sample. Women at risk for preterm deliveries benefited from the programs to the extent that the programs reduce the risk conditions that lead to poor birth outcomes (e.g., smoking). Thus, those populations with specific needs or higher than average risks may benefit more from these programs than others (Olds & Kitzman, 1993).

In a review of home visiting programs for families at social or economic risk, Olds and Kitzman (1993) found that the literature did not demonstrate positive outcomes from all programs. Less than half of the programs reviewed indicated cognitive gains in children or the parenting behaviors. Again, the programs varied in the risk factors associated with the families and on program measures such as intensity, duration, and the training of the staff. The Yale Child Welfare Project is an example of a program that provided some evidence of the positive benefits from parent-centered intervention (Seitz & Apfel, 1994; Seitz & Provence, 1990). Longitudinal evaluations of the program have shown that the experimental group of children demonstrated better school adjustment (not higher IQs). More impressive and hopeful was that these outcomes were also found in their younger siblings. That is, the program demonstrated that intervening at the parent level could create diffused effects and consequently those children who were born after the completion of the program also benefited (Seitz & Apfel, 1994). Thus, the better school adjustment of the siblings suggests that the program's facilitation of better parenting skills was an effective long-term strategy that may have promoted the development of younger children (Seitz & Apfel, 1994). Although these findings are promising, the program, though described as parent-centered, also provided other very important services. The families received pediatric care, social work, high-quality day care, and psychological services delivered by a continuous team of professionals. Most parenting education programs do not provide such an array of intensive services.

## Other Current Social Policy

Although the compensation/remediation framework has been employed most often in the construction of programs for low-income children and families, specific policies targeted at families of color also tend to reflect this framework. Our policies assume that these populations have a deficit, and therefore are created to correct the individuals' deficits. Bilingual education is one clear example of how social policies that target ethnic minorities are also based on a deficit paradigm.

Although the notion that nonnative English-speaking children need some special assistance to succeed in U.S. schools has been given credence, it is largely because we consider their inability to speak English as a deficit to be corrected through compensatory services. Although in theory bilingual education is meant to teach both English and the children's native language, nearly all programs emphasize learning English at the expense of the native language (Hakuta, 1986). This implies that when students' English-language use becomes adequate it is no longer necessary nor desirable to instruct children in their native languages (Laosa, 1984). Hakuta and García (1989) claim that the ultimate goal of bilingual education is to "mainstream students into monolingual English centered classrooms with maximal efficiency." Consequently, it not surprising that evaluations of bilingual programs have focused on how well these students have learned English, rather than their overall or more general academic achievement (Hakuta & García, 1989). In fact, most schools do not provide bilingual classes; instead they provide classes to help these children learn English, such as English as a Second Language or Limited English Proficient instruction (Hakuta, 1986).

The compensation/remediation paradigm is especially apparent when we realize that immigrant education is an invisible policy issue. Independent of immigrant children's need to learn English, these students are not considered a distinct group in need of any unique services (McDonnell & Hill, 1993). Policymakers have defined immigrant students' academic achievement in relation to their lack of English skills, rather than as impacted by larger social, structural and cultural factors imbedded in the histories of different linguistic minority groups within the United States (Hakuta & García, 1989).

Another interesting example of how the compensation/remediation paradigm is manifested in the lives of the children of color was offered by McLaughlin & Heath (1993). Their work was based on extensive fieldwork with youth programs in three cities. They asked the leaders of these programs and the youths to define the problems of youth in deteriorating urban environments. Each gave different responses. The leaders discussed the individual deficiencies of the children such as low motivation or the deficiencies of their families such as lack of parental care. The youths themselves understood and defined their problems in terms of the "failure of institutions which compose their social contexts" (p. 213). McLaughlin and Heath concluded that to be effective, youth programs needed to build on the youths' strengths, consider their own voices, and take into account the many contextual factors that influenced their lives.

## POLICY APPROACHES TO POVERTY

Current social policies for families in poverty are not limited to child and parent education. Federal money provides relief to families with low incomes in the form of Aid to Families with Dependent Children (AFDC). However, the way in which we have structured these programs have indicated that as a nation we are willing to provide only a small amount of relief from poverty to families, without providing a way out of poverty. Welfare, as we know it today, raises the standards of living only minimally for poor families. It provides a certain monthly income to mothers and their children; however, the amount that they receive leaves them well below the official poverty line. Edin's (1995) research found the average welfare mother fell short over three hundred dollars each month trying to meet her expenses using only welfare payments. Consequently, most women receiving aid sought out additional sources of income or in-kind contributions from friends and family members.

Although recent state and federal efforts have been made to promote or even require education and job training, AFDC has yet to be a strong force in the promotion of self-sufficiency (Smith, Blank & Collins, 1992). The assumption that a transition from welfare dependence to work brings about an increase in economic well-being ignores the fact that low-paying jobs neither lead to better jobs nor pay enough to remove a family from poverty (Edin, 1995). Programs often define the solution to welfare dependence as "labor force participation in any kind of job" (Edin, 1995, p. 4). Ironically, most job-training participants can at best move their family only slightly above the poverty line, and these programs have limited success rates in moving families off the welfare roles (Herr, Halpern & Conrad, 1991).

Welfare mothers in Edin's study had learned two seminal lessons from their previous work experience: first, that the types of jobs they could get did not make them any better off financially than receiving welfare payments, and second, that the jobs they attained would not lead them to better jobs or promotion. The employment they secured did not pay well, did not offer benefits, required irregular hours, and often involved intensive physical labor. This situation was described by the mothers as the "$5 an hour ghetto" (Edin, 1995, p. 5).

Programs that help participants receive high school equivalency degrees are also problematic. In an evaluation of Project Match, a welfare-to-work program, Herr, Halpern, and Conrad (1991) characterized GED placements as "unhelpful" and "unrealistic." They argued that most jobs that pay enough to support a family require more training and skills than provided by a high school equivalency degree. Furthermore, they noted that most participants in the GED classes dropped out before taking the exam.

In summary, it has not been on our agenda to help children or families who live in poverty to get out of poverty. We have expected that they find their own way out of poverty, even facing difficult labor markets and racism. We have tried to help poor children without helping their families, at first by creating alternate institutions in which to impart supposed lacking critical skills, and later by teaching their parents how to adapt to situations, rather than actually improve them.

## PARALLELS BETWEEN RESEARCH AND SOCIAL POLICY

This focus on remediation and compensation in the construction of social policy has been paralleled by a trend in theory research that emphasizes the deficient nature of the poor families and populations of color. To point out parallel trends is not to suggest that our policies, as we might hope, reflect our knowledge base. Rather it is more probable that social policy, theory, and research with poor children and children of color reflect the dominant ideology of our present historical and cultural context (de Lone, 1979; Grubb & Lazerson, 1982). That is to say that both fields are embedded in a larger ideology that influences the way in which we conceptualize the research we conduct and policy we construct for children of color (de Lone, 1979; García Coll & Magnuson, in press).

### Deficit Models

Most research conducted with children and families of color has been based on a set of assumptions and premises similar to those utilized by policymakers. The foremost assumption of researchers has been that low-income families and children of color have behavioral, cognitive, linguistic, and motivational deficits (McLoyd & Randolph, 1985). The causes of these deficits have varied, but mostly they have been attributed to either genetic or cultural factors. Although the bulk of the work that has emphasized a biological deficit in children of color was produced early in the twentieth century, there has remained a persistent argument throughout this century attributing the academic failure of these populations of color to biological or genetic inferiority of their "race" as measured through such indicators as IQ scores (García Coll et al., 1996).

Jensen's 1969 article in the *Harvard Educational Review* was one of the most clearly articulated pieces written about the biological/genetic deficiency of children of color. Jensen argued that the difference between blacks' and whites' IQ scores is due to genetic factors: "No one has yet to produce any evidence based on a properly controlled study to show that representative samples of Negro children and white children can be equalized in intellectual ability through statistical control of environment and education" (p. 82). In spite of this lack of definitive proof, Jensen proposed that the preponderance of evidence was in line with a genetic explanation of intelligence. He implied that blacks were cognitively inferior to whites, because intelligence is determined more by hereditary factors than environmental ones.

Jensen's ideas are revisited most recently in Herrnstein and Murray's *The Bell Curve,* published in 1994. By sifting through previous studies on IQ distributions and cognitive tests the authors argued that both genetics and environmental conditions contribute to the lower cognitive abilities of blacks in the United States. They further argued that lower cognitive abilities of blacks to a large extent explains their lower socioeconomic status within United States society. Finally, the authors proposed that those who are disadvantaged by their low cognitive abilities are not likely to be aided by intervention efforts targeted to increase their cognitive capacities. Consequently, Herrnstein and Murray suggested that educational research should shift its focus and spend more effort exploring the physiological basis of intelligence.

Although the genetically deficient model has been most often employed to compare blacks and whites, its theoretical underpinning is broad and has been used to describe other populations. For example, this framework was employed by Dunn (1987) to explain the lower IQ scores of Puerto Rican children. Dunn referred to and supported the work of Jensen (1969) by stating that genetics contributed to the Puerto Ricans' lower IQ scores through the mixing of the Spanish and African races. Although the work of Jensen, Herrnstein and Murray, and Dunn has been strongly contested, their ideas still reverberate throughout society.

Researchers who found the genetically based differences unpalatable and untenable proposed an alternate explanation of the lower cognitive abilities of populations of color that stressed the critical role of early experiences in the process of development. They attribute the failure of these populations to the environmental conditions of their development, with an emphasis on the transmission of cultural traits, and point out that these populations display different behaviors than middle-class mainstream families. This difference in behavior became understood as a "deprivation" and "pathological"

(Moynihan, 1965). Thus, this paradigm labeled children who were raised in families that did not display middle-class white mainstream behavior as "culturally deprived" because they lacked the benefits and advantages of Anglo, middle-class American child rearing. Although historically this paradigm seemed progressive, in that it no longer attributed biological or genetic "race" as a basis for cognitive deficits, it continued to locate a deficit and the causes of that deficit within low-income families and families of color.

This cultural deficient paradigm, like its genetic counterpart, was applicable to all low-achieving populations, but was most clearly applied to blacks and Hispanics. The two most well-known studies were Oscar Lewis's (1965) anthropological work *La Vida* and Daniel Patrick Moynihan's (1965) *The Negro Family*. These works suggested that cultural characteristics of a population were better indicators of outcome than contextual and systemic variables. In *La Vida*, a family study of Puerto Ricans in San Juan and New York, author Oscar Lewis wrote that "the remarkable stability in some of the behavior patterns . . . suggests that we are dealing with a tenacious cultural pattern. [This pattern included] more negative elements and pathology than I am willing to grant" (p. xxvii).

Another manifestation of this paradigm was found in the scholarly work of the 1964 Research Conference on Education and Cultural Deprivation, organized by the University of Chicago's Department of Education (Bloom, Davis & Hess, 1964). The final paper of the conference, which was based on participants' working papers, sought to generalize what was known "about the nature of cultural deprivation" and its impact on "disadvantaged children." The report covers a number of environmental conditions that were considered pivotal in the low-scholastic and developmental outcomes of these children; however, the roots of the problem were believed "in large part to be traced to their experiences in their homes which do not transmit the cultural patterns necessary for the types of learning characteristic of schools and the larger society" (Bloom, Davis & Hess, 1964, p. 3). In particular, the cultural handicap that the "Negro child" faced included "lack of books, lack of emphasis on reading in the home, the dialect the child learns from his family, and the level of parental interest in education" (Bloom, Davis & Hess, 1964, p. 21).

## Finding Deficits

In the process of finding deficits with families and children of color, the preponderance of research has sought to compare these populations with white middle-class families and children (McLoyd & Randolph, 1985). In particular, the developmental literature involving African Americans and Puerto

Ricans has focused on cross-race comparative research rather than intrarace research (Graham, 1992; McLoyd & Randolph, 1985). This is troublesome given the very small amount of normative developmental research conducted with populations of color (Graham, 1992). Similarly, research with Asian or Native American children is largely unavailable (García Coll, 1990).

This type of research limits our knowledge of children of color in several ways. First, it stresses outcomes rather than the processes that lead to differences in outcome (García Coll & Magnuson, in press). As Graham (1992) described, "it is not clear at all . . . that psychologists have achieved better understanding of the intellectual potential of Black children or their repertoires of adaptive social behaviors by relying on empirical literatures that simply chart their gains and losses relative to those of a White comparison group" (p. 634). Furthermore, by not addressing the mechanisms that lead to different outcomes, researchers have tended to disregard intragroup variability and consequently have often confounded cultural differences with differences in socioeconomic status (García Coll, 1990; Laosa, 1984).

Cross-cultural comparisons of outcomes also ignore the fact that the relationships between variables and the pathways by which these variables affect development may vary across contexts (García Coll & Magnuson, in press). This outcome comparative approach assumes a homogeneity within groups and among the relationships between variables across different contexts that is often unfounded if not erroneous.

Finally, in cross-cultural research, values of family functioning and normative child development based on white middle-class families are used as standards for outcomes in all families. Thus, diverse family structures, nontraditional two-parent homes, single head of households, and diverse family functioning as well as nontraditional competencies are interpreted as nonfunctional systems. Consequently, the variant experiences between groups have been systematized into "risk factors" by researchers (Swadner & Lubeck, 1995). As a result, families and children of color have been perceived as being inherently deviant, intellectually inferior, culturally deficient, and pathological (McLoyd & Randolph, 1985; Swadner & Lubeck, 1995). Even though studies address the contributions of stress, poverty, or the lack of social support, the literature's emphasis still remains on negative developmental outcomes (García Coll et al., 1996). Barbarin (1993) noted that most research on African American and Latino school-age children has focused on aggression, delinquency, attention deficits, and hyperactivity, but has not informed such areas as emotional development and resiliency. Consequently, the bulk of research has conceptualized low-income or minority children and families as in need of compensation or remediation services.

## Challenges to the Deficits

In recent years, the notion that low-income children and particularly children of color demonstrate deficits has been challenged repeatedly (e.g., Cole & Brunner, 1974; Labov, 1970; Tulkin, 1972; for a review of the contribution that research with children of color has made to psychology *see* Miller-Jones, 1988). Scholars in diverse fields have argued that families and children of color as a group do not manifest any deficiencies, cognitive, linguistic, or otherwise. They maintain that children of color are neither genetically inferior, culturally deprived, nor any less intellectually or cognitively capable upon entering schools. This criticism thus strikes at the very basis of compensation and remediation programs, and questions the assumptions of our knowledge base and intervention efforts.

Labov's (1970) work on the linguistic patterns of ghetto children is one of the most forceful attacks on the concept of deficits. He introduced his work by acknowledging that the poor performance of children in ghetto schools has been attributed to a cultural deficit resulting from their exposure to an impoverished environment in their early years. He claimed that the concept of verbal deprivation has achieved widespread acceptance by educators and psychologists. He concluded, however, that the notion of verbal deprivation has "no basis in social reality. . . . They have the same basic vocabulary, possess the same capacity for learning and use the same logic as anyone else who learns to speak English" (p. 153–154). Labov critiqued those who suggest the personal deficiencies of children and their home life as the source of their school failure and construct interventions based on this premise. He argued that such programs are bound to fail unless they address "the social and cultural obstacles to learning" that these children face.

Cole and Brunner (1974) use the work of Labov and others to further refute the notion that low-income children and children of color manifest deficits. Their critique was based largely on the argument that an individual's performance on psychological or educational tasks is not necessarily indicative of their competencies or capacities. They posited that the very assessment mechanisms that have been used to locate these deficits are themselves faulty. They explained that "the crux of the argument is that those groups ordinarily diagnosed as culturally deprived have the same underlying competence as those in the mainstream of the dominant culture, *the differences in performance being accounted for by the situations and contexts in which the competence is expressed*" (p. 870). By distinguishing between performance and competence they refocused the debate about educational failure on the context in which children develop, that is, the different situations to which children of various cultural groups apply their skills.

Other recent empirical work has also found that children of diverse backgrounds enter school with the same cognitive and developmental competencies as white children. For example, Enwisle and Alexander (1990) conducted a comparative study of math competencies in a group of urban black and white preschoolers. They found that these children were equivalent in verbal performance and math computational skills upon school entry. Their work also found that performances diverged after only one year of schooling, with the black children achieving less well than white children. The authors found this study persuasive evidence that school-based factors played a considerable role in explaining later performance differences between minority and majority populations.

Furthermore, recent work has also refuted the notion that low-income parents and families of color demonstrate deficits in their parenting behavior, especially in respect to imparting a drive or motivation for success (Arnold, 1995; Stevenson, Chen & Uttal, 1990). The findings from Stevenson, Chen, and Uttal's (1990) investigation of beliefs and achievement among different racial/ethnic groups led the authors to conclude that "despite adverse economic conditions and other social impediments, the black and Hispanic families represented in this study had enthusiastic attitudes about education and attempted to provide supportive environments for academic achievement in their young children" (p. 521). Likewise, in her study of Head Start children and their parents, Jones (1993) found that low-income parents had a strong desire to instill achievement motivation in their children. The parents emphasized the importance of teaching their children the skills, attitudes, and values that they would need to achieve regardless of the obstacles that they faced.

Finally, Cook and Fine's (1995) interviews with low-income African American mothers shed light on both the difficulties they encountered trying to raise their children in impoverished neighborhoods and their attempts to nevertheless promote their children's achievement. These mothers were actively involved in keeping their children out of trouble and in school, although the urban poverty in which they lived made it a constant struggle. Fine and Cook described these women as having "a fighting spirit and proactive mindset in making a difference in their child's social and educational lives" (p. 129).

## Mediating Variables

The second important parallel trend between child development research, theories, and social policy has been to understand developmental outcome as mediated by immediate personal, individual, or familial contextual factors rather than systemic or macro level influences, such as poverty and racism (Caplan & Nelson, 1973). It has been the nature of psychology and behavioral scientists to attribute causal significance to person-centered variables rather than situation-centered variables (García Coll & Magnuson, in press; McLoyd & Randolph, 1985).

An illustration of this phenomenon was provided by Caplan and Nelson (1973). They studied the first six months of psychology abstracts for 1970 that dealt with black Americans, "the most frequently studied group in a problematic relationship to the rest of society" (p. 203). Of the abstracts studied, 15% of the studies reported an association between problem characteristics and a personal characteristic, 19% presented such information in a correlated rather than an associated manner, but left the reader with a sense that the personal variable under consideration is at least a plausible causal variable. Forty-eight percent of the abstracts dealt with correlations between group memberships and personal characteristics, largely employing cross-racial comparisons that portrayed blacks in an unfavorable light. In conclusion, Caplan and Nelson found that 82% of the classifiable psychological research dealing with black Americans lent itself, either "directly or by implication, to interpreting the difficulties of black Americans in terms of personal shortcomings" and completely overlooked other kinds of forces that operate on black Americans (p. 204).

Another clear example of how our understanding of development is based on immediate variables is Belsky's (1984) process model of the determinants of parenting (see Figure 11–1). The model represents how we think of not only parenting but also child development. Belsky's model lists a number of variables that interact to create parental functioning and, as such, child development. The model places considerable emphasis on what parents themselves bring to the parenting process, inclusive of their developmental history, social support network, work, marital relations, and personality. Belsky argues that "personal psychological resources" are the most influential determinant of parenting (Belsky, 1984, p. 91).

Belsky's model is very indicative of how we think about a child's development. In this model, the child is situated solely within the context of their parents, and the parents exist only in relation to each other and the child. Consequently, the children are somewhat indirectly influenced by a small number of contextual variables mediated through their parents, but almost the entire process of parenting and development takes place within the family. As long as our conceptual models focus on individual and immediate contextual variables, then our research and public policy programs will also be targeted at the individual and the immediate context (family)

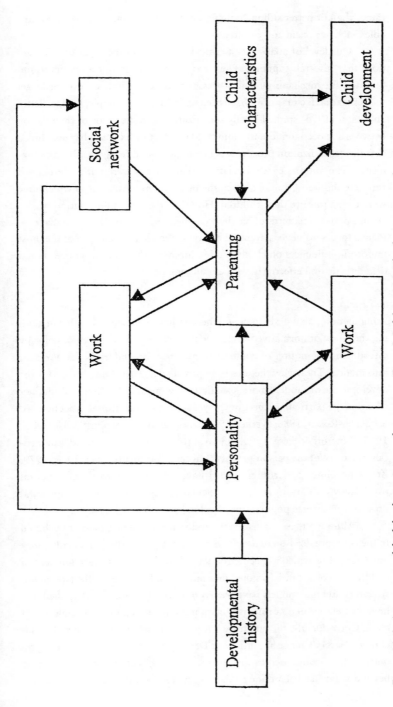

Figure 11–1. A process model of the determinants of parenting. (From J. Belsky, 1984, The determinants of parenting: A process model. Child Development, 55, 83–96.)

rather than or better still in conjunction with other macro or systemic variables such as racism and poverty.

Our level of analysis is a critical influence on the types of interventions that research supports. Thus it is crucial that in our attempts to understand the mechanisms and processes of development, we do not forget the contextual factors, as we have been apt to do. For example, Dodge, Pettit, and Bates (1994) studied family socialization as a mediator of the relation between socioeconomic status and child conduct problems. They concluded that the "socialization process was breeding ground for aggressive development." The authors carefully claimed that parents were not to be blamed for their children's conduct, given the difficult circumstances in which they were trying to raise their children. However, their recommendation was to change parental patterns of harsh discipline. Yet, if we truly believe that ecological forces influence parenting behavior, which in turn is one of the most important influences on children's development, then our programs should deal directly and effectively with eliminating poverty.

## Contextual Factors

A number of global developmental theories have had heuristic value in guiding the study of normative developmental processes in children of color by introducing the notion of contextual influences on children's development into models. These new theories have provided a general framework for the development of models more specific to low-income families and families of color. In particular, the interplay of the organizational (Cicchetti & Schneider-Rosen, 1986; Werner, 1948), transactional (Sameroff & Chandler, 1975; Sameroff & Fiese, 1990), life span (Lerner, 1989), and ecological theories (inclusive of the person-process-concepts) (Bronfenbrenner, 1977, 1979; Bronfenbrenner & Crouter, 1983) have contributed to developmental psychology's ability to address particular issues critical to developmental processes in diverse populations of color.

Although these mainstream developmental models have contributed to the conceptualization of developmental processes in children of color, they have not yet provided a specific framework with which the development of children of color can be studied and understood optimally. To date, mainstream contextual models have been too narrowly defined and applied and have not elaborated considerations unique to populations of children of color. Consequently, the literature has proven to be more exclusive than inclusive (García Coll et al., in press). Developing more inclusive models requires the rigorous specification and integration of contextual influences far beyond what has been done to date in mainstream theories (e.g., transactional and ecological). Finally, one of the most critical omissions in this work has been the influence of social mechanisms of stratification such as racism, prejudice, and discrimination (García Coll et al., 1996).

However, recent conceptual frameworks and empirical findings that emphasize the strengths of populations of color and the critical importance of macro-level structural forces on family processes and children's developmental outcomes have been recently developed (García Coll et al., 1996; Harrison et al., 1990; Slaughter-Defoe et al., 1990).

A broad framework that brings contextual factors explicitly into our understanding of development is Ogbu's (1981) cultural-ecological cross-cultural or universal model of child rearing. The very premise of this model is that people's effective environment shapes their child-rearing behaviors, the effective environment being defined as those aspects of the environment that directly affect subsistence quests and protections from physical violence (Figure 11–2). The thrust of Ogbu's argument is that parents inculcate and children acquire instrumental competencies that are determined by the context in which they develop inclusive of their sociocultural history. Consequently, Ogbu's entire model of child rearing is saturated with the notion that the context in which children develop is not only important but critical to understanding the process of child development and the achievement of instrumental competencies. For example, Ogbu applied his model to inner-city ghettoes and claimed that "the marginal participation of ghetto residents in the conventional economy and their participation in the street economy affect the way in which they organize their childrearing" (Ogbu, 1981, p. 424). In addition, in Ogbu's model, extrafamilial variables are not just important in shaping the competencies that people seek to instill in their children, but they can also act as independent sources of influence. Ogbu noted that "experiences in the street, church, school, and other settings may reinforce or change the course of development" (Ogbu, 1981, p. 424).

García Coll et al. (1996) proposed an integrative and comprehensive model for the study of child developmental competencies in children of color (Figure 11–3). The model is unique in that it draws from both mainstream developmental frameworks as well as models specific to children of color. It addresses two major considerations: constructs salient only to populations of color that contribute unique variance to their developmental processes and constructs that are relevant to developmental processes in all children, but differentiated on the basis of individual factors.

The model gives social position variables such as race, social class, ethnicity, and gender a preeminent position. These position traits represent social addresses that influence or create alternative developmental pathways

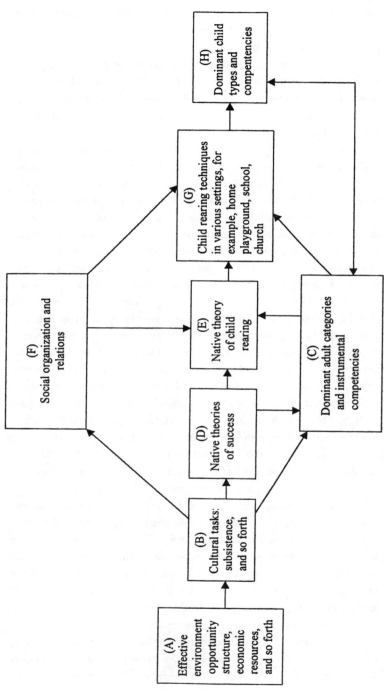

*Figure 11–2. Ogbu's cultural-ecological model of child rearing. (From J. Ogbu, 1981, Origins of human competence: A cultural ecological perspective.* Child Development, 52, 413–429.)

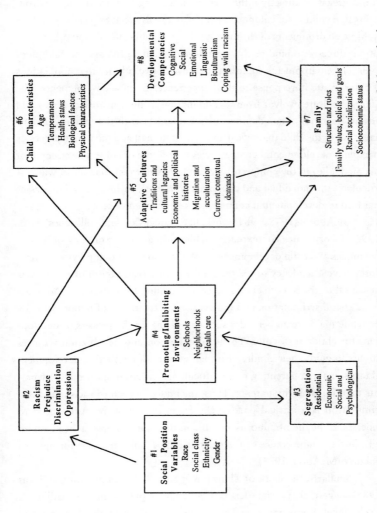

Figure 11–3. *An integrative model for the study of developmental competencies in children of color. From C. T. García Coll, G. Lamberty, R. Jenkins, H. P. McAdoo, K. Crnic, B. H. Wasik & H. A. Vázquez García, 1996. Child Development 67 (5), 1891–1914.*

to competence in these children. Although the role of social position in the model is crucial, its influence is not direct. Rather these characteristics are mediated by the pervasive social mechanisms of racism, prejudice, discrimination, and oppression. These factors in turn create segregated environments (inclusive of residential, economic, social, and psychological dimensions). This segregation directly influences the inhibiting and promoting environments that children of color experience. Children's social experiences in these multiple environments of the family, school, neighborhood, and other institutions directly and indirectly affect developmental processes in children of color. The environments contribute to the adaptive cultures that populations of color create in response to their experiences in these environments. The adaptive culture evolves from a combination of both historical forces and current demands. The adaptive culture interacts with the individual characteristics of the child (biological and constitutional) and the family processes to explain developmental competencies in children of color. The strength of this model lies in the comprehensive and yet still exact manner in which it articulates the individual and contextual variables, pathways, and processes that lead to developmental competencies in children of color.

McAdoo's (1978, 1981) work, like García Coll and colleagues' work (1996), incorporates contextual variables into an understanding of minority families and child development. McAdoo also noted that previous frameworks have a tendency to see the family, rather than racism or poverty, as the causal factor of each child's success or failure. In contrast, McAdoo asserted that discrimination and the derogatory treatment of minority life by the white mainstream pervades society and shapes the process of development for children of color. This discrimination and devaluation requires parents to guide their children through a series of conflicting developmental tasks, making parenting more difficult and frustrating for minority parents than for majority parents. Thus, the added burden of racism and discrimination is a critical part of the framework that McAdoo used to understand the life of minority families in the United States and to gain insight into the importance of the extended kin family structure for upward mobility (McAdoo, 1981).

Similarly, the work of Thornton et al. (1990) and Boykin and Toms (1985) suggests that racial socialization is a large part of minority children's development. For instance, in Thornton et al.'s (1990) study of sociodemographic and environmental correlates of racial socialization by black parents they found that race was a primary element of the socialization practice. Furthermore, the primary goal of racial socialization is to prepare children to cope with an oppressive environment. Thornton et al. identified three areas in which this socialization was important: the recognition of racial restrictions, of one's race as perceived by others, and the development of appropriate coping styles to deal with minority status. Boykin and Toms also highlighted three cultures into which parents must socialize their children: mainstream, African American, and minority. The implication of this work is that racial constructs are important not just for children of color, but for all children. If we know that racism and discrimination are central in the lives of minority children, why should it be any less important for nonminority children? Thus, all children's developmental outcomes are influenced by their experience of developing in a society that devalues and discriminates against people of color.

McLoyd's (1990) analytical framework of how poverty and economic loss affect black children is a more specific example of a contextually situated model (Figure 11–4). McLoyd began this model with the variable of economic loss and poverty. The model includes all of the developmental or immediate variables found within Belsky's model. However, McLoyd has clearly placed the family and individuals within a contextual setting. Conceptually, this is an important distinction because it explicitly demonstrates that the family and the child are situated within and influenced by larger forces. Parenting behavior is not any less important than in Belsky's model; however, it is also understood as the moderator or mediator of the parents' economic context on the child's development. The implication of this model is that economic status of parents, be it deprivation or affluence, is critical in understanding developmental processes and outcomes.

Also significant is that within the domain of social support and controls, McLoyd listed the community as a source of influence. McLoyd's discussion of important community/neighborhood characteristics that influence a child's development included the age and transient nature of the residents, the ethnic composition of the neighborhood, the proximity of the parents' social support network, and the available professional resources such as health service providers. Thus, McLoyd noted that ecological forces as well as the more traditionally considered developmental variables have an impact on the children. Although researchers have begun to investigate correlates between environmental factors and parenting behaviors (e.g., Kelley, Power & Wimbush, 1992), McLoyd concluded that "our understanding of the particular features of neighborhoods/communities that influence parenting and black children's development has lagged, despite the obvious importance of these issues and longstanding appeals for such work" (p. 337).

An ecological framework is apparent in a number of other studies on the impact of poverty on children's development. In a special issue on pov-

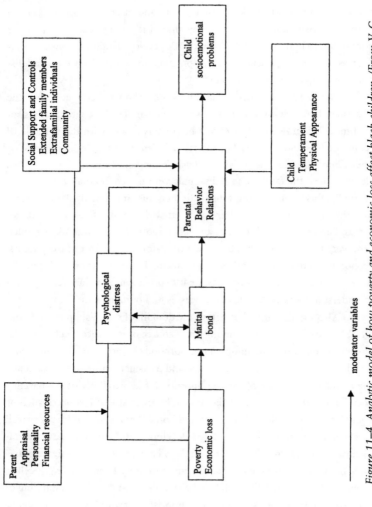

▶ moderator variables

*Figure 11–4. Analytic model of how poverty and economic loss affect black children. (From V. C. McLoyd, 1990. The impact of economic hardship on black families and children: Psychological distress, parenting, and socioemotional development.* Child Development, 61, 311–346.)

erty, the journal *Child Development* (*see* Huston, McLoyd & García Coll, 1994) published several articles investigating the processes by which poverty has an impact on developmental processes and outcomes in children. In general, researchers argued that poverty indirectly affected children by contributing to maternal depressive symptomology and thus negatively influencing these mothers' interactions with their children. The punitive nature of the mother-child interactions in turn manifested itself in both internalized behaviors such as cognitive distress (McLoyd et al., 1994) and externalized behaviors such as delinquency and behavior problems (Leadbetter & Bishop, 1994; Sampson & Laub, 1994).

Laosa's (1982a) research on the differences between Mexican American and Anglo teaching strategies suggests that discrepancies in parenting behavior can be accounted for by parents' levels of formal schooling, rather than cultural differences or economic indices. Laosa found that although Chicano mothers were less likely to use praising and inquiring teaching strategies than Anglo mothers, when the mother's level of formal education was statistically controlled for, differences between the groups' teaching tactics disappeared. Therefore, Laosa concluded that mothers with more years of formal education used more praising and inquiring than mothers with less education, who were more apt to use modeling techniques. Simply controlling for parents' occupational status did not account for the variance in didactic strategies. Together these articles emphasize the importance of unraveling the contextual factors that contribute to parenting behavior, be it income level, economic stress, or educational opportunities and thus understanding children's developmental outcomes as situated within the broader context of economic well-being.

In summary, recent work on low-income populations and populations of color indicate that parenting and child developmental processes and outcomes are influenced by many contextual factors, especially access to educational and economic opportunities and experiences with racism. The argument, consequently, is not that parenting is any less important for a child's development than previously thought, but that the context in which families raise their children has an impact on parenting patterns and practices. This is clearly illustrated by Cook and Fine's (1995) description of low-income African American mothers living in violent crime-ridden neighborhoods. Extensive interviews with mothers of adolescents detailed the difficulties they faced living in urban poverty. The stress and difficulties they face as parents were phenomenal: inadequate housing, dangerous neighborhoods, illnesses, job layoffs, long work days for minimal pay, few social supports or resources, and dependence on social structures they did not trust or have any power over. As Cook and Fine described, "These women cannot fanta-size the bullets away, can't promise safety, can't unambivalently invite their children to report any problem to the police" (p. 124). The context in which these women struggle to survive, protect, and nurture their children has an impact on both their ability to parent and their child's development.

## RECONCEPTUALIZING SOCIAL POLICY

Recent work that acknowledges and articulates the importance of contex-tual variables, especially less access to opportunity structures because of poverty and racism, and questions the notion of deficits in families and chil-dren of color's capacities, provides a new base on which to build social poli-cies and prevention/intervention programs. If we begin to see parents' be-havior as at least in part a mediating mechanism through which ecological forces operate, then our social policies and programs shift dramatically. That is, if our purpose is to bring lasting change to the lives of families and chil-dren, we must focus our efforts on promoting the development of both chil-dren and parents. Our policies cannot merely focus on the mediating vari-ables, such as parenting behavior, without considering the contextual forces that have an impact on these variables. We cannot understand the develop-mental processes and outcomes of low-income children without understand-ing their parents, nor can we understand parenting practices without under-standing the challenges of poverty and racism. This reconceptualization compels us not merely to reform current policies, but rather to be innova-tive and create new policies that reflect our slowly advancing research and theoretical work with these populations.

An understanding of the role that macro structural forces play in shap-ing family environments and developmental outcomes suggests that social policy's goals should be to make radical structural and social changes. To most effectively promote developmental outcomes for children of color, poli-cies must contend with the elimination of racist practices, which support, perpetuate, and undergird the pervasive inequality within United States so-ciety (Hare, 1987). Furthermore, this calls for broad-based change in the structure of our economy. Only when adequate educational and employment opportunities exist, so that all parents can provide for their families' basic needs, will our society be promoting the development of all children.

Unfortunately, by all indications, our society and policies are not sup-portive of this sweeping type of change (Halpern, 1990). Instead, we are witnessing an ideological and political shift that emphasizes personal achieve-ment and responsibility. Consequently, until broad societal changes are achieved, we should also construct programs to provide a variety of services to families and parents that will support them in their individual struggles to escape poverty and to cope with the detrimental effects of prejudice, discrimination, and segregation.

The types of policies that provide services to low-income families should move beyond the remediation/compensation paradigm. The programs and policies should foster the simultaneous educational and economic development of the family as well as the development of children. Fostering parents' and families' access to opportunity structures would improve the ability of programs to maintain the gains achieved by the child-centered or parent education services. Grubb and Lazerson (1982) summarized that "although public institutions promise to provide for children when their parents cannot, it proves impossible to separate children from their parents, either physically or conceptually. Providing for poor children, therefore, means providing for their parents at the same time" (p. 189).

Finally, it is not enough to shift our programs to understand children's well-being within the context of family and community well-being. We must also redefine our aspirations for these families. To bring lasting change to the lives of children we must do more than increase the family from the status of welfare dependency to working poor. Our policies must promote appropriate opportunities out of poverty altogether and provide the appropriate resources to enable families to cope with the stresses caused by poverty until that time. We must begin to seek optimal versus incremental growth.

In fact, we are provided with good examples in two-generation intervention programs, which usually integrate two types of family supports. First, they provide services to promote the development of young children, such as early childhood education and parenting skills programs. In addition, they also provide services designed to improve parents' education and employment status (Smith, Blank & Collins, 1992). The comprehensive array of services is offered in an integrated and preventive manner. That is, these programs link together different types of services for children and families, in an attempt to address the growing child within the context of their family. The range of services offered are intended to promote personal growth of all members of families (Weissbourd & Kagan, 1989) and to eliminate barriers to labor market participation, such as the costs of child care, medical care, education, and training. In doing this, the programs attempt to increase family functioning and enhance children's development. The hope is that families can be provided with services that promote self-sufficiency through employment, and thus break the cycle of poverty.

In the past, two-generation programs predominantly have been demonstration projects, and as such have taken a variety of forms. We will highlight two such promising programs as described by Smith, Blank and Collins (1992) in their book *Pathways to Self-sufficiency for Two Generations*. The first is the New Chance Demonstration project, which has been started at 16 sites and is designed for disadvantaged young mothers and their children (Quint et al., 1994; St. Pierre, Layzer & Barnes, 1995). It combines a highly structured adult education and vocational training program along with unusually strong child development and health services. Parents are required to spend at least five months involved in on-site educational activities, although some spend longer completing their GED. In connection with the federal- and state-mandated JOBS program, New Chance participants are also provided with either vocational or postsecondary education opportunities, case managers, counselors, and support groups. Child development is promoted by on-site child care for infancy through age six, and the parents are also required to spend time with the children in the care facility. The breadth of the comprehensive services provided seem to offer the appropriate combination of elements to promote the development of the entire family.

Likewise, recent Head Start initiatives have taken a comprehensive approach to serving families. Our second example is Operation Family, a Comprehensive Child Development Program funded by the U.S. Department of Health and Human Services located in Kentucky, which is linked to the state's JOBS programs. This project differs from the New Chance Demonstration in that the service delivery is less center-oriented and more case management–oriented. Case managers work closely with families and combine biweekly home visits and center-based visits (St. Pierre, Layzer & Barnes, 1995). The thrust of New Chance's efforts is to help parents meet personal and parenting goals. In addition, the case managers serve as advocates to help parents negotiate existing social support networks, as well as provide crisis management and problem-solving assistance. Consequently, through this case management system, parents gain access to such services as developmental child care, health care, and employment training. While Operation Family provides assistance in locating supportive services for families, the JOBS program helps to fund the supportive services including transportation and child care (Smith, Blank & Collins, 1992).

Two-generation programs and the comprehensive and developmentally appropriate services they provide are crucial in creating healthy families. Research with children, specifically children of color and their families, indicates that contextual factors exert a strong influence on a child's development. In light of our societal unwillingness to implement broad and far-reaching social and economic change to eliminate poverty and racism, policies should at least contend with these issues on an individual level.

Two-generation programs have begun to do just that. They provide comprehensive support and services to both parents and children, thus enhancing the cognitive development of children and thus taking a step toward enabling families to negotiate their own pathways out of poverty.

While two-generation programs make attempts to support families, the evaluations of these have been less positive than researchers and policymakers had hoped. An ongoing evaluation of the New Chance program is currently being conducted by the Manpower Demonstration Research Corporation (Quint et al., 1994). Interim findings indicated that the experimental group of participants did not demonstrate much more positive outcomes in several domains than the control group. In fact, the results were so mixed that in some instances the effects were even in the opposite direction than had been anticipated. However, positive outcomes were found on indicators such as having the children in regular care arrangements, day-care centers, or preschools, and mothers' attainment of GEDs. A review of two-generation program evaluations (St. Pierre, Layzer & Barnes, 1995) reported a similar pattern of findings: small short-term effects on measures of child development, scattered short-term effects on measures of parenting, an increase in the use of relevant social and educational services, and an increase in the rate of GED attainment. Although the long-term results are still unknown, it is questionable whether long-term results will be found in the absence of short-term results (St. Pierre, Layzer & Barnes, 1995).

The fact that two-generation programs seem to be able to produce only small short-term gains highlights the importance of contextual influences on human development and the difficulties that programs have in making an impact on or overcoming contextual influences. The ability of any program to enable their participants to reach self-sufficiency is limited often by the very scope of the programs. St. Pierre, Layzer, and Barnes's (1995) review of two-generation programs suggested that when implemented, two-generation programs' approaches to service delivery result in lower intensity single-component programs (e.g., child development component or parent employment training); this in turn produces smaller results. As they summarized, "Two-generation programs are in danger of taking a broad-based approach that does not provide enough of any single service to be effective" (p. 90). If effective programs are to be built on promoting the development of both parents and children, then we must make sure that the programs we establish really do provide enough support to parents and families to augment their efforts to reach self-sufficiency.

Finally, the ability of two-generation programs to have an impact on families is limited by the chosen target level of intervention, the individual.

If human development is impacted by many contextual factors, as our re-search and theories now suppose, then any intervention targeted solely at individuals will demonstrate only limited success. To bring both meaning-ful and lasting change into the lives of families we need to contend with con-textual and structural changes. We need to continue to articulate and begin to address the larger forces that influence the lives of low-income families and people of color. Although the services that two-generation programs may provide are a crucial component of promoting the growth of family mem-bers, growth in the absence of available jobs and adequate wages, and in the face of discrimination, racism, and prejudice, will continue to be lim-ited. These programs may help some struggling families and may increase the cognitive development of some children in modest ways, but these pro-grams will also fail to help others until both growth and opportunities are present in the lives of all families.

## CONCLUSION

Essentially, it is hard not to be skeptical of the ability to provide effective services without harming the population we intend to promote. In the past, our policies have been ineffective, and even detrimental. We have provided services when families need income, and created a population that is depen-dent rather than empowered (McKnight, 1991). In light of our previous fail-ures and our own skepticism we offer some precautions to be taken.

Programs should be congruent with and complementary to the par-ticular strengths of the population being served (Delgado-Gaitan, 1993; McAdoo, 1978; McKinney et al., 1994; McLoyd, 1994). Constructing poli-cies in this manner will allow the achievement of more long-lasting success-ful outcomes (Washington, 1988). Imposing a policy created only by out-siders without regard to the particular sociocultural history and strengths of the community increases the possibility that it will be ineffectual or harm-ful. In addition, we need to establish partnerships with the implementors of programs to evaluate the effectiveness of these programs (McKinney et al., 1994). Program evaluation is a critical step in the process of policy creation, and the inappropriate use of evaluation tools will continue to either perpetu-ate ineffective programs or mask the benefits of successful programs (Laosa, 1982b).

Because social policy responds to both ideological pressure and data, researchers need to learn how to communicate with policymakers and to provide the necessary data to support the development of programs that are effective in addressing the impact of poverty and racism. Given that the U.S. political climate currently emphasizes personal responsibility and individual-level analyses, researchers need to be more vocal about their knowledge and disseminate the findings which prove that this type of approach has limitations. At the same time that we disseminate proof of the limitations of programs that seek change at the individual level, we need to clearly and consistently articulate the importance of macrostructural forces. Finally, if we are serious about promoting the well-being of children, we as researchers should in the very least aspire and work to eradicate poverty and racism.

## REFERENCES

Arnold, M. S. (1995). Exploding myths: African-American families at promise. In B. B. Swadner & S. Lubeck (Eds.), *Children and families at promise* (pp. 143–162). Albany: State University of New York Press.

Baratz, S. S. & Baratz, J. C. (1970). Early childhood intervention: The social science base of institutional racism. *Harvard Educational Review, 40* (1), 29–50.

Barbarin, O. A. (1993). Coping and resilience: Exploring the inner lives of African American children. *Journal of Black Psychology, 19* (4), 423–446.

Barnett, W. S. (1995). Long term effects of early childhood education programs on cognitive and school outcomes. *The Future of Children, 5* (3), 25–50.

Belsky, J. (1984). The determinants of parenting: A process model. *Child Development, 55,* 83–96.

Bloom, B. S., Davis, A. & Hess, R. (1964). *Compensatory education for cultural deprivation.* Chicago: Department of Education, University of Education.

Boykin, A. W. & Toms, F. D. (1985). Black child socialization: A conceptual framework. In H. P. McAdoo & J. H. McAdoo (Eds.), *Black children: Social, educational, and parental environments* (pp. 33–51). Newbury Park, CA: Sage.

Bronfenbrenner, U. (1977). Toward an experimental ecology of human development. *American Psychologist, 32,* 513–531.

Bronfenbrenner, U. (1979). *The ecology of human development.* Cambridge, MA: Harvard University Press.

Bronfenbrenner, U. (1986). Ecology of the family as a context for human development: Research perspectives. *Developmental Psychology, 22* (6), 723–742.

Bronfenbrenner, U. & Crouter, A. C. (1983). The evolution of environmental models in developmental research. In W. Kessen, *Handbook of child psychology (4th ed.): Vol. 1. History, theory, and methods* (pp. 357–414). New York: Wiley.

Brown, B. (1985). Head Start: How research changed policy. *Young Children,* July, 9–13.

Caplan, N. & Nelson, S. D. (1973). On being useful: The nature and consequences of social research on social problems. *American Psychologist, 28,* 199–211.

Ceglowski, D. (1994). Conversations about Head Start salaries: A feminist analysis. *Early Childhood Research Quarterly, 9* (3–4), 367–386.

Cicchetti, D. & Schneider-Rosen, K. (1986). An organizational approach to childhood depression. In M. Rutter, C. E. Izard & P. B. Read (Eds.), *Depression in young people: Developmental and clinical perspectives* (pp. 71–134). New York: Guilford.

Cicirelli, V. G., Evans, J. W. & Schiller, J. S. (1969). *The impact of Head Start: An evaluation of the effects of Head Start on children's cognitive and affective development,* vols. 1–2. Athens: Westinghouse Learning Corporation and Ohio University.

Cole, M. & Bruner, J. S. (1974). Cultural differences and inferences about psychological processes. In J. W. Berry & P. R. Dasen (Eds.), *Culture and cognition: Readings in cross cultural psychology* (pp. 231–246). London: Methuen.

Connell, R. W. (1994). Poverty and education. *Harvard Educational Review, 64* (2), 125–149.

Cook, D.A. & Fine, M. (1995). "Motherwit": Childrearing lessons from African-American mothers of low income. In B. B. Swadner & S. Lubeck (Eds.), *Children and families at promise* (pp. 119–142). Albany: State University of New York Press.

Delgado-Gaitán, C. (1993). Research and policy in reconceptualizing family school relationships. In P. Phelan & A. L. Davidson (Eds.), *Renegotiating cultural diversity in American schools* (pp. 139–158). New York: Teachers College Press.

de Lone, R. (1979). *Small futures: Children, inequality, and the limits of liberal reform.* New York: Harcourt Brace Jovanovich.

Dodge, K. A., Pettit, G. S. & Bates, J. E. (1994). Socialization mediators of the relation between socioeconomic status and child conduct problems. *Child Development, 65,* 649–665.

Duncan, G. J. (1991). The economic environment of childhood. In A. Huston (Ed.), *Children in poverty* (pp. 23–50). New York: Cambridge University Press.

Dunn, L. M. (1987). *Bilingual Hispanic children in the U.S. mainland: A review of research on their cognitive, linguistic, and scholastic development.* Circle Pines, MN: American Guidance Service.

Edin, K. (1995). The myths of dependence and self sufficiency: Women, welfare, and low-wage work. *Focus, 17* (2), 1–9.

Enchautegui, M. E. (1995). *Policy implications of Latino poverty.* Washington, DC: The Urban Institute.

Entwisle, D. R. & Alexander, K. L. (1990). Beginning school math competence: Minority and majority comparisons. *Child Development, 61,* 454–471.

Florin, P. R. & Dokecki, P. R. (1983). Changing families through parent and family education. In I. E. Siegal & L. Laosa (Eds.), *Changing families* (pp. 23–64). New York: Plenum.

García Coll, C. T. (1990). Developmental outcome of minority infants: A process oriented look into our beginnings. *Child Development, 61,* 270–289.

García Coll, C. T., Lamberty, G., Jenkins, R., McAdoo, H. P., Crnic, K., Wasik, B. H. & Vázquez García, H. A. (1996). An integrative model for the study of developmental competencies in minority children. *Child Development, 67,* 1891–1914.

García Coll, C. & Magnuson, K. (in press). Cultural influences on child development: Are we ready for a paradigm shift? In C. Nelson & A. Masten (Eds.), *Minnesota Symposium on Child Psychology, Vol. 29.*

Graham, S. (1992). "Most of the subjects were white and middle-class": Trends in published research on African Americans in selected APA journals, 1970–1989. *American Psychologist, 47* (5), 629–639.

Grubb, W. N. & Lazerson, M. (1982). *Broken promises.* New York: Basic Books.

Hakuta, K. (1986). *Mirror on language: The debate on bilingualism.* New York: Basic Books.

Hakuta, K. & García, E. E. (1989). Bilingualism and education. *American Psychologist, 44* (2), 374–379.

Halpern, R. (1990). Poverty and early childhood parenting: Toward a framework for intervention. *American Journal of Orthopsychiatry, 60* (1), 6–18.

Hare, B. R. (1987). Structural inequality and the endangered status of black youth. *Journal of Negro Education, 56* (1), 100–110.

Harrison, A. O., Wilson, M. N., Pine, C. J., Chan, S. Q. & Buriel, R. (1990). Family ecologies of ethnic minority children. *Child Development, 61,* 347–362.

Haskins, R. (1989). Beyond metaphor: The efficacy of early childhood education. *American Psychologist, 44* (2), 274–282.

Head Start, Appendix A. (1995). *The future of children, 5* (3), 212–213.

Herr, T., Halpern, R. & Conrad, A. (1991). *Changing what counts: Re-thinking the journey out of welfare.* Evanston, IL: Center for Urban Affairs and Policy Research.

Herrnstein, R. J. & Murray, C. (1994). *The bell curve.* New York: Free Press.

Hess, R. D. & Shipmann, V. (1965). Early experiences and the socialization of cognitive modes in children. *Child Development, 36,* 869–886.

Huston, A., McLoyd, V. C. & García Coll, C. (1994). Children and poverty: Issues in contemporary research. *Child Development, 65* (2), 275–282.

Jensen, A. (1969). How much can we boost IQ and school achievement? *Harvard Educational Review, 39* (1), 1–123.

Jones, D. J. (1993). The culture of achievement among the poor: The case of mothers and children in a Head Start program. *Critique of Anthropology, 13* (3), 247–266.

Kelley, M. L., Power, T. G. & Wimbush, D. D. (1992). Determinants of disciplinary practices in low-income black mothers. *Child Development, 63,* 573–582.

Labov, W. (1970). The logic of nonstandard English. In F. Williams (Ed.), *Language and poverty* (pp. 153–189). Chicago: Markham.

LaFromboise, T. D. & Low, K. G. (1989). American Indian children and adolescents. In J. T. Gibbs & L. N. Huang (Eds.), *Children of color: Developmental interventions with minority youth* (pp. 115–147). San Francisco: Jossey-Bass.

Laosa, L. (1982a). Families as facilitators of children's intellectual development at three years of age. In L. Laosa & I. Siegal (Eds.), *Families as learning environments* (pp. 1–45). New York: Plenum.

Laosa, L. (1982b). The sociocultural context of evaluation. In B. Spodek (Ed.), *Handbook of research in early childhood education* (pp. 501–520). New York: Free Press.

Laosa, L. (1983). Parent education, cultural pluralism, and public policy: The uncertain connection. In R. Haskins & D. Adams (Eds.), *Parent education and public policy* (pp. 331–345). Norwood, NJ: Ablex.

Laosa, L. (1984). Social policies toward children of diverse ethnic, racial, and language groups in the United States. In H. W. Stevenson & A. E. Siegal (Eds.,) *Child development research and social policy* (pp. 1–109.) Chicago: University of Chicago Press.

Lazar, I. & Darlington, R. B. (1982). Lasting effects of early education. *Monographs of the Society for Research in Child Development, 47* (2–3).

Leadbetter, B. J. & Bishop, B. (1994). Predictors of behavior problems in preschool inner city Afro-American and Puerto Rican adolescent mothers. *Child Development, 65,* 638–648.

Lerner, R. M. (1989). Individual development and the family system: A life-span perspective. In K. Kreppner & R. M. Lerner (Eds.), *Family systems and life-span development* (pp. 15–31). Hillsdale, NJ: Erlbaum.

Lewis, O. (1965). *La Vida.* New York: Vintage.

Lubeck, S. (1994). Children in relation: Rethinking early childhood education. *Urban Review, 26* (3), 1994.

Maccoby, E. E., Kahn, A. J. & Everett, B. A. (1983). The role of psychological research in the formation of policies affecting children. *American Psychologist, 38* (1), 80–84.

McAdoo, H. P. (1978). Minority families. In J. Stevens (Ed.), *Mother/child, father/child: Relationships* (pp. 177–195). Washington, DC: National Association for the Education of Young Children.

McAdoo, H. P. (1981). Upward mobility and parenting in middle-income black families. *Journal of Black Psychology, 8* (1), 1–22.

McDonnell, L. M. & Hill, P. T. (1993). *Newcomers to American schools: Meeting the educational needs of immigrant youth.* Santa Monica, CA: RAND.

McKinney, M. H., Abrams, A., Terry, P. A. & Lerner, R. M. (1994). Child development research and the poor children of America: A call for a developmental contextual approach to research and outreach. *Family and Consumer Sciences Research Journal, 23*, 26–42.

McKnight, J. (1991). Services are bad for people: You are either a citizen or a client. *Organizing,* Spring/Summer 1991, 357–360.

McLaughlin, M. W. & Heath, S. B. (1993). Casting the self: Frames for identity and dilemmas for policy. In S. B. Heath & M. W. McLaughlin (Eds.), *Identity and inner-city youth: Beyond ethnicity and gender* (pp. 210–239). New York: Teachers College Press.

McLoyd, V. C. (1990). The impact of economic hardship on black families and children: Psychological distress, parenting, and socioemotional development. *Child Development, 61*, 311–346.

McLoyd, V. C. (1994). Research in the service of poor and ethnic/racial minority children: Fomenting change in models of scholarship. *Family and Consumer Research Journal, 23*, 56–66.

McLoyd, V. C., Jayaratne, T. E., Ceballo, R. & Borquez, J. (1994). Unemployment and work interruption among African-American single mothers: Effects on parenting and adolescent socio-emotional functioning. *Child Development, 65*, 562–589.

McLoyd, V. C. & Randolph, S. (1985). Secular trends in the study of Afro-American children: A review of *Child Development.* In A. B. Smuts & J. W. Hagen (Eds.), History and research in child development. *Monographs of the Society for Research in Child Development, 50* (4–5, Serial No. 211).

Miller-Jones, D. (1988). The study of African-American children's development: Contributions to reformulating developmental paradigms. In D. T. Slaughter (Ed.), *Black children and poverty: A developmental perspective. New Directions for Child Development* (pp. 75–92). San Francisco: Jossey-Bass.

Moynihan, D. (1965). *The negro family: The case for national action.* Washington, DC: Office of Policy Planning and Research, U.S. Department of Labor.

Ogbu, J. (1981). Origins of human competence: A cultural ecological perspective. *Child Development, 52*, 413–429.

Olds, D. L. & Kitzman, H. (1993). Review of research on home visiting for pregnant women and parents of young children. *Future of Children, 3*, 53–92.

Parker, S., Greer, S. & Zuckerman, B. (1988). Double jeopardy: The impact of poverty on early child development. *Pediatric Clinics of North America, 35* (6), 1227–1240.

Quint, J. C., Polit, D. F., Bos, H. & Cave, G. (1994). *New chance: Interim findings on a comprehensive program for disadvantaged young mothers and their children.* New York: Manpower Research Demonstration Corporation.

Sameroff, A. (1993). Risk and resilience in children: Identifying targets for service to young children. [Summary]. *Translating research into practice: Implications for serving families with young children, summary of the conference proceedings of the 2nd national Head Start research conference,* 44–48.

Sameroff, A. J. & Chandler, M. (1975). Reproductive risk and the continuum of caretaking casualty. In F. D. Horowitz, E. M. Hetherington & S. Scarr-Salapatek (Eds.), *Review of Child Development Research,* Vol. 4 (pp. 187–244). Chicago: University of Chicago Press.

Sameroff, A. J. & Fiese, B. H. (1990). Transactional regulation and early intervention. In S. J. Meisels & J. P. Shonkoff (Eds.), *Handbook of early childhood intervention* (pp. 119–191). New York: Cambridge University Press.

Sampson, R. J. & Laub, J. H. (1994). Urban poverty and the family context of delinquency: A new look at structure and process in a classic study. *Child Development, 65*, 523–540.

Schorr, L. B. (1992). Effective programs for children growing up in concentrated poverty. In A. C. Huston (Ed.), *Children in poverty: Child development and public policy* (pp. 260–281). New York: Cambridge University Press.

Seitz, V. & Apfel, N. H. (1994). Parent focused intervention: Diffusion effects on siblings. *Child Development, 65,* 677–683.

Seitz, V. & Provence, S. (1990). Caregiver-focused models of early intervention. In S. J. Meisels & J. P. Shonkoff (Eds.), *Handbook of early childhood intervention* (pp. 400–427). New York: Cambridge University Press.

Siegal, I. E. (1983). The ethics of intervention. In I. E. Siegal & L. Laosa (Eds.), *Changing families* (pp. 1–22). New York: Plenum.

Slaughter-Defoe, D. T., Nakagawa, K., Takanishi, R. & Johnson, D. J. (1990). Toward cultural/ecological perspectives on schooling and achievement in African- and Asian-American children. *Child Development, 61,* 363–383.

Smith, S., Blank, S. & Collins, R. (1992). *Pathways to self-sufficiency for two generations: Designing welfare to work programs that strengthen families and benefit children.* New York: Foundation for Child Development.

St. Pierre, R. G., Layzer, J. I. & Barnes, H. V. (1995). Two generation programs: Design, cost, and short-term effectiveness. *Future of Children, 5* (3), 76–93.

Stevenson, H., Chen, C. & Uttal, D. H. (1990). Beliefs and achievement: A study of black, white, and Hispanic children. *Child Development, 61,* 508–523.

Swadner, B. B. & Lubeck, S. (Eds.) (1995). *Children and families at promise.* Albany: State University of New York Press.

Thornton, M. C., Chatters, L. M., Taylor, R. J. & Allen, W. R. (1990). Sociodemographic and environmental correlates of racial socialization by black parents. *Child Development, 61,* 409–410.

Tulkin, S. R. (1972). An analysis of the concept of cultural deprivation. *Developmental Psychology, 6,* 326–339.

Washington, V. (1988). Historical and contemporary linkages between black child development and social policy. In D. T. Slaughter (Ed.), *Black children and poverty: A developmental perspective. New Directions for Child Development* (pp. 93–105). San Francisco: Jossey-Bass.

Weiss, H. B. (1993). Home visits: Necessary but not sufficient. *Future of Children, 3* (3), 113–128.

Weissbourd, B. & Kagan, L. (1989). Family support programs: Catalyst for change. *American Journal of Orthopsychiatry, 59* (1), 20–31.

Werner, H. (1948). *The comparative psychology of mental development.* New York: Harper & Row.

Zigler, E. (1993). On the front lines: Federal contributions to Head Start research [Summary]. *Translating research into practice: Implications for serving families with young children, summary of the conference proceedings of the 2nd national Head Start research conference,* 25–28.

Zigler, E. & Styfoco, S. J. (1994). Is the Perry Preschool better than Head Start? *Early Childhood Research Quarterly, 9* (3–4), 269–289.

# 12 ETHNIC MINORITY FAMILIES AND THE MAJORITY EDUCATIONAL SYSTEM

## AFRICAN AMERICAN, CHINESE AMERICAN, HISPANIC AMERICAN, AND NATIVE AMERICAN FAMILIES

*Melvin N. Wilson*

*L. Michelle Piña*

*Raymond W. Chan*

*Desiree D. Soberanis*

The family serves an important function in many societies; however, the role of the family is especially crucial in minority cultures, since the family is the means by which that culture is passed on to future generations. Unlike Anglo American children, who are able to explore the richness of their culture in many domains, such as school, television, books, and celebrated holidays, minority children seldom have this luxury. Minority culture is learned at home, or it may not be learned at all. As such, family roles and dynamics, emphasis on certain behaviors, and familial expectations all serve to inform minority children of their home culture, a culture that may be vastly different than that found outside of the home. Sometimes conflict of cultures results in children who may have to vault many hurdles before attaining the advantages that majority children may take for granted, especially in academic achievement, and perhaps, then, job availability and stability, and hence the ability to support future generations may be more difficult.

The causes of academic underachievement are many and varied; however, it may be that academic underachievement among some minority students is at least partially explained by differences between majority and minority families. That is to say that families of minority children reinforce goals and attributes that may be different from mainstream Anglo American middle-class culture, thus rendering minority children disadvantaged in acquiring the skills necessary to achieve in American classrooms. For instance, in 1988 the Native American high school dropout rate was 36%, compared to 28.8% for the U.S. population as a whole, and some observers estimate that the Native American dropout rates are actually as high as 52% (O'Brien, 1992). Furthermore, 75% of those Native American children who graduate from high school and enter college will eventually drop out without earning a degree (Beuf, 1975; NEA, 1992). That is, 9% of Native American adults have completed four years of college, compared to 20%

of the U.S. population (O'Brien, 1992). In addition to startling dropout rates, Native American children are also underrepresented in gifted and talented programs and overrepresented in learning disabled programs (NEA, 1992). Finally, almost 30% of Native American children have repeated a grade, the highest rate of any minority group (O'Brien, 1992).

Among Hispanic Americans, underachieving is closely tied to issues of language barriers. Children whose parents speak Spanish in the home confront language discrimination in school. That is, many schools have unwritten rules of no-Spanish and English-only policies; some localities have begun attempts to enact legislation that would permit English as the only language of instruction in schools. Although Hispanic Americans have made substantial gains in education, they are more likely than are non-Hispanic Americans to have less than five years of schooling (McKay, 1988). Educational differences also exist among Hispanic American groups; in 1993, only 50% of Mexican Americans completed four or more years of high school, compared to 76% of Puerto Ricans and 84% of Cubans.

Among Chinese Americans, the popular focus has been on their attainment of high achievement: 21.6% of Chinese Americans are college graduates, as compared to 13.9% of white Americans, and 19.1% of Chinese Americans earned a postgraduate or professional degree, as compared to 7.7% of white Americans (U.S. Bureau of the Census, 1993). However, the 1990 census also reports that 16.8% of Chinese Americans have less than a ninth grade education, compared with 8.9% of white Americans. Clearly there exists a polarized distribution of educational attainment. Furthermore, despite relatively high educational attainments among some Chinese Americans, Chinese Americans continue to be absent from executive, supervisory, and decision-making positions (Hsia, 1988, as cited by Wong, 1995). Given the language barrier, many Chinese Americans tend to concentrate in fields such as mathematics, science and engineering, or entrepreneurship, using risk-aversive strategies to deemphasize English skills. This approach curtails managerial and decision-making career opportunities where communication skills may be as important or more important than analytic and mathematical skills (Miller, 1992).

Recent reports indicate that among African American students high school completion rates have improved over the past decade. Data also reveal that girls do better academically at the high school level than African American boys (Washington & Newman, 1991). However, the same report also asserts that African Americans have experienced "sporadic increases, then consistent declines, in opportunities to participate in higher education" (p. 19). According to the study, African American men, on the whole, are least likely to apply to college. Most middle-class African Americans have a high school diploma, while working-class African Americans have at least a secondary education (Wilson, 1987). However, less than half (44%) of inner-city residents have a high school diploma (Wilson, 1987). Washington and Newman (1991) refer to three societal influences that may negatively affect school performance. First, the lack of male role models for African American boys could be a negative factor in promoting education attainment. For instance, 83% of elementary school teachers are women, while only 0.2% are African American men, and among secondary school teachers, 46% are women and only 3.2% are African American men. Second, in many schools the curriculum is based on white middle-class concepts of competence. Many African American children perceive middle-class competence as going against the norm. Children who go against the norm are likely to be classified as at risk for negative outcomes. According to Ogbu (1991), at-risk groups are mostly composed of boys, particularly African American boys. Third, even when African American boys achieve higher academic goals, employment opportunities are not always offered to them (Washington & Newman, 1991).

## INTRA-ETHNIC VARIATION

Socioeconomic and historical contexts within each ethnic group create unique life experiences; however, there is still a striking lack of research that considers intra-ethnic diversity. To ensure a continually growing and up-to-date knowledge base on ethnic minority American peoples, the variations within cultural groups must be recognized and considered as data and not discarded as noise or minor variations. In this chapter we recognize that these differences exist, and thus we endeavor to avoid unnecessary generalizations to all members of any ethnic group.

In the case of Chinese Americans, the popular media has perpetuated the myth of the "model minority" (Peterson, 1966, as cited in Sim, 1992)—hard-working and academically successful. The notion of a "model minority" compelled Harvard University sociologist Nathan Glazer at one point to question the need for affirmative action programs to include Asian American participants (Kwong, 1987, as cited in Sim, 1992). However, differences among Chinese Americans do exist. The "Uptown Chinese"—the academically and professionally successful—are, in large part, children of Chinese Americans who immigrated to the United States in the 1960s (Sui, 1992). They are also by and large middle- to upper-class professionals from Taiwan and Hong Kong. Some recent immigrants who fit the "Uptown Chinese" profile are those who have adapted to the American culture and adjusted "successfully" from their immigration experience, often bringing substantial economic, professional, and intellectual resources with them from Asia. Graduate students from Singapore or medical doctors from Hong Kong, for example, are more likely to achieve "uptown" status than factory workers from the People's Republic of China who know little English.

During the 1970s and 1980s, the United States saw a new group of Chinese immigrants, many of them from developing nations such as the People's Republic of China, Vietnam, and Cambodia. These immigrants are often refugees of war and oppressive political regimes. Having spent their life savings on the immigration process (legal or otherwise), these Chinese Americans come with little to no financial or professional resources. Lacking a Western education and English skills, many of these recent immigrants are living in Chinese ghettos/tourist attractions known as Chinatowns in some major cities in the United States. Despite romanticized notions of tourists, Chinatowns isolate its residents from the majority culture as well as afford the protection of "safety in numbers," often accompanied by conditions of sub-optimal housing and economic hardship. Many of these new Chinese Americans face unique problems that are often not addressed by the American welfare system, and children of these Chinese Americans are remarkably unlike those "model minority" students touted by the media.

The stereotype of the "Uptown Chinese" often blurs the reality of the lives of "Downtown Chinese." Many Chinese Americans are in fact disadvantaged, economically, socially, and culturally, and they are rarely acknowledged within the social welfare systems. Here, we see one of the important intra-ethnic distinctions within the communities casually labeled "Chinese American."

Hispanic people, or Latinos, share a common ancestral home in Central or South America. The Hispanic label combines the offspring of colonized natives with the descendants of foreigners and with political and economic refugees under one umbrella. The term "Hispanic" is not universally accepted; some prefer the term "Latino" to better capture their ancestral ties to Latin America. However, sharp differences also exist among the cultures of Latin America. In the United States, active immigration keeps these differences alive: currently, Mexican Americans (64%) make up the largest distinct ethnic group among Hispanics; Puerto Ricans make up the second largest group (11%), followed by Cuban Americans (5%). The remaining 20% are various peoples from Central and South America. The traditional cultural values of most Hispanic Americans include familism (Sabogal, Marin & Otero-Sabogal, et al., 1987), simpatia (Triandis, Lisansky, et al., 1984) communalism (Kagan & Madsen, 1971), and machismo (Gonzales, 1982).

Hispanic Americans also emphasize respect toward elders and toward people in positions of authority (Triandis, Marin, et al., 1984).

Among all of the central Hispanic cultural values, familism is the one that receives highest regard; regardless of national origin, familism is the core cultural value (Sabogal, et al., 1987). Familism conveys the respect, sense of loyalty, and importance that is placed on the family in Hispanic culture. Family, not work, is viewed as the primary obligation of Hispanic adults. Children are also reared to regard family as the primary source of reference, support, and companionship. Because the African slaves' countries of origin were not recorded and voluntary migration from African, Caribbean, and other nonwhite countries was restricted until 1965 (Papademetriou, 1985; Pastor, 1985; Segal, 1987), the heterogeneity among African Americans is reflected largely by geographic and economic distribution within the United States rather than by migration history (U.S. Bureau of the Census, 1980, 1986). It is estimated that 96% of the African Americans are descendants of slaves from Africa, 3% are immigrants from Caribbean countries, and the remaining 1% are recent immigrants from African countries (Pastor, 1985). These population estimates do not include the estimated 300,000 to 650,000 black Caribbeans and Africans who reside in this country as illegal aliens (Papademetriou, 1985; Segal, 1987). From 1790 to 1920, most African Americans resided in the South. The exodus of large numbers of African Americans from the South to the North and from rural to urban areas of the country began during World War I. For example, 91% of African Americans resided in southern states in 1790, 89% in 1910, 77% in 1940, and 53% in 1970. The exodus was attributed to the pursuit of economic benefit in the North and the elusion of racial discrimination, segregation, and injustice. Initially, African Americans went to northern urban areas; later, a substantial number migrated to the western sections of the United States. Today, 85% of African Americans reside in urban areas, as compared to 71% of white Americans. Regionally, 40% of African Americans reside in the South, 24% reside in the Northeast, 22% in the Midwest, and 14% in the West. The majority of African Americans are either working-class or middle-class, and about one-third of the African American population lives below the poverty level.

Intra-ethnic variation is also evident within the Native American communities. There are about 500 different Native American tribes in the United States, and among them, there exists over 200 different Native American languages. In addition to variations in cultural and lingual heritage, the two million Native Americans reside in a variety of communities within the

United States: 25% reside on reservations, 300,000 live in urban areas, and the rest live in rural communities.

In terms of schooling, most (82%) Native American children attend public schools, 11% attend BIA (Bureau of Indian Affairs) schools, and 7% attend primarily church-affiliated private schools (NEA, 1992).

## HISTORICAL INFLUENCES

In addition to the considerations of intra-ethnic variations within ethnic groups, minority students' current status and relationships with the majority educational system cannot be well understood without the proper historical contexts. At its commencement, education was used as a way to "civilize" the Indians by converting them to Christianity; some observers have in fact argued that "education was used as a form of war" (Larimore, 1993). The schools were created by religious organizations and funded by the federal government. In response to public protest at the use of government funds for missionary schools, the government created Bureau of Indian Affairs (BIA) schools. These boarding schools, much like their predecessors, focused on transmitting Western thought and culture, with "no consistent attempts to incorporate the Indian languages or history " (Fuchs, 1973). BIA schools took children away from their homes and forced them to live long distances away from their families, almost always in another state, sometimes halfway across the continent (Nabokov, 1991). In addition, the students were forbidden to speak their tribal languages or practice their customs and religions as a requirement for becoming good Americans (Fuchs, 1973). One major critique of the BIA schools was that they were "overcrowded, rigid, overly demanding in their schedule of work and study, and deficient in health services and food" (Fuchs, 1973). Some tribes, such as the Cherokee, attempted to create their own schools and achieved great success, maintaining a 90% literacy rate.

However, until the 1960s, many tribes did not have the power to control their own education, and tribe-created schools were shut down by the federal government (Fuchs, 1973). It is unclear exactly what impact this history has had on Native Americans' contact with the schools today; however, Native American parents frequently cite the treatment of themselves and their ancestors as reasons leading to their distrust and suspiciousness of the American educational system. Further research is needed to empirically support these anecdotal claims.

Historically, the majority of Chinese people immigrated to America, the Golden Mountain, on a voluntary basis either as laborers (as early as during the building of the transcontinental railroad) or in more recent times, as professionals and students. As a group, most Chinese Americans came with an optimistic attitude and a strong belief that the hardships they faced would be only temporary and the reward—the ability to be like the white middle-class—would be close at hand. In addition, there is an implicit trust in the majority government and institutions. Chinese Americans believe in incorporating the best of both worlds and that the Chinese language and culture do not have to be given up in order to succeed in America. Chinese Americans recognize a social identity that they may be different but not necessarily excluded from majority America.

Given the trust in the majority institution and a high level of optimism, many Chinese American parents view themselves as compensatory partners to the schools in educating their children. Parents may not be partners in the traditional American way such as being the class mother or being school board members. Rather, Chinese American parents tend to take a compensatory approach. Instead of complaining to the school or the teacher about problems, parents would teach at home what they feel is lacking in the school system. This process is referred to as rules of facework (Cupach & Metts, 1994). Rather than embarrass the school system for its failure to provide appropriate educational materials and resources, which would violate the rules of facework, the parent makes up the school deficiency. For example, one mother who felt that her child's school was not assigning sufficient homework, especially in mathematics, would make up math problems to supplement her child's school work instead of complaining to the school system (Sui, 1992). Some may argue that it is a luxury that this mother has the time to make up additional homework problems; however, the mother believes that "Education is like a business, if you don't invest now, there is no return in the future" (Sui, 1992, p. 28).

Through this type of compensatory partnership, Chinese American parents are able to take advantage of the majority education system while keeping the children connected with traditional Chinese values. Learning the "best of both worlds" seems to be the goal of many immigrant and ethnic minority families in the United States, and Chinese American families are not an exception.

The lives of African Americans during the antebellum period were largely reflective of slavery and intense racial oppression. Fully 94% of African Americans living in the United States were slaves. During this period, education was largely prohibited for African Americans. The emancipation of slaves, which started in 1861 as military and presidential proclamations, was not finalized until 1865 by the enactment of the Thirteenth Amendment (Franklin, 1966). However, before the newly freed people could enjoy their prized possession of freedom, white Americans began enacting laws that would form the basis of Jim Crow segregation. After a period of vehement Ku Klux Klan intimidation, southern states forcibly discouraged African Americans from using their newly won franchising rights. Once disenfranchisement was enacted as law, whites proceeded to systematically decree a series of legislation that led to two separate and unequal societies of African Americans and whites. The Jim Crow laws were being enacted in the southern states in 1870. Toward the end of the century, African Americans were banned from many public, white establishments and were directed to follow a different protocol in using public facilities—separate and unequal facilities. Entering public buildings from the rear, seating in the rear or balcony, and attending entirely separate but low-quality facilities became the order of the day. The 1896 *Plessy* v. *Ferguson* Supreme Court decision upheld the separate but equal doctrine. Segregated public schools were established throughout the South, the main result of which was inferior education for African Americans. It would take nearly sixty years to overturn *Plessy* v. *Ferguson;* in *Brown* v. *Board of Education of Topeka, Kansas,* Justice Earl Warren would state in his opinion that "separate educational facilities are inherently unequal, thus depriving African Americans equal protection of the law."

The term "Hispanic" is a recent U.S. census label that is applied to a diverse population of Spanish descendants who migrated from Mexico, Puerto Rico, Cuba, and Central and South America. It is reported that nearly 200,000 Hispanic Americans legally migrate to the United States annually, making Hispanic Americans the fastest growing minority group in the United States (Garcia, 1992; Martinez, 1993). However, Hispanic Americans have had a long and conflicted history with the United States.

Despite the diversities in background, history, and national origin, there are commonalties that lend coherence to this group. The Hispanic population is unified by a common set of values, a common set of socialization practices, and a common experience as an ethnic minority population in the United States. Many Mexican Americans trace their ancestry as far back as the sixteenth century and to land that is today the United States; approximately 1.3 million Mexican Americans are descendants of Hispanic people who lived in what is now the southwestern and western United States. Today, Mexican Americans represent the largest group of Hispanic Americans, fully 61% of the Hispanic population.

Many of the Mexicans who came to the United States have done so to escape poverty and political upheaval. Due to discrimination, exploitative practices of employers who take advantage of some undocumented Mexican immigrants, and resentment of some Americans who feel a loss of job opportunities, Mexican Americans often remain in poverty and in dismal conditions (Chilman, 1993). Puerto Rico is a protectorate of the United States, and consequently, Puerto Ricans are able to enjoy many of the rights and privileges of American citizenship that may help them adapt to the majority culture. Puerto Rico became a colony, and later a commonwealth, of the United States as a result of the Spanish American War of 1898–1900. However, many Puerto Ricans continue to endure high rates of poverty and unemployment. In addition, there is resentment among some Puerto Ricans who feel that Puerto Rico should be an independent colony and not be subjected to exploitative policies of the United States.

There were relatively few Cuban immigrants to the United States until after the communist revolution. Many Americans, sympathetic to their plight, were more welcoming to Cuban immigrants. The first group to migrate en masse to the United States were dubbed the "Golden exiles." Cubans had a better reception than other Hispanic groups for two major reasons: They were leaving a governmental system that many Americans opposed, and Cubans who were the first to migrate were socioeconomically successful and were viewed as an asset to American society (Suarez, 1993).

There have been three waves of Cuban immigration to the United States. The first wave came immediately after the communist revolution; these Cubans were primarily successful professionals and entrepreneurs who contributed to the American cities that they resided in, thus bringing with them the image of successful and desirable immigrants. Each successive wave of Cubans who entered the United States were less socioeconomically stable. In addition, because each successive wave of Cuban immigrants were also from nonwhite ancestry, racism and classism became factors for the more recent Cuban immigrants in their adjustment to majority America. Although Cubans were originally regarded highly by Anglo Americans, the perception of Cubans has changed for some, and consequently, the attitudes and behavior toward Cubans have become less positive.

Thirty-one percent of Native American eighth-graders live in single-parent households (second only to African Americans, 47% of whom live in single-parent households) (O'Brien, 1992). Furthermore, 42% of Native Americans report family incomes of less than $15,000 per year (again, second only to African Americans, where 47% of families report incomes below $15,000) (O'Brien, 1992). Overall, an average 30.3% of Latino children live in poverty; by ethnic group, Puerto Rican children and Mexican American children experience the highest level of poverty, while other Hispanic groups' poverty rates are similar to white Americans.

It is interesting to observe that the mention of "Chinatown" often conjures up romantic notions of exotic cuisines and unbeatable bargains for those who do not live in these ghettos. Ironically, no such romanticized notions or tourist attractions exist in Harlem and Bedford-Stuyvesant in New York City, or Tenderloin in San Francisco—ghettos for other ethnic minority groups today. Chinatowns work on a very specific organizational structure; they are rooted in Chinese traditions and are often unofficially governed by kin-based clans, benevolent associations based on provincial origin, and gangs and secret societies. All three types of Chinese organizations exist based on common goals: to protect and assist its members in an often hostile society; however, the means to accomplish this end varies a great deal among these organizations (Wong, 1995). Nonetheless, all of these organizations make loans to its members in times of need or for starting a business, act as arbitrators during disputes, and often arrange initial housing and employment for immigrants. There has also been a strong presence of religiously affiliated benevolent associations run by missions and churches, usually of the Christian faith. It is perhaps due to these organizations that much of the poverty among Chinese Americans is hidden from the majority society; Chinese Americans would often turn to kin-based benevolent associations or the secret societies for financial help before turning to the public welfare system—a practice grounded in traditional beliefs about pride and shame, keeping one's troubles among one's kin, and not to appear destitute in the eyes of the majority society.

Even Chinese Americans who are not in financial difficulty continue to lag behind their Anglo American and Japanese American peers in terms of mean income. Chinese American men average $28,852 annually and Chinese American women average $13,583 annually. Discrimination based on perceived language barriers continues to be rampant as more and more Chinese American students are preparing to bump against the glass ceilings of corporate America (Miller, 1992).

Poverty is often considered a major cause of chronic stress and thus often presents major difficulties for African American families (Gephart & Pearson, 1988). Although most are not poor, a significant proportion of African American families has always lived below the poverty level (Duncan, 1968; Duncan & Hoffman, 1986; Reid, 1982). Since 1960, the average rate of poverty for African American families has been 30.8%, which is on average 3.8 times higher than the proportion of white American families living below the poverty level (Reid, 1982). Among single-parent families, poverty is particularly evident: 52.9% of single-parent African American families as compared to 27.4% of single-parent white families were classified as poor.

Hispanic Americans are the most economically disadvantaged ethnic population in the United States (Trueba, 1991). Although many Hispanics migrated to the United States to escape economic hardship in their home countries, the economic condition that they have met in the United States has not proved to be substantially different; 1992 statistics reveal that 26.2% of Hispanic families live below the poverty level, and fully 38.8% of Hispanic children live below the poverty level.

## Interacting with the Educational System

Historical and socioeconomic factors discussed thus far become crucial when we examine how ethnic minority children interact with the majority educational system. It may be that the reasons for minority underachievement stem from the clash between enculturation (the induction into the home or family culture) and acculturation (the induction into the majority culture). That is, what children learn at home, in terms of behavior, language, and desired personality traits, are often at odds with the majority culture, which is omnipresent in the American school system. This culture clash may lead to the failure of educators to understand the effect of, for example, Native American culture on a student's personalities and behaviors. Leary (1985) contends that "often the activities and behavior of the minority culture child are misinterpreted or unrecognized within the majority culture system of education, resulting in the application of misappropriate instructional strategies, assessments, and rededication" (p. 16). For example, for Native American children, deference is displayed by an avoidance of eye contact. This may be easily misinterpreted by Anglo teachers as resistance or lack of motivation (Ponterotto, 1990). Furthermore, Native American (and Hispanic) children tend to not raise their hands in class in order to avoid attracting attention to themselves; though this behavior occurs even when the child is fully prepared, the reluctance of these children to raise their hands is often construed as a lack of preparation (Ponterotto, 1990). Leary (1985) comments that this type of clash between educators and Native American children leads to discontinuity, a lack of match between the dominant system and its minority parts. He argues that these discontinuities lead to "miscommunication, misunderstanding, lowered attention, comprehension, and low achievement" (p. 4).

One student encapsulated these problems as follows:

> Navajos learn that time is infinite, collaborative and cooperative behavior is prized, submissiveness and humbleness are rewarded, and working to satisfy present needs and to be in harmony with nature is vital. Those belief systems clash with the qualities emphasized in

Anglo schools, where it is expected that deadlines should be met, aggressive and competitive behaviors are positively rewarded, future gratification is extolled, and the mastery of nature is assumed. (Payton, 1985, p. 79)

The misunderstanding between Native American children and the majority educational system is further illustrated in the case of history textbooks. For example, these books rarely devote more than a couple of pages to the history of Native Americans, even though their presence in America spans thousands of years, as opposed to the only hundreds of years for Europeans. Furthermore, descriptions of Columbus's arrival to the Americas frequently uses words such as "the New World" and "the discovery," again, disregarding the rich cultural heritage, variety in scope, language, and customs present before the time of Columbus. In addition, textbooks rarely describe the wholesale genocide against the Native American peoples by Columbus and his companions. Instead, European attacks on Indian peoples are referred to as "defense," whereas Indian attacks are referred to as "slaughters." In summary, Native Americans, "like all American students, [are required] to revere those whose fame was won by the decimation of their people" (Leary, 1985, p. 11).

Finally, textbooks rarely address the situations of modern Native Americans in the United States. Because of this, schoolchildren as well as some teachers tend to believe that Native Americans can be found only in the movies, that they are long dead and no longer contributing to the fabric of current American society. For example, a Native American student in a university sociology class responded to a professor's comment on the lack of reliance on the extended family in the United States by reporting that, in his community, a great importance is placed on the extended family. The professor dismissed the comment by stating that the student was simply incorrect (Larimore, 1993).

Boykin (1984) has suggested that some of African American children's difficulties may lie in the serious incongruence between the child's home environment and the school environment. He observed that African American culture emphasizes emotional expressiveness, communal bonding, movement, rhythm, and percussiveness. These aspects of African American culture, taken together, indicate a high level of sensate stimuli in the familial environment. This is manifested by regular and frequent visiting and contacting behaviors, presence of lively and varied physical activity, and the functional assistance provided by relatives (Allen & Boykin, 1991; Boykin, 1979; Wilson, 1989). According to Boykin (1979, 1984), the psychological and behavioral verve of African American children is consistent with their familial environment, which is filled with a heightened level of activity and stimulation variability.

History has taught African American people to not speak out, not to get a good education, and not to associate with white people (Fordham & Ogbu, 1986). For example, slaves who tried to learn to read were beaten, civil rights leaders who demanded humane treatment were hosed down, and African American men who spoke to white women were lynched. Thus, many African Americans kept to themselves, kept quiet, and were often uneducated. From this, strong ties within groups were formed and a strong group identity was developed. Fordham and Ogbu (1986) called this a "fictive kinship"; protection was creating and maintaining boundaries between African American and white people. African American people avoid behaviors that white people engage in and in turn engage in those behaviors that whites do not.

If one can conceive of achieving academic success as something whites do and can do, but that African Americans do not or cannot do, it becomes more obvious how underachievement by African American children plays a role in maintaining group identity or the fictive kinship. Low-income African American children in the Washington, D.C., schools believe that "acting white" is to betray one's fictive kinship (Fordham & Ogbu, 1986; Ogbu, 1991). Speaking standard English, listening to "white" music, going to the opera, and getting good grades are things that the Washington, D.C., students believe only white people do. To do these things would thus be to betray the fictive kinship and to embrace the white culture. Getting good grades, therefore, creates cognitive and affective dissonance. One might want to achieve, but to achieve is seen as a betrayal, and is also often met by peer rejection. One clear result is underachievement among low-income African American children.

Among Chinese Americans, on the one hand, there is a voluntary and optimistic historical and social context, and on the other hand cultural values also contribute to Chinese American children's academic experience. Stevenson and Lee's research (1990) show that Chinese children's identities are almost always intimately tied to their academic achievements, as academic achievement is valued above all other types of achievements. Key Confucian values taught within the family also demand respect and grant power to educators and teachers. Children are taught, often using shaming, to respect and obey authority figures. These values, combined with an implicit trust of the majority institutions, help students to avoid some of the obstacles in the way of learning and achieving in majority schools. For instance, many primary school teachers equate obedience with a good student, and so Chinese American children who are taught at home to be obedient to authorities have an advantage in the elementary classrooms over those students who question authority and assert their independence (Koslowski, 1994).

In addition to obedience, effort and an internal locus of control are stressed over innate abilities or fairness. Academic failure is blamed on the self rather than on hard teachers or unfair tests; academic failures also place Chinese American children in the position where they have failed in fulfilling their obligations toward the family. Chinese American students often work on a "do better" system, rather than a "good job" system (Sui, 1992). That is to say that high achievement and perfection are not extraordinary acts; rather, they are the ordinary expectations. It is believed that a high level of expectation, combined with an internal locus of control, gives Chinese American students self-motivation in achieving academically. However, many Chinese American youths living in Chinatowns are anything but the glamorized "models" portrayed by the media (Sue & Okazaki, 1990). For youths living in these ghetto conditions, barriers as basic as language and communication skills bar many of these new Americans from attaining the academic and economic successes that their "uptown" peers often enjoy. Far from the university campuses, many of these Chinese American youths are working long hours as semiskilled laborers to support their families in their new lives in the United States. Furthermore, Chinese American students who do not adjust successfully to the life-changing event of immigration usually choose to remain living in Chinatowns, where, despite the lack of economic or academic opportunities, there is perceived security. Thus, many completely fail to take advantage of the system of higher education in the United States.

Chinese youths in these ghettos are just as at risk as those from the much politicized inner cities of the United States. In reality, new Chinese Americans not only face the usual financial hardships and lack of opportunities, but they also face the basic barriers of language and cultural expectations. Indeed, Chinese traditional values such as facework (Cupach and Metts, 1994) and stoicism lead to silent struggles for many Chinese American students that go unnoticed by unaware schoolteachers. The "speak up if you need help" approach in traditional American teaching often leads educators to believe that the quiet Chinese American students face little or no problems (Sim, 1992).

The educational status of Hispanic students has been a consistent cause for concern (Garcia, 1992). The overall high school dropout rate for Hispanic Americans in 1992 was 33.9%, 38.3% for boys and 29.6% for girls. In 1993, 53.1% of Hispanic Americans completed high school and only 9% completed four years of college or beyond. Educational statistics on Hispanic Americans reveal that the high school dropout rate has been steadily increasing, levels of academic performance have been persistently lower than other ethnic groups, and graduation rates and entrance into colleges and universities have been lower than any other group.

The discrepancy between Hispanic Americans and other groups on academic achievements has led to considerable research. Garcia (1992) suggests that the cultural differences between Hispanic homes and majority American schools attended by Hispanic children may lead to the difficulties seen in adjustment and achievement. Garcia suggests that the same cultural clash in values and expectations that lead to lower performance among African Americans, poor whites, Hawaiians, and Navaho Indians may also lead to academic troubles for Hispanics. The underlying theory is that exposure to clashing expectations may lead to an "educationally harmful dissonance."

Prior attempts at improving the academic performance of Hispanic American students have included the implementation of ethnocentric and ineffective policies. Attempts to "Americanize" Hispanic students have included requirements to exclusively use English in instructions and examinations and to replace Hispanic values with American values (Garcia, 1992).

## COOPERATION VERSUS COMPETITION

There exists other aspects of the educational system that tend to exaggerate the differences between the majority and the minority culture, which thereby creates a possibility for confusion and alienation in the classroom for minority students. For example, Native American culture focuses heavily on the group, not the individual, and thus the competitive atmosphere in American classrooms is in direct conflict with Native American emphasis on cooperation (Luftig, 1982). Students trained to value cooperation and discourage competitiveness can be confused and frustrated in an environment that emphasizes competitiveness. Competition is an important aspect of American society, as the economic system of the United States is based on competition. Competition in all areas, from sports to business, is also encouraged and rewarded in the educational institutions of America. Cooperation, on the other hand, is reinforced in Mexican villages as well as in Mexican American communities through rituals, ceremonies, and "cultural control" (Kagan & Madsen, 1971). The difference in competitive behavior between Anglo Americans and Mexican Americans is manifested as early as age four. Kagan and Madsen (1971) reported that overall Hispanic children were much more cooperative than Anglo American children. Many researchers believe that by making schools more cooperative, educators can help reverse the poor academic achievement levels of Native Americans and Hispanics, and may even lead other students to superior performance.

The feeling of alienation due to teachers' ignorance of minority culture, prejudice, and textbook bias may contribute to minority underperformance. The argument is not for a direct cause of underperformance, but rather that alienation serves to create a hostile learning environment. While many children may be alienated from the classroom because of personal characteristics (e.g., poor social skills), alienation is almost institutionalized with minority children. Minority status imparts on these children a wealth of characteristics that may serve to alienate them from the classroom, and thus prevent achievement from becoming a part of minority children's sense of self-worth. In other words, children will not identify with school and therefore will not perform well in school if school is a place of pain and discouragement (Steele, 1992).

## IDENTITY

The development of an ethnic identity within a majority culture is a relatively unexplored area of research, and the impact of identity on school achievement is still open to speculation. In the case of Chinese American students, research is limited to the "Uptown Chinese," those of the middle to upper socioeconomic classes (see Ou & McAdoo, 1993; Rosenthal & Feldman, 1992). Through this limited research, scholars have found that by age seven, Chinese American children are aware of their ethnic difference from children of majority background. Younger children who are from bilingual homes tend to have more positive self-concepts; their parents also have more positive attitudes toward Chinese culture and beliefs, exposing their children to Chinese culture and traditions, and maintaining bilingual and bicultural identities. In contrast, monolingual Chinese American children tend to have a lower self-concept and lower racial awareness.

The development of bicultural or multicultural identities needs to be studied and fleshed out. Successful adjustment to the immigration process also depends on the ability to assimilate and accommodate the majority cultural expectation with home cultural expectations. The ability to build a bicultural identity would help Chinese American children succeed socially as well as academically.

Studies of Native American identity are not as extensive as they are with some other minorities. Doll preference studies have indicated that Native American children are more likely to prefer a white doll and say that a white doll looked most like them in the presence of a Caucasian experimenter. However, with a Native American experimenter, Indian children preferred the Indian doll and indicated that the Indian doll looked most like them (Corenblum & Wilson, 1982). The authors suggested that the reaction to experimenter effects may be due to the fact that ethnic identity is not part of self-identity until the children are somewhat older. The impact of identity on educational achievement among Native American children remains relatively unexplored.

Ethnic identity is an important issue for Hispanic Americans. Hispanic culture is highly regarded among adults who migrate to the United States; parents continue to instill the values and customs of Hispanic culture in their children. Yet cultural differences between the home environment and the majority United States society often become a source of extreme intrafamilial and intergenerational conflict, as children become acculturated at a much faster pace than their parents (Szapocznik & Kurtines, 1993).

Ethnic identity for Hispanic Americans has often been categorized dichotomously: Hispanic Americans who speak Spanish and maintain ties to the Hispanic community (activities, values, etc.) are distinguished from those who speak predominantly English and who have adapted to the values and customs of the majority society. Cortes, Rogler, and Malgady (1994) suggest that researchers and clinical professionals should make a more concerted effort in acknowledging and assessing biculturality: becoming involved in American society does not necessarily mean that one forsakes one's own Hispanic culture. He argued that it is likely that individuals can operate effectively, fluently, and comfortably in both cultures.

Spencer (1977) has argued that there is a difference between the social motives of Mexican Americans and Anglo Americans. When faced with a variety of behavioral opportunities, Mexican American children are more likely to choose alternatives that promote group enhancement rather than individual rewards. That is, Mexican American children are more likely to play cooperatively and/or altruistically (Madsen & Shapira, 1970; Kagan & Madsen, 1971), and they are more likely to avoid overt conflict during role playing and when responding to hypothetical situations.

Other differences between Hispanics and Anglo Americans emerge during social relations. Social relations within the Hispanic culture are governed by the cultural value of simpatia (Triandis, 1984a). Simpatia is a social script that characterizes Hispanic social relations as warm, personal, and sincere. A great deal of emphasis is placed on positive social relations. Objectivity and reserved social responses, however, tend to be the norm within the American culture, especially during encounters between acquaintances. This may lead to interpersonal conflict between Hispanics and non-Hispanics, and serve as an obstacle to networking and obtaining promotions.

This cultural script may affect interpersonal relations and the perceptions of interpersonal interactions (e.g., among coworkers and supervisors) in the work force. Hispanic Americans tend to see neutral relationships as negative and positive relationships as neutral. There are cultural differences in familial orientations to the job market (Triandis, 1984b). The general population experiences a push out of the family, a pull toward family, and a pull toward work roles, the total sum of these forces favoring work roles. Hispanic Americans, on the other hand, experience no push out of the family, strong pull toward the family, and ambivalent perception of work roles. Results indicate that relative to the mainstream, Hispanics see a warmer, supportive family environment and a colder, hostile work environment. (Triandis, 1984a).

Accordingly, Harrison (1985) asserts that in order to understand the development of identity for African American children, we have to study the social systems within which they grow and develop. For instance, several researchers (Johnson, Shireman & Watson, 1987; McRoy, et al., 1982, 1984; Shireman & Johnson, 1986) have found that African American children who are raised in transracially adopted homes showed no differences in African American identity development and self-esteem. However, Spencer and Markstrom-Adam (1990) suggested that families are essential in establishing a sense of personal and racial identity. They suggest that the familial environment provides cultural beliefs and practices that permit children to develop important strategies for bicultural survival. In other words, African American children must rely on their families for a source of knowledge about their ethnic group (McAdoo & Crawford, 1990).

Many researchers have suggested that children without a positive sense of group identity are caught between rejecting their own ethnicity and being ostracized by the majority group (Harrison, 1985). Previous research shows that as early as age four a child is capable of distinguishing between different ethnic groups (Aries & Moorehead, 1989; Carr & Mednick, 1988). Thornton and his associates (1990) showed that 63% of a sample of 2,107 guardians and parents had informed their children about racial and group identity. Those youngsters from two-parent homes who lived in a racially mixed neighborhood were more likely to receive earlier racial socialization (Thornton, et al., 1990).

It seems that as African American boys get older, racial group identity becomes more important, while socioeconomic status and academic achievement become less important. For example, Aries and Moorehead (1989) revealed that ethnicity was most predictive of overall identity status and was seen as the most important factor for self-definition among African American students. Ethnicity was viewed as being more important to self-definition than occupation, ideology (religion and politics), or sexual and interpersonal attitudes and behavior. The findings of other studies indicate that racial group identification is strongest among older African Americans (Baldwin, Bell, & Duncan, 1987; Broman, Jackson, & Neighbors, 1988). Of those children who have not developed a positive ethnic identity, McAdoo (1982) suggested that positive reinforcement bolstered white American children's feelings of esteem and ethnic attitudes and preferences but did not promote feelings of esteem and ethnic attitude in African American children. Thus, among African American students, academic achievement may not factor as heavily in their identities when compared to other minority groups.

## CONCLUSION

To address issues surrounding academic achievement among ethnic minority students, it is important that we not only account for their differences with mainstream Caucasian culture but we must also consider their group-specific concerns as well. Put another way, there is no single minority-relevant recommendation that can be made. Each group must be addressed on its own merit and not as a part of a larger minority contingent. For instance, in order to accommodate Native Americans, whose perception of time is quite different from that of mainstream Caucasian culture, it has been recommended that there be flexible time limits and untimed examinations (Ponterotto, 1990). In addition, it may be wise not to judge ability by assertiveness, as this quality is rarely valued in children in Native American homes. Similarly, when oral examinations are possible (and granted, they often are not) educators may want to consider this method of assessing children's understanding of the material, as an oral tradition is emphasized much more than a written one in Native American families (Ponterotto, 1990). In addition, in research and assessments, Native Americans are often labeled as "other," which may lead to a paucity of information regarding their educational experiences and needs.

Regarding Chinese Americans, education is one of the major obligations children have toward their families; the duty of children to invest in education and achieve academically is as deeply ingrained as facework and filial piety. As discussed earlier, Chinese American students seem to be well represented at some of the top-ranked universities and colleges in the United

States; these achievements are in no way accidental nor are they necessarily representative of all Chinese American students. However, to understand the educational underachievement as well as achievement of Chinese American students, one must consider the educational history of the Chinese Americans, the values of Chinese American families, as well as societal factors such as family economics and opportunities. Educators need to become sensitive to issues surrounding pride and shame for the Chinese American student and not fall into the trap of ignoring individual differences in circumstance and opportunities. For instance, with a misconception about the Chinese Americans' "natural" superior ability in mathematics remaining widespread (e.g., Lynn, 1991), it is not difficult to conjure up the image of the stereotypical "Chinese statistics nerd," a stereotype that is not necessarily helpful to all Chinese American students.

Many of the tests in our present-day school system have proven to be biased. As a result, there has been a recent trend to place large numbers of African American students in special education classes (Wyche & Novick, 1985). The problem lies with the fact that our school environment tends to reflect the values and beliefs of the mainstream culture. Therefore it is impossible to think that people who don't belong to the mainstream culture can fully understand it and do well on tests that incorporate it. The problem is that many students may come from a culture that may not introduce or nurture the concepts, skills, behaviors, and abilities that go along with school success as defined by the white culture. Therefore they start at a disadvantage.

Tests should cover material that is familiar to all cultural groups. When a test is used to measure aptitude, it should not depend on high-level achievements in areas that are unfamiliar to the test taker. This is why we need programs to help educators make tests that can be understood by people from all cultures. The only way that this can be achieved is for researchers to start looking at the African American culture as legitimate, strong, and one that is separate from the mainstream.

Another problem that adds to the academic underachievement of African Americans and is the result of ignorance of the African American culture is the cultural-ecological influences on schooling (Fordham & Ogbu, 1986; Ogbu, 1991). The ecological aspect stems from mainstream society's belief that African Americans are by nature not as intelligent as other racial groups. As a result African Americans have been given substandard schooling, based on the mainstream's perceptions of the educational needs of African Americans.

Minority children from Native American, Chinese American, Hispanic American, and African American families are diverse; however, all groups face challenges as they interact with the majority education system in the United States. In order to understand these challenges and to begin remedying the underachievements among minority students, we must consider these minority families' historical as well as socioeconomic contexts, while at the same time, not losing sight of individual differences and abilities.

REFERENCES

Allen, B. A. & Boykin, A. W. (1991). The influence of contextual factors on Afro-American children's performance: Effects of movement opportunity and music. *International Journal of Psychology, 26,* 373–387.

Aries, E. & Moorehead, K. (1989). The importance of ethnicity in the development of identity in black adolescents. *Psychological Reports, 65,* 75–82.

Baldwin, J., Bell, R. & Duncan, J. (1987). Assessment of African self-consciousness among black students from two college environments. *Journal of Black Psychology, 13* (2), 27–41.

Beuf, A. H. (1975). *The home of whose brave? Problems confronting Native Americans in Education.* Paper presented at the annual conference of the National Association for Women Deans, Administrators, and Counselors, Philadelphia, PA.

Boykin, A. W. (1984). Reading achievement and the social frame of reference of Afro-American children. *Journal of Negro Education, 53* (4), 464–473.

Broman, C., Jackson, J. & Neighbors, H. (1988). Racial group identification among Black adults. *Social Forces, 67* (1), 146–158.

Carr, P. & Mednick, M. (1988). Sex role socialization and the development of achievement motivation in Black preschool children. *Sex Roles, 18* (3–4), 169–180.

Chilman, C. S. (1993). Hispanic families in the United States: Research perspectives. In H. P. McAdoo (Ed.), *Family ethnicity: Strength in diversity* (pp. 141–163). Newbury Park, CA: Sage.

Corenblum, B. & Wilson, A. E. (1982). Ethnic preference and identification among Canadian Indian and White children. *Canadian Journal of Behavioral Science, 14* (1), 50–59.

Cortes, D. E., Rogler, L. H. & Malgady, R. G. (1994). Biculturality among Puerto Rican adults in the United States. *American Journal of Community Psychology, 22,* 707–721.

Cupach, W. R. & Metts, S. (1994). *Facework.* Thousand Oaks, CA: Sage.

Duncan, G. J. & Hoffman, S. D. (1986). Welfare dynamics and the nature of need. *Cato Journal, 6,* 31–53.

Duncan, O. D. (1968). Inheritance of poverty or inheritance of race? In D. P. Moynihan (Ed.), *On understanding poverty.* New York: Basic Books.

Fordham, S. & Ogbu, J. U. (1986). Black students school success: Coping with the burden of "acting white," *The Urban Review, 18,* 176–206.

Franklin, J. H. (1996). *From slavery to freedom.* New York: Knopf.

Fuchs, E. (1973). *To live on this earth: American Indian education.* New York: Anchor Press/Doubleday.

Garcia, E. D. (1992). Hispanic children: Theoretical, empirical and related policy issues. *Educational Psychology Review, 4* (1), 69–93.

Gephart, M. A. & Pearson, R. W. (1988). Contemporary research in the urban underclass. *Items: Newsletter of Social Science Research Council, 42* (1/2), 1–10.

Gonzales, A. (1982). Sex roles of the traditional Mexican family. *Journal of Cross-Cultural Psychology, 13* (3), 330–339.

Harrison, A. O. (1985). The black family's socializing environment: Self-esteem and ethnic attitude among black children. In H. P. McAdoo & J. L. McAdoo (Eds.) *Black children* (pp. 174–193). Beverly Hills, CA: Sage.

Johnson, P. R., Shireman, J. F. & Watson, K. W. (1987). Transracial adoption and the development of black identity at age eight. *Child Welfare League of America, 66,* 45–55.

Kagan, S. & Madsen, M. (1971). Cooperation and competition of Mexican, Mexican-American, and Anglo-American children of two ages under four instructional sets. *Developmental Psychology,* 532–539.

Koslowski, B. (1994). Personal communication.

Larimore, J. (1993, 1994). Personal communication.

Leary, J. (1985). *School success or school failure: An Indian example.* Paper presented at the annual meeting of the American Educational Research Association, Chicago, IL.

Lee, E. (1982). A social systems approach to assessment and treatment of Chinese American families. In M. McGoldrick, J. K. Pearce & J. Giordano (Eds.), *Ethnicity and family therapy* (pp. 527–551). New York: Guilford.

Luftig, R. L. (1982). *The effect of schooling on the self-concept of Native American students.* Paper presented at the annual meeting of the American Educational Research Association, New York.

Lynn, R. (1991). Educational achievements of Asian Americans [Comment: Lynn on Sue & Okazaki]. *American Psychologist, 46* (8), 875–876.

Madsen, M. C. & Kagan, S. (1973). Mother-directed achievement of children in two cultures. *Journal of Cross-Cultural Psychology, 4* (2), 221–228.

Martinez, E. A. (1993). Parenting young children in Mexican American/Chicano families. In H. P. McAdoo (Ed.), *Family ethnicity: Strength in diversity* (pp. 184–195). Newbury Park, CA: Sage.

McAdoo, H. P. (1982). Stress absorbing systems in black families. *Family Relations, 31* (4), 479–488.

McAdoo, H. & Crawford, V. (1990). The black church and family support programs. *Prevention in Human Services, 9,* 193–203.

McKay, E. G. (1988). *Changing Hispanic demographics.* National Council of LaRaza, Washington, DC. Office of Research Advocacy and Legislation (ERIC Reproduction Services No. ED329640).

McKay, E. G. (1993). *The forgotten half: An Hispanic perspective.* National Council of LaRaza, Washington, DC. Office of Research Advocacy and Legislation (ERIC Reproduction Services No. ED361431).

McRoy, R. G., Zurcher, L. A., Lauderdale, M. L. & Anderson, R.N. (1982). Self-esteem and racial identity in transracial and inracial adoptees. *National Association of Social Workers, 27,* 522–526.

McRoy, R. G., Zurcher, L. A., Lauderdale, M. L. & Anderson, R.N. (1984). The identity in transracial adoptees. *Social Casework: Journal of Contemporary Social Work, 65,* 34–39.

Miller, S. K. (1992, November 13). Asian-Americans bump against glass ceilings. *Science, 258,* 1224–1228.

Nabokov, P. (1991). *Native American testimony.* New York: Penguin.

National Education Council (1992, September). *Focus on American Indian/Alaska Native education.* Washington, DC: Author.

O'Brien, E. M. (1992). *American Indians in higher education.* Division of Policy Analysis and Research (Research Briefs, Vol. 3, No. 3). Washington, DC: American Council on Education.

Ogbu, J. (1991). Immigrant and involuntary minorities in comparative perspective.

In M. G. Gibson & J. U. Ogbu (Eds.), *Minority status and school* (pp. 3–37). New York: Garland.

Ou, Y. S. & McAdoo, H. P. (1993). Socialization of Chinese American children. In M. P. McAdoo (Ed.), *Family ethnicity: Strength in diversity* (pp. 245–270). Newbury Park, CA: Sage.

Papademetriou, D. G. (1985). Illegal Caribbean migration to the United States and Caribbean development. In R. A. Pastor (Ed.), *Migration and development in the Caribbean* (pp. 207–236). Boulder, CO: Westview.

Pastor, R. A. (1985). Introduction: The policy challenge. In R. A. Pastor (Ed.), *Migration and development in the Caribbean* (pp. 1–40). Boulder, CO: Westview.

Payton, C. R. (1985). Addressing the special needs of minority women. *New Directions for Student Services, 29.*

Ponterotto, J. G. (1990). Racial/ethnic minority and women students in higher education: A status report. *New Directions for Student Services, 52,* 45–59.

Reid, J. (1982). *Black America in the 1980's, 37* (4), 1–37.

Rosenthal, D. & Feldman, S. S. (1992). The nature and stability of ethnic identity in Chinese youth: Effects of length of residence in low cultural contexts. *Journal of Cross-Cultural Psychology, 3* (2), 214–227.

Sabogal, F., Marin, G. & Otero-Sabogal, R. (1987). Hispanic familism and acculturation: What changes and what doesn't? *Hispanic Journal of Behavioral Sciences, 9,* 397–412.

Segal, A. (1987). Caribbean exodus in a global context. In B. B. Levine (Ed.), *The Caribbean exodus* (pp. 44–66). New York: Praeger.

Shireman, J. F. & Johnson, P. R. (1986). A longitudinal study of Black adoption. Single parent, transracial, and traditional homes. *National Association of Social Workers, 31* (3), 172–176.

Sim, S. C. (1992). Social service needs of Chinese immigrant high school students in New York City. *Asian American Policy Review, 3,* 35–54.

Spencer, K. (1977). Social motives and behaviors of Mexican American and Anglo-American children. In J. L. Martinez (Ed.), *Chicano Psychology* (pp. 45–86). New York: Academic Press.

Spencer, M. B. (1990). Parental values transmission implications for the development of black children. In H. E. Cheatham & J. B. Stewart (Eds.), *Black families: Interdisciplinary perspectives* (pp. 111–130). New Brunswick, NJ: Transaction.

Spencer, M. B. & Markstrom-Adams, C. (1990). Identity processes among racial and ethnic minority children in America. *Child Development, 61,* 290–310.

Steele, C. M. (1992). Race and the schooling of black Americans. *Atlantic Monthly* (April), 68–78.

Stevenson, H. & Lee, S. (1990). *Contexts of achievement.* Chicago: University of Chicago Press.

Suarez, Z. E. (1993). Cuban Americans: From golden exiles to social undesirables. In H. P. McAdoo (Ed.), *Family ethnicity: Strength in diversity* (pp. 184–195). Newbury Park, CA: Sage.

Sue, S. & Okazaki, S. (1990). Asian-American educational achievements: A phenomenon in search of an explanation. *American Psychologist, 45,* 913–920.

Sui, S. F. (1992). How do family and community characteristics affect children's educational achievement? The Chinese-American experience. *Equity and Choice, 8,* 46–49.

Szapocznik, J. & Kurtines, W. M. (1993). Family psychology and cultural diversity: Opportunities for theory, research, and application. *American Psychology, 48* (4), pp 400–407.

Thornton, M. C., Chatters, L. M., Taylor, R. J. & Allen, W. R. (1990). Sociodemographic and environmental correlates of racial socialization by Black parents. *Child Development, 61,* 401–410.

Triandis, H. C., Lisansky, J., Marin, G. & Betancourt, H. (1984). Simpatia as a cultural script of Hispanics. *Journal of Personality and Social Psychology, 47,* 1363–1375.

Triandis, H. C., Hui, C. H., Lisansky, J. & Ottati, V. (1984). Role perceptions of Hispanic young adults. *Journal of Cross-Cultural Psychology, 15,* (3), 297–320.

Trueba, H. T. (1991). Reconsidering anthropological explanations of ethnic school failure: Commentary. *Anthropology & Education Quarterly, 22* (1), pp. 87–94.

U.S. Bureau of the Census (1980). Social and economic status of the black population in the U.S.: An historical view, 1790–1978. *Current Population Report,* Series P-23 No. 80. Washington, DC: U.S. Government Printing Office.

U.S. Bureau of the Census (1986). Household and family characteristics: March 1985. *Current Population Report,* Series P-20, No. 411. Washington, DC: U.S. Government Printing Office.

U.S. Bureau of the Census (1993). *1990 census of population, Asian and Pacific Islanders in the United States* (CP-3-5). Washington, DC: U.S. Government Printing Office.

Washington, V. & Newman, J. (1991). Setting our own agenda: Exploring the meaning of gender disparities among blacks in higher education. *Journal of Negro Education, 60* (4), 19–35.

Wilson, M. N. (1989). Child development in the context of the Black extended family. *American Psychologist, 44,* 380–385.

Wilson, W. J. (1987). *The truly disadvantaged: The inner city, the underclass, and public policy.* University of Chicago Press.

Wong, M. G. (1995). Chinese Americans. In P. G. Min (Ed.), *Asian Americans: Contemporary Trends and Issues* (pp. 58–94). Thousand Oaks, CA: Sage.

Wyche, L.G. & Novick, M. R. (1985). Standards for educational and psychological testing: The issues of testing bias from the perspective of school psychology and psychometrics. *Journal of Black Psychology, 11* (2), 43–48.

# Author Index

## A

Aber, J. L., 39, 40, 46
Aboud, F. E., 111, 115
Abrams, A., 250, 253
Abrams, B., 165, 182
Abrams, L., 18, 22
Agency for Health Care Policy and Research, 213
Ahearn, Jr. F., 105, 115, 189, 201
Ahmed, P. I., 105. 116
Alarcon, O., 38, 51
Albee, G. W., 56, 69
Aldous, J., 125, 216
Alexander, G. R., 148, 156
Alexander, K. L., 235, 252
Allen, B. A., 268, 277
Allen, L., 6, 20
Allen, W., 210, 216
Allen, W. R., 25, 50, 63, 69, 242, 255, 274, 279
Amaro, H., 164, 165, 166, 181, 182
Anderson, R. N., 274, 278
Anzovin, S., 201
Apfel, N. H., 227, 255
ARC, 81, 90
Arciniega, T. A., 108, 116
Argys, L. M., 29, 46
Aries, E., 274, 275, 277
Arnold, M. S., 235, 251
Aronowitz, M., 98, 115
Asarnow, J. R., 138
Aschenbrenner, J., 210, 216
Astone, N. M., 18, 23
Athey, J., 105, 115, 189, 201
Atrash, H. K., 148, 149, 156, 164, 181
Azibo, D., 8, 20

## B

Backlund, E., 123, 124, 125, 140
Baker, K., 107, 118
Baker, L. G., 141, 157
Baldwin, A. L., 109, 115
Baldwin, C. P., 109, 115
Baldwin, J., 275, 277
Bandura, A., 64, 69
Baral, D. P., 98, 115
Baratz, J. C., 221, 222, 225, 251
Baratz, S. S., 221, 222, 225, 251
Barbarin, O. A., 233, 251
Barnard, K. E., 31, 46
Barnes, H. V., 248, 249, 255
Barnes-McGuire, J., 38, 46
Barnett, W. S., 233, 251
Baruth, L. G., 113, 115
Bates, J. E., 238, 252
Baumrind, D., 35, 46
Baydar, N., 27, 46
Becerra, J. E., 148, 149, 156, 164, 181
Becker, J. A., 127, 138
Becknell, C. E., 78, 90
Bell, R., 275, 277
Belsky, D., 109, 115
Belsky, J., 31, 46, 236, 251
Benasich, A. A., 32, 46
Bennett, L., 14, 20
Bennett, M., 194, 201
Bennett, N., 211, 216
Berlin, L. J., 46, 33
Betancourt, H., 30, 46, 101, 119, 260, 273, 274, 280
Beuf, A. H., 257, 277
Bialik-Gilad, R., 195, 202
Bibace, R., 129, 138
Bieri, M., 105, 119

# F

Fairchild, H., 10, 14, 21, 24
Falicov, D., 101, 116
Family Support Act of 1988, 18
Feagin, J., 15, 21
Feldman, S. S., 272, 279
Felice, M., 155, 157
Felix-Ortiz, M., 137, 139
Ferguson, J., 33, 50
Fernandez, M., 198, 203
Fiese, B. H., 221, 238, 254
Finch, W. A., Jr., 195, 202
Fine, M., 235, 245, 252
Fisher, L. E., 12, 21
Fishman, J. A., 78, 90
Fix, M., 95, 96, 116
Flor, D., 11, 21
Florin, P. R., 226, 252
Fong, R., 188, 190, 192, 193, 202
Fordham, S., 269, 276, 277
Fortes, M., 210, 216
Fossett, M., 211, 216
Franklin, J. H., 263, 277
Freeman, R. B., 27, 48
Frey, W., 207, 216
Fried, L. E., 164, 181
Fritz, J., 205, 209, 217
Fuchs, E., 262, 277
Fukuyama, F., 200, 202
Furstenberg, F. F., Jr., 27, 28, 39, 46, 47, 48

# G

Garbarino, J., 55, 70
Garcia, H. A. V., 206, 216
García Coll, C. T., 8, 15, 19, 22, 25, 35, 36,
    38, 39, 44, 48, 49, 51, 100, 109,
    112, 113, 116, 205, 206, 216, 220,
    230, 233, 236, 238, 239, 242, 245,
    252, 253
Garcia, E. E., 107, 117, 228, 252, 264, 270,
    271, 277
Garcia, M., 165, 182
Garcia-Castro, M., 30, 51
Garfinkel, I., 29, 50, 211, 217
Garmezy, N., 98, 100, 116
Gay, J., 79, 91
Gelfand, D. E., 195, 202
Gephart, M. A., 266, 277
Gerrity, P. S., 129, 140
Gerton, J., 112, 117
Gibbs, J. T., 6, 16, 17, 21, 54, 55, 63, 70
Gibson, M. A., 81, 91
Gilbert, M., 165, 182

Gillis, A. R., 63, 70
Ginsburg, H., 91
Ginzburg, E., 124, 139
Gladney, D., 190, 202
Glauberman, N., 10, 22
Glymph, A., 67, 72
Gold, S. R., 68, 70
Golden, M. P., 139
Goldenberg, C., 108, 116
Golding, J. M., 109, 116, 125, 140
Gonzales, A., 260, 278
Goodnow, J. J., 31, 50
Goodyer, I. M., 32, 48
Gordon, R., 39, 44, 47, 49
Gould, J., 164, 182
Gould, S. J., 14, 21
Graham, S., 4, 5, 6, 7, 9, 10, 21, 233, 252
Grant, K., 32, 50
Green, M., 105, 118
Greenberg, M. T., 31, 47
Greenfield, P. M., 101, 117
Greer, S., 39, 50, 220, 254
Griffin, T., 33, 51
Gross, R. T., 31, 47
Grubb, W. N., 220, 221, 225, 226, 247,
    252
Grusec, J. E., 126, 139
Guendelman, S., 148, 149, 157, 165, 182
Guerra, A. M., 127, 129, 133, 140, 157
Gunnarsson, L., 205, 210, 216
Guo, G., 27, 47, 48
Guthrie, R. V., 4, 21

# H

H'HANES, 150, 157
Habenstein, R., 217
Hacker, A., 10, 11, 19, 21
Haffner, S. M., 127, 134, 139
Hagan, J., 63, 70
Hagen, J. W., 5, 6, 10, 21
Hakuta, K., 107, 117, 228, 252
Halfon, N., 152, 157
Hall, E. T., 80, 91
Halpern, R., 221, 229, 230, 246, 252, 253
Hamburg, B. A., 29, 49
Hamburg, D. A., 104, 117
Hammond, W. R., 18, 21
Haney, W., 95, 97, 117
Hansen, J. F., 91
Hare, B. R., 63, 66, 70, 246, 252
Harjo, S., 210, 217
Harris, K. M., 27, 28, 48
Harris, M., 4, 8, 9, 23
Harris, S. M., 68, 70

# SUBJECT INDEX

## A

academic achievement
  and Hispanic students, 271
academic underachievement, 257, 258
acculturation, 42, 43, 96, 267
  and health risk behaviors, 165
  levels of, 188
  maternal, 136, 137
  measurement of, 136
achievement
  levels of, 107
  motivation, 83, 235
adolescence
  as a transitional period, 67
  coping opportunities, 54
adolescent mothers, 35
adolescents
  and academic performance, 65
  and affluence, 63
  African American, 54, 58, 62, 64
adolescents, African American, 54, 64
adolescents, Anglo American, 64
advocacy groups
  access to research findings, 214
African American boys
  and racial identity, 274
  lack of role models, 259
African American children
  and sensate stimuli, 268
African American students
  and dropout rates, 258
African American community, 63
African Americans, 3, 10, 11, 14, 17, 65,
    67, 108
  and birth weight, 161
  and policies affecting children, 215
Aid to Families with Dependent Children,
    229

Al Bienestar del Niño Study, 125, 126
  details of 127
alienation
  from teachers, 272
American immigration policy, 187, 188
American-born Chinese, 188
Americanization, 165, 169, 179
  and perinatal outcomes, 180
analysis
  social address model, 14
Asian, 3
Asian Americans, 141
assessment tools
  culturally appropriate, 38
asset approach, 100
attitudes
  anti-immigrant, 195, 201
  autonomy, 67

## B

baby boomers, 4
belief systems
  cultural, 15
biculturism, 112
bilingual education, 228
bilingualism, 107
birth weight, ethnic differences, 175
black American culture
  and patron-client strategy, 77
black Americans, 77
black children, 53, 62
Black English, 74, 85, 87
black poverty, 89
black youth, 53
Boas group, 12
Bureau of Indian Affairs schools, 262
Burlingame Treaty, 193

# C

California Tomorrow, 143, 145, 145
Cambodians, 161
caregiving environment, and community
  variables, 40
child centered programs, 225
child development
  comparative study of, 89
  convention approach, 88
child development research
  policy implications, 19
child migration risks
  language proficiency, 107
  loss of family ties, 105
  low self esteem, 106, 107
  parental support, 104
  racism and discrimination, 108, 109
  traumatic life events, 105,106
child rearing practices
  Hispanic, 209
  Native Americans, 209
children
  African American, 5, 60, 61
  and poverty, 219
  and social policy, 219
children of color
  research agenda, 213
Children's Defense Fund, 215
Chinese, 81
Chinese Americans,164
  and dropout rates, 258
  heterogeneity of, 189, 190
  and immigration policy, 193
  and the myth of model minority, 259
  and poverty, 266
  and stereotypes, 276
Chinese American parents
  and the compensatory approach, 263
Chinese cultural values, 191
Chinese Exclusion Act, 187, 193
Chinese immigrant
  from Hong Kong, 189
Chinese immigrant children
  and gang involvement, 198
  and intergenerational conflict, 198, 199
  mental health issues, 197
  and self-identity, 198
  and suicide, 198
Chinese immigrants, 260
Chinese people
  and value of children, 192
co-habitation rates, and ethnicity, 29
communication channels, 79
communication codes, 79

compensation
  definition of, 221
compensation/remediation approach, 221,
  222, 228
competence
  individual, 77
  definition of, 82
competitiveness, 271
Comprehensive Perinatal Program
  description of, 166
  findings from, 169–179
concentrated poverty area, 43
Confucian values, 269
Confucianism, 191
context effects, 55
contextual characteristics, 58
contextual factors
  and children's development, 238
coping strategies
  identity-linked, 57
  reactive, 57
coping skills, 56
  maternal, 31
coping, modes of, 56
country of origin, importance of, 211
cross-cultural research, 233
cross-cultural studies, 74
cross-race comparative research, 233
Cuban American, 97
cultural ignorance, 19
cultural deficient paradigm, 232
cultural context, 35
  and children's development, 89
  and language, 86, 88
  of mathematical skills, 79
  of spatial orientation, 80
  of time orientation, 80
cultural equivalence
  definition of, 26
cultural frame of reference, 80, 81
cultural validity, 11
culture
  components of, 74, 75
  concept of, 82
  definitions of, 74
  and family life, 211
  influence on behavior, 76

# D

de facto racial segregation, 10
dependency, 105
depressive symptoms, 32
deviance, 16
disciplinary styles, 209

Mexicanos, 89
middle-class perspective, Eurocentric, 73
migration, 261
migration risks, 100
minority
   diversity of classifications, 146
minority children
   as deviant, 8, 9
   stressors, 16
minority culture, 257
minority families
   poverty and racism, 221
minority issues
   opulation changes, 207
minority status, 62
   economic aspects, 18
mother-child interaction patterns, 40
multiculturalism, 206
   policy implications, 212–213

# N

Native American, 13, middle school children, 265
   Native Americans
      heterogeneity of, 261, 262
   Native American children
      and history books, 268
Navajo, 78
need achievement, 84
neonatal mortality
   causes of, 148
New Chance Demonstration Project, 248
nutrition
   children's knowledge of, 129, 135

# O

Operation Family, 248
oppression, racial and ethnic, 12
optimum infant health outcome score, 175, 176
outcome comparative approach, 233

# P

parent education, 225, 226, 227
   and parent-child relationships, 226
   goals of, 226
parenting
   process model, 236
parenting behavior, 32, 33
   authoritarian, 35
   authoritative, 35
   disengaged, 35

permissive, 35
parenting practices
   and children's knowledge of nutrition, 135
   the internationalization model, 126, 136
peer relationships, 67
performance-competence distinction, 234
Phenomenological Variant of Ecological Systems Theory, 56, 57, 58
physical maturation, 66
police, perceptions of, 67
policy implications, 114
population growth, 3
post-traumatic stress disorder, 106, 145
poverty, 245
   and African American children, 220
   childhood rates, 4
   and Hispanic American children, 220
   neighborhood, 39
   and Puerto Rican children, 220
   rates of, 17, 144
pregnancy outcomes
   and blacks, 164
   and Hispanics, 164
preoperational period, 61
prevention programs
   evaluation of, 18
program evaluation
   need for, 250
protective factors, 100
   coping, 112
   cultural supports, 111
   ethnic identify, 111
   family supports, 109
pubertal status
   and stress, 66
Puerto Rican children
   and IQ, 231
Puerto Rican women
   types of cancer, 124
Puerto Ricans, 43, 97
   and chronic illness, 154
Punjabis, 81

# R

race and ethnicity effects
   mediators of, 14, 15
race-comparative studies, 10, 12
   external validity of, 11
race-homogeneous studies, 12
racial differences
   children's perceptions of, 111
racial socialization, 242